Leading and Managing Nonprofit Organizations

TEXT AND WORKBOOK

Roger M. Weis

Robert F. Long

Special thanks to

Dr. Vernon W. Gantt for his assistance in establishing the foundation of this work through research and previous collaborative publications.

eddie bowers publishing co., inc.
Post Office Box 130
Peosta, Iowa 52068-0130 USA

www.eddiebowerspublishing.com

ISBN 1-57879-089-0

Dedication

This book is dedicated with love to
Stefani, my wife
Clint, my son
Annika, my daughter in law
Riley, my granddaughter
Ryder, my grandson

~ Roger M. Weis

This book is dedicated with love to
Patricia, my wife
Chayo and Eric, my daughter and her husband
Paco and Beto, my sons
Dorothy, my mother
and in memory of my father Robert F. Long, Sr.

~ Robert F. Long

Authors

Roger M. Weis

Roger Weis is Campus Director and Professor for the Youth and Nonprofit Leadership program at Murray State University, where he has twice been selected as student advisor of the year. He has published numerous journal articles and manuals regarding career development and service learning and has written seven books, including six textbooks on various aspects of leadership in nonprofit organizations.

As director of the AH program at MSU for the past twenty one years, he has served as the Chair of the American Humanics Director's Association for two terms and as a member of the National AH Board of Directors for two terms and he was the first recipient of the AH National Award of Excellence in Leadership. He is the founding chair of the local Campus Connection Volunteer Center and the Big Brothers Big Sisters program, and the founding chair of the MSU Center for Service Learning and Civic Engagement, Health Matters for Students and founding co-chair of the Service Learning Scholars program. Prior to working at MSU, he was a program director and director for the Boys and Girls Clubs of America in Norfolk/Virginia Beach, VA and the Chief Executive Officer for the Leukemia Society of America for the state of Virginia. Weis received his B.A. and M.A. from Marshall University and his Ed.D. from the University of Kentucky.

Robert F. Long

Bob Long is the Visiting Distinguished Professor of Nonprofit Leadership with the Youth and Nonprofit Leadership program at Murray State University. He has published and presented extensively in the areas of youth leadership, service learning, community empowerment, nonprofit education, and philanthropy.

Prior to joining Murray State University in 2009, he served for sixteen years in a variety of leadership roles with the W. K. Kellogg Foundation in Battle Creek, Michigan. He helped build the Philanthropy and Volunteerism Program area and served as its Vice President for Programs from 2001 to 2007. His portfolio included the Building Bridges Initiative to increase the number and variety of nonprofit management education programs in the United States and Latin America and the Unleashing New Resources Initiative to increase philanthropy through innovations in technology, support systems, and partnerships. His professional engagements include serving as faculty and chair of four Salzburg Seminars in Austria focused on the role of nongovernmental organizations in emerging democracies, founding board member of Grantmakers for Effective Organizations, and team member of the Orava Project to develop public education in Slovakia. He has served as a program leader with the 4-H youth development program in Illinois and Nevada and as a director of a nonprofit outdoor education center.

Long holds faculty appointments with centers for philanthropy and nonprofit leadership at Arizona State University, Grand Valley State University, and Indiana University. He received his B.S. from Western Illinois University and his M.S. and Ph.D. from the University of Illinois.

Preface

Most reports indicate there are well over two million different private nonprofit organizations in the United States and tens of thousands of new positions open in youth, human service, and other nonprofit organizations each year. The primary purpose of this introductory text is to present information relevant to a number of competencies required to be leaders/managers in these organizations. Another purpose is to provide opportunities to develop skills in these competency areas through classroom activities, simulations, and service learning projects. The competencies selected for discussion in the chapters to come were selected through numerous processes including surveys and reports developed by the Nonprofit Leadership Alliance, formerly known as American Humanics. NLA is an organization of colleges, universities, and nonprofits preparing undergraduates and graduates for careers with youth, human service, and other nonprofit organizations. The organization headquarters is located in Kansas City, Missouri.

The first chapter of the text discusses the history, purpose, and importance of the nonprofit sector throughout history. The next chapter presents theories, models, and studies on leadership and management and the development of each as well as discussing the connection between leadership, character, and ethics. Following this, Chapter 3 is an in-depth look at staff, board, and volunteer development. Chapter 4 includes information on various theories of human development essential to future leaders in the nonprofit sector, and presents information on a number of trends and issues--important information to have prior to designing programs. Developing programs from beginning to end is covered in Chapter 5 and includes information on marketing and promotion of programs. Chapter 6 presents an overview of financial processes including accounting, budgeting, and financial development. The importance of risk management and developing a risk management plan, along with a discussion on the importance of insurance is covered in   Chapter 7. Chapter 8 discusses different theories related to organizational development and support. The final chapter, Chapter 9, provides information on assessing oneself relative to a career in the nonprofit sector and information on developing effective resumes, cover letters, interview and networking techniques.

The authors would like to acknowledge and thank a number of individuals who made a contribution to this book. These include Christopher R. Edginton, Susan D. Hudson, and Phyllis M. Ford, who authored *Leadership in Recreation and Leisure Service Organizations*, which served as a model for a portion of this text. Another author, Thomas Wolf, provided a significant foundation for some of the technical aspects of this text with his book *Managing a Nonprofit Organization*. Special thanks go to Susan Ellis and Katherine Noyes for their book *By the People: A History of Americans as Volunteers*, which served as a foundation for Chapter 1 and to Dr. Vernon Gantt, co-author of *Knowledge and Skill Development in Nonprofit Organizations* which serves as a foundation for much of the work ahead. Acknowledgement also goes to personnel at the Independent Sector for providing statistical information and to various individuals with the Nonprofit Risk Management Center for their assistance with risk management and insurance. And recognition goes to Robin Esau who researched and prepared Appendix A and layout/design specialist Linda Pierce for their expertise and commitment to the project.

Last, we would like to express our appreciation to those closest to us, our family members: Stefani Weis, Clint Weis, Annika Weis, Riley Weis and Ryder Weis along with Patricia Mendez Long, Chayo Long-Mendez, Eric Renner, Paco Long-Mendez, Beto Long-Mendez, and Dorothy Long.

Contents

1 Understanding the Nonprofit Sector: Purpose and History

In order to become the best employee, leader and/or manager one can be in any organization, it helps to have a basic understanding of the purpose and history of the sector that organization is a part of. The nonprofit sector is large and diverse and many times citizens don't realize just how involved each individual is with nonprofits throughout a lifetime. For instance, many youngsters are involved in 4-H, Boys and Girls Clubs of America, Boy or Girl Scouts of America, participate in youth programs at a local YMCA, attend a private, nonprofit school and/or have received swim lessons through the American Red Cross.

As adults we may rely on that same American Red Cross for disaster relief, safety education or blood transfusions and we and our families may participate in a local church, synagogue or mosque. Other adults may be attending private nonprofit colleges and universities and also participating in recreational and other types of activities at local YWCAs or Jewish Community Centers. Still others may rely on the services provided by national health organizations such as the American Cancer Society or the American Heart Association. In the first chapter we will look at the overall purpose and general criteria of the nonprofit sector as well as its rich history.

Throughout history, societies have made special provisions to address the needs of the young, the aged, the weak, the sick, and the disabled. In earlier times, families and neighbors were often charged with the care of these individuals. But as time advanced and individual needs became more and more specialized and complex, families and neighbors could no longer address these needs effectively. In some countries, the government has provided for such needs as education, health care, and retirement, to mention several. In other countries, these needs are met through a network of private, charitable organizations. And in still others, like the United States, various needs of the citizenry are addressed through a complex combination of government programs and private, nonprofit organizations with essentially public purposes.

There is a Middle Eastern legend about a sparrow lying on its back in the road, when a journeyman comes along and asks the sparrow what he is doing. The sparrow responds that he has heard that the heavens were going to fall on that day. The journeyman looks at the sparrow and asks the sparrow if he really thinks he can hold up the heavens with his spindly little legs, and the sparrow responds, "One does what one can, one does what one can" (Ellis and Noyes 1978, 31). The government is not designed to address actively all of the needs of each individual citizen but private, nonprofit organizations are designed specifically to meet certain needs of various citizens and do an amazing job in that respect.

There are approximately 2 million nonprofit organizations in the United States, and the first section of Chapter 1 offers an operational definition of nonprofits and provides several explanations for their tax-exempt status (Internal Revenue Service data Book 2008). This chapter includes a number of examples of different types and categories of nonprofit organizations, along with a list of criteria characteristic of these organizations. The history of the nonprofit sector is rich and diverse. The remainder of the chapter deals with an exploration of philanthropy and service, from its early colonial beginnings involving the Pilgrims, patriots, and Native Americans, to its involvement with relief efforts for the victims of the horrendous terrorist attacks of September 11, 2001, the aftermath of Hurricane Katrina in new Orleans in 2005, the Tsunami in Indonesia in 2007 and the devastating earthquake in Haiti in 2010. Included in this section is the sector's involvement with various areas of American life: health care, education, recreation, politics, social welfare, conservation, and religion, to mention several. The nonprofit sector has been an integral factor in a number of turning points in the history of the United States, including the colonization of the country, the Great Awakening, and the American Revolutionary War. The establishment of private institutions of higher education, the Civil War, child welfare, women's suffrage, World War I, the Great Depression, World War II, civil rights, the Korean War, the Vietnam War, Desert Storm, 9/11, Hurricane Katrina and the earthquake in Haiti are all examples of important historical events in which nonprofit organizations have played a significant role.

■ What is the Nonprofit Sector?

The **nonprofit sector** is a collective name used to describe organizations that are private, nonprofit entities with public purposes. These organizations are neither government, nor businesses incorporated for a profit. Other names for the sector include the **voluntary sector,** the **not-for-profit sector**, the **third sector**, the **independent sector,** the **charitable sector,** the **philanthropic sector** and **non-governmental organizations** (**NGOs**), for those organizations outside the United States. There are approximately 2 million organizations in this country that belong to this sector that have made the enhancement of the lives of people in their community the sole purpose of the organization (Internal Revenue Service Data Book 2008). These privately incorporated organizations range from educational, cultural, and religious institutions, to recreational, service, and character development organizations, to hospitals and wellness centers, and many others.

The term **nonprofit organization** signifies that the organization can charge fees for memberships and services, but cannot make a profit for owners or investors. In other words, these organizations are committed to programs to meet specific missions, and any revenue that is generated above expenses must go back into supporting the operation of the organization. And in spite of the term nonprofit, these combined organizations have an approximate $3.4 trillion in assets (Wing, Pollak, and Blackwood 2008). The 2 million organizations have combined annual revenues of approximately $1.1 trillion making the sector an integral part of the country's overall economy (US Department of Labor Bureau of Labor Statistics). Nearly 13 million people work in the nonprofit sector (Wing, et al, 2008) or about one in ten Americans work in a nonprofit organization

Figure 1.1
Sample Nonprofit Organizations

4-H

AFL-CIO

American Cancer Society

American Heart Association

American Humanics, Inc.

American Red Cross

Boys and Girls Clubs of America

Ford Foundation

Girl Scouts of America

Jewish Community Centers

Metropolitan Museum of Art

National Association for the Advancement of Colored People (NAACP)

National Collegiate Athletic
Association (NCAA)

National Geographic Society

Planned Parenthood

Pop Warner Little League

The American Civil Liberties
Union (ACLU)

The Brookings Institution

The National Rifle Association

W.K. Kellogg Foundation

Yale University

YMCA

YWCA

and over fifty percent of American adults volunteer in a nonprofit organization each year (Independent Sector 2002). A list of some of the leading organizations, along with a brief history, purpose statement, various programs, career opportunities, and contact information can be found in **Appendix A.**

Nonprofit organizations have received a limited **tax-exempt status** throughout history for several reasons (Independent Sector 2002):

- **They provide assistance in place of government**. The thousands of day-care centers, hospitals, schools, and shelters that nonprofits offer relieve the government from providing these services. Government, in turn, provides a tax-exempt status for the many benefits nonprofits offer. Nonprofits also provide services that governments wouldn't be required to provide anyway, such as encouraging civic involvement and other community enrichment activities.
- **The taxation process would be problematic**. According to lawyers and economists, deciding what income would be taxable would be difficult, and taxation would make it even more difficult for nonprofits to operate efficiently.
- **Tax-exemption for religious organizations protects separation of church and state**. Making religions tax-exempt prevents government from using taxation as a way of favoring one religion over another, or of putting one religion out of business. The tax-exempt status of nonprofit organizations will be discussed in more detail in the section below.

Some sample nonprofit organizations are listed in Figure 1.1.

■ Characteristics of a Nonprofit Organization

Most nonprofit organizations have similar characteristics or meet a number of criteria (Weis and Gantt 2002).

- **Maintain a legal, incorporated status.** Although some nonprofit organizations exist as ad hoc, informal groups, most nonprofit organizations have a legal designation as a corporation chartered under state laws. This is significant in that it allows the organization to enter contracts and frees the officials of the board from financial entanglements and personal financial responsibility of the organization's obligations.

- **Private but provide a public service mission.** Private, nonprofit organizations are institutionally separate from government, but may still receive significant government support. The general purpose of all nonprofit organizations is to serve the public in some manner. Because the purpose is often very broad, nonprofits designate a number of **goals** to accomplish as part of the mission.

    Organizational goals often have a number of **objectives** or outcomes within the framework of a goal. For instance, a nonprofit that has as its mission the enhancement of the lives of children in the community could have educational enhancement as a major goal, and literacy improvement as an objective beneath that goal. Private citizens or community organizations initiate and develop nonprofit organizations to serve the public good. Nonprofits attempt to fill the huge gap between services provided by public organizations and those provided by businesses for profit.

- **Governed by a voluntary board of directors.** In order to keep cost down and maintain expertise in a number of different areas, nonprofit organizations enlist the help of volunteer staff members and consultants. Key volunteers for a nonprofit organization are often referred to as the board of directors. Boards act as a governing body for nonprofits and their function and purpose will be discussed in detail in Chapter 3. Organizations such as the National Charities Information Bureau and the Council of Better Business Bureaus' Philanthropic Advisory Service are charged with monitoring the activities of nonprofits, while a division of the IRS (the Tax Exempt/Government Entities division) is responsible for insuring that organizations comply with the requirements for maintaining their tax-exempt status.

- **Funded primarily through individual and corporate fees and/or contributions.** Financial support for these organizations comes through a variety of measures. Individual and corporate donations make up a significant portion of the funding for nonprofits. Allocations from the United Way, membership fees, program fees, special events, and grants and governmental contracts are additional ways in which these agencies are funded.

- **Operate under a financial system without profit.** Although more than a trillion dollars are exchanged each year within nonprofit organizations in the form of fee payments or contributions, revenue that exceeds expenses cannot be used for personal profit, but must go back into the support of the organization. Revenue above expenses may be used as a **contingency fund** for special situations or

Figure 1.2
Types of Tax-Exempt Organizations in the United States

Tax Code Number	Type of Tax-exempt Organization
501 (c) (1)	Corporations organized under an act of Congress
501 (c) (2)	Title-holding companies
501(c) (3)	Religious, charitable, educational, etc.
501 (c) (4)	Social welfare
501 (c) (5)	Labor, agriculture organization
501 (c) (6)	Business leagues
501 (c) (7)	Social and recreational clubs
501 (c) (8)	Fraternal beneficial societies
501 (c) (9)	Voluntary employees' societies
501 (c) (10)	Domestic fraternal beneficiary societies
501 (c) (11)	Teachers' retirement fund
501 (c) (12)	Benevolent life insurance associations
501 (c) (13)	Cemetery companies
501 (c) (14)	Credit unions
501 (c) (15)	Mutual insurance companies
501 (c) (16)	Corporations to finance crop operation
501 (c) (17)	Supplemental unemployment benefit trusts
501 (c) (18)	Employee-funded pension trusts
501 (c) (19)	War veterans' organizations
501 (c) (20)	Legal services organizations
501 (c) (21)	Black lung trusts
501(d)	Religious and apostolic organizations
501(e)	Cooperative hospital service organizations
501(f)	Cooperative service organizations of operating educational organizations
521	Farmers' cooperatives

Source: Internal Revenue Service, Annual Report

emergencies, or it may be placed in a **reserve fund** that can be used for the purchase of new equipment, renovations, or growth of any kind. Sometimes these funds are combined and labeled as either contingency or reserve.

- **Possess a tax-exempt status from the IRS (Exp.: 501 (c) 3)** Nonprofit organizations are exempt from federal corporate income taxes and most are exempt from state and local property and sales taxes. Because of the great diversity of this sector, there are at least twenty-six different sections under which nonprofit organizations can claim exemption from federal income taxes. They are not exempt from withholding payroll taxes and they must pay taxes on income that is not directly related to their mission, such as the income from a university owning a retirement home and receiving revenue from that home. This exempt status can be traced back through medieval England to ancient times. Various types of tax-exempt organizations operating in the United States are included in Figure 1.2.
- **Conduct an annual, independent audit.** Conducting an annual, independent

audit by a competent, certified accounting firm provides insight for nonprofits to operate efficiently, ethically, and legally. The *independent* aspect of the audit signifies that the audit is done by accountants without close ties to the organization being audited, thereby avoiding the possibility of a conflict of interest. The annual audit provides valuable information to the organization, its members, potential donors, and accrediting organizations.

■ Sub-categories of Nonprofit Organizations

Charities. Nonprofit organizations that are exempt under Section 501 (c) (3) of the income tax law are sometimes referred to as charities, although they offer a lot more services than sheltering and providing food to the poor. These organizations include hospitals, art centers, schools, advocacy groups, public radio and television stations, wellness centers, disaster relief organizations, various recreational centers and many others (Independent Sector 2002).

An organization must have a broad base of financial support to be considered a public charity before applying to the IRS for tax-exempt status. Individuals and corporations may receive tax deductions for making contributions to public charities, but an accountant is generally consulted regarding any possible deductions.

Foundations. About fifty-thousand individuals, families, corporations, and/or communities have established foundations for the purpose of providing funding for support of various causes while operating as a 501 (c) (3) entity and receiving tax breaks. Some of these foundations are subject to strict regulations, being required to contribute at least five percent of investment assets each year and being required to pay approximately two percent excise tax on net earnings. Some common types of foundations are listed below:

- **Private** foundations are typically funded by an individual, a family, or a business and use investment income to make contributions to nonprofit organizations. The W.K. Kellogg Foundation, the Ford Foundation, and the Carnegie Corporation are good examples of private foundations.
- A **corporate** foundation is a type of private foundation that receives funding from and make grants on behalf of a corporation. Many corporate foundations provide grants to community organizations, as well as to employees and their family members, for educational and other purposes. The Metropolitan Foundation and the Starbucks Foundation are examples of corporate foundations.
- **Operating** foundations are yet another form of private foundations that use the majority of their resources to fund their own service programs, rather than funding other programs. Examples of operating foundations include the Carnegie Endowment for International Peace and the J. Paul Getty Trust.
- **Community** foundations receive contributions from many donors and then focus their grants on specific cities or regions. Community foundations are classified as publicly supported charities by the IRS and are therefore not subject to excise taxes or distribution restrictions like private foundations. Individual donations to community foundations are generally tax deductible. The Cleveland Foundation and the New York Community Trust are examples of community foundations.

Nonprofit organizations such as hospitals and colleges often create related 501 (c) (3) organizations, referred to as foundations, whose sole purpose is the support of the parent or sponsoring organization. These foundations are fund raising in nature rather than grant making, and all of the proceeds go toward the parent organization.

Social Welfare Organizations. Advocacy organizations, such as the NAACP and the National Rifle Association (NRA) are exempt entities under Section 501 (c) (4) of the tax code. Social welfare or advocacy organizations have greater freedom in legislative advocacy, lobbying, and political campaign activities so contributions to 501 (c) (3) organizations are generally not tax-deductible.

Professional and Trade Associations. Organizations that promote business or professional interests, such as chambers of commerce, usually qualify for tax exemption under 501 (c) (6) of the tax code. Donations to these organizations are not tax-deductible, but membership dues should qualify as a business expense.

In addition to donations, United Way allocations, special events, grants, program and membership fees, nonprofit organizations can also receive funding from the government in the form of grants or as contracts for providing services.

One of the most important and distinctive aspects of the United States is the important role that has been left to private, nonprofit organizations and the way in which these organizations have changed and benefited the American way of life. Millions of Americans have learned to swim, received blood transfusions, turned their lives around at "safe" houses, learned a trade, developed character, been rehabilitated, or just had fun at one or more of the hundreds of thousands of nonprofit organizations across the land. But how did all this begin? The history of the nonprofit sector is rich in detail and scope and certainly worth examining.

■ How Did the Nonprofit Sector Begin?

According to Stephen Ott (2001) the emphasis on community and social responsibility goes all the way back to Greco-Roman days and to the Judeo-Christian ethic of individuals helping each other in their communities..

The concept of American benevolence or **philanthropy**, as it is often called, is generally considered to be an imported product originating in Europe before the colonization of America began (Worth 2009). However, the concern for the well-being of others in the United States stretches all the way back to the seventeenth century, when no one individual could overcome the harshness of the new land. White settlers received enormous assistance from Native Americans, and this cooperation often meant the difference between life and death. In the winter of 1620-21 in Plymouth, Massachusetts, one Indian in particular, Squanto, proved to be especially helpful when he taught the weary Pilgrims how to plant corn, where to fish, and how to procure other commodities that were necessary for survival. Squanto also guided the Pilgrims in their exploration of the new land and stayed by their side until his death. Many Native Americans followed in Squanto's footsteps, assisting the settlers in adjusting to conditions that few had ever encountered before. American benevolence was influenced by European experience and theory, and for many years American institutions practically mirrored those of Europe. These institutions also sought and received financial support from abroad. American philanthropy took root almost immediately and grew rapidly, probably because the colonization of America coincided with one of the greatest periods of European philanthropy. A number of missionary enterprises, a renewed interest in charitable works, and the development in England of tax-supported poor relief in the seventeenth century all inspired similar goals in the New World.

A more detailed account of the history of philanthropy and the nonprofit sector follows and is derived primarily from several sources, including *Historical Perspectives on Nonprofit Organizations* by Hall, and *Leadership and Program Development in Nonprofit Organization* and *Knowledge and Skill Development in Nonprofit Organizations* by Weis and Gantt. Ellis and Noyes conducted unparalleled, historical research regarding nonprofit organizations in this country and much of what follows is a selected chronology of their work, *By the People: A History of Americans as Volunteers.* More information on each of these references and others can be found in the reference section at the end of this chapter.

New Beginnings and Colonization:
Philanthropy and Service Take Root in the 1600-1700s

In 1620, the Pilgrims developed the **Social Compact** as a declaration of their determination to achieve mutual, civic goals. This document resulted in a covenant that tied the Pilgrims to the mutual care of other community members. This covenant was supported by the doctrines of **Puritanism** that consisted of a strict moral code and an active concern for the members of the church and the community. According to the tenets of Puritanism, man was born evil, but could obtain Grace by positive actions and deeds. These doctrines had a profound influence on the behavior of the settlers. Farmers often combined their efforts to clear land, plant crops, build barns, and to defend against any and all assaults by nature or man. While the men did most of the strenuous work, the women and children assisted and also prepared communal meals (Weis and Gantt 2004).

The largest church in a particular area often directed the social welfare activities of the community. For example, the **Quakers** in Pennsylvania would hold meetings that dealt with both church and community issues; the tradition was referred to as **Meeting Day**. Members of the church would prioritize what needed to be done for the poor, for the maintenance of the city, and for other community needs, and volunteers from the church would initiate appropriate action. In most cases, even the church buildings were built by voluntary community effort. A religious revival referred to as the **Great Awakening** swept the colonies between 1740 and 1760 and was as much a social and political revival as a religious one. The evangelicals promoted liberties and organized voluntary associations such as the **Sons of Liberty**, which eventually played a role in resisting the British. With the support of Benjamin Franklin, secret organizations like the **Juntos,** artisans who met weekly to discuss politics and other issues, and the **Freemasons,** a club formed for mutual improvement, began to establish themselves as leaders in the collective movement for independence from Britain (Hall 1994).

During the colonial period in New England, the strong, Puritan ethic maintained that individuals were first responsible for their own well-being, and there was often a lack of "organized charity" (Ellis and Noyes 1978). Alms giving to the poor was looked down upon, and people who provided handouts were considered to be fools. In spite of this culture, the need for an occasional charitable act was recognized, and families were considered the first line of assistance for members, poor relatives or close friends. These activities were not necessarily voluntary actions, since the colonies eventually adopted the provisions of the **Elizabethan Poor Law** that framed these activities and others as requirements of the citizenry (Hall 1994).

Oftentimes the elderly and those with serious illnesses were kept in private homes, and the host families were paid through tax collections. In some communities, families would take turns taking care of indigents and the infirm for a couple of weeks each year; a term referred to as **taking in.** When the population grew in the cities, these informal systems of care became less and less effective and **almshouses** were initiated to assist the poor and the needy, the first in Boston in 1662 and in Philadelphia in 1732. In addition to almshouses, clubs, societies and fraternal orders began to develop with the primary purpose of providing assistance to others.

Medical care was also important during colonial days, the quality of which left much to be desired and the few doctors that were available were much in demand. In an effort to establish medical standards, the **Weekly Society of Gentlemen in New York** was formed in 1749, and it later evolved into the **Medical Society of the State of New York** in 1794. Colonies did not have health organizations, as such, but when a medical crisis did occur, a committee of citizens with a physician at the head was appointed to address the situation; these committees were usually referred to as **boards of health.** When epidemics occurred, individuals or families were treated in **pest houses**, which were little more than shelters built in a remote area because of the need to quarantine. The first colonial hospital was the **Philadelphia Hospital**, built in 1751 as a nonprofit, philanthropic enterprise.

During the period when the colonies were developing, most educational institutions in Europe were supported by the church, and few were actually state supported. Accordingly, the first educational institutions in this country were initiated and developed by the churches. Children, however, were often put to work at home or in industries, and when educational activities did take place, they occurred in log cabins, in seacoast churches or in sod houses along the prairie. The first schoolhouses were generally built through a cooperative effort, such as the "Old School House" in Mount Holly, New Jersey; constructed in 1759 by a group of citizens who also bought the land the schoolhouse was built on (Ellis and Noyes 1978). In 1794, the **Society of Associated Teachers** was formed in New York City to improve the education of teachers and to set and regulate standards for teaching. This prompted some of the initial instructional activities for teachers in the early part of the 1800s.

Advanced degrees were also desirable, but candidates were forced to consider expensive, European universities until 1636, when a group of clergy founded the first college in the New World. The success of this college was insured when John Harvard left the developing college a large sum of money and hundreds of books from his own library; the school honored Harvard by naming the institute **Harvard College**. Following this, a group of Connecticut clergy founded **Yale University** in 1700 by offering books from their own, personal libraries and embarking on a successful fundraising campaign; hence two of America's most prestigious, private, nonprofit institutes of learning were firmly established (Ellis and Noyes 1978).

As the population expanded in the cities the potential for fire and the need for effective fire fighting equipment and personnel became more and more important. In 1736, Benjamin Franklin in Philadelphia pioneered the first voluntary fire department that became an immediate and extraordinary success and the idea spread quickly through the colonies. It was not until the late 1700s that fire departments started to become staffed with professionals as well as volunteers.

In the eighteenth century, America was mainly an agricultural society and it was important that farmers understood the most efficient methods of farming and had the most modern equipment. To this end, voluntary organizations such as the **Society for the Promotion of Agriculture** were formed in 1785. This organization provided farmers with the latest results in agricultural testing and supported them with reports regarding other activities. In 1786, the **Patriotic Society in Virginia** began which combined agricultural activities with political initiatives; such as blending different methods of fencing with the preservation of timber (Ellis and Noyes 1978).

There was such a strong emphasis on farming and farming societies and associations, that business and trade associations didn't fully develop until the mid-1800s, with some exceptions. Two noteworthy exceptions were the **New York Chamber of Commerce** established in 1792 and the **New York Stock Exchange** initiated in 1792.
For obvious reasons, these organizations were primarily concerned with economic profit and activities designed to enhance commerce but were also actively involved with civic and community enrichment.

A Century of Paradox:
Service Opportunities Abound in the 1800s

The end of the Revolutionary War brought a great number of opportunities and challenges; a unified government was formed and the original frontier was moved further and further west. In spite of the development of a unified government, there were many limits to what government could accomplish, and social welfare, education, the arts, and many other local issues often had to be handled by local citizen groups and community organizations (Weis and Gantt 2004).

Small towns expanded into cities, and as factories and industrial trades grew, labor organizations were created to provide sick benefits and voluntary assistance to widows and orphans. In the early 1800s, a number of these **benevolent societies** began in the state of New York. In 1811, child labor had not yet become a major issue, but the **Manumission Society** was organized with the primary function of encouraging legislation that would regulate the horrible working conditions for chimney sweeps, who tended to be juvenile boys.

A different form of assistance for children began to form in the mid-1800s: **day nurseries**, which are now referred to as children's day care centers. Organizations such as the **Children's Aid Society** and the **National Conference of Charities and Correction** worked diligently to develop an effective structure for child care. These nurseries were usually located in large, urban centers and were sponsored by the wives of wealthy men, who could plan charity balls, fairs, and other activities in support of the nurseries. Nurseries usually employed a large number of women and were sometimes part of settlement houses, churches, or adjuncts of family welfare agencies, and they were almost never publicly supported. In addition to providing child care, day nurseries offered a number of services including employment and training. Staff from the nursery would match individuals looking for domestic work with some of the local, wealthy families, and individuals would train to be domestic workers or child-care providers under the supervision of more experienced staff members.

It was also around this period that a concern grew for the separation of the juvenile court system from the adult justice process. Volunteer associations, such as the **Cook County Woman's Club** in Illinois, lobbied with parent-teacher associations and many other such associations across the country, and in 1899 the first juvenile courts were established in Chicago and Denver. These were typically staffed by volunteers until the early 1900s.

Prior to the turn of the century, **free schools** did not exist for poor children, most of whom were laboring at home or in an industry. This problem was particularly true for children in urban areas who did not have the time for or the money to pay for private schooling. This problem was also prevalent in Europe, where they began the first **Sunday Schools** established for reading and religion. They were held on Sunday, when children did not labor in the factories. This idea soon spread to the United States, where citizens volunteered their time and their money to provide educational experiences for the poor. **School societies** began forming throughout large cities and on the East Coast, providing educational opportunities for children. They were supported completely by voluntary contributions and voluntary instruction. These societies became the basis for tax-supported, public school systems that made their appearance around 1840.

Another popular and successful method of instruction was the **Lancastrian** method, named after Joseph Lancaster, who developed the system in London in the late 1700s. This system was brought to this country around 1800, and it involved teachers teaching a lesson to older students, who would then present the lesson to their younger classmates. This method of using students as resources was highly successful and cost effective and thrived between the early 1800s and 1825.

In the early 1800s, private, nonprofit institutions of higher education came under attack by members of the Jeffersonian party who wanted to convert the privately founded **Dartmouth College** to a state institution. In 1816, the New Hampshire legislature passed a bill reorganizing the college under state control (Hall 1994). The old trustees of Dartmouth, represented by Daniel Webster, appealed to the United States Supreme Court in 1818 and won on the basis that property and money had been contributed to the trustees for the purpose of establishing a private college; the Constitution prohibited states from passing laws breaking contractual agreements (Hofstadter and Smith 1961).

The education of slaves in the 1800s was extremely limited. In spite of the fact that teaching slaves to read or write was illegal, many individuals would risk being arrested. Family members of the master's house would sometimes teach slaves to read and write, and in turn the educated slaves would teach others. A strong interest in adult education also developed in the 1800s and the **Lyceum Movement** began in 1820. This was a fairly formal way of educating the adult population in which philanthropic, humanitarian organizations and corporations would sponsor libraries, museum collections, seminars, and debates for self-improvement.

Between 1862 and 1877, the war between white settlers and Native Americans reached a fever pitch which led to the federal government taking over Indian land and forcing entire tribes to live on reservations. A number of whites were so affected by this injustice that they formed the **Indian Rights Association** in 1882. This organization joined with the **Women's National Indian Association** and lobbied successfully for educational centers for Native Americans. Boarding schools were instituted on most reservations, first run by missionaries and then by government-contracted instructors.

In the late 1800s, education underwent a significant renaissance, public school systems began to out-number private educational systems, and the demand for adult educational opportunities increased. As a result of this demand, there was an increased need for efficient public libraries, and in 1876 the **American Library Association** began in Philadelphia. Members of this group initiated the cataloguing and circulation systems that remain in existence today and began raising funds to build more and start libraries.

The system of higher education also went through a number of changes in the late 1800s due in large part to a committee of university presidents who worked together to change what they considered to be an already inefficient higher education system in America. Working individually and collectively, these presidents brought about revisions in curriculum and then founded universities supported by state funds. They established technical and professional schools, graduate education, co-education, and education for blacks. They also encouraged philanthropic gifts that led to creating laboratories, purchasing new equipment, and building libraries and museums. This period of growth encouraged scholars to form nationwide associations in many branches of research, including the **American Chemical Society**; the **American Ornithologists' Union**; the **American Catholic Historical Association**; the **American Climatological Society**; the **Association of Economic Entomologists**; and the **American Psychological Association** (Ellis and Noyes 1978).

Several events late in the century led to the encouragement of increased contributions to private colleges, universities and other nonprofit organizations and to a support system for college-educated women. In 1874, **Harvard** defended its tax exemption to the Massachusetts General Court so eloquently that the court raised the ceiling on the amount of property that could be exempted from taxation, and it expanded exempt institutions to include educational, charitable, benevolent and religious organizations (Hall 1994). This was great news for nonprofit organizations, which grew at an enormous rate in the latter part of the nineteenth century. Then, in 1882, a group of the first college-educated women joined together to form the **American Association of University Women**. Still in existence today, this association supported other women in seeking college degrees and worked diligently to make colleges co-educational.

Religion continued to be a significant part of the lives of the early citizens, and the Protestant dominion was preserved through collaborative participation in various causes. Organizations made up of different denominations, such as the **Connecticut Moral Society,** also began to appear throughout New England and the Midwest in the early 1800s with purposes such as moral development, missionary pursuits and educational activities.

Early missionary societies served the American family, settlers, and the Native Americans. Missions were established throughout the Midwest and the Southwest, with a primary purpose of converting Indians to Christianity. This was usually a dangerous mission with little progress, until Congress authorized ten million dollars to fund religious groups working with various tribes. As a part of these missionary activities, thousands of Bibles were distributed and an outgrowth of this movement was the establishment of the **American Bible Society** in 1815 with chapters beginning in hundreds of locations in just a few years.

Religious growth was also occurring in the south, where preachers would hold services for slaveholders and their families in the morning, followed by similar services for their slaves on Sunday afternoon. Sometimes even the master of the plantation would hold services, but eventually black religious leaders began to emerge and mostly black churches began to come into existence. A similar occurrence began with urban slaves who became very active in religious life, taking on more leadership roles with the churches. Free blacks and slaves also combined forces to develop associations, such as the **Free African Society** in Philadelphia, for the purpose of developing leadership in black churches and other cities soon followed suit.

In spite of the fact that religious freedom was a legal right in most states, prejudice, particularly against atheists and Jews was rampant and organizations such as the **Native American Party** began in the 1830s and reflected hatred and divisiveness for anyone who was different. But most religious organizations had much more positive purposes. For instance, following the Civil War, the American missionary movement grew rapidly and contributed evangelical efforts, humanitarian aid, and commercial ventures throughout Latin America, the Middle East, Africa, Hawaii, and the Far East in the 1980s and 1990s.

In the early part of the 1800s, medical practices were relatively unstructured, with few standards, and doctors often served as druggists and visiting nurses as well. Initially, women provided medical assistance in most areas and often prescribed and even formulated their own remedies. Most wagon train leaders also served as surgeons as pioneers headed westward and the need for removing bullets and treating snakebites became prevalent.

Local counties were allowed to institute boards of health to coordinate efforts regarding matters of health. As a result, free vaccination clinics begin to form, and New York established a **Vaccination Institute** in 1802, with Boston following in 1803. These clinics provided essential services and were generally staffed with volunteer doctors. The first visiting nurse service in the country, called the **Ladies' Benevolent Society**, was established in 1813 in Charleston, South Carolina, with medical care primarily for the sick poor. Volunteers established specialized institutions, such as the **Asylum for the Deaf and Dumb** in 1827, the **New York Institute for the Blind** in 1831, and the **New York Ophthalmic Hospital** in1852. In 1892, the **Pennsylvania Society for the Prevention of Tuberculosis** was created and became the first organization in which lay and medical persons worked together toward the prevention and cure of a specific ailment. Medical societies played a significant part in establishing standards for medical practice and the **American Medical Association,** started in 1847, was at the forefront of this movement. Its purpose was to insure the quality of licensure and to improve instructional methodology.

Although the Civil War had been tremendously divisive, it also united citizens of the North and South as never before. Northern women organized themselves into **Ladies' Aid Societies** to assemble bandages and other items of medical aid. Several of these societies were eventually merged into the **Women's Central Relief Association for the Sick and Wounded of the Army.** The association encouraged the formation of the **U.S. Sanitary Commission**, which soon became the largest private relief organization of the war. This organization stockpiled huge warehouses of food, clothing, and medical supplies for future distribution, and it maintained houses where traveling federal soldiers could find meals, rest, lodging and comfort. Following the war, the commission also found jobs for soldiers who returned disabled and for their wives and mothers. Another commission, the **Christian Commission**, was established in 1861 in order to present evangelical opportunities to soldiers, distributing Bibles and religious tracts, and providing food kitchens.

Black contributions to both sides of the war were numerous and invaluable. Although some slaves remained loyal to their masters even after the Emancipation Proclamation, records indicate that thousands of slaves helped the Union cause by engaging in work slowdowns, serving as spies, and by not participating in the Southern Army. They also provided food and shelter to Northern soldiers whenever possible. The **Loyal League**, for instance, helped escaped slaves and spied for the North. The **Underground Railroad**, used primarily by runaway slaves to escape from the plantations, was also used by Northern soldiers as an escape route from Confederate incarceration.

The 1800s were such a turbulent time, and the population of the country was growing so rapidly, that a staggering number of associations and nonprofit organizations came to be following the end of the Civil War. One of the first of these organizations was the **Freedmen's Bureau**, established in 1865 to coordinate the monumental mitigation efforts for former slaves. The bureau's main concern was to make emancipation a reality through programs of education, employment, and land acquisition. The Freedmen's Bureau joined with other such organizations to recruit teachers and acquire school buildings for providing educational opportunities for the newly freed Southern blacks. It has been estimated that about 90,000 black men, women, and children attended 1000 schools supported by the bureau in the year 1866 (Ellis and Noyes 1978).

Manufacturing flourished following the Civil War, and new production methods for steel and oil added to increased jobs and consumer demand. As manufacturing increased, so did the demand for stronger and stronger unions to address issues such as unfair wages, lack of benefits, and unsafe working conditions. Groups such as the **Sovereigns of Industry**, the **Industrial Brotherhood**, and the **Knights of Labor** came to the forefront of workers' rights and made their demands felt through strikes and other work stoppage methods. It was out of this support for the labor movement that the **Young Women's Christian Association (YWCA)**, established in the mid-1800s, grew much stronger in the late 1800s. Churchwomen in cities throughout the East developed more YWCAs to provide housing, recreation, and training for women, particularly women who were working in the sweatshops in the Eastern cities. This organization continues to empower women through health, education, and enrichment programs and operates in all fifty states.

Because of the proximity of some manufacturing companies to one another, competition existed for raw materials and customers, and trade unions were founded to fix prices and discounts, and to allocate materials. The first such recognized union was the **American Brass Association**, founded in 1853 in Connecticut. Since local efforts were not always enough to manage business problems, trade associations began to create national ties. Local Chambers of Commerce joined together in 1868, forming the **National Board of Trade** to represent this country's business interests nationally and internationally. And by the end of the century, other business groups were coming together for the purpose of economics and professionalism, such as the **American Association of Public Accountants**, established in 1887, and the **National Association of Life Underwriters**.

Farmers also felt a need to organize, and the **Grange** association was established in 1867 in Washington, D.C. The Grange was supported by the Department of Agriculture. The Grange provided opportunities for forums on new scientific agricultural techniques, recreational activities, and other communication opportunities for farmers and their families to share their knowledge and interest. Grange organizations had a tremendous impact on formal education and lobbied for more curricula relevant to farming. A Cornell University professor initiated a process of naturalist pamphlets for young people in country schools in 1898 and assisted in organizing nature studies. This eventually led to the formation of the **4-H** organization in partnership with the U.S. Department of Agriculture. The purpose of 4-H is to help young people acquire knowledge and develop life skills and it has served over 40 million boys and girls nationwide.

Another group that was feeling the need to organize during this period was women. Women had always worked together before and during the Civil War, and women's associations of one kind or another had existed for a long time. Women's groups began to develop strong interests in child welfare, public education, divorce reform and other civic concerns. The **Women's Christian Temperance Union** sought legislation prohibiting the sale of alcohol, and the **General Federation of Women's Clubs** became a strong force for a number of social issues. The **National Woman Suffrage Association** was considered a radical group devoted to women's rights at almost any cost, and the **American Woman Suffrage Association** developed as a more conservative group devoted to women's issues. Women's rights, particularly for the working class, became of paramount importance, and feminist leaders urged the formation of independent unions, such as the **Working Women's Association** and the **Protective Association for Women**.

One woman in particular who made a big difference during this time was Clara Barton, a Civil War battleground nurse who founded the **American Red Cross (ARC)** in 1893. Barton thought there should be an organization with volunteers trained to handle disasters during war as well as during peacetime and trained to prevent, prepare for and respond to different kinds of emergencies. Devastating forest fires in Michigan and floods along the Ohio and Mississippi provided the Red Cross its first tests, tests that the organization handled wonderfully. Congress chartered the Red Cross in 1905 (Boylston 1955).

Philanthropy in general was undergoing change in the 1800s, and contributing money to charities had reached monumental levels, but it was unorganized and highly competitive. Eventually, the **American Charity Organization Society** was established in Buffalo in 1877 to provide an organized system of fund raising and by 1893 there were dozens of similar organizations across the nation. In addition to fund raising, the society established a process referred to as **friendly visitors**, in which volunteers would interview individuals and families to determine eligibility for charitable funds. This process evolved into the profession of **social work**, and individuals received training and payment for their investigative efforts.

Following this, the **Young Men's Christian Association** and the **Jewish Federation** joined in 1887 in conducting fundraising activities that eventually led to the formation of the **United Way of America**. Initiated by four clergymen in Denver, the idea of a coordinated, unified, fundraising campaign for nonprofit organizations spread across the country, and there are currently over two thousand United Way offices nationwide. In the last quarter of the nineteenth century, wealthy citizens such as Andrew Carnegie and John D. Rockefeller were looking for ways to more effectively use money to get at the real root of problems, and the concept of **grant-making foundations** was born. Instead of operating programs, foundations would fund organizations that were addressing the issues that interested the foundations. However, while Carnegie and Rockefeller were sold on the concept, they were slow to move, and credit for establishing the first foundation went to a lesser-known individual, Margaret Olivia Slocum Sage (Hall 1994).

Another organization active in the late 1800s was the **Salvation Army**, which originated as an integral part of the **Social Gospel** doctrine and was first involved with evangelistic efforts. It then expanded to operating shelters, food warehouses, and employment agencies. Organizations were also formed for the care and prevention of cruelty to animals, and in 1873 the **Society for the Prevention of Cruelty to Animals (SPCA)** was established, and volunteers for the organization distributed millions of pamphlets nationwide. In its early days and in a dramatic and unusual act, the SPCA brought a beaten child to court in a case that spurred the formation of the first **Society for the Prevention of Cruelty to Children** in New York in 1875.

Recreational and cultural activities increased following the Civil War with the advent of **playgrounds**, recreational centers, community centers, music and drama groups, theaters, bands, and orchestras. Recreation was becoming more and more a part of church related activities and the **YMCA**, first founded in England in 1844 and then established in the United States in 1852, became a leader in offering organized sports. The first **Girls Club** came to be in 1854 in Connecticut, with the purpose of providing safe havens and social and educational centers for workers in northeastern mill towns during the industrial revolution. The Girls Club would change its name to **Girls Incorporated** in 1990 and maintain its purpose of empowering girls and young women to be self sufficient and personally fulfilled. The **Boys Club** was established in the late 1860s in New England as a place for boys to be able to get off the streets and to have a safe and inviting place to play. The idea spread quickly, and by 1906 there were fifty clubs nationwide that banded together to become the **Boys Clubs of America**. The Boys Clubs gradually began inviting girls to participate in their programs, finally becoming known as the **Boys and Girls Clubs of America** in the 1980s.

As the industrial, urban lifestyle increased, so did the interest in outdoor activities, and camps began springing up across the country. YMCAs, settlement houses, and private individuals founded a number of camps in the late 1880s and the YMCA established itself as a leader in outdoor activities. A conservation movement also developed and grew during this time. The **American Forestry Association** was formed in Chicago in 1875 by a committee of horticulturists and concerned community members. This first organized conservation initiative was not able to have much influence with Congress at the time, but it did manage to have an impact on the public's perception of conservation. These energies also led to the establishment of **Arbor Day**, a national day of planting trees. To foster geographic knowledge, thirty-three men who had occupations ranging from explorer to meteorologist founded the **National Geographic Society** in 1888. The Society promotes research projects and then disseminates information about the physical and social world through publications. The **Sierra Club** was founded in 1892 to protect California's forests and wildlife. It soon became clear that there were limits to what local actions could achieve, so eventually the Sierra Club became a national venture. The **Audubon Society** was established in the late 1800s with a mission of conserving wildlife; colleges and universities soon began offering classes in forestry.

National and International Challenges: The 1900s and Beyond

The depression of the 1890s was a devastating period, but individuals, families, and communities seemed to bounce back quickly. The citizens of the United States entered the twentieth century with a great deal of optimism, and the country established itself as an industrial leader at home and overseas. While the country as a whole was prospering, wages, benefits, and working conditions were still problems for the urban poor, and middle-class, progressive, social reformers began to organize groups into coalitions to bring about change (Weis and Gantt 2004).

Not all voluntary organizations had socially redeeming intentions. One group that opposed this progressive movement was the **Ku Klux Klan**. Having been organized in the 1800s and then disappearing into the background for a while, the Klan re-emerged in the 1900s. First operating as vigilante groups to protect the tobacco farmers in Kentucky and Tennessee, the Klan became a national, fraternal order made up of men who believed in protecting the "Anglo-Saxon" way of life and who set themselves against Catholics, Jews, blacks and foreigners. World War I briefly interrupted the growth of the Klan, but in the 1920s the Klan made a second re-birth in the North, the Midwest and the Southwest and actually organized some charitable activities in places where they were present. Southern Klans often participated in vigilante activities and used lynching as a deterrent to those they opposed. The **Southern Women for the Prevention of Lynching** organized interracial committees in the 1930s, and by 1933 the **National Council of Women**, representing twenty different women's groups and totaling five million women, held the **International Congress of Women**, which worked to abolish lynching.

Women began to develop a collective social conscience for various concerns, and the **General Federation of Women's Clubs** emerged, with an interest in child welfare, public health, the protection of women in industry, growth of educational institutes, and the reform of civil service. The question of women's suffrage was a continuing issue and women's clubs began educating women regarding the need for change and the importance of the vote. In 1913, the **National Women's Party** was established and led the movement to introduce the first **Equal Rights Amendment** in 1923.

The issue of child welfare was another major issue for women and men and the **Big Brothers Association** began in 1903 in Cincinnati, with the purpose of matching adult mentors with needy boys, many from single parent families. Soon afterward, the **Big Sisters** program was formed in 1908 in New York City, with the mission of working with court-referred, delinquent girls. Volunteers first operated both organizations, but social workers were eventually hired to manage the matches and other administrative duties. These two organizations would later merge to become the **Big Brothers Big Sisters of America**. The **National Child Labor Committee** was formed in 1904 and worked both to prohibit children under fourteen from working and to limit the hours and time of day that fourteen- and fifteen-year-olds could work.

In 1912, the **Children's Bureau** was initiated by a group of women concerned with the welfare of mothers and infants, and it was placed under the control of the Department of Labor. The organization grew rapidly and was designed to assist poor mothers in finding adequate shelter and work. Another nonprofit organization began in 1919, **Junior Achievement**, with the purpose of providing young people with economical education programs and experiences in the competitive private enterprise system (Weis and Gantt 2002). This program has provided tens of thousands of children with opportunities to create and develop products and to learn effective ways to market and sell the products they have developed. And in 1939, **Little League Baseball** was organized to teach the game of baseball and the value of sportsmanship to youngsters. It would go on to exist in all U.S. states and territories as well as twenty-nine foreign countries.

Blacks were also looking for a voice in the early 1900s, and in 1905 a group of college-educated blacks formed a coalition to encourage brotherhood and end racism that was to become the **Niagra Movement**. Although this movement lasted only a few years, it laid the foundation for the creation of the **National Association for the Advancement of Colored People (NAACP)** in 1909. The organization was interracial and was established to address discrimination. A conference held in 1910 specifically to address issues pertaining to blacks living in New York City eventually led to the formation of the **National Urban League**. The National Urban League was also an interracial organization and often joined with the NAACP in the battle against unfair practices of discrimination.

Health and social welfare issues were of paramount importance in the early years of the 1900s; there were a number of discoveries made in medical science and a number of national voluntary health organizations began to form. **Goodwill Industries** began in 1902, with the purpose of assisting and enriching the lives of the disabled, and the **National Association for the Study and Prevention of Tuberculosis** was formed in 1904 by a group of doctors dedicated to the elimination of tuberculosis. As tuberculosis was brought under control, the organization expanded its work to fight other lung diseases and pollution and adopted the name **American Lung Association.**

Maryland Association for the Colored Blind was formed in 1913 for the purpose of assisting and enriching the lives of the disabled, and. the **American Foundation for the Blind** was established later, in 1921, and was recognized as Helen Keller's cause. When Edgar Allen's son was injured in a trolley car accident in Elyria, Ohio, and died from lack of sufficient medical help, Allen vowed to never let anyone die from lack of care in his hometown again. He quit his job and began raising funds that led to the establishment of the Elyria Memorial Hospital in 1908. He soon began raising funds throughout the state and enlisted the aid of the local Rotary Club to form the **Ohio Society for Crippled Children** in 1919, which evolved into the **Easter Seals Society**.

Cancer also caused increasing concern, and the **American Cancer Society** was formed in 1913 by a group of doctors and concerned citizens. The organization joined forces with women's clubs across the country and raised public awareness of the disease and promoted interests in finding a cure. Also concerned with health-related issues, John D. Rockefeller, financier, and Frederick T. Gates, Baptist minister, joined to establish the **Rockefeller Foundation** in 1913. The foundation began funding millions of dollars for medical research and soon became a model for well-organized, effective philanthropy. The numbers of those suffering from the disease of alcoholism grew steadily, following the depression of 1929, and a New York stockbroker and an Ohio surgeon, who had been hopeless alcoholics for years, founded **Alcoholics Anonymous (AA)** in 1935. It grew from two members to over 2,000,000 members today and is the largest self-help group for alcoholism in the country.

The **Leukemia and Lymphoma Society of America** was established in 1949 as the Villiers Foundation and was later renamed. The organization is dedicated to eradicating leukemia and related cancers and improving the lives of patients and their families. Another national health organization, the **Juvenile Diabetes Foundation** began in 1970 with the purpose of providing funds for research for the cure, treatment, and prevention of diabetes and its complications.

Social welfare organizations also continued to increase and one result of this growth was the **Junior League**, which began as a way for girls to learn about charity and community responsibilities in their neighborhoods. A national school lunch program was initiated in the early part of the century, and the **Parent Teacher Association (PTA)**, the **Junior League**, and the **American Legion** joined forces to provide volunteers and equipment; a decade later the program was providing a hot meal a day to over nine million school children. **Catholic Charities USA** began in 1910 with the goal of reducing poverty, supporting families, and building healthy communities throughout the country. Today, Catholic Charities USA serves approximately ten million people in need.

Camps and public parks increased in the early part of the twentieth century, and the Sierra Club and similar organizations encouraged the growth of the National Park Service and the Forest Service. The **National Conservation Commission** was established in 1908 to influence legislation that would protect environmental interests. The **Boy Scouts of America** was the primary boys' organization at the start of World War I, with over 300,000 scouts and 8,000 volunteer Scout Masters (Ellis and Noyes 1978). It began as an organization to develop character and practical skills with a membership made up mostly of middle- and upper-class boys, but later its members included immigrant and Native American youth, as well. Both the **Girl Scouts of America** and the **Camp Fire Girls** began in the early part of the 1900s with similar purposes as the Boy Scouts. The **National Collegiate Athletic Association (NCAA)** would form in 1906 and serve young adults by setting guidelines and fostering sportsmanship for collegiate athletic competition. Other youth-serving, recreational organizations appeared on the scene later, such as the **Ski Patrol** in 1936, the **Cub Scouts** in 1937, and the **Little League** in 1939.

World War I brought tremendous collaborative efforts among the nation's major nonprofit organizations. The **YMCA, YWCA, National Catholic War Council (Knights of Columbus), Jewish Welfare Board, Salvation Army** and the **American Liberty Service** all worked together to assist soldiers overseas and at home, as well as the general public. The **American Red Cross** was recognized as the preeminent disaster-relief organization in the United States in the early 1900s and had begun to develop nursing programs and training for first aid. At the start of WWI, the Red Cross organized fifty-eight military hospitals overseas and managed forty-seven ambulance companies to transport injured soldiers. The Red Cross also handled the assignment of thousands of nurses, provided field directors for counseling, served as a communication link between servicemen and their families, and maintained over 700 canteens where servicemen and women could shower, use a telephone and generally relax.

With WWI at an end, the nation entered a period of prosperity. Employers and employees began a time of relative harmony, and farming cooperatives and agricultural youth programs grew in popularity. Such organizations as the **Young Farmers**, **Junior Farmers**, and **Future Farmers of America** provided information, activities and support for young people who were interested in agriculture. Businesses also begin to organize around the common cause of safety of all kinds--home, industrial, and automobile. The **National Safety Council** took the lead in educating the public concerning safety issues and organizing community committees around the country to meet and develop action plans for implementing safety plans.

When the stock market crashed in 1929, the nation experienced a nearly devastating depression, and soup kitchens and bread lines were established by a number of charitable organizations. To offer cooperative help for citizens, many of the national service and religious organization joined forces just as they had done during WWI. The Catholic Church, in particular, fared very well during this period, forming the **National Catholic Welfare Conference** to increase the parameters of its secular services. Ecumenical organizations such as the **Committee on Religion and Welfare Activity**, made up of churches of different denominations, joined forces during this time to provide a coordinated effort of services for citizens affected by economic hardships. And private, charitable think tanks, like the **Brookings Institution**, played a pivotal role in public initiatives by helping to draft the Social Security Act. Although unrelated to the depression, the **National Wildlife Federation** began in 1936 with the purpose of educating and inspiring individuals and organizations to conserve wildlife and other natural resources and to protect the Earth's environment.

As the Second World War in Europe began to heat up, communities all over America initiated steps to prepare citizens for conflict. Many community businesses subsidized young men who joined the National Guard or participated in some other government sponsored military endeavor. The **Green Guard**, an all female militia organized to defend the homeland, was initiated in North Carolina, and the **Military Training Camps Association** offered military training to middle-class professionals and businesspeople who would be good candidates as officer reserves. The **American Women's Volunteer Service** was founded and had over 200,000 members who assisted with military activities at home, such as driving trucks and chauffeuring Army and other military officers and instructing housewives and others how to cope in case of an air-raid. A number of women, however, became involved in the pacifist movement, and even the Girl Scouts changed their uniform color from military khaki to a neutral green as a means of protest.

Prior to entering WWII, many Americans felt compassion for the French and English, and the American Red Cross raised over seven million dollars in aid money. Employees at Lockheed donated their own time and used their own money to construct and pay for a new Hudson airplane as a Christmas gift to the Europeans. As America entered WWII, a massive shortage of farm workers ensued, but thousands of volunteers from the **YWCA**, the **High School Victory Corps**, and the **American Women's Voluntary Service**, pulled together to operate the farms successfully. Many farmers cooperated with the **Farm Security Administration** in a movement called "An Acre for a Soldier," in which a farmer would donate the money raised from an acre's crop to the war effort.

In 1942, a nonprofit organization called the **Seaman's Service** was founded, and it collaborated with the **YMCA**, **Travelers' Aid Society**, and the **Red Cross** to provide housing, medical care, counseling and recreation to seamen stationed on shore. American business was actively involved in supporting war efforts, and the **American Society of Association Executives** was created to coordinate activities such as selling war bonds as a funding source, encouraging gasoline conservation, and providing technical assistance to government agencies that needed help. The **American Red Cross** recruited over 71,000 nurses for military duty and provided volunteer staffing for a number of military hospitals, clubs, and mobile club units for servicemen abroad in rest and recreation areas. Americans supported the Red Cross by donating more than $785 million for these efforts (Ellis and Noyes 1978).

Following WWII, the country became forever linked to the world community as witnessed by the creation of the **United Nations** in 1945, and one voluntary organization, the **General Federation of Women's Clubs**, was recruited for input. Urged by the Federation, the **Commission on Human Rights** was included in the United Nation's Charter. Congress chartered the **Civil Air Patrol** in 1946 as a nonprofit organization with a humanitarian focus, and the **Red Cross**, the **Salvation Army**, and the **Veterans of Foreign Wars** agreed to a collaboration to provide disaster relief, air and ground searches, and instruction for aerospace. The business community encouraged the growth of **Chambers of Commerce**, and in a landmark decision in 1952, the New Jersey Superior and Supreme Courts declared that financial gifts by business corporations to institutions of higher education were legal and desirable and did not constitute an endorsement of the business on the part of the educational institution (Hall 1994). Business contributions to education were therefore sanctioned, and future involvement was insured.

A large number of nonprofit organizations established themselves or grew significantly in the 40s and 50s, and ninety percent of nonprofits currently in existence were established following WWII. The **School Safety Patrol** was formed with guidelines from the **AAA**, **National Committee on Safety**, and the **National Safety Council**. The **Red Cross** assisted in pursuing those missing in action after the end of WWII and in helping families reunite in spite of political complications. This organization also began to coordinate large-scale relief operations following major disasters. The **American Heart Association** grew from a group comprised totally of health professionals to a voluntary health organization with community members, and the **National Association for Mental Health** was established in 1950. The **National Epilepsy League** began in 1948 (Ellis and Noyes 1978). That same year, H. Roe Bartle, the Mayor of Kansas City, Missouri, would initiate the **American**

Humanics (AH) program. AH is an affiliation of colleges and universities that prepare students for leadership roles with youth, human service, and other nonprofit organizations (Taylor 1995). The **Muscular Dystrophy Associations of America** began funding research in 1950, and the **Fellowship of Christian Athletes,** an evangelical group associated with sports, started in 1954. The **Cystic Fibrosis Foundation** was organized in 1955 to provide support for researching a cure for cystic fibrosis**,** and **Parents Without Partners**, a self-help support group for single parents was established in 1957.

Another significant aspect in the growth of nonprofit organizations during this period was the role the government played. Prior to the 1940s, the government had already been the largest source of revenue for nonprofit organizations in the fields of culture, education, health, and social welfare. This role became enhanced when the **National Science Foundation** and the **National Institute of Health** made grants on a huge scale to private hospitals and universities. During this same period, the **GI Bill**, passed in 1948 and renewed in 1952, combined with the **National Defense Education Act** of 1958 to provide massive federal funding in the form of student aid to private colleges and universities (Hall 1994).

In the period between the 1940s and the 1970s, the civil rights movement became a major factor in the political landscape of the country. Thousands of volunteers joined in interracial activities, such as boycotts and sit-ins, and a visible militancy emerged. The Montgomery, Alabama, boycott of 1955 involved over 50,000 black residents who avoided using local busses in opposition to segregation and discrimination. This boycott was supported by the **Montgomery Improvement Association**, with Rev. Martin Luther King as the president. Other civil rights groups included the **Southern Christian Leadership Conference (SCLC)**, founded in 1957 by clergy members and committed to the concept that the church should provide key leadership in the civil rights movement, and the **Congress of Racial Equality (CORE)**, which was an interracial, urban group committed to civil rights for all.

In spite of the 1957 **Civil Rights Act**, white supremacy groups often intimidated black voters, and organizations such as the **Mississippi Summer Project of 1964** were created to conduct campaigns to build up voter registration for blacks. Following the march on Washington in 1963, things moved rapidly and a number of black student unions and heritage awareness groups began to form, such as the **American Society of African Culture**. Some militant groups, such as the **Black Panther Party**, advocated armed resistance as the primary method for achieving racial equality. On the other side, white supremacy groups, such as the **Citizens Council**, made up mostly of professionals and business groups, did everything possible to fight discrimination laws.

The Vietnam War also elicited strong sentiments from the majority of the population, and a number of protest groups formed all over the country. The **American Friends Service Committee**, for instance, advocated a pacifist stance and organized citizens to resist the draft. The **Women's Strike for Peace** and the **Veterans and Reservists to End the War** were other groups opposing the Vietnam War that organized citizens to oppose and demonstrate against the government's position. Local and national demonstrations proliferated, and some anti-war groups such as the **Students for a Democratic Society (SDS)** took a militant stand and even attacked Selected Service offices. There were also groups who supported the war, such as the **National Committee for Responsible**

Patriotism, who organized demonstrations of loyalty toward the troops overseas and the cause they represented.

In the middle of the civil rights movement and prior to the controversy surrounding the Vietnam War, President Kennedy initiated a corps of dedicated and skilled Americans to volunteer for positions in the world's developing countries. The **Peace Corps** was established in 1961, and it provided idealistic Americans with productive outlets for their idealism. Though publicly funded, the Peace Corps sparked an interest in serving others. Another famous American, entertainer Danny Thomas, fulfilled a pledge to St. Jude Thaddeous, patron saint of the hopeless to whom he had prayed for direction, by establishing **St. Jude Children's Research Hospital** in 1962 in Memphis, Tennessee. This unique hospital is devoted to curing catastrophic diseases in children. Thomas almost single-handedly raised the money to build the hospital, and today it is the seventh largest health care charity in the country. The same year St. Jude's Hospital was founded, a migrant farm worker named Cesar Chavez organized the **National Farm Workers Association (NFWA)** to lobby for fair wages, benefits and shelter for the thousands of crop pickers harvesting grapes, apples, lettuce, oranges and other produce in southern California. Chavez incorporated nonviolent measures, such as fasting, picketing and boycotts, against the powerful Teamsters Union and the California Growers Association, and the NFWA was eventually victorious in the fight for fairness, thanks to Chavez's quiet resolve and determination (Weis and Gantt 2004).

A few years following the establishment of the Peace Corps, President Johnson initiated **Volunteers in Service to America (VISTA)**, a publicly funded organization that provided citizens opportunities to work in projects in the United States. These government supported volunteer programs have been hugely successful, in spite of some objections to the volunteers' receiving a basic subsistence allowance and a modest stipend. Another organization with a Kennedy name attached was founded in the early 1960s. **Special Olympics** was initiated by Eunice Kennedy Shriver to provide year-round sports training and athletic competition in a variety of Olympic-type sports for children and adults with mental retardation. Those who become involved in Special Olympics develop physical fitness, a sense of belonging and accomplishment, and friendships with fellow competitors and volunteers in their community. While the Peace Corps, VISTA, and to some extent, Special Olympics tended to attract young and often college-educated people, the **Serve and Enrich by Volunteer Experience (SERVE)** was developed in New York to attract senior citizens. This experiment grew to over forty-two pilot programs in New York and eventually inspired the creation of the **Retired Senior Volunteer Program (RSVP)**, which provided seniors with volunteer opportunities nationwide.

President Nixon sought to organize and stimulate the nation's volunteer efforts even further, so in 1971 he created **ACTION**, which was to serve as an umbrella organization for six volunteer organizations: the Peace Corps, VISTA, the Foster Grandparent Program, RSVP, the Service Corps of Retired Executives (SCORE), and the Active Corps of Executives (ACE). Founded during the presidency of Jimmy Carter, **Habitat for Humanity International** was organized by Millard and Linda Fuller in 1976 to provide affordable housing for families in need. This was a cause that President Carter later embraced, and he became actively involved in recruiting volunteers, raising funds, and assisting in the actual building of homes for people of low-income. This was also the decade that brought the **Independent Sector** into existence. The Independent Sector would become a national clearinghouse, of sorts, for information regarding all private, nonprofit organizations, and it would also serve to represent the viewpoint of the nonprofit sector to the public.

In the 1980s, President Reagan proposed that citizens rely less and less on the federal government and more on nonprofit, service organizations. In an economic, belt-tightening move, the president also cut a significant amount of funds for federal programs. This cut in funding had the opposite effect of supporting the efforts of nonprofit organizations, since a number of these organizations received federal support in the form of grants or contracts for performing program services. Ironically, the **Alzheimer's Association** was founded in 1980 to provide patient aid support and research for Alzheimer's disease, a disease that eventually afflicted President Reagan himself. Although federal dollars were less attainable during the Reagan era, the president's efforts to involve corporations with nonprofit work brought forth a tremendous amount of cash through the concept of **cause related marketing.** Cause related marketing involves tying in a nonprofit cause with a specific product. This produced and still produces hundreds of collaborations between the for-profit and nonprofit sectors, providing a great deal of publicity for for-profit businesses and millions of dollars for nonprofit entities (Hall 1994).

An area of service that found deeper roots in the 1980s was the area of service learning, in which students incorporate learning objectives in community service projects. National organizations such as **Campus Outreach Opportunity League** and **Campus Compact** took the lead in encouraging service on college campuses across the country, whether as extra-curricular activities or curriculum-based activities, such as with service learning (Weis and Gantt 2004).

Although there have been occasional scandals involving charities, they usually had no more than a local impact. This changed in the 1980s and 1990s with a series of breaches in trust. First, the **Covenant House**, which provided a safe haven for children, was rocked when the CEO and founder was found to be misusing funds and sexually abusing clients; then, the national **United Way** was besieged when the leading executive was accused of obtaining unreasonable perks and benefits; a series of scandals beset televangelists who had misused organizational funds for personal gain; and the **Blue Cross** experienced a number of different scandals across several states (Hall 1994). These breaches of trust sparked a series of laws that more closely regulated charitable giving and charitable organizations.

In the late 1980s and the early 1990s, President Bush encouraged national service with his **Thousand Points of Light** initiative, which led to financial support for thousands of community service projects across the country. President Clinton signed the **National and Community Service Act** in the early 1990s, which was followed by the creation of **Americorps.** Americorps provides thousands of citizens the opportunity to engage in community service across the country, while receiving financial assistance to register for college coursework. Although not as heralded as President Kennedy's Peace Corps, Americorps is much larger than the Peace Corps and has proven to be a valuable asset for fulfilling community needs, as well as for providing service opportunities and college tuition for citizens who may not have been able to afford college otherwise.

Following the controversial election of 2000, President George W. Bush took a strong and unique stand on involving citizens in community service by offering to fund "faith-based" organizations that fulfilled tasks that the federal government could not or would not be able to do. Though a number of politicians and citizens argued that this position endangered the separation of church and state, a number of eligible, nonprofit organizations actively sought funding to expand their service base. Following the tragic terrorists attacks of September 11, 2001, a number of national, nonprofit organizations such as the **American Red Cross,** the **United Way,** and the **Salvation Army** took the lead to raise funds and provide services for the thousands of citizens that were affected by those events. Millions of citizens across the country contributed blood, money, and other support to the thousands of nonprofit organizations that bonded together to work cooperatively in support of the relief efforts following the terrorist attacks (Weis and Gantt 2004).

Millions of citizens and nonprofit organizations joined together again to assist the victims of Hurricane Katrina in and around the state of Louisiana in 2005, the victims of the tragic Tsunami that occurred in Indonesia in 2007 and the hundreds of thousands of individuals affected by the devastating earthquake in Haiti in 2010.

■ Summary

The nonprofit sector includes educational, cultural, religious, recreational, service, and character development organizations, along with foundations, hospitals, wellness centers, and other privately incorporated organizations that serve a public mission of some kind. These organizations can take in revenue, but any money over and above expenses must go back into the organization in some manner. Nonprofit organizations provide assistance to citizens that the government cannot or does not provide, and they receive a special tax-exempt status, which differs with the type of nonprofit organization. Other characteristics include being governed by a voluntary board of directors and conducting an annual, independent audit of financial processes and records.

The sector's roots can be traced back to the benevolence that existed between the Pilgrims, patriots, and Native Americans and to the importation of philanthropic ventures from Europe and even to Greco-Roman days. The combination of a strong Puritan ethic of concern for family and community and the Elizabethan Poor Law, which framed some community activities as requirements, made for a fertile ground for service. For instance, the elderly and infirm were often boarded in private homes, for which families were paid through tax collections, and religious institutions were often the center of many other community service initiatives in Colonial times.

The end of the Revolutionary War brought a number of opportunities and challenges as the country pushed westward and towns became cities. Industrialization brought on the need for organizations that would encourage safe and fair working conditions for laborers, particularly children. Educational processes became more and more sophisticated, public education systems began to outnumber private ones, and adult education grew in importance. Health care also became more sophisticated with the founding of a number of private, nonprofit hospitals. The Civil War created a need for establishing a number of nonprofit organizations as support systems during the war and as relief organizations following it. Charitable giving became more organized and grant making foundations were born. Recreational activities and organizations increased significantly following the Civil War, as the industrial urban lifestyle involved more people.

Women began to develop a collective social conscience for various concerns, and a number of women's groups and associations began forming in the 1900s. Because child welfare was one of these concerns, a number of youth organizations were formed throughout the twentieth century. A number of discoveries in medical science were made in the 1900s, and a number of national health care organizations formed to support further research and patient aid. World War I brought tremendous cooperative action among the nation's major nonprofit organizations, as did the stock market crash of 1929. In the early 1940s the Second World War in Europe began to heat up, and a number of nonprofit organizations developed to prepare citizens for support efforts of the war. As America entered the war, support and relief efforts provided by nonprofit organizations were highly significant, and a large number of organizations established themselves or grew at an unparalleled pace following the war.

The passing of the GI Bill and the National Defense Education Act in the 1950s provided massive federal funding in the form of student aid to private colleges and universities. A large number of organizations were involved in the civil rights movement between 1940 and 1970. The Vietnam War evoked strong emotions from most citizens in the 1960s and 1970s, with a number of people and nonprofit organizations ending up on both sides of the conflict. The Peace Corps, which provided opportunities to volunteer for positions in the world's developing countries, and VISTA, which provided opportunities for volunteers to work in projects in the United States, were established by Presidents John F. Kennedy and Lyndon B. Johnson, respectively, in the 1960s.

President Richard M. Nixon put his own stamp of support on nonprofit organizations in the 1970s with the creation of ACTION, which was designed to bring a number of successful, nonprofit organizations under the same umbrella. In the 1980s, President Ronald Reagan encouraged citizens to depend less on government and more on nonprofit organizations. President George Bush established the Thousand Points of Light initiative that led to financial support for thousands of community service initiatives; President William J. Clinton signed the National and Community Service Act in the early 1990s, which led to the establishment of Americorps. Americorps provides thousands of citizens the opportunity to engage in community service across the country while receiving financial assistance from the government to register for college course-work. In 2001, President George W. Bush offered to fund faith-based organizations that fulfilled tasks that the federal government could not or would not be able to do.

This chapter addressed, in part, the Nonprofit Leadership Alliance Certification Competency Requirements of Historical and Philosophical Foundations.

Two books that include a description of the history of nonprofit organizations are suggested:
- *By the People*, by Susan Ellis and Katherine Noyes, Prestegord and Company, 1978.
- *The Jossey-Bass Handbook of Nonprofit Leadership and Management*, edited by Robert D. Herman & Associates, Jossey-Bass, 1994.

■ Reflection and Application

1. Why do nonprofit organizations receive a tax-exempt status?

_____

_____

_____

_____

2. How did the Social Compact of 1620, Puritanism, and the Elizabethan Poor Law affect the lives of the early settlers?

_____

_____

_____

_____

3. Describe medical care in the 1700s?

_____

_____

_____

_____

4. What role did religion play in black churches in the 1800s?

_____

_____

_____

_____

5. Describe the role nonprofit organizations played during the Civil War.

_____

_____

_____

_____

_____

6. What role did nonprofit organizations play during World War I? During the stock market crash of 1929? During World War II?

_____

_____

_____

_____

_____

7. Contact a nonprofit organization in the community to see how closely their characteristics parallel those listed in Chapter 1 and the types of services they provide?

_____

_____

_____

_____

_____

■ References

Beard, M. R., ed. (1933). *America Through Women's Eyes*. New York: Macmillan Company.

Boylston, H. D. (1955). *Clara Barton: Founder of the American Red Cross*. New York: Random House.

Christenson, R. M. (1970). *Challenge and Decision*. New York: Harper Row.

Coalition of National Voluntary Organizations and National Council on Philanthropy (1979). *To Preserve an Independent Sector: Organizing Committee Report*. Washington, D.C.: Coalition of National Voluntary Organizations.

Croly, H. (1909). *The Promise of American Life*. New York: Macmillan Company.

Ellis, Susan J., and Noyes, Katherine H. (1978). *By the People*. Philadelphia: Prestegord and Company.

Epler, P. H. (1919). *The Life of Clara Barton*. New York: Macmillan Company.

Fosdick, R. B. (1952). *The Story of the Rockefeller Foundation*. New York: Harper Collins.

Hofstadter, R. and Smith, W., eds. (1961). *American Higher Education: A Documentary History*. Chicago: University of Chicago Press.

Hall, P. (1994). Historical perspectives on nonprofit organizations. In Robert Herman and Associates, eds. *The Jossey-Bass Handbook of Nonprofit Leadership and Management*. San Francisco: Jossey-Bass.

Hansmann, H. (1981). Why are nonprofit organizations exempted from corporate income taxation? In Michelle J. White, ed. *Nonprofit Firms in a Three-Sector Economy*. COUPE Papers. Washington, D.C.: The Urgan Institute Press.

Hicks, J. D. (1941). *The American Nation: A History of the United States from 1865 to Present*. Cambridge, Massachusetts: The Riverside Press.

Hodgkinson, V., ed. (1990). *The Nonprofit Sector (NGOs) in the United States and Abroad: Cross-Cultural Perspectives – 1990 Spring Research Forum Working Papers*. Washington, D.C.: The Independent Sector.

Hodgkinson, V., Weitzman, M., Toppe, C. M., Noga, S. M. (1992). *Nonprofit Almanac 1992-1993: Dimensions of the Independent Sector*. San Francisco, CA: Jossey-Bass.

Hopkins, Bruce, R., (1989). *The Law of Tax-Exempt Organizations*. 5th ed. New York: John Wiley and Sons.

Hunt, G. (1914). *Life in America One Hundred Years Ago*. New York: Harper and Brothers.

Independent Sector (1998). *America's Nonprofit Sector: Facts and Figures on the Independent Sector*. Washington, D.C.: Independent Sector.

_____(1990). *Giving and Volunteering in the United States, 1990*. Washington, D.C.: Independent Sector.

_____(2002). *The New Nonprofit Almanac In Brief*. Washington, D.C.: Independent Sector.

Independent Sector and National Center for Nonprofit Boards (2001). *What You Should Know About Nonprofits*. Washington, D.C.: Independent Sector.

Internal Revenue Service, "Tax-Exempt Organization and Other Entities Listed on the Exempt Organization Business Mater file, by Type of Organization and Internal Revenue Code Section, Fiscal Years 2005-2005," *Internal Revenue Service Data Book 2008.*

Lacour-Gayet, R. (1969). *Life in the United States Before the Civil War.* New York: Frederick Ungar Publishing Company.

Laidler, H. W. (1968). *Boycotts and the Labor Struggle.* New York: Russell and Russell.

Levy, J. E. (1975). *Cesar Chavez: Autobiography of La Causa.* New York: W. W. Norton and Company, Inc.

Lundberg, E. O. (1947). *Unto the Least of These: Social Services for Children.* New York: Appleton-Century-Crofts, Inc.

Macleod, C. W. (1928). *The American Indian Frontier.* New York: Alfred A. Knopf.

McMaster, J. B. (1884). *A History of the People of the United States.* New York: D. Appleton and Company.

O'Connell, B. (1983). *America's Voluntary Spirit: A Book of Readings.* New York: The Foundation Center.

O'Hare McCormick, A. (1956). *The World at Home.* New York: Alfred A. Knopf.

Renz, L. (1990). *Foundations Today.* 7th ed. New York: Foundation Center.

Salamon, L.M. (1992). *America's Nonprofit Sector.* The Foundation Center, John Hopkins University.

Salaman, L., and Abramson, A. (1981). *The Federal Government and the Nonprofit Sector: Implications of the Reagan Budget Proposals.* Washington, D.C.: Urban Institute.

Schlesinger, A. M. (1925). *New Viewpoints in American History.* New York: Macmillan Company.

Schouler, J. (1882). *History of the United States of America, Under the Constitution.* New York: Dodd, Mead and Company.

Starr, P. (1982). *The Social Transformation of American Medicine.* New York: Basic Books.

Sullivan, M. (1935). *Our Times: The United States, 1900-1925.* New York: Charles Scribner's Sons.

Taylor, J. B. (1995). *Down Home With the Chief and Miss Maggie.* Prairie Valley, KS: Leathers Publishing.

US Department of Labor Bureau of Labor Statistics, "Employment, Hours, and Earnings from the Current Employment Statistics survey (National): Financial Activities," *http://data.bls.gov/PDQ/servlet/SurveyOutputServlet?&serives id=CEU5500000001.*

Van Dyke, H. (1910). *The Spirit of America.* New York: The Macmillan Company.

Veblen, T. (1918). *The Higher Learning in America.* New York: B.W. Huebsch.

Wade, R. C. (1964). *Slavery in the Cities: The South, 1820-1860.* New York: Oxford University Press.

Warner, A. G. (1908). *American Charities.* New York: Thomas Y. Crowell.

Weis, R.M. and Gantt, V.W. (2004). *Knowledge and Skill Development in Nonprofit Organizations.* Peosta, IA: Eddie Bowers Publishing Company.

Weis, R. M. and Gantt, V. W. (2002). *Leadership and Program Development in Nonprofit Organizations.* Peosta, IA: Eddie Bowers Publishing Company.

Weisbrod, B. (1978). *The Voluntary Nonprofit Sector.* Lexington, MA: Lexington Books.

Wing, T., Pollak, T., and Blackwook, A. (2008). *The Nonprofit Almanac 2008.* Washington, DC: The Urban Press 2008.

Worth, M.J. (2009). *Nonprofit Management: Principles and Practices,* Thousand Oaks, CA: Sage Publications, Inc.

Wright, Louis B. (1955). *Culture on the Moving Frontier.* New York: Macmillan Company.

2 Foundations of Leadership, Character, and Ethics

Leadership is about inspiring, motivating, guiding, directing, and influencing others to reach goals and to make a positive impact on the organization's mission. The mission is the most important resource for nonprofit organizations, from the focus on the public purpose it provides to the legal reason for IRS support (Brinkerhoff 2009). The critical responsibility that leaders have to serve as stewards of the public missions of nonprofit organizations is a key reason that leadership needs to be seriously examined.

Leadership is more art than science. While there are theories, principles, and approaches that can help improve effectiveness, leadership is the art of achieving goals and missions with and through groups of people. Whether by design or by circumstance, effective leadership is accomplished in many different ways. From individual actions to collaborative efforts and from carefully designed strategies to unplanned and spontaneous initiatives, leadership is about moving in a positive direction toward chosen goals. Leaders must consider a wide range of factors that impact every aspect of the context, the culture, and the people engaged in the process. This is particularly true in nonprofit organizations, where the purpose of the institution is to strive toward a public mission, and individuals at every level--administration, board, program staff, support staff, volunteers, organizational members, and constituents and participants--have an opportunity to be a part of the endeavor. With approximately twelve percent of the workforce employed by nonprofit organizations and more than fifty percent of all individuals volunteering, it could be said that nonprofit organizations are the country's largest employer, and effective leadership is essential (Nonprofit Almanac 2008).

Whether undertaken by individuals or groups, leadership in the nonprofit sector means strengthening individuals and communities by developing influence through collaborative and trusting relationships. Leading others involves skills, character, and a good moral compass that includes an accepted system of principles and ethics. Personal character implies traits and values that make each person who he or she is. It is an essential ingredient in the formula for successful leadership, as is a personal system of ethics that helps an individual make effective moral decisions and commitments, and in so doing, inspire others to positive actions.

■ Fundamentals of Leadership

Leadership opportunities in the nonprofit sector are diverse and exist in many different forms and at many different levels. Consider a Senior Citizen Center fitness director, a Substance Abuse Center education program coordinator, a Girl Scout field director, a Good Will Industries training supervisor, and a American Red Cross CPR trainer, among others. In all of these types of roles, leaders in one capacity or another are the essential individuals responsible for providing people with services and supporting those services once they are established. Consider the groups of staff and volunteers serving a Boys & Girls Club program committee, a Big Brothers/Big Sisters annual fund raising campaign, a Nature Center public education initiative, and a Coalition Against Sexual and Domestic Violence intervention education program, among others. Whether working in a

positional leadership role or as a part of a group process, quality leadership provides the expertise, direction, guidance, support, inspiration, enthusiasm, and motivation needed to successfully pursue the mission. Regardless of the assigned role, the most effective leaders have the capacity to help a group arrive at a **shared vision** and the ability to contribute to the development and implementation of a quality plan of action to realize that vision (Collins 2001). Nonprofit organizations need leaders who are excited about working in this cooperative and collaborative context, who inspire and motivate others to action, and who are eager to share leadership with others. If skills and character can be developed, as is the belief of the authors, then individuals can develop as leaders when they see needs that should be addressed and aspire to acquire characteristics and skills that are important in influencing others to meet those needs. Effective leaders understand that leadership is a journey that requires commitment to continuing to learn and grow.

Effective leaders know that the ultimate success of their organizations is dependent on their followers, and therefore they work hard to **empower** others by providing them with training, support, and encouragement. By providing others with opportunities to lead and have influence themselves, a leader can provide perhaps the strongest base for success, a base of **empowerment**. Individuals who are empowered can operate confidently and competently, especially when they are encouraged to use their own initiative. In his book Developing the Leader Within, John Maxwell writes, "The one who influences others to lead others is a leader without limitations." (2001, 141)   Investing in building the capacity of others to lead, and trusting them to do so, is the mark of a true leader. One key evidence that a person has become a successful leader is found when leadership is fully given to others.

One essential aspect of empowering individuals is the function of **delegation**, or providing individuals with opportunities to share in responsibilities and authority. Out of both necessity and trust, leaders realize they must share responsibilities and authority in order for the organization to succeed. Effective leaders then monitor the progress of individuals who have been delegated responsibilities and make adjustments when necessary; a process referred to as **responsible delegation**. There has been a long-running discussion regarding the differences between managers and leaders (Weis and Gantt 2004). In most cases, **managers** are considered to be individuals who direct, control and organize tasks and people within organizations, whereas **leaders** may be considered individuals who inspire others to reach toward a vision and are willing to accept the risks involved in being at the forefront of reaching toward that vision. In his early work, Hitt (1988) combined the two labels to illustrate the need for individuals who have the knowledge and ability to organize as well as the ability to inspire individuals to realistic, yet challenging, heights, or **leader-managers**.

The ability to function effectively in both roles is often a necessity in smaller organizations, like many in the nonprofit sector, that do not have the resources of a large, diverse staff.

■ What is a Leader?

A leader is concerned with the purpose, vision, and direction of the organization. Worth writes that leadership is "...more concerned about the 'where' and the 'why' rather than the 'how'." (2009, 92) He describes leadership as interactive and based on the relationships among those serving the organization's mission. By contrast, Worth describes management as generally concerned with the ongoing operation of the organization and the effective implementation of policies, procedures, rules, and processes, or the "how" the organization functions. Considering this distinction, the authors support the framing that a leader is someone who inspires others to engage their character, purpose, and passion in a collective effort to pursue the mission that brought them together around the vision of an organization (Weis and Gantt 2009).

Leadership surfaces in a wide variety of ways in the day-to-day work of nonprofit organizations. At any given time, a leader needs to be able to call on a wide range of skills, capacities, and commitments in response to the needs of the organization, the staff and volunteers, and the constituents it seeks to support. A leader may provide guidance for individuals to meet their goals as a part of the mission of the organization. For example, a leader in a performing arts setting can offer suggestions on various classes that individuals could consider in order to develop competencies in the arts. Once a person becomes involved in a program, a leader can offer directions and instructions on how to learn and perform in a particular artistic area. For instance, a dancer might be directed in various movements or exercise techniques. Leaders recognize an opportunity or a need that should be addressed and are willing to accept the responsibility and risks involved in leading and influencing others to meet certain challenges.

What are some characteristics necessary for successful leadership? Because of the increasing complexity of operations and programs in nonprofit organizations and the mission focus of their contributions to the public good, it is particularly important that leaders demonstrate the following (Weis and Gantt 2004):

- **Commitment.** The focus of a nonprofit organization is on the purpose or public good mission of the organization. The mission becomes a beacon of light for the public and members of the organization toward which all activities and energies are directed. In other words, all activities are directed toward the perceived organizational purpose. Leaders of nonprofit organizations must have a strong belief in the purpose of their organization and must inspire and guide others to the realization of that purpose.
- **Concern.** Leaders of nonprofit organizations must have a genuine interest in the well-being of the people in their community. Members of nonprofit organizations describe effective leaders as individuals who express a real interest in their lives and demonstrate that interest through programs and other actions.
- **Competence.** Nonprofit leaders must have competence in human relations and in technical and conceptual skills in order to provide effective programs and services as well as the support for these programs and services.

- **Flexibility.** Because of the complexity and difficulty of tasks involved, nonprofit leaders must be able to coordinate a number of different tasks, often at the same time. They must be able to develop and utilize a variety of resources, and they must be able to coordinate and sometimes initiate change.
- **Determination.** Staff and volunteer members are faced with a number of hurdles on a daily basis. By focusing on the mission of the organization, staff members and volunteers need to work together to overcome whatever obstacles develop in working to fulfill that mission.
- **Integrity.** Establishing a tradition of trust and responsibility encourages confidence from members of the community that is important for successful practices and programs.
- **Communication.** Understanding what the community needs in relation to the organization's mission and then communicating the organization's intentions to the community is essential for the realization of goals and mission. The purpose and intent of the organization must be continually monitored and communicated to the community.
- **Motivation.** It is important that nonprofit leaders understand the nature of human motivation. Understanding motivational concepts can lead to the establishment of a **motivational environment**. Staff, board, volunteer and organizational members clearly expect something for their participation and performance, and an effective environment can provide positive reinforcement for all of these groups. This is particularly true of volunteers who are neither paid a salary nor receive services from the organization.

In addition to understanding characteristics of effective nonprofit leadership, it is also important to understand the **processes** and **responsibilities** that leaders engage. The early work by Sessoms & Stevenson (1981) offers a quality list of the "things leaders do" to help their organizations succeed:

- build camaraderie and cohesiveness.
- identify and define goals.
- develop methods and procedures to achieve goals.
- organize the work of others.
- motivate others.
- evaluate the work of others.
- represent the group.
- develop group members.
- establish the group atmosphere.
- promote the ideals of the profession.

All the stakeholders involved in the work of nonprofit organizations expect more than good management skills and commitment to the mission, they expect leadership. In Governance as Leadership, Richard Chait and his colleagues complement the early work of Sessoms & Stevenson when they write the range of what is expected of nonprofit leaders today, "Constituents expect (nonprofit) CEOs to articulate clearly and persuasively the organization's mission, beliefs, values, and culture. Both the process and the substance should galvanize widespread commitment towards those ends." (2005, 3) They report that

these leaders are expected to inspire and guide the organization by:
- shaping agendas, not imposing priorities.
- allocating attention, not dictating results.
- defining problems, not mandating solutions.

The processes and responsibilities involved with leadership are numerous and challenging. Most leaders in the nonprofit sector fulfill many of these responsibilities simultaneously, adding to the complexity of their roles. They work across the organization, among the many related organizations in their community, across the various sectors (business, government, and nonprofit), and within the various fields of practice and professions of which their work is a component. Leaders must be able to apply these types of facilitating skills in order to marshal all forces in the successful accomplishment of their organization's mission. Crutchfield and McLeod (2008) studied high-impact nonprofit organizations and their leaders and report that they work with and through others to create impact beyond what they could do alone. They offer the following framework of what these great nonprofit organizations and leaders do:

1. **Advocate and serve.** To accomplish the broadest possible impact, they work to both deliver the highest quality programs and services while also working on access government resources and change public policies.
2. **Make markets work.** They build partnerships with businesses to help them become more socially responsible and develop joint ventures to earn income.
3. **Inspire evangelists.** They engage volunteers in meaningful experiences that connect them with the mission and core values, to promote deeper relationships across the community.
4. **Nurture nonprofit networks.** They move beyond competitive relationships and invest significant resources in collaborating.
5. **Master the art of adaptation.** They are willing to adapt and modifying their tactics as needed to increase success, responding to changing circumstances with one innovation after another.
6. **Share leadership.** They empower others by distributing leadership throughout their organization and networks.

The most effective nonprofit leaders do all of this while keeping their eyes on the ultimate prize of successfully serving the mission of their organization.

The question is often asked, **"How do individuals become leaders?"** Shrivers (1980) suggests that people become move into leadership roles by one of the following methods:
- **Appointment.** Individuals often attain leadership roles through an appointment based on their level of skills and knowledge. This type of appointment is usually officially sanctioned by the organization.
- **Election.** In some cases, nonprofit leaders are selected through some sort of elective process. Elected leaders are generally people who are valued, respected, and capable of fulfilling the requirements of the position. Those who elect them have confidence in their abilities to take on the leadership role.
- **Emergence.** Emergent leaders become leaders when there is a void in the leadership position, and these individuals have the experience and motivation to fill a particular role.
- **Charisma.** Sometimes individuals are so well-liked and respected that they are

selected by group members to be a leader. These people lead with intangible qualities and a demeanor that are desired by other group members. These individuals tend to be persuasive and influential in a likable way.

Each of these ways of moving into leadership roles can be found in the nonprofit sector. Demonstrated skills and knowledge, proven effectiveness and resulting support and respect, and the appreciation by others involved in an organization combine to identify and connect people to leadership opportunities.

■ Leadership and Power

A correlation exists between successful leadership and the use of power to get things accomplished. Some people perceive power as a negative thing, but when it is equated with the positive influence involved in leading nonprofit organizations it becomes one of the most desirable aspects of leadership. Nonprofit leaders who understand this correlation and strategically use the right type of power in the appropriate situation can improve their effectiveness. Power can come from several different sources as illustrated by Stojkovic, Kalinich, and Klofas (2007), who describe the following types of power: **reward, coercive, legitimate, referent, and expert**. A discussion of the use of each type of power in the broad context of the nonprofit sector follows:

- **Reward Power.** Reward power means a person believes that they are going to get some type of reward if they do what they are being asked to do. Being in a position of offering a reward for desirable behavior can be very effective. Rewards can take the form of tangibles and intangibles, from pay to days off, from improved work conditions to access to additional program budget support, from a pat on the back to public recognition, and so on.

- **Coercive Power.** Coercive power means that a person believes that there will be a form of loss for not doing what they are being asked to do. Leaders can and should incorporate the threat of such loss to get some things done effectively. This power can be particularly important in enforcing practices that have to do with safety and health or in dealing with areas of member or client confidentiality, among other sensitive program and service delivery issues. Coercion can take the form of loss of position, control, funding, and access. This power, however, is sometimes misused, resulting in hostility, distrust, and turmoil.

- **Legitimate Power.** Legitimate power means that a person believes that what they are being asked to do is based on a foundation of power assigned to a position or office of the person providing the direction. The importance of influencing others from an official position should not be underestimated. The authority that goes along with a position is particularly important in hierarchical organizations where there are pronounced superior-subordinate relationships. Regardless of the organizational structure, people depend on the legitimate power of those with whom the work in order to value and follow the directions being given.

- **Referent Power.** Referent power is when a person has an attraction somehow to the person giving the direction. Individuals sometimes arrive at a position of leadership based on their level of energy and desirability as perceived by others. These individuals lead through the strength of their personality and usually develop a loyal following.

- **Expert Power.** Expert power is when a person believes that another person has so much expertise in an area that they believe what they are being told and follow the directions given based on this belief. Individuals who have significant knowledge and skills in particular areas are often influential, and their advice and counsel are highly sought after by other members of the organization.

These powers can influence behavior when used individually or collectively. Nonprofit leaders who understand and use these powers effectively have a greater potential for making a positive difference in people's lives.

■ Leaders and Followers

Leaders must aspire to develop certain characteristics and competencies in order to be effective. Good leaders also understand that the base of their support is from their followers; without followers there could be no leaders. As a matter of fact, some of the best training for leadership is to follow others. Individuals learn from modeling the behavior of successful leaders and also learn, in some cases, what not to do in particular situations from unsuccessful leadership practices. To be a good leader, it is important to understand the benefits of cultivating an active **leader-follower** approach to leadership. Hollander (2009) defines this approach as inclusive leadership that involves an essential leader-follower relationship that requires building a two-way flow of influence between the two. He refers to the benefits of upward influence and makes the case that a two-way operation of leadership and followership must involve the four "Rs" of inclusive leadership: **Respect, Recognition, Responsiveness, and Responsibility** in both directions.

Understanding the many reasons that people may identify their role in an endeavor as one of follower may also help a leader develop productive, quality relationships. Individuals become followers in certain situations because their needs are being fulfilled. Sometimes it is easier for an individual to be a follower; it takes less time and energy. At other times it is a matter of comfort with the current leadership, and at still others it may have something to do with comfort and previous experiences. Being aware of the different reasons that individuals become followers should help in making a leader more responsive and effective.

■ Leadership Development

Former White House Fellow, Thomas Cronin, writes that leadership cannot be taught, as such, but that individuals can learn in their own minds the strengths and limitations of leadership (Wren 1995). An integrated approach to developing leadership that incorporates study, modeling, sharing, and practice in intentional and strategic ways, is the best way to develop as a leader. There are typically four ways to develop as a leader: (1) examining theories and models, (2) assessing the lives of past leaders, (3) mentoring with effective leaders, and (4) engaging in service learning activities. **Examining leadership theories, studies, and models** provides a theoretical and academic foundation for learning about leadership. **Assessing the actual lives of leaders** can provide understanding and inspiration for self-development. Another process, **mentoring**, allows current leaders opportunities to pass on their knowledge of leading to the next generation. And finally, **service learning,** a field experience that combines community service with specific learning objectives, provides individuals with opportunities to perform meaningful service while developing knowledge, skills, and character, all important for effective leadership (Weis and Gantt 2004). These aspects of leadership development will be discussed in the next four sections.

■ Leadership Theories and Models

The literature on leadership is rich, diverse, and continuing to evolve. Some leadership theories maintain importance because they have withstood the test of time and are worthy of consideration. Others gained importance as they have demonstrated their usefulness in practice, become integrated with other theories, and supported effective response to changing dynamics in the need for leadership across context, culture, and regions of the globe. Emerging leadership theories and frameworks add to the understanding and continuing development of effective practice. Some of the foundational theories are presented here, followed by a discussion of evolving and emerging thinking about leadership.

Classical Organizational Theory

Frederick Taylor (1967) suggested that natural work, completing tasks in a natural manner, was uneconomical and inefficient; he stated that organizations needed to plan, organize, direct, and control in order to be successful. Taylor determined that there was really only one right way to complete a task and any other way was inefficient. Dividing tasks up into different processes, and training an individual for each part of the task seemed much more efficient to Taylor than having one individual complete an entire task alone. As the employee became more skilled at a particular task, according to Taylor, the more efficient production became overall. This theory was reinforced by the behavioral movement in psychology and by B. F. Skinner, who emphasized the importance of behavior alone in the work place. A great deal of the traditional organizational framework for nonprofit organizations was informed by this theory.

Great Man Theory

Eugene E. Jennings (1960) developed the Great Man Theory based on the idea that leaders develop in relation to the situations and the times with which they are confronted. According to Jennings, past leaders such as George Washington, John F. Kennedy, and Martin Luther King developed their platform for leadership and power because of specific circumstances they were passionate about and were successful in their response. In the nonprofit sector there are a number of individuals throughout history who have recognized various needs in the community and have gone about initiating an organization of people to respond to those needs. Clara Barton recognized a need to respond to casualties of war and natural disasters, and she developed the American Red Cross. Juliette Gordon Low thought young girls should have an opportunity to expend their energies in productive and character developing ways and founded the Girl Scouts of America. Sir Robert Baden-Powell believed these same kinds of opportunities should exist for boys and started a scouting program in England that eventually led to the Boy Scouts of America, founded in this country by William D. Boyce.

Sessoms and Stephenson developed the great man theory further by introducing categories of great men (1981, 23-26).

- **Princes.** Develops a strong base for personal power, often for their own self-aggrandizement.
- **Democratic Hero.** Draws power from the support of the electorate.
- **Great Average Person.** Recognizes needs in the family or community and quietly organizes support to meet those needs.
- **Receptive Person.** Perceives that there is a need for change, recognizes that he or she has the ability to make these changes, and then takes advantage of the opportunity to lead others in making a difference.
- **Eventful Person.** Can change the course of history by doing what he or she thinks is right, regardless of the consequences. These individuals lead with integrity and often by example.
- **Nietzsche's Superman.** A self-starter who likes to develop power so that he or she does not have to depend on others. This individual is not a conformist and looks past society's constraints in order to develop to the fullest.
- **The Superior Person.** Leads from a platform of personal strength and self-respect and a high level of self esteem. Although leadership is based on individual power, this type of leader is prepared to return to the role of a follower, if it would be more beneficial.

When we consider some of the enormously complex situations that have occurred throughout history and the number of leaders who have risen to the occasion, one of these categories of the great man theory can seem to be at work. The nonprofit sector has its share of founders and current leaders who illustrate this theory in practice.

Group Theory

The primary basis for the group theory of leadership comes from the exchange theory of George C. Homans. Homans (1950) states that before an individual seeks a leadership role in a group, the individual and the group members must perceive that the rewards for both the leader and the follower must exceed the costs. With this theory, the leader fulfills a role expectation and assists group members in reaching their goals. This relationship is reciprocal: the leader is rewarded with the status of being in charge and opportunity to influence organization direction, and progressing toward their goals rewards the group members. There are three interrelated factors necessary for the exchange theory to be successful:

1. **Activities.** Tasks implemented jointly by the group members and the leader.
2. **Interactions.** Communication within the group when individuals reach goals, resolve conflict, and coordinate the work.
3. **Sentiments.** Level of attraction and degree of bonding that group members develop for one another.

Homans suggested that the more interaction within the group, the stronger the bonding, and the stronger the bonding, the greater the sentiment among group members that would enhance the quality of activities. The group theory provides a link between group and leader effectiveness and overall satisfaction with the process and the results. This theory is often present at some level in nonprofit organizations as groups work together toward a shared goal.

The Trait Theory

The trait theory (Northouse 2010) attempts to identify and explain what traits might be helpful for individuals to be leaders. The great man theory of leadership provided the stimulus for this theory and a number of studies indicate that certain characteristics correlate with successful leaders. Traits that are considered important for effective leadership include:

- **Intelligence.** Able to think critically and creatively.
- **Desire for Achievement.** Need to achieve goals and willing to work tirelessly toward that end.
- **Decisiveness.** Thoroughly study the situation and then carefully weigh the pros and cons in making a decision.
- **Maturity.** Trusted and counted on for their experience, knowledge, and responsibility.
- **Confidence.** Gives a sense of quiet strength without appearing overbearing or flashy.
- **Ability to Work with Others.** Work cooperatively with others and provide support, encouragement and inspiration.
- **Initiative.** Initiating tasks and activities from an inner sense of what is necessary and appropriate, rather than from an outside source.
- **Flexibility.** Able to adapt to new trends, issues, activities, and individuals readily and effectively.

Traits are present in other theories and useful in many leadership styles and models. For example, the above traits are clearly woven into the six practices of high-impact nonprofits and their leaders identified by Crutchfield and McLeod Grant in their book *Forces for Good* (2008).

Behavior Theory

With origins in the 1950s and 1960s, behavior theory focuses on the concept that leaders develop an understanding of what a group shares as its vision and then encourage group members to focus on and work toward that vision. (Northouse 2007) Leadership is considered the way in which an individual behaves or acts in directing the group toward their vision.

Leadership is the pattern of interpersonal processes that occur between the leader and group members, and understanding the ways in which a leader influences group members in reaching their goals is the focus of the model. Leadership is understood to be the processes the leader uses to influence others in reaching their goals.

Situational Theory

Situational theory (Bass 2008) is based on the idea that the leader takes into account different aspects of a situation prior to deciding on a leadership approach. A good leader will consider a number of variables, such as the skills and abilities of the group members and the kind of task involved, before deciding upon a particular approach. Additional variables, such as social, political, cultural, and financial considerations, may also be figured into decision making process.

Depending on the circumstances, a leader may decide to take a highly disciplined, authoritative style of leadership, if this approach seems appropriate for the group in the context of the tasks at hand. Or in a different situation, the leader may take a more democratic approach to leadership and invite input from group members before making a decision on how to reach goals. According to the theory, the best approach is the one that works best for a particular situation, and effective leaders are consistently successful at selecting which approach works best for any given situation. The situational framing has great utility in the nonprofit context with its many diverse stakeholders and potential for changing circumstances where flexibility and responsiveness are valued.

Humanistic Theory

The humanistic theory's underlying assumption is that all individuals naturally seek responsibility and that external stimulus affects behavior, rather than personality traits or internal motivation. Humanistic theorists are interested in developing organizations that are structured to motivate individuals to seek responsibility and to realize their full potentials. (Nevid and Rathus 2005) As individuals realize their full potential, they will invariably assist the organization in realizing its goals.

The humanistic leader's purpose, therefore, is to develop organizations that provide guidance, support, and encouragement for individuals to reach their full potential and to acquire expertise in various areas of importance. As individuals mature in the levels of expertise, the leader will provide less guidance but continue with support and encouragement.

Excellence Theory

Appearing in the literature in the 1970s, the excellence theory was articulated further and brought to the forefront of leadership concepts in the next decade by the works of Peters and Waterman (1982). According to the theory, an organization can excel only when individuals aspire to individual and organizational excellence. The theory pulls from the transactional/transformational model of leadership, in which leaders and followers motivate each other to reach higher and higher levels of quality in service and products.

In this concept, a leader works actively with followers to complete tasks and reach goals. One way to do this is to incorporate a process referred to as **managing by walking around**. This process can lead to a strong rapport between leaders and followers, it can ensure more effective communication, and it can assist in addressing problems before they become significant. If enacted effectively, it can build camaraderie and even increase morale for leaders and followers. The cooperative nature of many volunteer-based nonprofit programs and organizations frequently promote and benefit from this theory's framework.

The Principle Theory

Character traits, such as honesty and patience, have often been mentioned as essential aspects of good leadership. Stephen Covey (1989) took this concept in a specific direction in the 1980s and 1990s with his idea that effective living and leadership could only be achieved if individuals integrated principles character into all aspects of their lives. The principles Covey selected were based in all the major religions and include *integrity, fairness, honesty, service, human dignity, excellence,* and *potential*, among others. Covey believed people could develop and maintain these principles by processes he referred to as *habits.* He referred to habits as purposeful systems that involve knowledge, skills, and desires, and once formed and practiced would be difficult to let go.

Incorporating habits based on principles, Covey thought people would be able to take charge of their lives; they would set goals and priorities based on what is truly important and act accordingly. This process would encourage all parties involved in situations to feel as if they are winning. It would also encourage leaders to listen and understand individual input from group members, provide a way to enhance collaborative creativity and energy, and give some direction on keeping that energy fresh.

Jim Kouzes offers a Foreword to the Jossey-Bass Reader on Nonprofit and Public Leadership (Perry 2010) in which, after providing a long list of world leaders across the ages, he asks what do they have in common. Kouzes writes, "...the list is populated by people with strong beliefs about matters of principle. They all have, or had, unwavering commitment to a clear set of values. They all are, or were, passionate about their causes. The lesson from this simple exercise is unmistakable. People admire most those who believe strongly in something, and who are willing to stand up for their beliefs. If anyone is ever to become a leader whom others would willingly follow, one certain prerequisite is that they must be someone of principle."

Emerging Thinking about Leadership

Over the past twenty years or so a number of ideas about leadership have begun to evolve and emerge from a diverse set of perspectives, experiences, and interactions among existing theories. They grow out of examinations of the intersections of traditional theories like those presented above, views from other regions and cultures of the world, and creative new thinking about human dynamics. During these two decades, Margaret Wheatley (2005), among others, has encouraged leaders to explore the limits of the current leadership practice. She opens her 2005 collection of essays on leadership with the following:

> Western cultural view of how best to organize and lead (the majority paradigm in use in the world) are contrary to what life teaches. Western practices attempt to dominate life; we want life to comply with human needs rather than working as partners. This disregard for life's dynamics is alarmingly evident in today's organizations. Leaders use control and imposition rather than self-organizing processes. They react to uncertainty and chaos by tightening already feeble controls, rather than engaging our best capacities in the dance. Leaders use primitive emotions of fear, scarcity, and self-interest to get people to do their work, rather than the more noble human traits of cooperation, caring, and generosity. This has led us to this difficult time, when nothing seems to work as we want it to, when too many of us feel frustrated, disengaged, and anxious. (1 and 2)

The cautions and concerns presented here are shared by others and are informing some of the emerging frameworks for a different way of thinking about leading. For example, in the early 1990s Peter Senge began to offer a vision of a **learning organization** as a group of people committed to continuously improving their capabilities to create what they want together.

An important element of this emerging thinking is a shift from the view of leadership as being the role of one person to the belief that leadership is the role of all members of the group. This notion finds roots in indigenous cultures around the world and influences in more recent examinations of human interaction. To be most effective with approach, the following must be considered (Seagal and Horne 1997):

- Differences in individual communication and learning styles are important in the building and functioning of groups.
- Differences in the wide range of human dynamics promote the ability to work effectively within groups, from the continuum of emotional, physical, and personality to the benefits of diversity of culture, language and tradition.

Considering the differences among individuals in groups creates the potential for more creative, cohesive, and successful group action. Even the illustrations used to depict these frameworks have generally shifted from traditional top-down organizational charts shaped as pyramids to circles and clusters of circles connected by lines to illustrate relationships. Even the language used to describe any one person designated as a key leader is often changed to the describing the leader as a coach or facilitator (Senge, 1994). Among other things, this means that a leader is no longer expected to have the answers but to be skilled at helping the group find the answers. This emerging thinking has greater potential as groups learn to work collaboratively and collectively without the need of a coach or facilitator.

Others are continuing this journey with their study of less controlling and more cooperative principles like shared leadership, collective leadership, participation, and engagement. Cashman (2003) tells a story of a traditional Western leaders transformation as he is guided by a Eastern-based philosophy in *Awakening the Leader Within*. Quinn (2000) blends the models of global leaders who have transcended narrow views of leadership in providing a framework for "How Ordinary People Can Accomplish Extraordinary Results", which is the subtitle of his book, *Change the World*. The years ahead offer exciting opportunities as the nonprofit sector capitalizes on the rich history and emerging thinking about leadership as it seeks to engage and serve the needs of an increasingly diverse society.

Efforts to better understand leadership are important in order to continue to improve the effectiveness of nonprofit organizations. Reflecting on key studies, styles, and models offers a foundation for effective practice.

The Lewin, Lippin and White Studies

A number of studies were conducted by Lewin, Lippin and White in the 1930s that involved young boys who were members of a hobby club (1939). The boys took part in a number of activities involving different kinds of crafts, and the studies examined the effectiveness of various leadership styles. The styles that were identified are explained below:

- **Democratic Leadership Style.** Members in this group are asked for their input on goals, processes, and even the individuals they may wish to work with. An attempt is made to treat individuals fairly and equally.
- **Authoritarian Leadership Style.** During this type of leadership, the leader directs group members toward the goals of the organization, the processes involved to reach those goals, and the individuals with whom members would work. The leader often maintains a distance from the group and can appear to be aloof, but not hostile.

- **Laissez Faire Leadership Style.** There is very little guidance or direction involved with laissez faire style of leadership. Although the leader may provide some of the supplies and materials, he or she does not provide guidance and support. There is also little monitoring or feedback provided by the group leader.

Comparisons were made among the different styles of leadership, and it was determined that members in the authoritarian-led group were more hostile and aggressive than the members of the democratic group. Members reported positive feelings toward the democratic and laissez faire leaders when compared with the authoritative leader. The Lewin, Lippitt, and White studies have been considered ground-breaking research into understanding the nature of leadership, and the results have been the foundation for training, teaching, and further research. Their findings also provide support to the emerging thinking about more collaborative approaches to leadership reported in the previous section.

The Ohio State Studies

The Bureau of Business Research at Ohio State University initiated a series of studies on leadership in 1945 (Stogdill and Coons 1957). A group of researchers involved with these studies developed an instrument referred to as the Leader Behavior Description Questionnaire. The instrument was designed to assess a leader's conduct in a number of different work settings, including the armed forces, manufacturing, civil service, and education. Two important areas of leadership behavior were identified as a result of the studies, *initiating structure*, and *consideration*.

- **Initiating Structure.** The way in which the leader determines group goals, group structure, and role expectations.
- **Consideration.** The relationship that develops between the leader and group members regarding their ideas and feelings. This consideration may be weak or strong depending on the level of trust and respect that exists between the group leader and group members.

University researchers Halpin and Weiner conducted a study in which 83.2% of a leader's behavior was determined by combining these two factors (Stogdill and Coons 1957). Prior to this, it was thought that leaders were either task-oriented or people-oriented, but the results of the Ohio State Studies indicated both factors should be considered when examining leadership styles and models.

**Figure 2.1
A Leadership-style Model
Portraying the Ohio State
Studies' Dimensions**

Reproduced by permission

Figure 2.1 (above) demonstrates the different combinations of the factors of *consid-*

eration and *initiating structure. Initiating structure* has been designated as task orientation and *consideration* has been designated as human relations orientation. Each of the four quadrants represents a possible leadership style. For instance, a leader with a high human relations orientation and a high task orientation would be interested in doing a good job while at the same time establishing good relationships with employees. This study did not suggest which of the styles was most effective, just that the styles occurred under certain circumstances.

The New Managerial Grid

Robert R. Blake and Jane S. Mouton (1978) developed another leadership style model, the New Managerial Grid, in the 1950s. This model includes two dimensions: concern for production and concern for people. Concern for production might include completing orga-

Figure 2.2
Blake and Mouton's Managerial Grid

1,9

Country Club Management
Thoughtful attention to needs of people for satisfying relationships leads to a comfortable friendly organization atmosphere and work tempo.

9,9

Team Management
Work accomplishment is from committed people; inter-dependence through a "common stake" in an organizational purpose leads to relationships of trust and respect.

5,5

Organization-Man Management
Adequate organization performance is possible through balancing the necessity to get out work with maintaining morale of people at a satisfactory level.

Impoverished Management
Exertion of minimum effort to get required work done is appropriate to sustain organization membership.

Authority-Obedience
Efficiency in operations results from arranging conditions of work in such a way that human elements interfere to a minimum degree.

1,1

9,1

Concern for People (vertical axis, 1 Low to 9 High)

Concern for Production (horizontal axis, Low 1 2 3 4 5 6 7 8 9 High)

Source: Robert R. Blake and Jan Srygley Mouton, The Managerial Grid Figure from *The New Managerial Grid*, © 1978, Houston: Gulf Publishing Company, p. 11.

nizational tasks and meeting various quotas. Concern for people would include developing effective employee benefits packages and activities to enhance employee morale.

These two variables are placed along two axes (Figure 2.2, on the previous page). Concern for production is positioned along the horizontal axis, and concern for people is placed along the vertical axis. A high concern is represented by the number 9 and a low concern by the number 1. Blake and Mouton identified five different leadership styles using this grid.

- **1,1 Impoverished Management.** This individual has little interest in getting work done and little interest in developing relationships. This leader essentially manages in name only.
- **1,9 Country Club Management.** With a high concern for relationships but little concern for accomplishing tasks, this person would spend his or her time effecting positive relationships with others.
- **9,1 Authority-Obedience.** This individual would have a strong interest in completing tasks but little interest in the ideas or feelings of employees. This individual usually uses a leadership position within the organization to control others and to get the job done.
- **5, 5 Organization-Man Management.** This person tries to take a middle-of-the-road approach to leadership, often compromising both production and employee needs.
- **9, 9 Team Management.** This individual attempts to reach organizational goals through trusting and effective relationships with employees. Creating a sense of interdependence and commitment to organizational goals can do this.

Blake and Moulton suggest that the first four styles listed are ineffective. A leader can only be effective by concentrating on a high level of achievement and by developing trusting and respectful relationships with employees. Again, the study provides additional support for the emerging thinking about leadership as a group process of shared vision and action presented earlier.

The University of Michigan Studies

The University of Michigan Survey Research Center started investigating leadership behavior in 1947, with a focus on determining factors that might lead to group achievement and satisfaction. The results of this study suggest that leadership behavior could be plotted on a continuum. At one end of the continuum, the leader encourages ideas from employees and includes these ideas in decision-making processes. This individual would be people-oriented and interested in the satisfaction of individuals in the organization. At the other end of the continuum, the leader is task-oriented and focuses on overall organizational achievement. This person would be more interested in achieving organizational goals and developing strategies for reaching goals.

Conclusions derived from the study indicate that employee satisfaction was contingent on the presence of an employee-centered leader and that the level of productivity was less important when compared to the importance of the relationship between employees and leader.

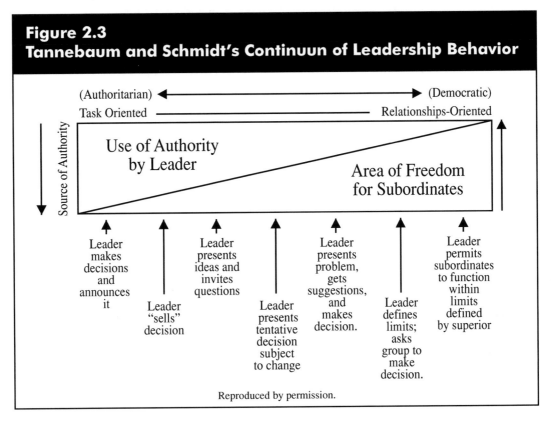

Figure 2.3
Tannebaum and Schmidt's Continuun of Leadership Behavior

(Authoritarian) ◄——————————————► (Democratic)

Task Oriented ——————————————— Relationships-Oriented

Source of Authority

Use of Authority by Leader

Area of Freedom for Subordinates

| Leader makes decisions and announces it | Leader "sells" decision | Leader presents ideas and invites questions | Leader presents tentative decision subject to change | Leader presents problem, gets suggestions, and makes decision. | Leader defines limits; asks group to make decision. | Leader permits subordinates to function within limits defined by superior |

Reproduced by permission.

Tannenbaum and Schmidt's Leadership Continuum

Tannenbaum and Schmidt developed a leadership model that organizes leadership style along a continuum (1973, 166). At one end of the continuum (Figure 2.3, above), the leader would make decisions with little or no employee input and would direct most of the actions of his or her subordinates. At the other end of the continuum, the leader would encourage employee input in decision-making, planning, and other aspects of the organization. The leader would allow a certain range of freedom of action based on pre-established agreements.

A leader may select the style of leadership based on any number of variables. For instance, if the leader has faith in the abilities and motivational level of the employees involved in a task, a democratic style of leadership might be selected for that task. On the other hand, if the leader is unsure about the skill or motivational level of employees, and if time is a consideration, then he or she may choose a more autocratic style.

The authors of the study suggest that leaders remain flexible regarding which style to select, and they state that no style is necessarily better than another; the best approach depends on the situation and circumstances involved.

Transactional/Transformational Leadership

Burns (1978) incorporated the social exchange theory developed by Hollander (1978) to advance the concept of transactional/transformational leadership in the 1970s. Burns used the exchange theory as a foundation, stating, "Leadership occurs when one person takes the initiative in making contact with others for the purpose of an exchange of valued things. The exchange could be economical, political, or psychological in nature" (156). Burns thought that leadership involved mutually shared influences as perceived by followers.

Transactional Leadership. This type of leadership involves the exchange of something of value between the leader and someone who may be thought of as a follower. For instance, a leader may exchange a salary for an employee's time and expertise in a particular area. In a nonprofit setting, individuals often exchange money for the opportunity to participate in a program, to develop a skill, to learn something, or experience something else of significance.

At one level, a transaction may seem like a practical and effective exchange process, but it can also have a negative connotation if more meaningful processes are not present. Exchanges that do not involve other meaningful processes can lead to a "carrot and stick" mentality where individuals are rewarded if they provide the right exchange, but might be punished if the exchange is inadequate. This process could lead to a "wage mentality" in a work environment where individuals compete solely for the highest salaries at the expense of feeling proud of accomplishing something worthwhile. The process of treating people according to their productivity can also lead to a negative environment of hostility between employees and between leaders and employees.

Transformational Leadership. Burns suggested that individuals could motivate each other toward higher levels of job satisfaction and wrote that transformational leadership occurs "when one or more persons engage with others in such a way that leaders and followers raise one another to higher levels of motivation and morality" (1978, 20). Authors Peters and Waterman (1982) proposed that leadership is a system of transforming individuals and organizations to pursue excellence. Using the transformational model, a leader would empower employees and inspire them to work together to achieve greater heights.

Transformational leadership assumes that individuals need commitment and self-fulfillment, which might actually enhance personal productivity. It is a leadership process that is based on fairness and trust and as Burns wrote, "Transformational leadership is elevating" (1978, 455). This type of experience "can take place in many aspects of our personal, professional, and moral lives. These transformations can be physical, intellectual, aesthetic, psychological, social, civic, ecological, transcendental, moral, spiritual, and holistic" (Rost 1993, 126). With this process, individuals are important in and of themselves and are encouraged to pursue a more visionary approach to productivity. As Peters and Waterman (1982) noted, individuals will commit a great deal of themselves to efforts they deem worthwhile.

Tri-Dimensional Leader Effectiveness Model

Hersey and Blanchard (1977) incorporated elements of the Ohio State Studies (human relations orientation and task orientation), in developing a situational leadership theory called the **tri-dimensional leader effectiveness model.** This model is based on the idea that leadership style should be determined based on three variables: (1) the demands of a particular situation or tasks , (2) the type of supervision needed or relationship, and (3) the level of maturity of the individual. A mature individual is described as someone who sets high goals, accepts responsibility for attaining those goals, and has the knowledge and skills

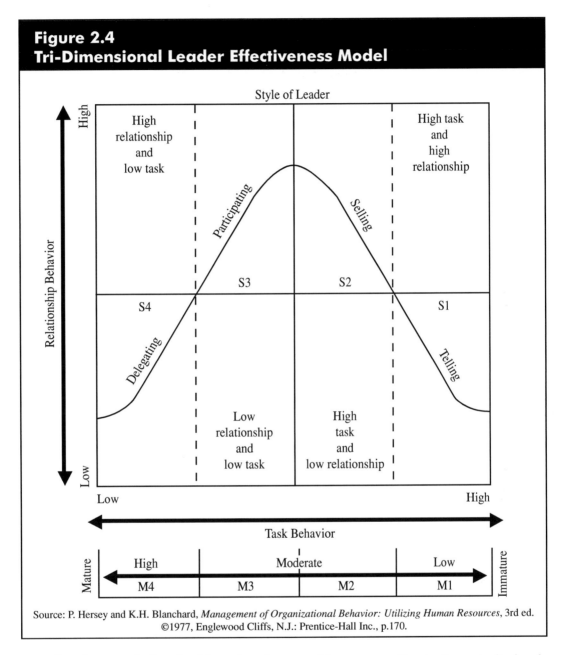

Figure 2.4
Tri-Dimensional Leader Effectiveness Model

Source: P. Hersey and K.H. Blanchard, *Management of Organizational Behavior: Utilizing Human Resources*, 3rd ed. ©1977, Englewood Cliffs, N.J.: Prentice-Hall Inc., p.170.

to realize those goals. Leadership styles, then, would vary according to the maturity levels of group members (Figure 2.4).

Four different leadership styles are suggested: telling (S1), selling (S2), participating (S3), and delegating (S4). The telling quadrant involves a high task and low relationship orientation. Selling involves a high task and a high relationship orientation. Participating includes a high relationship with a low task orientation, and delegating involves a low relationship with a low task orientation. As an individual progresses in their level of responsibility, knowledge, and skills, they would move from a low level of maturity to a higher level, resulting in a leader changing styles accordingly.

An example of how this process might work would be an employee who is relatively new to an organization and who has not had a great deal of practice in using skills relevant for a particular project. A leader using this concept might adopt an S1 or S2 style of leadership while the individual is developing competence and confidence. As both competence and confidence are enhanced, the leader might assume an S3 or S4 position, encouraging the employee to take more initiative while still monitoring his or her progress.

An employee who reaches a high level of maturity in one project may not reach the same level under different circumstances, and it is important for a leader to adjust leadership styles accordingly. The bell shaped curve running through the quadrants is a continuum, and a leader can go back and forth on this continuum, depending on the circumstances and the maturity level of the employees. The model is particularly relevant as a guide to leading and guiding people on an ongoing basis, where context and experience may influence the need for regular supervision. This finds relevance in the staff and volunteer work of nonprofit organizations.

Hitt's Model of Leadership

Hitt (1988) proposed a simple model of leadership in which a leader would create a vision for an organization and then develop a plan of action to reach that vision. The process of leadership, then, would be in creating a desirable vision and developing an effective plan for people to follow to achieve success.

Hitt suggested that the leader must both create a vision and develop an effective plan to follow in order to motivate others, and he refers to these qualities as dreaming and doing. In the two-dimensional model below (Figure 2.5), Hitt designates the four possible types of leadership styles:

- **Victim.** This person has little vision or initiative and often complains about unfair practices within the organization.
- **Dreamer.** The dreamer has a lot of vision but few implementation skills.
- **Doer.** This individual will work hard at implementing the vision of others.
- **Leader-Manager.** This person is high on vision as well as implementation.

The victim is someone with little motivation and vision and remains happy regarding almost everything within an organization. The dreamer is an individual

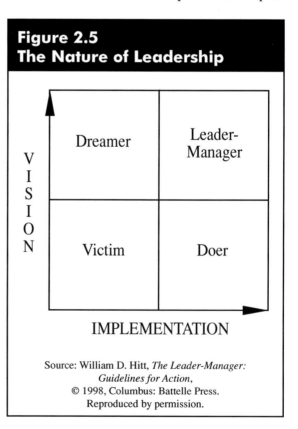

**Figure 2.5
The Nature of Leadership**

Source: William D. Hitt, *The Leader-Manager: Guidelines for Action,*
© 1998, Columbus: Battelle Press.
Reproduced by permission.

who has high goals but little ability to reach those goals. The doer will work diligently to reach the goals of others. The leader is someone who can create an exciting and worthwhile vision and can motivate group members toward a plan of action to reach goals.

Collaborative Leadership

Collaborative leadership involves people coming together to build trust, cooperation, and communication as they work toward a shared vision and common goals. This is a contemporary style of leadership that continues to evolve. When it emerged in the early 1990s it was described as what was happening when a leader brought people together in a synergistic mode to develop leadership in groups who are working together to make decisions and solve problems. More recent framings of the style shift the focus from the actions of an individual leader to the collective efforts of the members of the group. Archer and Cameron (2009) write about the strategic use of collaboration with the focus on capitalizing on the mutual responsibilities and benefits within the group and the resulting interdependence that strengths the partnerships formed among the group members. They write about success being based, to a great extent, on the attention given to deciding when to collaborate and when not to collaborate. This style of leadership emphasizes sharing ideas and listening, understanding, and supporting the group in acting on the input of those involved. Collaborative leaders are empowering leaders who bring people together for discussion and reflection; then they encourage individuals to accept responsibilities and take actions, depending on situations and levels of professional expertise.

In their book, *The Flight of the Buffalo,* Belasco and Stayer (1993) developed an interesting model of collaborative leadership based on analogies to geese. Belasco and Stayer describe the way geese communicate with each other and change leadership positions in flight when one becomes tired or the situation changes in some other way. Accordingly, in the discussion presented by the authors, effective communication and trust is encouraged as is the sharing of leadership. Individuals are encouraged to accept positions of leadership at opportune times, when their personal strengths and capacities are most appropriate and when others need support and encouragement when their strengths and capacities are challenged or wane. This sharing of leadership responsibilities results in a strong commitment to the goals of the group. Like the smooth transitions observed as the flight of geese seem to shift roles with ease and without significant communications, a quality team of people shift roles and responsibilities naturally as the needs of the group change as work unfolds.

Comprehensive Approach to Leadership

For a leader to be effective, it is essential to be aware of important variables associated with a particular project or activity. A flexible and responsive approach to leadership requires consideration of factors such as the particular situation, group members, and the leader are important in the selection of a leadership style and are depicted in Figure 2.6. (Mondy, Holmer and Flippo 1980) These three factors are interrelated and are discussed in detail next.

Situation. The term *situation* has to do with the task at hand and the process involved in accomplishing the task. Consideration needs to be given to:

- **External Forces.** External forces are those forces that individuals have little or no control over, such as weather conditions, political conditions, cultural preferences, customs, and traditions. Knowledge of these circumstances can help in the selection of a leadership style.

- **Group Goals.** Having a clear understanding of organizational goals can be helpful in selecting a leadership style and determining the process for reaching those goals.
- **Methods and Procedures.** There are a number of different methods that a leader can choose from to achieve results. For instance, programs can take the form of leagues, special events, seminars, classes or workshops. Different situations call for different approaches.
- **Type of Environment.** Environments can be more or less stable, depending on circumstances. A more stable environment calls for a more task-oriented leadership style, whereas a less stable environment might call for a more people-oriented style.

Group Members. Understanding the background and qualifications of each group member is essential in selecting a style of leadership. A number of factors should be considered:

- **Knowledge, Skills, and Abilities.** A leader must have an understanding of individual areas and levels of expertise in order to match this expertise with specific, correlating tasks.
- **Needs Disposition.** Group members are each motivated differently, so a leader must have knowledge of individual interests, needs, and desires prior to developing a plan of supervision.
- **Experience.** Members of a group who have had a broad range of experience may require a less direct approach than members with minimal experience.
- **Task-relevant Maturity.** Individuals who have proven to be responsible and/or high achievers may require less supervision than individuals with less task-relevant maturity.

The Leader. The leader is the key in pulling all of the elements together for successful programs and organizations. Some of the factors important in the development of a successful leadership style are detailed below:

- **Knowledge, Skills, and Abilities.** Being aware of one's own strengths and weaknesses is important when selecting a leadership style.
- **Needs Disposition.** The leader's own interests, needs, and desires are significant factors, since a leader operates according to his or her own motivational factors and comfort levels.
- **Experience.** The leader who has had previous experience working with group members can use this experience in making decisions in the future.
- **Style Flexibility.** The degree to which a leader can adapt to different leadership styles should also be a factor in selecting a style of supervising.
- **Source of power.** The ability of a leader to incorporate sources of power (mentioned previously in this chapter) is important in selecting leadership style. A leader who is charismatic may need to take a more relaxed style, while an individual who is comfortable with a legitimate or authoritative style may be more directive in supervising others.

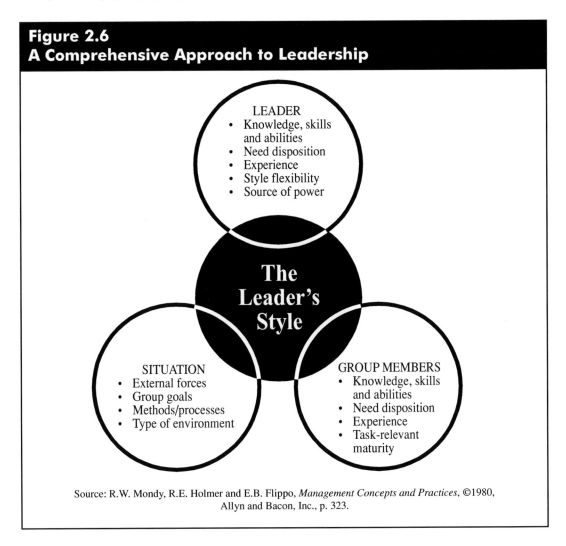

Figure 2.6
A Comprehensive Approach to Leadership

Source: R.W. Mondy, R.E. Holmer and E.B. Flippo, *Management Concepts and Practices*, ©1980, Allyn and Bacon, Inc., p. 323.

Being able to evaluate each of these areas effectively – the situation, group members, and the leader – provides the leader with valuable information in selecting the best leadership style. Many effective approaches to nonprofit leadership seem to naturally incorporate deliberate consideration of such factors in framing a response or action plan.

Systems Thinking Framework

Growing out of the learning organization perspective (Senge 1994) and its relationship to the body of work on human dynamics (Seagal and Horne 1997), **systems thinking** is organized around the basic notion that everyone involved in an organization can think, work, and lead together on behalf of the organization's mission. Aspects of many of the theories, models, and studies presented in this section are present in the life of all organizations and play their appropriate role in applying the principles of system thinking.

Systems thinking requires groups to commit to valuing each member in the generative process of creating new ways of working in pursuit of the mission. The term **generative** is central to the process as it is counter to the natural tendency to solve problems as a part of leading. It expects people to think together about what they want for the future, rather than what they do not want. This often proves difficult and requires creative approaches to helping groups move into the generative space.

Senge (1994) and many others have developed a large collection of processes to help groups move into this generative leadership space (Klimek, Ritzenhein and Sullivan 2008). One of the more useful processes that has grown out of this movement is the application of a Creative Tension Framing (Figure 2.7). It offers a collective way of engaging a group in responding to a gap between an organization's current reality and vision for the future. In Western-based theories and frameworks, effective problem solving is of great importance.

Figure 2.7
Creative Tension Framing

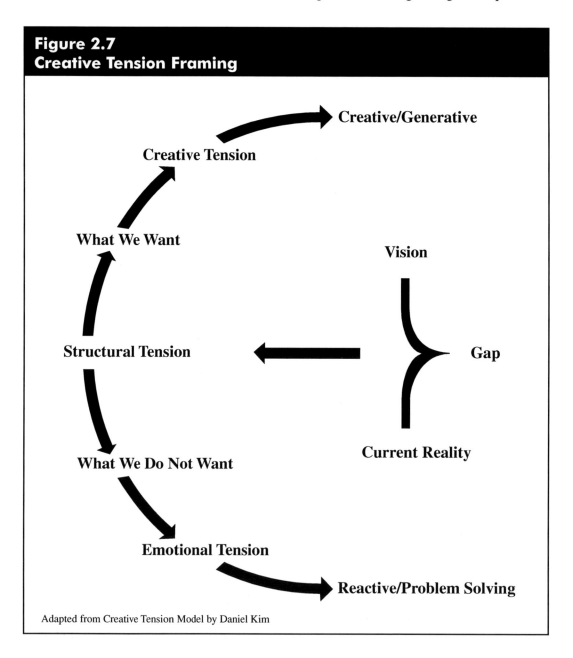

Adapted from Creative Tension Model by Daniel Kim

Leaders are valued for their problem-solving capacities, often without regard to the methods engaged. The Creative Tension Framing asks groups to abandon the tendency to solve problems and the orientation to work on "what we do not want" in favor of a more generative and creative approach to determining "what we want." (Corey and Kim 2003) (Kim)

Identifying the gap between the current reality and the vision for the future creates structural tension within the group. This tension is not negative or positive. It is just the fact that there is a difference between the vision and reality, and the group wants to move toward the vision. If the group responds to this structural tension by focusing on "what it does not want," it experiences emotional tension and shifts into a problem solving mode. The context in which they are now working tends to be negative and limits the creative capacity of the group to consider or generate new ways of working toward the vision. The experience can lower the vision for the future or eliminate it completely. It can also slow progress toward the vision, causing the gap to widen. If the gap becomes too great, the emotional tension will cause the connection to the vision to break. If instead the group responds to the structural tension by focusing on "what it wants," it shifts to a creative space where every idea is valued and new ways of thinking about the gap and the future are generated through the group experience. It tends to be positive and promotes creative tension and group synergy that generates new ideas and advances the vision for the future.

There is an ethical basis for leadership to provide the organization with a framework for making decisions. How the question is asked makes an enormous difference in the discussion and responses. If the question presented by leadership is "What is wrong with the situation and what are we going to do to fix it?" then a problem-solving orientation will be taken. If the question presented by leadership is "What do we want for our future?" the door is open to a wide range of creative and generative responses. The context in which the question is being asked can influence the responses that will come from the group. Even irrelevant information presented in the discussion framing can influence the process and responses. Leaders must consider the setting, the context, the information provided, the tone of the assignment, and the type of questions being asked. The design or selection of a decision framework should be taken very seriously by leaders as an ethical responsibility to the organization's mission (Kahneman and Tversky 2002). It is a key responsibility of leadership to take the framing process seriously for the potentially significant impact it has on the process and the results.

The various theories, models, and studies continue to inform the developing of the next approaches to leadership. Improving understanding of the context, culture, and human dynamics of the nonprofit sector will continue to be a challenge for leadership in the quest to improve the quality of life for the people it serves. Therein lies the motivation for continuing the leadership learning journey for the field, as well as all those who are called to serve a public mission and vision for a better future.

∎ The Connection between Leadership, Character and Ethics

Too often, leadership models fail to include the importance of character and ethics in the overall scheme of leading and influencing others. Aristotle identified *ethos* as a central element in understanding how one person influences another. He contended that our perception of another is based heavily on our perception of that person's virtues, wisdom, and good will (Kennedy, 1991). **Character** includes the beliefs, traits and values that distinguish one person from another. It is being true to a standard or standards a person has set to govern his or her life. **Ethics** is a system of moral principles and values and moral duty and obligation; it not only deals with what people believe about how they should act, but what they *should* believe (Jeavons 1994). Leaders must have the kind of character it takes to represent the organization effectively and the type of ethical system that allow them to lead with a strong moral compass. An examination of a leadership model that includes character at the center will be followed by review of a concept for maintaining ethical standards in nonprofit organizations. (Weis and Gantt 2004)

The Integrated Leadership and Character Model

The Integrated Leadership and Character Model (Figure 2.8) focuses on the importance of character in leadership (Weis and Gantt 2004). The model identifies critical skills and knowledge areas and illustrates the central function of personal character. According to the model:

- To be successful, organizations must have leaders with traits and values (personal character) that are important to the overall development of the organization.
- Leaders must also possess or develop an effective level of conceptual, technical, and human relation skills.
- The interaction and effectiveness of these three skill areas is dependent on the personal character of individual leaders within the organization.

To develop and implement effective programs in a nonprofit organization, a leader must have an idea of what individuals need and want (conceptual skills); skills in planning and implementing programs (technical skills); and be able to inform and motivate staff members to implement programs and know how to encourage constituents to participate in the programs (human relations skills). The more determined an individual is to make a program work, and the more trusted the leader (personal character), the more likely the program is to succeed.

This same concept can be effectively applied to any process or procedure being undertaken in a nonprofit organization. For instance, in developing and implementing a budget, a leaders must have an understanding and a vision of financial matters. They need to be knowledgeable and skilled in developing the technical aspects of the budget and the budgeting process, along with being able to communicate budgetary procedures effectively to others. And, personal character is critical in making certain all of the skill areas are working effectively and that the processes are moving along smoothly.

There are three important **implications** to consider in the context of this model:

1. Consider the model in the context of oneself. It provides a framework for individuals to go by to assess and develop their own character and skills for any given circumstance being addressed.
2. Consider the model as a framework for individual leaders to use in selecting and training staff and volunteer members.
3. Consider the model as a useful frame of reference in determining the types of programs and support systems that may be helpful for organizational members.

Figure 2.8
Integrated Leadership and Character Model

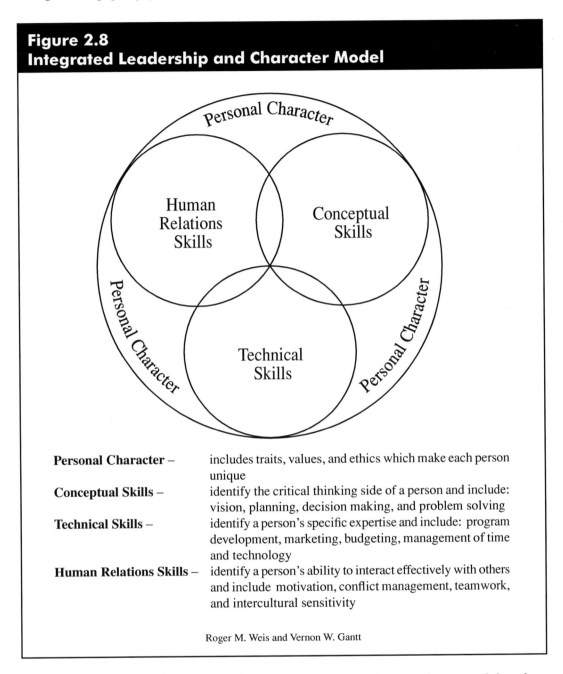

Personal Character –	includes traits, values, and ethics which make each person unique
Conceptual Skills –	identify the critical thinking side of a person and include: vision, planning, decision making, and problem solving
Technical Skills –	identify a person's specific expertise and include: program development, marketing, budgeting, management of time and technology
Human Relations Skills –	identify a person's ability to interact effectively with others and include motivation, conflict management, teamwork, and intercultural sensitivity

Roger M. Weis and Vernon W. Gantt

Recognizing that individuals need to be competent in these three skill areas and that character is the key element in the overall scheme of things provides nonprofit leaders with guidelines for personal development, staff and volunteer development, and the development of constituents.

In realizing that character consists of **traits, values, and ethics**, it is important to examine these attributes to discover how they enhance character. While each person might identify a slightly different list of **personal traits** and **values** that make up their character, **Character Counts!** (http://www.charactercounts.org/) a nonpartisan, nonsectarian coalition of 454 schools, communities, and nonprofit organizations, works to advance character education by teaching what it calls the **Six Pillars of Character:**

1. **Trustworthiness** implies that an individual can be depended upon. When a person is considered to be trustworthy, his or her word means something. He or she can be expected to do everything possible to assist the organization and the individuals in the organization in succeeding. It is important to be able to work alongside people we believe in and that we can trust.

2. **Respect** includes valuing the contributions, the differences, and the feelings of others. It is only possible to value someone else's ideas and feelings through a genuine effort of understanding. Understanding means making an attempt to gather as much information as possible regarding another person in order to empathize and collaborate with that person.

3. **Responsibility** means accepting a degree of ownership for all areas of an organization and accepting strong ownership for particular areas of an organization. Accepting responsibility is important for the overall health and success of an organization. Leaders of good character do not waste time blaming others, but rather work cooperatively to ensure success.

4. **Fairness** involves full consideration of all information to assure that all parties in a situation are listened to and dealt with without favoritism. Being fair is not always popular or necessarily expedient, but it is always just and equal. Fairness is a trait that, when perceived, brings with it the trust and loyalty of others.

5. **Caring** for others is essential in a nonprofit organization and includes compassion and concern for others. Members of nonprofit organizations report that good leaders are those who care about their needs, concerns, and feelings. Members are not so concerned about the behind-the-scenes activities of organizations, but they are concerned about leaders who exhibit a genuine interest in their well-being.

6. **Citizenship** means taking an active and thoughtful interest in the community. Leaders of nonprofit organizations have an opportunity to incorporate their position to make things happen in the community. They also have the opportunity--and perhaps obligation--to involve staff, volunteers, and members in community action, when appropriate.

Organizations such as the YMCA, Big Brothers/Big Sisters, and Girls, Inc., often have other traits and values they associate with character, and these traits and values may differ from individual to individual and from culture to culture. The important consideration is that character is critical to effective leadership, especially in the nonprofit sector. Greater attention should be given to the role character plays in leadership, regardless of context. Doing the right thing for the right reasons as opposed to doing what works is the subject of the next section, ethics.

The Role of Ethics in Nonprofit Leadership

Staff members, volunteers, and constituents often look to positional leaders to set the standards for moral thought and behavior in the nonprofit sector. Nonprofit organizations benefit when they have an established ethical culture to guide their work toward their public good mission. It needs to include key ethical *obligations* that the organization believes must be embraced and pursued. Jeavons (1994) suggests five such obligations necessary for developing an **ethical culture**: *integrity, openness, accountability, service,* and *charity.*

Integrity implies that the organization and individuals within the organization can be depended upon to do what they have stated they intend to do. In other words, their deeds match their words. Integrity is critical for establishing

> ## *We are discussing no small matter, but how we ought to live.*
>
> **Socrates**
> - as reported by Plato
> in the *Republic* (ca.390 B.C.)

trust within the organization and between the organization and the community. Integrity can be demonstrated in a number of different ways. Organizational literature such as promotional brochures, fundraising materials, and other reports should match actual situations. In other words, documents should never be embellished for organizational gain. If actual performance in an area does not match the degree to which it is billed, then mistrust develops between the organization and its constituents and other members of the community.

Another way integrity can be demonstrated is to have leaders who represent the values and mission of the institution effectively. In other words, trustworthiness can and should be demonstrated on a daily basis. In 2001 the American Red Cross generated hundreds of millions of dollars to assist the victims of the terrorist attacks of September 11th. When it is was revealed that a small portion of the money contributed would go elsewhere, the public was outraged and the organization quickly reverted to its original plan and worked hard to rebuild the public trust that may have been lost with the incident. Some donors may have been lost or slow to return as a result. Nonprofit leaders have an obligation to be as honest as possible with the public as well as with their own staff members. Attempts to disguise facts or offer misleading information can create dramatic results often with far-reaching consequences.

Openness may not accurately qualify as a "moral" value, but for organizations operating in the public sphere, maintaining openness to public observation and scrutiny is certainly virtuous and even practical. For organizations that provide public services or advocacy and have impact on community life, operating in secrecy would arouse skepticism regarding motivation. Part of this skepticism is historical in nature, since a small number of service organizations from time to time have operated with ulterior motives. The most successful nonprofit organizations operate effectively and welcome inquiries regarding any area of their operation.

Organizations that are concerned with maintaining a culture of interest and excitement realize that maintaining a climate of trust is essential to this interest and excitement and that operating openly is the best way to develop trust. Another reason to maintain openness is that many nonprofit organizations began as volunteer associations with a rich, populist, democratic background, and maintaining openness and democratic ways helps to insure that tradition. Maintaining openness in decision making, programs, financial matters and other issues relevant to the overall operation of an organization is key to maintaining the trust of the community. Transparent and open communications are a key to maintaining integrity for nonprofit organizations.

Accountability means that not only should organizations maintain an openness regarding all operations, but they must also be able to explain and be accountable for their activities. Nonprofit organizations often solicit tax-deductible contributions, or at least receive a tax-exempt status, and with that they have an obligation to perform public service as effectively and as efficiently as possible. These tax benefits are contractual in nature and obligates organizations both ethically and legally to perform according to promise and to be evaluated accordingly.

By accepting the privilege of tax-exempt status or the opportunity to solicit tax-deductible contributions, organizations accept the obligation to be evaluated not only by their constituents but also by the public at large. This also obligates organizations to pursue the stated mission and purpose of the institution and to be accountable to the membership in working toward that end. The need for accountability has motivated more and more states to pass laws mandating financial disclosures and regulating fundraising activities for nonprofit organizations. Additionally, "watch-dog" groups such as the National Charities Information Bureau and the Better Business Bureau's section on nonprofit organizations are taking a closer look at organizational finances and other operations. Nonprofit leaders have an obligation to insure that the organization and all individuals within the organization--are accountable to their constituents, their board members, and to the broader public.

Service is similar to accountability in the sense that nonprofit organizations exist, and are granted special privileges, because of their commitment to serve the public, or at least to the membership. The social contract they receive, which provides them with special privileges, obligates them to work toward a mission of public good; the membership dues, program fees, special event money, contributions, volunteer time and other resources these organizations receive also obligate them ethically toward service.

This service ethic must also be manifested in the leaders of nonprofit organizations, who can certainly work toward their own advancement, but, without sacrificing personal well-being, they must always place the cause of the organization and the well-being of the people the organization is serving uppermost in their priorities. The idea of leaders seeing themselves as servants for the cause of the organization and for their constituents is critical in focusing others within the organization on the needs of the members. Nonprofit organizations are by nature altruistic, and it is therefore necessary for the leaders of these organizations to lead with a philosophy of selflessness and service.

Charity is one of the most important ethical obligations of all, since the word "charity" comes from the Latin *caritas*, which means more than giving to those in need (Jeavons 2006). Originally, the translation of the word "charity" was "love," but not romantic love. Rather, it meant the kind of love a neighbor shows for another neighbor in need. It also meant to be caring, putting the welfare of others above one's own, and sharing one's resources with others out of a sense of concern and social obligation rather than a sense of pity.

From an organizational standpoint, an ethical obligation to the principle of charity is derived in part from reciprocity. In other words, nonprofit organizations benefit from the generosity of others and are therefore obliged to express generosity themselves. The motivation of the supporters of many of these organizations comes from the idea that the organization is committed to caring for others. Additionally, individual service recipients often indicate that they believe that they will receive more personable and more caring service from private, nonprofit organizations than from public entities. The leaders of these organizations must be selected for their character traits that include a caring and respectful nature. Leaders often set the tone for all operations within the organization and a caring and giving person will influence the way the organization operates.

The elements of character, ethics, and purpose, among others, are central to the notion of effective leadership for the good of others. The Integrated Leadership and Character Model offers a straightforward framing of how these elements can be thoughtfully and intentionally woven into a more holistic approach to bring the full range of human emotions, commitments, and skills to the responsibilities of leadership. (Weis and Gantt 2004)

■ Leaders through the Ages

Assessing the lives of effective leaders provides understanding and inspiration for leadership development. Following are brief profiles of leaders across eras, regions, and perspectives that offer a range of experiences for considering and exploring leadership in action:

Lao-Tzu was a Chinese sage who lived in sixth century B.C. and described leadership as providing a service in a selfless manner. According to Lao-Tzu, a leader should place the well-being of others above oneself and accordingly, these acts of selflessness would actually enhance oneself. He compared an enlightened leader to water that "cleanses and refreshes all creatures without judgment (Wren 1995)." A leader is yielding, like water, and if a leader does not push forward too severely, group members will not resent or resist being led. He thought leadership should be a nourishing experience and that leaders should be humble and direct credit for successes to others. He imagined leaders as facilitators who would lead with as little direction as possible.

Lao-Tzu also compared the process of leadership to being a midwife, in which the leader is merely facilitating another person's process. The leader needs to be reminded that it is basically someone else's process and that the leader should guide the process with as little intrusion as possible. If the leader trusts the other person in the process, according to Lao-Tzu, that person will also trust the guidance of the leader. Just as a midwife assists at someone else's birth, a leader should facilitate what is happening, rather than what he or she thinks should be happening. And if the leader must take the lead from time to time, the leadership should be such that the group member is assisted, yet still feels a sense of autonomy.

Plato lived between 428-347 B.C. and was a student of Socrates. He founded the Academy in 387 B.C., and this was the first permanent institution in Western civilization completely devoted to education and research. Plato often expressed disappointment in the excesses of liberty and democracy and, writing in his *Republic,* suggested these excesses often led to tyranny and anarchy. He thought wise philosophers, selected for their love of philosophy and knowledge, should lead the state. These philosopher-kings should rule the state based on their natural inclinations and should set themselves apart from their followers in order to rule more objectively with their intellect.

Plato thought these philosopher-kings would be discovered as individuals who naturally wished to study philosophy and who would also exhibit leadership qualities. These individuals would be intelligent, noble, gracious, courageous and temperate, and they would therefore appear different from the rest of the citizenry. These philosophers would be able to focus on the eternal nature of truth and justice without varying from generation to generation and without being led astray by corruption.

 Aristotle (384-322 B.C.) was the gifted student of Plato, yet he disagreed with his teacher and mentor regarding the selection of philosopher-kings as leaders of the state. Aristotle believed all citizens should have an opportunity to govern and to be governed. He believed that all men should experience being governed in order to be more effective as leaders themselves. Aristotle thought all men should be treated equally by the state and that all men should have an equal chance to govern. These were concepts he believed to be essential in order for the state to survive. Anything else would lead to anarchy and revolution and the demise of the state.

Aristotle stated that it was impossible for any one class or group of citizens to assume a place of superiority over another. According to Aristotle, it was the charge of the state, therefore, to provide education that would allow a citizen to learn to be a good citizen, to learn obedience and at the same time to learn to command. Obeying and commanding were both honorable in themselves, as long the intentions and the end results were good.

 Niccolo Machiavelli (1469-1572) was trained as a humanist and served as a diplomat for Florence prior to being exiled. While in exile, he wrote his infamous *The Prince*, which addresses the idea of gaining and maintaining individual power by any means. Although *The Prince* describes the importance of individual power, his other famous work, the *Discourses*, describes the important aspects of a republic. In *The Prince*, Machiavelli suggests that individuals should be merciful, gracious, upright and religious, whenever possible, but should revert to trickery and deceitfulness whenever it is necessary to gain power and to maintain authority.

Machiavelli postulated that individuals who used cunning measures when necessary to reach their goals accomplished more and would win over individuals who incorporated honesty in their dealings. He believed that men were generally dishonest by nature, and therefore a leader should not keep his (or her) word when it becomes advantageous to do otherwise. According to Machiavelli, whenever a leader succeeds in establishing and maintaining authority, regardless of the means of accomplishment, the leader will be judged honorable and be approved by all. Although this philosophy was timely for Machiavelli's day, its treatise resonates to present time and *The Prince* remains a classic in the study of leadership.

 Thomas Jefferson (1743-1827) was a brilliant statesman, scientist, architect, inventor, educator and public servant. (Koch and Peden 1993) He was the author of the Declaration of Independence, the founder of the University of Virginia, and the third president of the country. He was born into a Virginia family of means; his father was a wealthy plantation owner, and his mother was of distinguished English and Scottish pedigree. He took advantage of the opportunity for a formal education and eventually earned a law degree from William and Mary College in 1762.

Jefferson's interest in politics led him to become an accomplished statesman. His southern, aristocratic background and culture generally served him well, and he incorporated his vast knowledge and statesmanlike abilities to move the country toward the birth of its independence from England. This same culture, however, led to a contradiction for the man who wrote, "We hold these truths to be self-evident, that all men are created equal, that they are endowed by their Creator with certain unalienable Rights, that among these are Life, Liberty, and the pursuit of Happiness" in the Declaration of Independence. At the same time he bought, sold and owned slaves, and did so even later when he became president. In spite of this contradiction, Jefferson continues to be revered as one of the greatest leaders of the country and a champion of democratic ways.

Harriett Tubman (1820-1913) was born into a slave family in the Eastern Shore section of Maryland on a plantation owned by Edward Broadas. (Petry 1955) Growing up, Tubman learned what it meant to be a slave and was taught to say, "Yes, Missus," "No, Missus," to white women and "Yes, Mas'r," "No, Mas'r," to white men (Petry 1955, 21). At nighttime she would sometimes hear the hoofbeats of horses as slave owners would ride up and down the dirt roads looking for runaways. Runaways would sometimes be brought back shackled in chains and beaten, or worse, "sold South," a term that meant a slave was sold to a plantation in the deep South (Petry 9). As a young girl, Tubman worked in the fields of the plantation, often from dusk to dawn, but when hard times came to the plantation, she was sometimes hired out to other families for cleaning, weaving, watching trap lines and caring for their children.

Tubman later married a freed slave named John and was allowed to live in his cabin with him. But Tubman feared being sold South, and she plotted running away to the North. When John refused to accompany her, she left anyway. On her escape North, she was befriended and supported by people along the way. This assistance came to be known as the Underground Railroad, but it was little more than a loosely organized group of people who offered hiding and food. She soon found herself a free person in Pennsylvania, but missed her family and friends and made the dangerous journey back and forth to Maryland numerous times, always guiding a group of slaves North with her. Later in life, Tubman became a scout and a spy for the North, but she is remembered most as a conductor for the Underground Railroad. In later years, she had a difficult time financially and even sold produce door to door. In 1913, she died penniless, but free.

Clara Barton was born on Christmas day in 1821 in an unpretentious farmhouse in Oxford, Massachusetts. (Bolyson 1955) Barton was a shy student as a youngster but was something of a tomboy and relished the idea of jumping on a wild colt and racing across the Massachusetts countryside. It was during her early years that her younger brother David was injured in a fall, and she was asked to assist in his care. Barton was a natural nurse and completely took over the care of her brother until he was well. Later, she became a teacher, winning the admiration of her students for her caring ways and her ability to keep up with them in recreational pursuits. After teaching for a number of years, Barton left to work in the U.S. Patent Office in Washington, D.C. While she was there, war broke out between the states, and Barton accepted a nursing position and was able to go to the battlefront, where most of the casualties were. As a nurse, Barton saved countless lives, often working from daybreak to long past dusk.

Following the war, President Lincoln recruited Barton to assist in locating 22,000 missing soldiers, which she did for four long years. Afterward, tired and ill from her efforts, she sailed to Europe to recuperate. While in Europe, Barton learned of the International Red Cross, an organization designed to provide relief for people during a time of war. Upon returning from Europe, she began forming the American version of the IRC. In no time at all, Barton's organization was providing relief services for flood and fire victims, and in 1882 President Arthur appointed her as the first president of the National Red Cross, which later came to be known as the American Red Cross. Her desire to help others has changed the lives of millions, and in so doing helped to change the shape of an entire nation.

Geronimo (1829-1909) was born in the mountains of Arizona into a Bedonkohes Apache family. (Debo 1976) As a young man, Geronimo was very athletic. He played games that prepared him for a rigorous adult life, which often involved raiding the enemies of his people and then fleeing to the mountains for weeks at a time. He was considered stronger and wiser than his years and was admitted into the council of warriors for his skill and knowledge in battles at the early age of seventeen. He experienced a great personal tragedy a little later in life, when his entire family--mother, wife, and three children--were slain by the members of the Mexican Army. From that day forward, he vowed never to be killed by a Mexican bullet, and he managed to live to be over eighty and died of natural causes.

Geronimo became one of the most feared Indians ever and could ride a horse, handle a lance, and shoot a rifle better than anyone. Once with Geronimo at the lead, he and eighteen Apache warriors were able to confront and deter the forces of 5000 U.S. Troopers. Since there was no formal leadership structure with the Apache Indians, Geronimo led by example and was admired by his fellow warriors for his independence, integrity, courage, determination and ruthlessness. He was often very persuasive and led through this skill as well as by being trusted by the other Indians. He was a highly religious man, and his sense of honor and courage had been observed in battle on numerous occasions. They earned him the respect of friend and foe alike. Although Geronimo had been lied to many times by his enemies, he never broke his own code of honor. In fact, it could be said that the Apache culture itself was the style of leadership adopted by Geronimo.

George A. Custer was a West Point graduate who served as a general and became a true hero in the Civil War. (Utley 1988) As one of the leaders for the Michigan Wolverines, he and his troops defeated the Confederate cavalry General Jeb Stuart at Gettysburg and defended the Union Army from attack by General Pickett and over twelve thousand Confederate infantrymen. He and his troops also dogged General Robert E. Lee in his final retreat and eventually forced Lee to surrender. He was described by his superiors as a warrior who fought with audacity, courage, and an unparalleled fury and focus on winning. He was revered by most and considered to be one of the greatest military leaders of his time. In fact, had it not been for a place in Montana named Little Big Horn, Custer could very well have become President Custer.

Following the Civil War, millions of Americans moved West in search of cheap land

and encountered nearly 200,000 Indians, many of whom were determined to defend their territory. The dashing Civil War hero, Custer was sent along by his government to protect the pioneering Americans. Custer and the U.S. Army adopted a tactic referred to as total war, which meant that all Indians were viewed as dangerous and were to be attacked wherever and whenever possible. He again became a national hero for the successes of this tactic and planned his next attack against the Indians at Little Big Horn. But Little Big Horn was to be his undoing, and Custer and all of the men in his unit were killed by an enemy enraged by past brutalities. Brimming with confidence from his successes, he had tragically underestimated the spirit and experience of his enemy, and overestimated his own ability and the will of his troops.

 W.E.B. Du Bois (1868-1963) was one of the founders of the National Association for the Advancement of Colored People (NAACP) and is considered one of the fathers of the modern black militancy movement. His involvement in militancy came about, at least partially, as a reaction to the conciliatory methods of Booker T. Washington. Du Bois was also the founder of the Niagara Movement and wrote extensively, his most memorable work being *The Souls of Black Folk.* The first black man to receive his Ph.D. from Harvard, he believed the Negro race, as he referred to it, could only be saved by the Talented Tenth. This was the term given to exceptional blacks who needed to be selected from the population for their intellect, charisma, and potential and who would then be educated and developed into leaders, who in turn would provide direction and education for the masses.

Du Bois believed that the only way the Negro race could rise above the shame and degradation that slavery had brought them was to find exceptional blacks who would educate other blacks. He believed that only by being educated in a culture with its own thoughts, its own ideals, and its own leaders could the masses of Negro people flourish and rise above the history that had been forced upon them. He thought that if blacks did not furnish these leaders to be trained to educate and lead others within the race, then chaos and misdirection would abound. Du Bois also believed that if this group of talented individuals did not come to be, the Negro race would become a lost cause and would pull down other races of men with it. His idea was that his fellow blacks would be lifted up through education and work, and he believed that education should not only provide work-related knowledge, but it should provide knowledge in life skills as well.

 Mohandas Gandhi (1869-1948) was educated in law but devoted his entire life to helping the disadvantaged. He worked to bring an end to discrimination against the lower orders of India, known as the untouchables, he helped establish Hindu-Muslim unity, and he was instrumental in securing independence for his native India from Great Britain. But it was not so much the issues he was involved in but the method he used that brought him fame and the honorable title of Mahatma, which meant Great Soul. His use of passive resistance to organize his countrymen in the wake of overwhelming British odds is legendary. He believed that passive resistance should only be used for just causes, and individuals espousing passive resistance must be willing to suffer to the end for those causes.

For Gandhi, evil was only to be overcome by good, anger by love, and untruth by truth, and always through peaceful means. He believed that only the courageous could be passive resisters and that, in the long run, both the individuals involved in resistance and the individuals who were being resisted benefited from the process. Gandhi thought that men of integrity would disregard unjust commands from leaders, even if it meant putting their lives in jeopardy, and that in defying death they freed themselves from fear. He believed there was no one in the world so bad that they could not be converted by love. His example of practiced non-violence inspired millions of people to emulate his example for decades.

 Helen Keller was born in the small town of Tuscumbia, Alabama, in 1904 and had a pretty normal childhood until she reached the age of nineteen months, when she developed a fever that left her blind, deaf, and unable to speak. Because this left Keller with limited opportunities for effective communication, she became something of a behavior problem. Her parents were encouraged to take her to Dr. Alexander Graham Bell, a prominent teacher of the deaf and inventor of the telephone. Dr. Bell recommended that Keller receive schooling from Anne Sullivan, who had become nearly blind herself and had overcome many obstacles to become a teacher of the blind, the deaf and the mute. Under Sullivan's care, Keller began to read and write by using braille and became calmer as she grew in her communication skills. By the age of seven, Keller had mastered four alphabets: the manual one for the deaf, the square pencil script, raised letters, and Braille dots.

Eventually, Keller wrote her own story about growing up with so many complications and the story became a book, *The Story of My Life* (2005), which was printed in fifty different languages. Sullivan went on to encourage thousands of others with similar afflictions and was deeply involved in what was then a new organization, the American Foundation for the Blind. She also wrote *Teacher*, a tribute to her teacher and mentor, Anne Sullivan. Keller, with the unparalleled assistance of Sullivan, had overcome incredible obstacles to become a source of inspiration for millions of people worldwide.

 Cesar Chavez grew up in the small town of Gila Bend, Arizona, where his father and grandfather were local business and landowners. (Levy 1975) The depression of 1929 left the Chavez family nearly penniless, however, and they had to leave their home and begin a life of crop picking. The conditions in the labor camps where the Chavez family had to live were horrible; there was no heat, sanitation system, running water, or electricity. The school system where Chavez and his brother and sister attended was racist, and children were punished if they spoke Spanish during school hours. Outside of school their life consisted of picking walnuts, cherries, cotton, potatoes, apricots, melons, and grapes for meager wages and for labor contractors who often cheated the growers regarding the weight of their daily production.

Following a stint in the United States Navy during World War Two, Chavez began working for the Community Service Organization. His job was to register people to vote, and he learned about power, organizing agencies, and organizing sit-ins. Later, Chavez's determination and personal involvement was critical in organizing the National Farm Workers Association to work for better wages and conditions for crop pickers. He successfully incorporated nonviolent strategies, such as boycotts and picketing, against the powerful California Growers Association, represented by the Teamsters Union and the AFL-CIO.

When the Teamsters began physically attacking NFWA members, Chavez adopted the Hindu concept of fasting, which encouraged other NFWA members to commit to his nonviolent movement, and the NFWA was eventually victorious in its fight for fairness with the growers in California. Like Ghandi before him, Chavez put his beliefs and his life on the line again and again in support of the culture and people he loved.

 Dr. Martin Luther King, Jr. was born on January 15, 1929, in Atlanta Georgia the son of minister. (Frady 2002) Dr. King became the pastor of the Dexter Avenue Baptist Church in Montgomery Alabama when he was twenty-five years old in 1954. Educated at Morehouse College and Crozer Theological Seminary, he completed his doctoral studies in 1955 at Boston University. As injustice toward African Americans gained increasing attention across the country, Dr. King sought ways of helping move toward civil rights. His learning journey included being inspired by Mahatma Gandhi's success with nonviolent activism. Dr. King was inspired by a 1959 visit to Gandhi's birthplace in India that he returned to claim that "nonviolent resistance was the most potent weapon available to oppressed people in their struggle for justice and human dignity."

Dr. King inspired and informed the Civil Rights Movement in the United States with his leadership. From his organizing role in the 1955 Montgomery Bus Boycott after Rosa Parks refused to give up her seat to a white man to his 1963 "I Have A Dream" speech during the march on Washington, Dr. King was the guiding force and inspiration for a generation of people from all walks of life and across all races in pursuit of civil rights for all Americans. His list of accomplishments is long and the impact he had on the country and the world beyond measure. His leadership was recognized with the Nobel Peace Prize in 1964. He was martyred by an assassin's bullet on April 4, 1968, in Memphis. The night before he had expressed the commitment of his life to the cause of social justice when he responded to a reported bomb threat with what became known as the "I Have Been To The Mountain Top" speech (Montefiore 2006). He said,

> *"And then I got to Memphis. And some began to say the threats, or talk about the threats that were out. What would happen to me from some of our sick white brothers? Well, I don't know what will happen now. We've got some difficult days ahead. But it doesn't matter with me now. Because I've been to the mountaintop. And I don't mind. Like anybody, I would like to live a long life. Longevity has its place. But I'm not concerned about that now. I just want to do God's will. And He's allowed me to go up to the mountain. And I've looked over. And I've seen the promised land. I may not get there with you. But I want you to know tonight, that we, as a people, will get to the promised land. And I'm happy, tonight. I'm not worried about anything. I'm not fearing any man. Mine eyes have seen the glory of the coming of the Lord. (155)"*

These individuals represent a wide range of philosophies regarding leadership and provide insight for a variety of approaches. Aspiring nonprofit leaders should assess these approaches and their experiences when developing a philosophy of leadership.

■ Using Mentoring to Develop Leaders

U.S. tennis great Althea Gibson once said, "No matter what accomplishments you make, somebody helped you." This statement is a starting point for discussing **mentoring** – people helping people. Some of the more positive terms associated with the term mentoring include *counselor, consultant, expert, referee, advocate, motivator, coach, guide,* and *teacher.* Applebaum, Ritchie, and Shapiro (1994) point out that there is a close relationship between mentoring and leadership, but the defining characteristics are elusive. Mentoring provides opportunities for seasoned leaders to counsel and guide aspiring leaders in the nuances of successful organizational processes. Nonprofit organizations that support mentoring activities can benefit immensely from the results. Perhaps mentoring is best understood in terms of the relationship that exists, or should exist, between or among organizational members. For effective mentoring to occur in an organization, four desirable qualities must exist: **caring, sharing, correcting,** and **connecting** (Gantt 1987):

1. **Caring** involves a genuine concern for the well-being of others. For true mentoring to occur, the individual being mentored should feel that the mentor is highly concerned for his or her growth as a person and a leader. Successful mentors accept individuals for themselves, but recognize their potential and will work with them to achieve high results.

2. **Sharing** suggests helping a person to become knowledgeable in any and all areas relevant to the successful operation of the organization. This might also include the sharing of information that could help an individual avoid making mistakes. While learning from mistakes is important, it can also be detrimental if those mistakes are significant. Sharing some information can be risky, and the information could be used against the mentor, or in some other harmful way, so the mentoring process should be undertaken carefully.

3. **Correcting** implies that a mentor should be able and willing to point out   mistakes, misperceptions, and incorrect assumptions. Since correcting is   sometimes associated with criticizing, it must be handled carefully. The way in which situations are addressed may be just as important as the subject matter addressed, and an employee being mentored should feel that the mentor is addressing a specific situation for the benefit of the organization and the development of the employee. Correcting is about helping a person change, not about punishing someone for making a mistake.

4. **Connecting** means having an active level of consideration for whom a mentee needs to know or meet in order to be successful in the organization and which activities an employee should be involved in for professional growth.

When all four of these qualities exist in an organization, learning can best occur. When learning occurs, the employee is actively developing, and the organization benefits from this development, as do all of those served by the organization. According to Appelbaum, et al. (1994), there is a positive correlation between mentoring and career commitment and a negative correlation between mentoring and dissatisfaction on the job. Everyone benefits from successful mentoring.

Mentoring is a highly important companion to leadership. A leader must be able and willing to provide mentoring to aspiring leaders for the sake of their development and for the continued growth of the organization.

■ Developing Leaders through Service Learning

Another way of developing leaders is by providing individuals with activities that offer the opportunity for skill and character development through an experiential learning process. **Service learning** is a field experience that combines community service with various learning objectives (Weis and Gantt 2004). It is a way in which individuals can perform meaningful service to the community while incorporating theoretical constructs that can include skill and/or character development. It is a process that combines community service with personal growth, learning, and civic responsibility. Individuals learn and develop by using newly acquired knowledge and skills in actual community situations. This helps them develop a sense of caring and responsibility for others, while learning through real world applications of the principles and skills being studied.

One example of a service learning application is found in a college class that is learning about financial resource development in nonprofit organizations. Once the students have completed a thorough study of the processes of fund raising, they partner with a local nonprofit organizations to participate in the annual fund raising campaign. Using classroom time, the students work in groups to select fund raising methods, coordinate scheduling to complement the set of methods to be used, and launch the campaign. Working closely with the nonprofit partner, the student groups complete the fund raising and turn in the money raised. Then, the students return to the classroom and conduct a thorough evaluation of the experience, complete written reports of the findings, and spend time reflecting on what they learned from the process. The students provide a copy of the written report to the nonprofit partner. As a result, everyone involved benefits from the service learning project, including the students, the nonprofit partners, and the beneficiaries of the organization's programs and services.

Research on the effects of service learning indicates a number of positive benefits for the participants, several of which are included below (Caskey 1991):

- **Capacity for Action.** Makes a difference, meets real needs.
- **Self-worth.** Identify, moral development, humane values.
- **Citizenship.** Connections to leadership for community.
- **Academic Development.** Increased relevance, challenge to think critically.
- **Career Development.** Increases understanding of the world of work, as well as providing a familiarity with and knowledge of specific job skills.
- **Social Development.** Enhancing interpersonal skills.

The many benefits derived from service learning can be very useful in developing skill areas as well as character attributes important in leadership development. Introducing service learning projects into a community, an organization, or educational institution can produce the following kinds of benefits beyond those to the individual participants (Caskey 1991):

- **Educational Institutions**
    - **Engaged Learners.** Motivated, responsible for own learning.
    - **Collegiality.** Staff, participants, community working together as partners.
    - **Educational Excellence.** Enhanced climate, enriched curriculum, performance-based evaluation.

- **Community and Organizations**
  - **Valuable Service.** Unmet needs addressed, often uniquely.
  - **Citizenship.** Participants become active stakeholders, now and in future.

Research shows the positive impacts of quality service learning programs on all those involved. Most studies regarding service learning have been conducted in an academic setting. One such study involved 24,000 K-12 grade students participating in the Learn & Serve America program in Florida. In this study, Grade Point Averages improved for most of the students, attendance improved, and disciplinary referrals declined during the program period (Follman and Muldoon 1997).

A study at Murray State University compared students in a service learning experimental group with a control group who were not involved in service projects and found the students in the experimental group felt a stronger sense of achieving something important in their lives as well as a stronger sense that they had made a positive contribution to the community. They reported a belief that what they did made a difference for the population they served and for the community, as well as for themselves (Weis 1998).

Service learning is like a laboratory in which character and skills relevant to effective leadership can develop under supervision, while important needs in the community can be addressed. It is a very appropriate leadership develop strategy to present at the close of this chapter, because the basic nature of service as a teaching and learning technique is deeply woven into the fabric of the nonprofit sector. The sector was founded on the basic notion that people can organize a voluntary response to any opportunity or challenge that faces them. It is a basic motivation to serve that drives the continuing growth and improvement of the sector. Collaborating in building the response and insuring that the life in their community improves as a result is central to leadership for the public good. Leadership at all levels and of all types are found in the nonprofit sector, effectively combining the two elements of leadership and service. Greenleaf (2002) brings these two elements together in the **servant leadership concept**, in which the great leader is a servant first. Greenleaf writes that whether leader or follower, those who work together to make the world a better place are always searching, listening, and expecting the goal to be accomplished. They are optimists committed to a shared vision in which the world is better for them having been involved and in service. He believes that people will "freely respond only to individuals who are chosen as leaders because they are proven and trusted as servants." (24)

■ Summary

Leadership in the nonprofit sector means strengthening individuals and communities by developing influence through collaborative and trusting relationships. Quality leaders play a wide range of roles in helping others reach higher and higher goals. They provide what is needed in each situation, from inspiration and motivation to guidance and facilitation. They both direct others to action and empower others to lead, depending on what is best for the circumstances at hand. A combination of characteristics and criteria is necessary for successful leadership. Leaders become leaders by a number of methods including appointment, election, emergence, and charisma. It is suggested that one way that leaders influence the behavior of others is by using personal powers, including referent power, legitimate power, expert power, reward power, and coercive power. To be a good leader, it is important to understand some of the reasons that individuals follow others. The ultimate success of an individual leader is often evident when they have empowered others to lead.

For a better understanding of the concept of leadership, the authors have incorporated a framework of classic theories, beginning with the Classic Organizational Theory that is based on a scientific approach to getting things done. The Great Man Theory suggests that leaders emerge and develop as a product of the times in which they live. The Group Theory states that there are roles to be filled and specific traits that are important for effective leadership to occur. The Trait Theory includes a list of personal traits necessary for successful leadership, and the Behavior Theory implies that leadership is a pattern of interpersonal processes with a goal of influencing the group. The Trait Theory implies that individuals should take situational variables into account when selecting a leadership style. Another important theory, the Humanistic Theory, signifies the leader as someone who encourages others to reach their full potential. The Excellence Theory implies that individuals and organizations can be transformed to higher levels of excellence, and finally, the Principle Theory is a values-centered concept for effective leadership. The examination these theories was complemented with an exploration of emerging thinking about leadership that incorporates both established and new frameworks and perspectives.

Over the years, large numbers of studies have been undertaken to explain leadership more fully. The Lewin, Lippit, and White studies were helpful in determining classic styles of leadership such as Authoritative, Democratic, and Laissez-Faire. The Ohio State studies identified two different dimensions of leadership – initiating structure and consideration. The New Managerial Grid places achievement and people along two axes. The University of Michigan study places the same two components, achievement and people, on a continuum relevant to the situation.

The Transactional Leadership Model is based on the social exchange theory, and the Transformational Leadership Model suggests that leaders can work with others in such a way that both leaders and followers are transformed to higher levels of achievement and morality. The Tri-Dimensional Leader Effectiveness Model combines the level of maturity of the employee with the demands of the situation. Hitt's Model of Leadership combines the importance of leadership and vision, and Collaborative Leadership implies team-building and turn-taking in various situations. The Comprehensive Approach to leadership is suggested in considering differing styles of leading, depending on the circumstances. Finally, a number of models and frameworks for leadership that are emerging were shared to help points the way to a future in which new ways of thinking about and practice leadership will surely evolve.

Too often, leadership models fail to include the importance of character and ethics in the overall scheme of leading and influencing others. The Integrated Leadership and Character Model was developed to discuss the importance of character in leadership. The model emphasizes the importance of three interrelated skill areas--conceptual, technical, and human relations--and the significance personal character has in the effectiveness of these three areas. Personal character is made up of traits and values, including trustworthiness, respect, fairness, caring and citizenship. Putting values to work is the role of ethics, and it is suggested that an ethical culture can be created in a nonprofit organization by emphasizing five ethical obligations: integrity, openness, accountability, service, and charity.

It has been stated that leadership cannot be taught, but must be learned by individual examination and experience. Several ways to accomplish this would include studying the lives of leaders through the ages, being a part of a mentoring program, and participating in service learning activities. Studying leaders such as Lao-Tzu, Plato, Aristotle, Niccolo Machiavelli, Thomas Jefferson, Harriett Tubman, Clara Barton, Geronimo, George A. Custer, W.E.B. Du Bois, Mohandas Gandhi, Helen Keller, Cesar Chavez, and Dr. Martin Luther King, Jr. can provide insight for a variety of leadership approaches.

Being a part of a mentoring plan can encourage aspiring leaders through qualities of caring, sharing, correcting, and connecting. And finally, service learning, a field experience that combines community service with various learning objectives, provides individuals with opportunities to practice skills and develop character while addressing important needs in the community.

To close this chapter, consider the growing resources and energies committed to the development of the understanding of leadership and its effective practice on behalf of society at large. Many groups exist to promote higher quality leadership develop at the community level, including the Association of Community Leadership and the National Society of Leadership and Success, among others. Many civic and service organizations share in this commitment and work toward similar goals. The number of other organizations with a clear commitment to leadership development on behalf of civil society is enormous. For example, consider that the for profit business community is now represented by organizations like Business for Social Responsibility and the National Social Venture Network, each seeking to connect business enterprises to social good. There is a growing network of independent centers committed to the subject, like the Center for Effective Leadership, the Center for Creative Leadership, and the Center for Progressive Leadership, just to name a few. The advance a particular perspective on the practice of leadership and provide educational and support resources toward that end.

When considering the ongoing study of leadership within the nonprofit sector, there are many discipline-based associations that include connecting the research of their members to the sector, including two that are solely focused on the sector: International Society for Third Sector Research and the Association for Research on Nonprofit Organizations and Voluntary Action. Most higher education institutions have a commitment to leadership woven into their missions, a key part of their strategy for student development, and focused programs of study dedicated to the subject. According to the Nonprofit Academic Centers Council there are over 255 institutions offering coursework in nonprofit leadership and management, found online at www.naccouncil.org. The American Humanics national network of undergraduate programs has 70 member institutions, found at www.humanics. org.

Leaders and those concerned about improving leadership practice should consider the many resources available. It is reasonable to expect that the importance of the subject will continue to advance the commitment to improved understanding and practice for the nonprofit sector and society at-large.

This chapter addressed, in part, the Nonprofit Leadership Alliance Certification Competency Requirements of Personal Attributes, Human Resources Development and Supervision, and General Nonprofit Management.

■ **Reflection and Application**

1. Drawing on the leadership theories, models, and studies presented in the chapter, write a description of your personal approach to leadership.

_____

_____

_____

2. List characteristics necessary for successful leadership today?

_____

_____

3. How do individuals become leaders?

_____

_____

4. Define the five types of power used in leadership:

_____

_____

_____

_____

_____

5. Select someone who has influenced your life and identify and describe the leadership theory that best aligns with how they lead.

_____

_____

6. Using the Integrated Leadership and Character Model, describe your Personal Character using traits, values, and ethics that you believe make you unique. Then, list the strongest skill you have in each category. Finally, list the skill in each category you want to improve.

    _____

    _____

    _____

    _____

    _____

    _____

7. Describe the five ethical obligations that an organization must embrace and pursued in developing an ethical culture?

    _____

    _____

    _____

    _____

    _____

8. What are the positive benefits of service learning to the individual and to the community organization in which the service occurs?

    _____

    _____

    _____

    _____

    _____

■ References

Applebaum, S. H., Ritchie, S., and Shapiro, B. T. (1994). Mentoring Revisited: An Organizational Behaviour Constuct. *International Journal of Career Management.*

Archer D. and Cameron, A. (2009). *Collaborative Leadership: How to Succeed in an Interconnected World.* Oxford: Elsevier Ltd.

Bass, B. M. (2008). *The Bass Handbook of Leadership: Theory, Research, and Managerial Applications.* (4th Ed.) New York: Free Press.

Belasco, J. A., and Stayer, R. C. (1993). *Flight of the Buffalo.* New York: Warner.

Blake, R. R., and Mouton, J. S. (1978). *The New Managerial Grid.* Houston: Gulf.

Brinckerhoff, P. C. (2009). *Mission-Based Management: Leading Your Not-for-Profit.* (3rd Ed.) Hoboken, NJ: John Wiley & Sons, Inc.

Boylson, H. D. (1955). *Clara Barton: Founder of the American Red Cross.* New York: Random House.

Burns, J. M. (1978). *Leadership.* New York: Harper and Row.

Cashman, K. (2003). *Awakening the Leader Within.* Hoboken, NJ: John Wiley & Sons, Inc.

Caskey, F. (1991). Model Learner Outcomes for Service Learning. *Minnesota Department of Education.*

Chait, R. P., Ryan, W. P., and Taylor, B. E. (2005) *Governance as Leadership.* Hoboken, NJ: John Wiley & Sons, Inc.

Collins, J. (2001). *Good to Great.* New York: Harper Collins Publishing, Inc.

Constantinides, H. (2001). The duality of scientific ethos: deep and surface structures. *Quarterly Journal of Speech.* February 87(1).

Corey, D. and Kim, D. (2003). *The Creative Tension Model.* Learning Partners Training, W. K. Kellogg Foundation.

Crutchfield, L. R. and McLeod Grant, H. (2008). *Forces for Good: The Six Practices of High-Impact Nonprofits.* San Francisco, CA: Jossey-Bass.

Covey, Stephen R. (1989). *The Seven Habits of Highly Effective People.* New York: Simon and Schuster.

Debo, A. (1976). *Geronimo: The Man, His Time, His Place.* Norman: University of Oklahoma Press.

Epler, P. H. (1919). *The Life of Clara Barton.* New York: Macmillan Company.

Follman, J. and Muldoon, K. (1997). Florida Learn & Serve 1995-96: What Were the Outcomes? *National Association of Secondary School Principals Bulletin.*

Frady, M. (2002). *Martin Luther King, Jr.* New York: Penguin Group.

Gantt, V. W. (1987). Beneficial mentoring is for everyone: a reaction paper. Paper presented at the November 1987 National Communications Association Convention, Chicago.

Greenleaf, R. K. (2002). *Servant Leadership: A Journey into the Nature of Legitimate Power and Greatness.* (3rd Ed.) Mahwah, NJ: Paulist Press.

Hersey, P., and Blanchard, K. (1977). *Management of Organizational Behavior-utilizing Human Resources.* (3rd Ed.) Englewood Cliffs, NJ: Prentice-Hall.

Hitt, W. D. (1988). *The Leader Manager: Guidelines for Action.* Columbus, OH: Battelle Press.

Hollander, E. P. (2009). *Inclusive Leadership: The Essential Leader-Follower Relationship.* New York: Routledge, Taylor & Francis Group.

Homans, G. C. (1950). *The Human Group.* New York: Harcourt, Brace and World.

Independent Sector (2002). *The New Nonprofit Almanac In Brief.* Washington, D.C.

Jeavons, T. H. (2006). When management is the message: relating values to management practice in nonprofit organizations. *Nonprofit Management and Leadership.*

Jeavons, T.H. (1994). Ethics in nonprofit management: creating a culture of integrity. In *The Jossey-Bass Handbook of Nonprofit Leadership and Management.* R. Herman, Ed. San Francisco: Jossey-Bass.

Jennings, E. E. (1960) *Anatomy of Leadership,* New York: Harper.

Kahneman, D. and Tversky, A. (2000). *Choices, Values, and Frames.* New York: Russell Sage Foundation.

Keller, H., Shattuck, R., Herrman, D., and Sullivan, A. (2005). *The Story of My Life.* New York: Bantam Books.

Kennedy, G. A. (1991). *Aristotle On Rhetoric: A Theory of Civic Discourse.* Oxford University Press.

Kim, D.H. *Creative Tension Model: Transformational Dialogue for Public Education Orientation Guide.* Cincinnati, OH: Knowledge Works Foundation.

Klimek, K. J., Ritzenhein, E., and Sullivan, K. D. (2008). *Generative Leadership.* Thousand Oaks, CA: Corwin Press.

Koch, A., and Peden, P. (1993). *The Life and Selected Writings of Thomas Jefferson.* New York: Random House.

Kouzes, J., and Posner, B. (1995). *The Leadership Challenge: How to Keep Getting Extraordinary Things Done in Organizations.* San Francisco: Jossey-Bass.

Levy, J.E. (1975). *Cesar Chavez: Autobiography of La Causa.* New York: W.W. Norton and Company, Inc.

Lewin, K., Libbitt, R., and White, R. K. (1939). Patterns of aggressive behavior in experimentally created social climates. *Journal of Social Psychology,* (May).

Maxwell, J. C. (2001). *Developing the Leader Within You.* Thomas Nelson, Inc.

Mondy, R.W., Holmer, R.E., and Flippo, E.B. (1980) *Management Concepts and Practices.* Allyn and Bacon, Inc.

Montefiore, S. S. (2005). *Speeches that Changed the World: The Stories and Transcripts of the Moments that Made History.* London: Quercus Publishing.

National Center for Charitable Statistics. (2008). *Nonprofit Almanac.* Urban Institute.

Nevid, J. S., & Rathus, S. A. (2005). *Psychology and the Challenges of Life: Adjustment in the New Millennium.* Hoboken, NJ: John Wiley & Sons.

Northouse, P. G. (2010). *Leadership: Theory and Practice.* (5th Ed.) Thousand Oaks, CA: Sage Publications.

Perry, J. L. ed. (2010). *Jossey-Bass Reader on Nonprofit and Public Leadership.* San Francisco, CA: Jossey-Bass.

Peters, T. J., and Waterman, R. H. (1982). *In Search of Excellence.* New York: Harper and Row.

Petry, A. (1955). *Harriett Tubman.* New York: Thomas Y. Crowell Company.

Quinn, R. E. (2000). *Change the World: How Ordinary People Can Accomplish Extraordinary Results.* San Francisco, CA: John Wiley & Sons, Inc.

Richards, N. (1968). *People of Destiny. Helen Keller.* Chicago: Children's Press.

Rost, J. C. (1993). *Leadership for the Twenty-first Century.* Westport, CT: Praeger.

Seagal, S. and Horne, D. (1997). *Human Dynamics: A New Framework for Understanding People and Realizing the Potential in Our Organizations.* Waltham, MA: Human Dynamics International.

Senge, P. M. (1994). *The Fifth Discipline Fieldbook.* New York: Doubleday.

Sessoms, H. D., and Stevenson, J. L. (1981). *Leadership and Group Dynamics in Recreation Services.* Boston: Allyn and Bacon.

Shivers, J. S. (1980). *Recreational Leadership: Group Dynamics and Interpersonal Behavior.* Princeton, NJ: Princeton Books.

Stogdill, R., and Coons, A. (1957). *Leader Behavior's Description and Measurement.* Columbus, OH: Bureau of Business Research, Ohio State University.

Stojkovic, S., Kalinich, D., and Klofas, J. (2007). *Criminal Justice Organizations: Administration and Management.* Belmont, CA: Wadsworth Publishing Company.

Tannenbaum, R., and Schmnidt, W. H. (1973). How to choose a leadership pattern. *Harvard Business Review*, (May-June).

Taylor, F. W. (1967). *The Principles of Scientific Management.* New York: W. W. Norton and Company, Inc.

Utley, R.M. (1988). *Cavalier in Buckskin.* Norman: University of Oklahoma Press.

Weis, R. (1998). *Service Learning Training Manual for Faculty K-16.* Murray, KY: American Humanics, Murray State University.

Weis, R. M. and Gantt, V. W. (2004). *Knowledge & Skill Development in Nonprofit Organizations.* Peosta, IA: Eddie Bowers Publishing.

Weis, R. M. and Gantt, V. W. (2002). *Leadership and Program Development in Nonprofit Organizations.* Peosta, IA: Eddie Bowers Publishing Company.

Weis, R. and Gantt, V. (2009). *Leading with Character, Purpose, & Passion.* Kendall-Hunt Publishing, Inc.

Weis, R. M. (1996). *A Lifetime of Making a Difference: A Student Manual for Career Planning in Youth, Human Service and Other Nonprofit Organizations.* Kansas, City, MO: Clevenger and Company.

Wheatley, M. J. (2005). *Finding Our Way: Leadership for an Uncertain Time.* San Francisco, CA: Berrett-Koehleer Publishers, Inc.

Worth, M. J. (2009). *Nonprofit Management: Principles and Practices.* Thousand Oaks, CA: Sage Publications, Inc.

Wren, J. Thomas (1995). *The Leader's Companion.* New York: The Free Press.

3 Staff, Board and Volunteers: Leading Effectively

Many people look at nonprofit organizations and see small for-profit organizations and try to suggest that nonprofits need to be organized and run in the same way as a for-profit. While all organizations share many qualities and characteristics, there is a vast difference between the nonprofit and for-profit worlds. What is successful in one world will not automatically succeed in the other. What is good for General Motors may not be good for the American Red Cross. Much, if not most, of the product or service delivered by the for-profit organization is "created" through advertising and marketing. In the nonprofit world, most, if not all, of the services delivered result from an individual or community "need." The very assumptions about why organizations exist and the core values are very different. For-profit organizations exist, first and foremost, to make a profit. They are profitable or they die. Nonprofit organizations exit to help people. They help people or they die. While this characterization is really an oversimplification, it is necessary to set the stage for viewing the similarities that matter and the differences that matter when it comes to staff, board and volunteer fundamentals. (Weis and Gantt 2004)

All organizations depend on the successful integration of three key components: people, resources, and a service or product. No matter how important or needed the product or service of an organization, the absence of appropriate resources or qualified and motivated people will cause the organization to struggle and ultimately fail. It might help to visualize any organization as a stool sitting on three legs (one for people, another for resources, and another for the product or service). The seat represents the organization's mission or reason for being. If one leg is missing, weak, or flawed, the seat of the stool will be adversely affected. Ultimately, it will fail to support its share of the weight of the mission. A successful nonprofit organization, like any organization must have three strong legs for its stool to do the job for which it was intended.

Within the people component, for nonprofits, there is another three-legged stool. Those legs consist of the **staff**, the **board** and the **volunteers**. If any group is ineffective, less effective than needed, or just not willing to live up to its potential, the whole organization is at risk.

When looking for answers, people often turn to principles which stand the test of time. Choose a busy person to get the job done. Do to others as you would have them do to you. Walk softly and carry a big stick. While each of these statements has value, no one time-tested principle works in every case. One reason for this is that psychologists tell us that every person is unique. There is no one exactly like us! With 6.7 billion unique human beings in the world, what is a person to do?

People fall into general categories when it comes to the type of interaction they desire when engaging others, desire for working conditions, and their reactions to very stressful situations. There are many tools which help leaders understand the general categories and support their work with different people. One of those tools is the **Personal Profile Preview™** (Resources Unlimited 2010). The research by the developers of the Personal Profile shows that people fall into four general interaction styles, with all four styles interacting to produce a highly predictive tool for what happens when people interact at work, at home, or at play. Following is a review of the four general styles:

- **Dominance.** People who emphasize this style like to solve problems and get immediate results, question current methods, enjoy independence and varied tasks.
- **Influence.** People who emphasize this style enjoy persuading and influencing others, are highly verbal and open to expressing feelings, prefer to work with others.
- **Steadiness.** People who emphasize this style prefer a stable and organized work climate, usually are patient and listen well, enjoy working in groups more that directing others.
- **Conscientiousness.** People who emphasize this style want to achieve high personal standards, carefully weigh all sides of an issue, are diplomatic, desire clearly defined expectations with no surprises.

It is possible that the greatest risk of all is to offer suggestions as to how others can best do their jobs. It always seems easy to give advice to others. The advice tends not to work in the real world. The best way to view suggestions from others is to consider the suggestion as a choice rather than an answer. There is a line in the 2002 movie "Solaris" when the lead character is trying to determine if his true love is real or a figment of his imagination. He is told by a space station veteran that "There are no answers, only choices."

This chapter explores the role of leadership in human resource development, examine each group of people involved in nonprofit organizations – staff, board, volunteers (their role and how to recruit the best people and develop them), makes suggestions as to how best to assure the success of each group (how to integrate the roles of each group and how to evaluate each group), and examines the central role of communication skills needed by leaders to help insure a solid, effective stool (through evaluation and re-direction).

■ The Role of Organizational Leadership

The chief executive officer, who typically carries the title of Executive Director (ED), plays a key role in selecting, developing, and leading people in the organization. Remember, leadership is much more a matter of character than a matter of certain qualities (Weis & Gantt, 2004). Leadership qualities are critical, but leadership qualities alone are not sufficient. Character matters a lot! In the nonprofit sector, anyone can be a true leader. Martin Luther King, Jr. put it this way, "Everyone can be great because anyone can serve. You don't have to have a college degree to serve. You don't even have to make your subject and your verb agree to serve…. You only need a heart full of grace. A soul generated by love …." (National School and Community Corps 1998). However, not everyone who serves effectively can lead a nonprofit organization. What is expected of the ED?

Even with great character, experience and research teach that certain skills, strategies and attributes help define what employees consider to be a successful leader. Chapter 2 provides in depth treatment of the qualities and characteristics of effective leadership. In the context of developing the people that make a nonprofit organization successful, a better word for leader might be mentor. Being a good boss, someone with whom people enjoy working, should be the goal of every ED. How can an ED get the job done for the organization, the board, the clients, the staff and the volunteers? There are six key qualities:

1. **A person who works to ensure a feeling of inclusion** – The "good" boss treats people fairly but not necessarily the same. The inclusive ED seeks feedback, not just accepts it graciously, and encourages innovation and creativity as long as it is true to the organization's mission. An ED should want all staff, volunteers and board members to be engaged and feel as though they are an important part of the "business" of the organization. People do not feel included or think they have voice (being heard) in an organization by accident. A feeling of inclusion is produced for staff, clients, volunteers, and board members by action, by effort. Inclusion is felt when there is an environment of trust and respect where every effort is made to treat people fairly.

2. **A person with a sense of mission** – Every organization needs to do something well and of value to the community it serves. The ED should set the agenda for the organization, by identifying what it will be known for in the community. It may be a service – hot meals, on time by Meals on Wheels. It may be an attitude – compassion and caring from Hospice. The ED must be a good "business" person, known for running a "tight" ship, and also known as someone who inspires staff and volunteers to pursue the mission. Organizational skills are crucial for leaders, but there must be a touch of humanity and compassion. People want to work with and for someone who goes about doing the "right thing."

3. **A desire to learn and promote learning** – The freedom to make mistakes is a powerful freedom. The ED who allows, even encourages staff and volunteers to test innovations and advance their creative ideas, while learning from the mistakes that may occur is an effective leader. To stop learning is to stop growing and to eventually die professionally and intellectually. An ED must be willing to learn in order to encourage learning. New ideas and new technology are not just for the new employees, they are for everyone, even the volunteers. True learning cannot be forced, it is best encouraged and rewarded.

4. **A coach, counselor, mentor** – The very best EDs are the ones who **help** staff, volunteers, and board members become the best they can be. It takes less time to help a person grow than it does to correct errors, smooth over hurt feelings, or repair damaged relationships. In the long run, an ED must view coaching, counseling and mentoring as *investment time*, not lost time.

5. **A person who helps everyone position for advancement** – The greatest mistake a human being can make in dealing with another is to try to hold a person back, slow career development, or be jealous of someone who jumps past them in their career path. Helping others succeed is a leaders reward. If every person in an organization is prepared to advance and is committed helping others advance, the organization will have a great pool of qualified and motivated people for its

future. If only select people are prepared or supported in their advancements, the organization suffers. People may not be ready to advance when they are needed. Also if there is no clear career path, the best people will find another organization. They will find a way to succeed in spite of all efforts they think are holding them back.

6. **A person who personally learns from mistakes** – The best way to demonstrate that an organization values learning from mistakes is for the ED to be seen learning from mistakes in a very public way. Leaders should admit mistakes, talk about what was learned, and encourage others to talk about what they have learned from their mistakes. This is a sign of strength and not of weakness.

With these qualities of an effective ED in mind, what is the nature and function of those who make up the rest of the organization – staff, board, and volunteers?

■ Human Resource Development

In the nonprofit sector, people make or break the organization. Without good people, the most needed service can be underutilized. A great vision can be thwarted by an ineffective board. A visionary ED can be undermined by a staff unwilling or unable to keep pace with the changing nature of a dynamic community. A committed and dedicated staff can be frustrated and rendered impotent by an ED who will not allow them to do their job. It is easy to identify what can go wrong. How can all these very different and very capable human resources be melded together to produce a useful, dynamic, vision driven nonprofit organization which can make a difference in the lives of people who need help?

Staff

The **staff** of any organization often has more to do with the ultimate success of the organization than does the designated leader. While the vision of the organization and direction is the responsibility of the positional leader or ED, it is the day-to-day function of any organization that determines its success. The key to day-to-day success is the quality of the work of the paid staff. Fully developed **job descriptions** must exist for every paid position in the organization. All job descriptions should consist of **seven elements** – *position title, purpose of the position, credential requirements, to whom does the position report, responsibilities of the position, specific duties of the position, and evaluation timetable along with the criteria for that evaluation.*

The **most critical issues** with respect to staffing an organization are: *recruitment, selection, hiring, training, evaluation, termination and retention* (Weis and Gantt 2004):

- **Recruitment**

    Positioning the organization to be seen as a desirable place to work is essential to successful recruiting. If the organization's image in the community is positive, it is much easier to attract the best employees. Positive activities produce positive perceptions by the community and potential employees. There are several steps in the recruiting process.

    First, the best source for finding the "right" person for the position is through the people who know the organization and what is required for the position

– other staff, board members, satisfied clients, and financial supporters. The only danger here is that some of these people will recommend people based on their relationship with the person rather than what is best for the organization. Therefore, it is important to be cautious, but do not reject this type of recommendation without thoroughly considering the qualifications of the candidate.

Second, network with other nonprofit professionals and ask for suggestions they may have of possible candidates and other people to contact for recommendations. Often, a person who is not "right" for one organization or position is perfect for another. Networking can extend beyond the immediate community to surrounding communities and can include contacts within for-profit organizations and government departments. At times, highly qualified people want a change of scenery and will trade the for-profit or government worlds for the nonprofit world.

Third, advertise in organization publications – newsletters, job listings, journals, and online job markets. Use local newspapers, radio and television to get the word out.

Fourth, prospect and recruit from the whole community. Read the newspaper, listen to the radio, and watch television for new companies coming to the community. Watch the performance of volunteers in other organizations. A good volunteer for one organization could be a great paid staff member for another organization. Many nonprofit professionals started their careers as dedicated volunteers.

- **Selection**

Most application processes require the applicants to submit a **letter of interest**, a **resume**, and a set of three to five **references**. To select the candidates to be interviewed, compare each candidate's application materials to the requirements listed in the **job description**. If none of the applicants meet the requirements, continue the search. It is never a good idea to fill the position with a less qualified candidate, just because there is pressure to get someone on the job quickly. It is much better to cover the work of the vacant position with temporary staff assignments until the most qualified person is found.

Before a selection can be made, **three criteria** must be clearly determined and reflected in the job description: what training/education is required, what level of experience is required, and what personal qualities are required.

All necessary background checks should be completed at this stage. This involves a careful check of references, which can be a significant factor in making the "right" choice and reducing **risks**. The general process of **risk management** is discussed in detail in **Chapter 7**. Selecting the wrong person can be very costly to an organization, resulting in the delays of termination and conducting another search. Risk reduction is a critical consideration. No organization wants to risk exposing its clients to potential physical harm, and no organization wants to risk being accused of unfair or biased hiring practices, as just two of the potential risks encountered in the hiring process. Every applicant deserves full and fair consideration, but the organization must also protect its clients and itself.

- **Hiring**

    The best indication of future behavior is past behavior. Construct the interview to determine **three** things: *are the credentials accurate, will the person fit with others in the organization, and does the person's work experience predict success in the position being filled*.

    The more care taken at the hiring stage, the more likely the new employee will become a permanent employee. Mistakes made by not being careful here tend to turn into bigger problems as time goes on. Firing someone is never easy. It is much better to hire well.

- **Training**

    Organizational training should be considered an investment, not a cost. Hire for attitude and train for skills. The time and money involved with new and continuing staff training are essential investments that help insure that the organization will continue to deliver effective service.

    Training new staff in the "organization's way" helps everyone understand and adjust to the changes which will occur when a new person or new people join the team. Training must be presented to employees in such a way as to enhance productivity and to meet any legal requirements. People must find training useful for it to be worthwhile.

    When training is built into a mentoring process, it is often more effective and more relevant. Training inside the mentoring process tends to be delivered when and where it is needed, not on an arbitrary time schedule which meets the agenda of the trainer. It can be very comforting for a new employee to have an experienced employee as a mentor to help feel welcomed and to navigate the new organizational culture.

- **Evaluation**

    In the ideal situation, evaluation should be an ongoing **process**. When evaluation is treated as an event rather than a **process**, problems tend to arise. Even when a person is given a six-month probation period, they should not have to wait six months to learn that they have performance problems. **Evaluation** is the comparison of expectations to actual performance. Assessment should occur daily with feedback to the employee being provide to help insure that expectations are being met.

    With a well written job description and daily interaction about expectations and observed performance, evaluation is simple. If problems arise which are not covered by the job description, they must be addressed immediately and agreement reached as to how the issue will be addressed.

- **Termination**

    Anyone associated with an organization can be asked to leave. While an organization leader is well advised to work to get the best out of everyone - staff, board members and other volunteers - some people are just not right for some organizations. The central reasons for termination is that performance is not matching the expectations of the position. When a person is asked to leave because of another reason, like they cannot get along with others, it can reflect very badly on a leader's ability to lead, mentor, and monitor staff or volunteers. Effective leaders must find a way to help all personnel do the best they can to contribute to the mission. When that is done, everyone benefits. The payoff is worth the effort of quality leading, mentoring, monitoring, and evaluation.

Anyone can be terminated for any reason if there is no employment agreement. However, everyone from staff to volunteer should know that there is a problem and efforts should be made and sufficient time spent to correct problems. No person should ever be surprised with a notice of termination, regardless of the seriousness of the reason.

If termination is necessary for someone who has an employment agreement with an organization, there are **three justifications** for ending an employment: **incompetence, violating agency rules, and violating local, state or federal laws**. A person who cannot perform the required task after due training and coaching may be dismissed. A person who violates agency rules, such as leaving young children unattended in a dangerous location, may be dismissed. A person who breaks the law, like traffics in drugs or firearms, may be dismissed.

- **Retention**

    Efforts made to retain effective staff are never wasted. The key is to give people meaningful work to do, appreciate them for what they add to the success of the organization, and reward them for a job well done. Retention is also an issue for board members and volunteers.

    The relationship an ED establishes with each staff member, each board member, and each volunteer is critical to the success of the organization's mission. Since human beings are so adaptable and resilient, the importance of relationship is often down played. Naisbitt and Aburdene (1985) report research which points to the central importance of relationships to job satisfaction. They report 10 qualities that people want in their work – for profit or nonprofit. Notice that high pay, good benefits, and job security are not in the top 10. They are in the top 15. Here is what research suggests that people want from their work and workplace:
    - to work with people who treat them with respect
    - interesting work
    - recognition for good work
    - a chance to develop skills
    - to work for people who listen if they have ideas about how to do things better
    - a chance to think for themselves rather than just carry out instructions
    - seeing the end result of their work
    - working for efficient supervisors/managers
    - a job/task that is not too easy
    - to think they are well informed about what is going on (85-86)

    While the order of these qualities could vary among staff and volunteers, all ten represent what people want to see if they are to consider their work rewarding and meaningful. Can a person do well without these qualities? Certainly! The better question is what kind of organization would want to be known as an organization which provides for its staff the kind of environment where these qualities are absent. In fact, Levering and Moskowitz (2003) write in the January 7th issue of *Fortune* that the 100 best companies to work for are expanding and increasing benefits, in spite of difficult economic times. These organizations understand the importance of investing in building happy and satisfied employees.

What is the proper way to establish an **appropriate relationship** with others? An appropriate relationship is open, honest, caring and genuine. Appropriate relationships are professional. They are two-way, joint ventures in which both parties must want to participate and see rewards from participation. Openness includes the opportunity to talk freely, expressing feelings and ideas. Honesty requires that each person be willing to discuss difficult issues and share views even when different, but this must be done with compassion and sensitivity. Caring is best shown by attentive listening to another and especially listening to how a person feels, not just what a person thinks. Being genuine is shown by actually living the other three, and this is best shown by taking time to learn about and from another, admitting mistakes, enjoying common good times and sharing times of sadness or disappointment. A healthy relationship requires frequent and focused work to keep it going.

How does a person know if a relationship is decaying? While each relationship will have its own unique qualities and characteristics, signs of decay can help anyone take stock of any relationship so that discussion can occur to address any problems. If a relationship appears to be changing, ask questions. Is the change a natural and maturing progression? Is it really changing? Is the change comfortable? Is it uncomfortable?

Here is a list of "signs" of a decaying relationship. Remember, these signs can be adapted and applied to any relationship – personal or professional:
- Shorter encounters
- Increasing physical distance between parties
- Increasing time between interactions
- Less personal information exchanged
- Less relationship talk
- Fewer favors given and/or asked for
- More negative evaluations and absolutistic statements and fewer positive superlatives
- Less nonverbal immediacy – less eye contact, colder vocal tone
- Increasing concern for self rather than for the other person or the relationship
- Less compromise due to increasing win-lose orientation
- More individual activities rather than mutual activities
- Return to more formal language and formal etiquette instead of comfortable, informal language and action

If relationships are sound and appropriate, an organization will prosper. If staff relationships are neglected or ignored, an organization will suffer. This is just as true of board and volunteer relationships (Weis and Gantt 2004).

Board

A board of directors, board of trustees, or administrative committee, hereafter referred to as the **board**, is common in the governance of nonprofit and for-profit organizations. Great resources on board development are provided by Board Source and found online at www.boardsource.org. The board serves to monitor organizational operation, set and adjust policies, and assure the financial support for the programs and personnel of the organization. The board is responsible for: 1) approving the direction, mission (or vision) of the organization; 2) assessing the fit of programs with the organizational mission; 3) approving budgets; and 4) evaluating the effectiveness of the organizations programs in meeting the organizations mission.

Since board members work without pay, usually, they are volunteers. They are, in fact, key volunteers. Their role is important, but not more important than any other group in the agency – staff or other volunteers. They, in fact, need to be examined for inclusion on the organization's team in the same way as would be done in recruiting and selecting staff and other volunteers.

All boards have four primary roles: 1. legal and fiduciary responsibilities; 2. represent an interested community constituency; 3. monitor agency operations; and 4. assist in raising necessary funds. It is useful to examine each of these four broad roles.

Legal and fiduciary responsibilities include attending to local, state and federal laws which impact the operation of the organization. Board members most also guard against misuse of the assets of the organization. If something goes wrong in either area, a board member cannot claim ignorance as a defense. The law assumes the individuals will exercise due diligence when making decisions with legal or financial stewardship implications. In legal terminology, all board members have the ***duty of care*** (due care) which is usually defined as the "care that an ordinarily prudent person would exercise in a like position and under similar circumstances" (*Black's Law Dictionary*, 499).

Representational responsibilities include acting in the best interest of all who receive benefit from the organization. Each board member should give **voice** to one or more of the groups or viewpoints served by the organization. In addition to a particular expertise (financial, legal, visioning, advocacy, etc.) that a board member brings to the group, members should represent and give voice to those served. Great care must be taken to make sure the board members can represent the skills necessary for a board to do its job well. Every board should have members who have strong financial backgrounds, others who have knowledge of the laws governing nonprofits, others with strong programming experience, others with fund raising skills, all with strong ties to the community and genuine interest in the organization's success. A board member is never to receive personal benefit from board membership. This is a part of a board members ***duty of loyalty*** which is the legal standard of fairness. Said in another way, a board member must be true to the interests of the organization when making decisions which affect that organization.

Monitoring duties include assuring that the organization is effectively and efficiently run. This is part of the board member's ***duty of obedience*** in terms of each member's legal duty to be faithful to the organization's mission. The board is responsible for hiring and firing the chief executive officer/ED. It is also the responsibility of the board to periodically evaluate the ED's performance and provide constructive feedback. If changes need to be made, the board must clearly spell out what action is expected and in what time frame. The board must then follow-up on the action plan and time table for improvement.

Financial support responsibility does not mean board members must personally fund the organization. However, it is good practice to recruit board members if they have already demonstrated their belief in the mission of the organization by offering some financial support. Their most important role, aside from making sure the organization adheres to local, state, and federal legal requirements and remains solvent, is to be a magnet for donors. In other words, the board must set an example for the community and help those responsible for fundraising make contact with community members who are capable of making meaningful contributions. They must also support and speak for the organization's mission in such a way as to generate a positive image for the organization among potential donors.

Another way of describing the key roles of board members is presented in *Governance as Leadership* (Chait, Ryan and Taylor 2005) in which the terms fiduciary, strategic, and generative are used. The case is made that the organization will be more successful when the board has time to work with all three roles and to look for the interconnections among them.

Fiduciary or financial responsibilities are the core of the traditional role of board members. It has historically consumed the major of the time board members give to the organization, from fundraising to financial oversight. The expectations of financial stewardship weigh heavily on most board members and, therefore, get a great deal of attention. Legal compliance and financial health dominate most board agendas.

Board members also need to have the opportunity to contribute to the **strategic** development of the organization's pursuit of its mission. Time needs to be available for the board to contribute to the alignment of programs and services with the mission, to help make sure that constituent needs are being most effectively met. This can involve such things as strategic discussions about program evaluation results with staff, giving board members a chance to have input to future directions.

Finally, board members need the opportunity to participation in period **generative** discussions about the future. These exchanges involve stepping back from the daily operation of the organization and its delivery of programs and services to think together about the mission and the ways in which the organization can become more effective in achieving it. Generative thinking is a process that helps every board member share their wisdom, inspiration, and most creative ideas about the core issues and how they can be most effectively be addressed. Such discussions are often the source of new thinking about the future and creative strategies that may impact the way the organization pursues its vision of that future. Attention must be paid to providing board members with a balanced experience that includes sufficient time on the fiduciary, strategic, and generative roles in order to make sure that the organization is health and effective today and long into the future.

The members of the board represent various groups and constituents from the community. As new members rotate on and off the board, balance in representation must be maintained. There should be a staggered rotation of board members. The most common model is a three year rotation system with one-third of the membership replaced each year, for an established board. If a new organization is selecting it first board, one-third would serve one year, one-third for two years, and one-third for three years. This helps keep a board from becoming stagnant and unproductive.

Board members are assigned specific roles as officers or committee members as a way of organizing the work and guiding participation. Most often there are four board officers: **President, Vice President, Secretary, and Treasurer**. The duties of each office are the same as it would be for any organization. Specific or special responsibilities may be added due to the nature or mission of the organization. Officers should be eligible for re-election, but there should be some reasonable term limits or rotation of members through offices. This is not always practical. For example, the skills of the person who serves as Treasurer or Secretary may not be shared by all members of the board. Whatever system is chosen, a board does not need to be taken hostage by one or a few members and controlled for satisfaction of their egos over the best interest of the agency. A dominating board leader can destroy the effectiveness of an agency. (Weis and Gantt 2004)

The **President** is responsible for running meetings, assuring that board members receive the information to discharge their duties, appoint committees as prescribed in the organizations governing documents, preside over executive committee meetings, speak for the organization as appropriate and lead the annual review of the Executive Director.

The **Vice President** assumes the duties of the President when he or she is unable to discharge those duties. The Vice President serves on committees as appointed by the President and represents the organization at public meetings when appropriate. This person is often the next one to serve as President of the board, which allows a person to prepare for the position of President with proper orientation and training. This succession process is often employed to ensure a smooth transition of leadership.

The principle function of the **Secretary** of the board is to maintain accurate minutes of all board meetings. This is critical since in legal terms a board speaks through its minutes, which are maintained over time to record all significant actions. These minutes must be prepared in a timely fashion and distributed to all board members and other affected parties. Taking attendance for all meetings is the responsibility of this officer. The responsibility for the safekeeping of all official board records and documents is also the responsibility of the Secretary.

The **Treasurer** monitors the financial business of the agency to assure that sound and accepted accounting procedures are followed and that annual, external audits are conducted and reported to the board. The Treasurer must keep in touch with day-to-day fiscal activities of the organization, working closely with the staff that are managing the processes. The Treasurer must make sure that all legal and governmental regulations are observed with respect to payroll and other financial obligations of the organization.

An effective board is organized into committees to divide the workload and assure proper monitoring organization operations (Hardy, 1990). The number and size of committees varies by the size and scope of the organization, the number of board members, and the nature of the work to be done. In one respect, committees keep an eye on the "big picture" for the organization, doing work that complements and supports the work of the staff. It is a serious mistake for the board or its committees to become involved in micromanaging the organization and interfering with the work of the staff. At the same time, the board must be interested in and aware of the day-to-day activities of the agency.

A board can rely on committees to do its work as long as the following requirements are met (Berman 2010):

- the purpose, powers, procedures, and limitations of the committee are clearly defined in the organization's bylaws on in formal board actions
- the committee maintains and distributes minutes of its meetings and other records appropriate to its assignment
- the committee regularly reports its work to the board
- the membership of the committee is appropriate to the assignment
- the committee is meeting and addressing matters appropriate to its assignment

The typical board committees include:

- **Executive Committee** – This committee usually consists of the officers of the board. It can be expanded to include the chairpersons of standing committees or anyone else the board designates. Size is always an issue. An executive committee of more than seven would be large and potentially difficult to assemble for important functions. This committee makes recommendations for board action. It only has authority as authorized by the board. The board President serves as chair of the executive committee and calls necessary meetings between the regular meetings of the full board. The ED should be an ex officio member of this and all other committees.
- **Budget & Finance Committee** – This committee works with the ED to prepare and monitor the annual budget of the organization. The Treasurer serves on the committee and frequently serves as chairperson. If necessary, the committee recommends adjustments in the budget throughout the year to stay on track for financial good health. They also oversee fundraising and provide liaison with external funding sources such as the United Way. In some cases, the committee also plans capital campaigns, usually with the help of a consultant, and planned-giving programs to benefit the organization and its loyal supporters. In other cases, a subcommittee may be established to oversee fundraising in general or specific fund raising activities like capital campaigns and planned giving programs.
- **Strategic Planning Committee** – This committee should be an ongoing committee and not just one which functions every five years or in times of crisis. This is the vision monitoring and adjustment committee. They should not be distracted by day-to-day issues. They must always be looking to the horizon to recommend needed change. They must watch for community changes, need for program modification, trends in funding, facility needs, personnel issues, opportunities for expansion and growth of the agency mission, and board issues. They engage the whole board in strategic and generative discussions to help inform the long-range plans and the ongoing activities that help prepare for that future.
- **Program Committee** – This committee monitors the programs of the organization for effectiveness and recommends changes and updates after appropriate consultation with clients and community representatives and reviewing evaluation

activity conducted by the staff. Membership should include the ED and appropriate program staff along with one or two board members to serve as liaison with the full board. They should prepare a calendar of activities for each year. This can be distributed to board members, clients, media or any interested person.

- **Facilities or Property Management Committee** – This committee keeps track of needed repairs and renovations. They plan for long-term funding of maintenance and improvements, working with the Budget and Finance Committee and whole board to prepare for those costs. They need to assure that all facilities meet or exceed local codes and that all risks associated with the facilities are addressed in a timely fashion. It should monitor the inventory of equipment and facilities and periodically review related insurance coverage.

- **Human Resource Committee** – This committee is charged with developing appropriate written personnel policy for board approval. Policies, practices, and procedures typically include: affirmative action compliance, conditions of employment, probationary period, job descriptions and classifications, performance review criteria, working conditions and hours, benefits, vacations, expense reimbursement, promotion options, training and conference attendance requirements, leave policies – family, illness, military service, termination of employment and severance pay. The committee must also insure that meaningful and timely evaluation of all staff and volunteers occurs on a regular basis. A critical function of this committee is to assure the a benefits and compensations package for all positions is competitive with like organizations. Additionally, this committee must insure that appropriate training exists for all employees, volunteers and board members.

- **Marketing and Advertising Committee** – This is a year-round functioning committee charged with the promotion and marketing of all organization programs and services by working in support of the ED and appropriate staff. It insures that all activities are exposed to the community by using appropriate newspaper, radio, television, and magazine media to tell the story of the organization through press releases, flyers and the annual report. This committee works in consort with local civic organizations, like the local Chamber of Commerce, to increase the visibility of the organization in the community.

- **Legal Issues Committee** – This committee monitors all issues related to legal requirements, risk management, and insurance. The use of external specialists, like legal counsel and insurance agents, can be recommended by this committee if the situation warranted it.

- **Board Recruitment and Recognition Committee** – This committee constantly searches the community for potential board members who could make a positive contribution to the mission and vision of the organization. The committee prepares a process for member evaluation and recognition. It prepares a slate of officers for annual elections and recommend term limits and rotation of board members through appropriate board positions. It formulates and recommends to the board policies and actions for filling expiring terms of officers and other members. Members should be sensitive to the representational charge of the board.

- **Activities or Special Events Committee** – This committee may not exist in every organization, since its work may be handled by staff and volunteers. It can be the source of input and/or support for a wide range of activities that are important in the life of the organization, including such things as annual banquet to honor clients and volunteers, public relations events to promote new programs, or any other event outside the work of other committees.

Boards may have fewer or more committees or specialized committees to meet challenges of their work of the organization. The number and size of committees is largely determined by the size and complexity of the organization. Too many committees can get in the way of organizational effectiveness. Committees of more than nine people can become unwieldy and ineffective. In short, a board needs the committees required to make it effective, not a long list of committees in order to look as important as other agencies.

Volunteers

Volunteers are critical to most nonprofit organizations. **Volunteers** can save an organization or kill it. The key is how clearly the organization defines the role of each volunteer, evaluates each volunteer, and rewards each volunteer. Notice the use of "each" in the preceding statement. While it is always important to understand that each person is an individual with unique qualities, needs, drives, abilities, interests and skills, it is critical when working with volunteers. Remember, board members are key volunteers.

Why do people volunteer to work for no pay? The answer is, they never do! While it is true that people who volunteer do not expect to receive money for their efforts, they do expect to "get something" for their experience. Basically, volunteers are drawn to an organization because they see a need or they need to be involved. These altruistic motives help organizations fill positions without having to hire full-time people. Worth (2009) reports that volunteers come to an organization and stay over time because they have:

- a desire to serve the organizations' mission
- positive relationships with other volunteers
- a rewarding experience with the work of the organization
- learned new skills

Just like quality paid staff management practices, volunteers want clear expectations for their work with the organization and the amount of time involved. Volunteer job descriptions can help provide this information. Volunteers also need quality supervision to help insure that their contributions of time are most effectively utilized. However, most nonprofit organization leaders find it more difficult to terminate a volunteer or board member than to terminate a staff member. Since this tends to be true, great care must be taken when selecting volunteers and matching them to tasks within the organization. Three broad categories of volunteer management must receive special attention: **planning, recruitment**, and **integration**. (Weis and Gantt 2004)

Planning is certainly the first step in the process of meaningful use of volunteers for any nonprofit organization. While planning comes first, it must also be viewed as a continuous process for the life of the organization. The initial stage in planning is assessment of needs, asking:

- What positions can be filled by volunteers?

- How many are needed?
- How much supervision or oversight is required?
- How will the time required for oversight impact staff time constraints?
- Is the use of a volunteer of real value or just a way to hold down the number of paid staff?

Once the assessment is complete, the results must be discussed with all staff, not just those who are most directly affected. A common mistake is to assume that only those most directly affected by an organizational change need to know what is happening. In truth, if organizational leaders only share information with people who are directly affected by a decision, those not included might think that information is being hidden which gives rise to mistrust and feeds the rumor mill. With the assessment results discussed openly and honestly, the organization can secure staff concurrence. The time spent at this stage is time well spent. If the staff does not agree with or understand the need for volunteers, it is a waste of time to look for them. If they are a part of the decision, they will more actively support and engage volunteers as a resource to the organization.

The final stage in the planning step requires great care. Clear and thorough **job descriptions** for each volunteer position are paramount to the meaningful utilization of any volunteer. All job descriptions should include: position title, reporting line, how the position fits into the organizational pattern, essentials duties, training requirements/plans, expected time contribution, and benefits to the organization and the volunteer.

Recruitment is almost as important as planning. In addition to organizational needs, leaders need to consider the motivation of people to volunteer. People seek to volunteer for the same reasons that everyone seeks to be a part of any group or relationship. Humans have four impulses which cause them to seek the companionship of other humans: to receive stimulation, to share experiences, to assert oneself, and for the increased enjoyment of certain activities.

People are attracted to each other much as a volunteer is attracted to an organization. Volunteers are attracted to nonprofit organizations because of:

- **Reward or punishment** – The volunteer gets something from the relationship. The person may feel good about what they do for the organization or its clients. On the other hand, the volunteer may be compelled by guilt or some motive which is a form of punishment for the person. In either case, the volunteer is getting a return on their investment.
- **Proximity** – The opportunity to engage an organization is close to the volunteer and easily accessed or an organization is distant enough to remove the volunteer from some undesirable condition or influence.
- **Similarity or dissimilarity** – Volunteers may turn to an organization because they see themselves and the organization traveling the same road, wanting the same things in terms of helping people. On the other hand, they could see the organization doing something they have never done and they want to try. It may be that they see the organization going in the opposite direction to the one they have personally chosen.
- **Physical attractiveness** – The organization may be the place to be. It may be the one that all the best people choose to engage. It may be the community "golden

child." Volunteers may conclude that association with such an organization will improve their community standing or make them attractive to other organizations.

Whatever a volunteer's motives, the organization can benefit or suffer. The organization that chooses to engage volunteers must have volunteers who have motives which blend with and support its mission. The most effective volunteers are driven by service to the organization and not by service to themselves.

In addition, due diligence must be taken in selecting volunteers, as with staff, in order to reduce and manage any **risk** to the organization. General guidelines for **risk management** are discussed in some detail in **Chapter 7.**

Integration is the third consideration in the effective utilization of volunteers. The organization can have a great plan for the use of volunteers and recruit only people with motives which support the mission and still fail to retain the best or make optimal use of each person if the organization does not properly integrate the volunteers with its programs and paid staff. Just as with paid staff, volunteers must have meaningful work, appropriate recognition, helpful feedback as to the effectiveness of their contribution to the mission, regular opportunities for input based on their experience and wisdom, and the chance to expand their skills, if they so desire. The more thoroughly integrated volunteers become with the flow of the organization, the more likely they are to have a positive impact on the mission (Herman 2005).

■ Communication

Quality communication is central to effective leadership. Time invested in understanding and developing communication skills will improve the work of leaders and managers working at all levels in nonprofit organizations. With the mix of paid staff, board members, and volunteers, it can be challenging work. The quality of the relationships that are developed across the organization is the secret to the success of its team of staff and volunteers. And, the secret to successful relationship building is communication. A leading author on the subject of people helping families get along puts it this way, "Once a human being has arrived on this earth, communication is the largest single factor determining what kinds of relationships she or he makes with others and what happens to each in the world. How we manage survival, how we develop intimacy, how productive we are, how we connect with our own divinity – all depend largely on our communication skills" (Satir, 1988, p. xi). A brief review of the foundations of effective communication sets the stage for understanding quality practices in leading nonprofit organizations.

The reason it is so difficult to achieve effective communication is that too many people assume that success is as simple as creating clear and understandable messages. This is often referred to as the **conduit model**. The conduit model assumes that communication is the simple passage of messages from a sender to a receiver through a channel (or conduit). The **conduit model** is source oriented (Bokeno, 2002). Sometimes the idea of feedback is added as a way of checking with the sender to verify if the receiver clearly and "correctly" received and understood the message. Even when consideration of interaction or feedback is added, it is easy to see why people mistakenly oversimplify communication and reduce it to the sending and receiving of messages. If someone misunderstands, is the fault of the sender or receiver?   The fault most often lies in the search for simple answers to difficult questions. The heart of the answer is in the question. Here is a poor question, "Why didn't you do what I asked you to do?" Here is a much better question, "Did you understand what I asked you to do?"

Effective communication is all about understanding meaning. It is not just about sending clear messages. Satir (1988) offers a practical definition of communication which works as well in the workplace as it does in a family setting. She contends that communication evolves from "the ways people use to work out meaning with one another" (p. 4).

In order to be an effective communicator, it is necessary to understand the nature of interacting with others, to alter or adjust messages to achieve meaning, and that bridges must be built between and among individuals because of differences resulting from variables such as experience, culture, education, area of expertise.

The kind of communication which makes an organization really succeed comes from genuine dialogue. It is a learned art. All humans have a natural desire to understand and be understood. The most helpful way to learn to communicate more effectively is to observe and study individuals who are effective, ask questions, try different styles, and ask more questions.

There are **four communication truths** that can help prepare for daily interaction with people from a wide range of backgrounds, experience, and cultures. Taking these truths into consideration helps improve the effectiveness of leaders and supervisors working with staff, board, and volunteers in nonprofit organizations. (Weis and Gantt 2004)

1. **Understanding must precede any agreement.** Understanding is required if an agreement between two people is to result. Agreement implies that both people are clear on each other's assumptions, values and positions.

2. **Agreement without understanding is usually meaningless.** In order for two people to agree, they must be talking about the same issue, idea, emotion, or relationship. To say they agree is without any substance unless they are talking about the same issues, idea, emotion, or relationship.

3. **Genuinely disagreement is not possible without understanding why or how they disagree.** For disagreement to be genuine, it must be based on a clear understanding of the issue at hand – their positions, why they take the positions, and the implication of the positions for the relationship between the two people. Unless these conditions are met, genuine disagreement is not possible. It is not based in substance but is fueled by assumptions which may or may not be accurate. Understanding of another does not require agreement, but it does require a clear and accurate comprehension of the other person's position.

4. **Disagreement without understanding is almost always meaningless.** Just like statement number two, there is no meaning or substance to a disagreement based on potentially inaccurate or unclear information. If there is clear understanding, there can be disagreement. If there is no understanding, there can only be shouting, anger, assertion, name calling, or worst of all, violence.

Senge (1994, 242-245) provides a useful tool to help groups be attentive to these truths and to hold each other accountable to their application. A **Ladder of Inference** (Figure 3.1, next page) helps illustrate how easy it is for people to receive the same information and

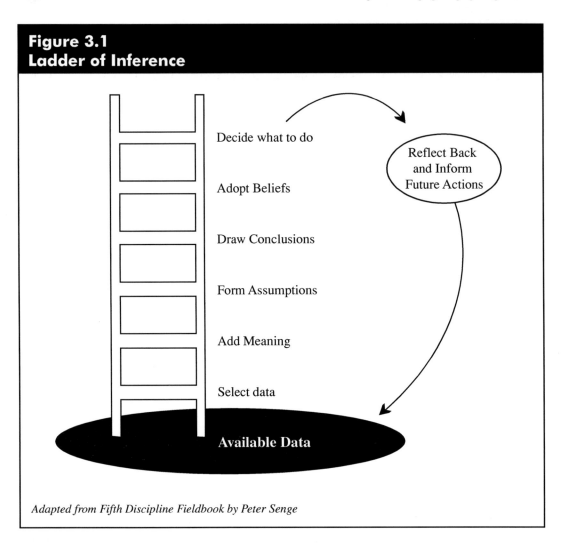

Figure 3.1
Ladder of Inference

Decide what to do

Adopt Beliefs

Draw Conclusions

Form Assumptions

Add Meaning

Select data

Reflect Back and Inform Future Actions

Available Data

Adapted from Fifth Discipline Fieldbook by Peter Senge

to come to very different conclusions and take very different actions. People can jump to assumptions and conclusions without checking the data they observe. It is a visual framework that, once accepted by a group, can be helpful in encouraging members to share their "available data and experiences" when expressing conclusions and beliefs and when taking actions. Improved understanding can follow. When put into practice, it becomes appropriate and comfortable for any member of the team to ask anyone else, regardless of position, for their "available data". This type of group commitment to clarifying communication, no matter what approach is taken, can improve all aspects of organizational development.

Deetz and Stevenson (1986) describe **five assumptions about communication** which can help a person determine what can be done to modify and build useful communication skills for any workplace:

1. Communication skills are learned.
2. Interpersonal skill needs change over time and situation.
3. Personal, situational and relationship needs determine the usefulness of various skills.

4. Individuals can exert considerable control over their communication behavior and skill development.

5. Self-esteem and healthy relationships require successful skill development or a person will enjoy only very limited personal and professional accomplishment. (p. 3)

Whether preparing a personal development plan for one employee or a board training program for that critical leadership group, these assumptions will help inform the design and deliver of the program.

In addition to such things as training and development, another factor in successful communication that must be considered is the **interaction environment**. When one person talks with another person, they use words which have meaning to them. Those meanings have evolved along with the person. The point is that the meaning of words is in the people who speak them, not in a dictionary. There are two factors affecting the interaction environment – the **cultural environment** and the **physical environment**.

- The **cultural environment** consists of the behaviors, attitudes and values which are shared by enough people to exert an influence on the messages we create. A person can begin to deduce the prevailing cultural factors by observing patterns of work, relationship styles, attitudes toward self-fulfillment and messages sent by the mass media.

- The **physical environment** consists of the natural and human constructions which frame our conversations and relationships. These frames include a person's idea of what constitutes appropriate formality, warmth, privacy, familiarity, constraint and distance.

Tools for groups to use, like the Ladder of Inference in Senge's *The Fifth Discipline Fieldbook* (1994), can promote the practice of checking with each other to ask for the meaning and the reasons behind it in clarifying and improving understanding. It is such group processes that help everyone learn to communicate more effectively together while learning about what each person brings to the interaction environment. When this happens, communication improves and the human resources of the organization become more effective in pursuit of the mission.

What are the essential communication skills and how does a leader use each one? There are **six** skills which are important for anyone working in nonprofit organizations: **listening, conflict management, decision-making, team building, coaching/counseling, and sensitivity to differences**.

Listening

Aside from our physical ability to hear sounds, perception is the most important variable in determining if a person is an effective listener. Frequently, the mistake is made in equating hearing and listening. If one person hears someone speaking to them, they consider that they are listening. Rarely, is that true. Even the fact that a person does not respond as expected does not mean that they are not listening. What is the difference between listening and hearing? Simply put, hearing is using the human senses to receive sensory data and store it in the brain. In its basic form, it is not listening. Listening, unlike hearing, which is a natural phenomenon, is **a learned skill**. It involves selecting, testing, and adding meaning to the sensory data that is being received. Any person can listen more effectively by understanding and acting on the following information (Weis and Gantt 2004):

- Effective, active listening is difficult, and practice and training can improve listening skills.
- There is no relationship between intelligence and listening skill. Highly intelligent people are often very poor listeners, because they jump to conclusions rather than hearing all that is being said.
- Listening is an active process. It requires a person's *participation* and *involvement*. Good listeners often notice a sense of fatigue after an intense listening experience.
- Personality plays an important role in how well a person listens. The more other-focused a person, generally, the better the listening skills.
- Effective listening requires the whole body. Proper eye contact and body posture facilitate effective, active listening.
- Feelings are often more important than the words spoken. People must look for the underlying feelings in any message. These feelings are often the _real_ message.

The practice of **active listening** can help improve communication. It involves listening for more than the apparent meaning of the words and includes listening for the feelings and emotions behind words or messages. There are **four** main **qualities of an active listener**:

1. Physical proximity or closeness
2. Appropriate, direct eye contact
3. An open mind
4. A demand for clarity as demonstrated by a willingness to ask questions to get clear meaning and to uncover underlying emotions and feelings

Conflict Management

Conflict is a naturally occurring phenomenon in the United States, indeed everywhere in the world. Hocker and Wilmot (1985) define **conflict** as "an expressed struggle between at least two interdependent parties who perceive incompatible goals, scarce rewards, and interference from the other party in achieving their goals" (23). As stress rises in society, conflict follows, and the workplace both reflects the results and provides a perfect place in which to address the negative impacts it has on people. Nonprofit organizations are a great place to manage conflict because they are more flexible and self-determined than the government and business sectors and the majority of the staff and all of the volunteers are involved by their own personal choices (Maravelas 2005). While many people try to avoid conflict, it can produce the following **positive rewards** that can help improve the nonprofit organization's efforts to develop human resources:

1. Conflict can produce a greater understanding by the people in disagreement and clarify their relationship.
2. Conflict can focus and clarify the similarities and differences between the people in disagreement.
3. Successful conflict management can help the people in disagreement discover better methods for dealing with future conflicts.

4. Conflict can expose areas where communication can actually be improved and strengthened.

The best way to look at the true value of conflict is to ponder the African proverb, "Smooth seas do not make skillful sailors." People must be tested and trained on the seas of conflict in order to know how to deal with it effectively. Experience working with conflict is the best way to improve the capacity to manage it.

Nonprofit organizations often operated in a context of limited resources. Most definitions of conflict include reference to the inability to share limited resources as a common source of disagreement. This source of conflict occurs frequently in nonprofit organizations. Another recurrent source of conflict in an organization with very diverse staff and volunteer groups, with different experiences and backgrounds, comes from communication rules violation. Communication rules define required, preferred and prohibited behaviors. The severity of the conflict often generates from the costs or rewards of rule violation. Understanding the communication rules of others helps to reduce conflicts over violations of rules. This can be even more pronounced when the diversity includes different roles, relationships, experience, and education that can often be found between staff and volunteers in nonprofit organizations.

Writers often suggest that conflict resolution should be a goal. In reality, conflict is rarely resolved. One conflict leaves a residue which is built upon through future conflicts. If that residue is basically negative, the subsequent conflicts start in a hole and tend to become more negative than the issue warrants. People typically choose from five options when they are faced with a conflict: **avoiding, accommodating, competing, compromising, or collaborating** (Borisoff and Victor, 1998). While each has its place and each has its advantages, the first four usually lead to more conflict or at least some unhappiness.

- **Avoiding** can be an appropriate approach to conflict if there is risk of harm. Otherwise, conflicts which are avoided tend to simply grow larger. Avoiding conflict does not solve anything and typically produces little satisfaction for any of the people involved since nothing is resolved. The main residual of avoiding conflict is to continue to avoid conflict even is it causes more harm.

- **Accommodating** can be very appropriate when the issue of the conflict is more important to one person than the other. If two co-workers are disagreeing over the best way to advertise a new program and one is insistent on the need for radio advertising while the other thinks newspaper advertising is enough, the one can accommodate the other by supporting radio advertising. It does not matter and if there is enough money in the budget, the costs of fighting may be too high. Accommodating involves one person giving in to the other. If a person uses this approach too often, it may lead to others taking advantage by cutting that person out of discussions where the issue may matter a great deal, expecting that they are not always going to accommodate.

- **Competing** is a common approach to conflict management in the United States and is a favorite of men. The objective is to win on the issue in question and have the other person lose. This approach can be effectively employed when there is a clear-cut solution with profound impact on an organization or when critical information for decision making is not fully available to all those involved. If there is no real justification for the competing approach, the result can be stifled ideas, weaker solutions, hurt feelings, damaged relationships, and little teamwork. In fact, since competing is so dominate in the U.S. culture, it is rarely justified. The main reason for its ineffectiveness is that it tends to promote compliance with power more than promoting open communication and effective conflict management. It can undermine efforts to build the positive relationships necessary for organizational success.

- **Compromising** involves all those involved giving some ground in order to move beyond the conflict. This approach is very appropriate when there is no clear-cut answer to an issue and no one has cause to impose a solution on others. The worst effect of compromise is that everyone may leave the conflict with some dissatisfaction which can dampen the enthusiasm for the results achieved by the compromise.

- **Collaborating** promotes discussing all perspectives in the creation of a solution which can make every party's satisfaction maximized. It focuses on issues, not positions. All the other approaches invite participants to adopt a position and stick to it. Collaboration, by its nature, invites all parties to look to the potential outcome as what will benefit everyone. This approach usually requires more time and effort but has the potential to produce high degrees of satisfaction and more creative solutions. It also creates a residual of success which in turns encourages those involved in a collaborative effort to have less fear of future conflict. There is a pattern of success to build upon. Collaborating is the most desirable approach in most situations.

There are **three skill sets** which help people **focus on a win-win prospective** that is central to the collaborating approach. These three tend to open a path to cooperation more than competition:

1. See the disagreement from the point of view of the other person
2. Actively listen to the other person, trying to hear their emotions and their meanings
3. Seek mutual problem solving with principled negotiation

Decision-making

Decisions can be easy to make but difficult to live with over time. People often forget that decisions are best made using a process which considers not only the final decision but the consequences of the decision. Research has produced and encouraged some useful models which help people remember the nature of the decision-making process.

Tuckman (1965) introduced a very useful four-stage description of the typical process used by small groups when they initially come together or are assigned a task: **forming, storming, norming, and performing.** The model has great usefulness for nonprofit organizations that are continually creating and reforming groups.

- **Forming** – Another word to describe this stage is confusion. Group members frequently have very different ideas as to why the group was put together and what it is to accomplish even when all have received the same written or oral instructions concerning the formation of the group. There are many questions at this stage. What are we doing here? Why are we here? What do they really want? Are we going to have any real power? Can we select our own leader? Why am I here? Why are you here? When do we have to present our report? Who is going to prepare it? There is little attention paid to process or protocol during this stage. Members often test the tolerance of each other and the appointed or emergent leader. At the other extreme there may be a great dependence on the leader and no one will participate until encouraged or forced to do so. This is particularly true when there is a high level of anxiety or suspicion among group members.

- **Storming** – Another word for this stage is uncertainty. While clarity of purpose and task direction improves, people have difficulty working together at this stage because they are positioning for power, influence, and recognition. Power struggles may appear, as well as alliances or factions. Relationship and emotional issues tend to take center stage. A clear focus on the task at hand is very important if the group is to continue to mature and begin to move toward a meaningful outcome. The leader may need to suggest compromise or encourage members to look for win-win solutions to conflict.

- **Norming** – The one word to describe this stage is stability. Work is now directed toward the goal(s) agreed to by the group. Decisions are made within the context of guidelines and processes understood and accepted by the members. Some decisions are made by the group as a whole while others are delegated to teams within the total group. The group may now take time for some fun or social outings to build quality relationships. Respect replaces uncertainty and suspicion. The uncertainties which still remain will usually be focused on the task and not on relationship or emotional issues. These uncertainties are understood as a natural part of group process and viewed as challenges which can be overcome.

- **Performing** – The word for this stage is productivity. The group has now answered most of the questions which arose in the first stage (forming). They now know why they are doing what they are doing. The group shares a vision of the desired outcome and is able to act without supervision in completing its assigned task. When disagreements occur, they are now handled within an understood process and managed according to accepted guidelines. The group finishes its task.

The time spent in each stage is not important. It must follow the natural progression needed by each group. The style of leadership employed by the appointed or emergent leader will largely determine how quickly and how well the group proceeds through the stages to become an effective, performing group. The more quickly a group can move to the performing stage the better, if they have satisfied all the behavioral obstacles inherent in the preceding stages.

One time-honored tool for groups is the **reflective thinking agenda** promoted by the American educational reformer, John Dewey, in the early 1900s. The **five step agenda**, when applied thoughtfully, can ensure higher quality decisions:

1. Clearly describe the problem
2. Analyze what is causing the problem
3. Establish criteria for solving the problem

    4. Brainstorm solutions which match the criteria

    5. Pick the solution or solutions which best fit the criteria

The decision making approach promotes groups working together to understand the situation and develop a shared and supported response. It is a traditional way that nonprofit organizations make decisions, while also promoting quality relationships and effective communications.

Elizabeth Dole, former president of the American Red Cross, demonstrated her understanding of effective decision making when she outlined the steps for making and selling decisions. She observed, "What you always do before you make a decision is consult. The best public policy is made when you are listening to people who are going to be impacted. Then, once policy is determined, you call on them to help you sell it." Her insight about public policy is just as applicable to any decision made by any nonprofit organization, at any level, with respect to any issue.

Team building

The old expression "two heads are better than one" could easily be changed in the 21st Century to the "teamwork." A very good website for resources on teamwork can be found at *www.teambuildinginc.com*. In addition to articles on important variables, there are links to other sources, a bookstore, teambuilding exercises, assessment tools and more. A great deal is known about teamwork. It seems obvious that working together improves productivity, discourages less productive activity, gives everyone an opportunity to get some of the glory, and provides encouragement and protection when someone makes a mistake or is simply discouraged.

It is common for leaders promoting teamwork to remind group members that "There is no 'I' in team." This does not mean there is no room for individual achievement since most of what a team is able to accomplish is magnified if all individuals are striving for what Senge (1990) calls **personal mastery**. As individuals work to be the best they can be, everyone they work with is made better. "Organizations learn only through individuals who learn" (139). Personal mastery is not achieved at the expense of other team members; it is achieved at the expense of personal effort.

Several concepts relate directly to successful team building, team success or teamwork. Excellent resources to support team building can be found at www.teambuildinginc.com, including Zoglio's (1993) identifies and describes seven keys for a successful team effort. They are commitment, contribution, communication, cooperation, conflict management, change management and connections:

    1. **Commitment** – In order for a group to become a team, they must understand what they are doing and why they are doing it. To achieve commitment, people need to work together to develop a mission for the team, a vision, and value statements which fit with the mission and still reflect the individual nature of the group. They need the experience of developing their measures of success and the chance celebrate their accomplishments.

    2. **Contribution** – Everyone must contribute to the team effort, but it is not necessary that they all contribute in the same way or the same amount. All members need strong technical and interpersonal skills and be willing to learn new skills

or improve current skills for the benefit of the team effort. Balanced contributions are more easily obtained when team members think they are included, have confidence, and are empowered. A person can be included by being allowed to talk and being asked to provide input if they seem reluctant. A team member's confidence can be enhanced through encouragement and coaching and by keeping past successes in front of the group. Empowerment comes from appropriate training, sufficient resources, showing respect, and involving members in decisions which affect the team (not informing them after a decision is made).

3. **Communication** – In order for a team to succeed, the most important key is the freedom to communicate openly and honestly. Members must be able to ask for help without feeling inferior, offer ideas that may appear to be off the wall without being laughed at, think out loud without being scolded for not considering the feelings of others, and risk making a mistake without being ridiculed. Trust must be built and maintained above all else. To improve communication, emphasize the importance of listening actively, using language with sensitivity, giving and receiving feedback with consideration for others, showing trust, and efficiently using meeting time. If some team members need training in interpersonal skills, provided it as enhancement not as punishment.

4. **Cooperation** – Very few programs or projects can be successful unless there is a great deal of interconnectedness. From for profit to nonprofit organizations, the information age relies on people sharing information and working together to meet goals and achieving organizational missions. Cooperation is highly valued in the nonprofit sector. An effective leader can stimulate cooperation by demonstrating and rewarding behaviors which facilitate cooperation among staff and volunteers. These behaviors include doing work accurately, doing it on time, keeping in touch with others who need to share information, being creative enough to not fear doing something a new way and promoting healthy, open, trusting relationships.

5. **Conflict Management** – Conflict happens!! It is natural. It is inevitable. It can be good! If conflict is well managed, it can, in fact, stimulate creativity and keep teams and individuals from becoming stale. If conflict is not well managed, future conflicts will be more intense or avoided all together, and neither response is ultimately constructive for individuals or the organization. Leaders can help team members reduce the damaging effects of conflict by teaching members to not avoid conflict and while giving them the skills needed to manage conflict in producing more constructive outcomes.

6. **Change Management** – For profit organizations thrive and survive on the basis of their ability to "stay out front" in their area of business. They must stay ahead of the competition to do well. Nonprofit organizations which best satisfy community and individual needs learn to act, not react. Change happens! The best way to survive change is not to try to avoid it and hold on to the past but to manage it. Leaders can help team members manage change by modeling a positive attitude toward any change and by continually supporting team efforts to change with resources and encouragement. Freedom to make a mistake or fail

in a change effort is critical if leaders want team members to believe that change is truly expected and desired.

7. **Connections** – It is important for any team to take a systems view of its own work and consider how its work is connected to mission of the organization, the work of other teams in the organization, and the issues and concerns of its own team members. The operative word here is *networking*. Two critical connections must be monitored continually: the connection to mission and the connection to feedback from constituents. Leaders can support these connections by helping to keep communication lines open to all levels of the organization and its clients. If people are rewarded and recognized for helping each other, they will tend to continue to help each other.

Alexander Graham Bell put it this way, "Great discoveries and achievements invariably involve the cooperation of many minds." If this is true for "great discoveries," how much more can people accomplish with respect to ordinary challenges and opportunities if they are approached with "many minds." Henry Ford described the value of teamwork and cooperation this way, "Coming together is a beginning, staying together is progress, working together is success."

Coaching/counseling

People frequently know they need to learn new skills to survive in their work but often do not know how to do it or just need a little help. Helping individuals succeed at work helps any organization succeed at its mission. If a person is unwilling or unable to do what is necessary for an organization to fulfill its mission, that person should be *freed* to find another job. If, however, a person is willing and able to improve, an organization should protect its investment and help improve the person's skills.

Skill improvement or enhancement can be achieved through the use of organizational training programs. When a person needs substantial help that can be provided by outside vendors or even through national affiliate organizations and professional associations, the local organization must invest in its people and cover the cost of the training.

When the improvement or enhancement needed can be addressed by local staff, it should be conducted at the local level. This assumes that someone is capable of helping the employee in need. This may be a coaching/counseling task. One of the most powerful coaching and counseling tools is **mentoring**. Mentoring is a process which occurs in the context of a relationship. To be successful, a mentoring relationship is best built from a base of genuine dialogue (Bokeno and Gantt 2000). Genuine dialogue is characterized by open interaction, a problem-solution mind set, an effort to generate new ideas (not just to choose the best from the past) and a joint-venture thought process. Mentoring is characterized by **caring, sharing, correcting,** and **connecting** (Gantt 1997).

Mentoring is *not* a program to be implemented, an initiative to be started, or an assignment to be discharged. Mentoring only works well when people have a trusting relationship where there can share without fear of punishment or sabotage, where refinement or correction can occur without defensiveness, and where genuine attempts are made to provide appropriate access to networks which will lead to advancement, development, or improvement. Other-centered communication is the basic building block of mentoring relationships. This simply means that both people in a mentoring relationship use communication skills and techniques designed to understand others rather than techniques or strategies intended to promote self-interest.

There are a lot of things that a mentor should do to help someone develop. Mentors should collaborate, not tell the other person what to do. Mentors should seek to construct solutions by working together, not by recycling past solutions which seem to fit the situation in question. Mentors should engage in critical reflection by "thinking out loud" and risking mistakes by openly discussing concerns, problems and issues, not by trying to make new problems fit old solutions or using past analysis as a standard for new solutions. Mentors fully and openly participate in dialogue; they do not sit back and wait until they are "needed." Mentors give "voice" to their protégé (Bokeno and Bokeno, 1998).

George Bernard Shaw provides a nice illustration of mentoring in his play "Getting Married." He writes, "I am not a teacher, only a fellow traveler of whom you asked the way. I pointed ahead – ahead of myself, as well as you." Thus mentoring, coaching and counseling, in their best form, become a joint venture between two people growing with help from each other.

If a person does not respond well to mentoring, the best way to proceed is to clearly define what behavior(s) is/are deficient, explain why change needs to occur, stipulate the consequences of a failure to change or improve, detail a plan for the person to demonstrate progress, and specify any appropriate rewards for achieving agreed upon goals. If change does not occur, change personnel!

Sensitivity to Difference

Diversity on all levels of life is a resource upon which to capitalize in order to enrich the relationships, generate creative thinking, and promote new ways of working together. To use an agricultural metaphor, hybrid vigor has unlimited potential when the members of the group are increasingly diverse. Many factors combine to promote this growing diversity, including changing demographics, accelerating communication, globalization, and multi-culturalism, just name a few. To capitalize on the potential of diverse groups, it is important to understand others in all their human conditions. William Schutz's theory of interpersonal needs (1966) identifies **three basic needs** all humans share:

- The need for **inclusion** can be satisfied by joining a civic club, church, fraternity or sorority; deciding to marry; attending a family reunion. What a person **wants** from others is **acceptance**. What a person **expresses** to others is **interest**.
- The need for **control** manifests itself in the choices mades in interactions with others. It is shown in attempts to influence others, positions of authority taken, or choices made which involve others. What a person **wants** from others is **guidance**. What a person **expresses** to others is **leadership**.
- The need for **affection** is defined as caring and respect for others. A person receives care and respect from others when care and respect for another is shown. What is person **wants** from others is **closeness**. What a person **expresses** to others is **liking**.

How each person behaves or shows these needs is influenced by age, gender, nationality, race, ethnicity, religion, etc.

Very often a person's failure to be sensitive to others who are different can be traced to one or more of the following misconceptions about communication in relationships. Any one of these **false assumptions** can limit the formation of a successful relationship with a person who is different because of age, ability, culture, education, ethnicity, experience, race, or sexual orientation. A person is asking for difficulty in any relationship when he or she assumes that (Weis and Gantt 2004):

- **Communication in a relationship is consistent**. Just as people change over time so does the need for different communication skills and different sensitivities with respect to others. The journey from the first meeting to working together occasionally, to working together regularly, to a deep, genuine friendship requires very different skills. Communication can vary significantly!

- **Communication has simple meaning**. Any interaction with another person is never simple, even if it is with someone well known. How much more complicated can interaction become if it is someone only known through work. Psychologists established many years ago that human brains react to sensory stimulation in three domains: the affective or feeling domain, the cognitive or intellectual domain, and the behavioral or action domain. Interactions with another person then are based on predictions that are based on psychological data which comes from how one **feels** about the person, the situation, self, past interactions, or potential for future interactions. Interactions with another person are also based on our intellectual abilities or what the person **thinks** they know, can understand, or can explain. Finally, interactions with another are based on personally established rules for what is right and wrong or appropriate and inappropriate. Communication is complex!

- **Communicators are independent**. Every person is connected to each and every person he or she has ever met, talked with, worked with, dated and so on. No relationship is ever truly ended except by death of one or both of the parties. Every communicator is influenced by others and influences others. Communication is dependent on many factors!

- **Communication behaviors have obvious causation**. Nothing is ever obvious. Some things appear to be obvious. It is human nature to try to explain everything observed. If someone smiles, most people want to know why. If someone yells, most people think they must be angry. Since there are many explanations for the smile or the yell, it is very dangerous to assume the reason for any communication behavior is obvious. There is nothing wrong with speculating and trying to think of causes. The error is not in speculating; it is in being convinced that we *know* the *correct* cause. Communication is complicated!

- **Communication interactions have a final point**. Interactions may have a temporary end or pause but not a final point. With every interaction, there is a residual, something left over, something unfinished, something to build on for the future. If there were a true final point to interactions, everyone would have to start all relationships and interactions from the beginning each time there was a new contact. All interactions are built on previous interactions. Communication is continuous!

Sensitivity to diversity is not just the politically correct thing to do; it is necessary for success in nonprofit organizations that seek to engage and serve the community. The arrogance of one race, one generation, one nation, or one group of people claiming to have the best answers to all the important human questions is not only very narrow and limiting, it can lead to the ineffectiveness or death of any organization. Diversity challenges assumptions, opens minds, and unlocks potential to solve problems. Being sensitive to what others bring to the relationship enriches everyone's life.

Valuing diversity in teams of staff and volunteers comes from knowing and appreciating individuals for what they are bringing to the group. In fact, the only way to have unity is to appreciate diversity. If a diverse group is unified, it is capitalizing on its diversity with everyone adding their distinctive perspective – way of thinking and way of acting – to each and every challenge faced. Being sensitive to differences is essential for success in groups. Going beyond sensitivity and valuing what each person brings to the group capitalizes both on each member as individual assets and on what the group does differently for having them as members.

■ A Final Thought

This deep exploration of communication skills illustrates how important these are in all aspects of nonprofit organization leadership, human resource development, and program and service delivery. Without effective communication, nonprofit organizations would fail to accomplish their missions. It is essential that nonprofit leaders commit to working on quality communications throughout the organization on a continuous basis.

■ Summary

Effective leadership is no accident. All organizations live or die based on their use of three key components: people, resources and service or product. The people component of an organization is the heart of successful leadership. Character is the variable which separates the effective leader from the efficient one.

The Executive Director (ED) must be effective in managing the staff, the board and the volunteers. In each group clear expectations are essential. Meaningful work is required. Regular and appropriate feedback is indispensable. Reward for a job well done is appreciated.

The glue that holds the work of the ED together and makes it successful and effective is communication. The goal of all interactions should be to understand and then to be understood. In order to do that, an organizational leader must develop, refine, and hone skills in attentive listening; fair conflict management; meaningful decision making; cooperative team building; compassionate coaching; counseling and mentoring; and, authentic sensitivity and valuing of differences.

This chapter addressed, in part, the Nonprofit Leadership Alliance Certification Competency Requirements of Communication Skills, Personal Attributes, Board/Committee Development, Human Resources Development and Supervision and General Nonprofit Management.

■ **Reflection and Application**

1. Make a list of the qualities an effective Executive Director needs to lead the staff, board, and volunteers of a nonprofit organization:

   _____

   _____

   _____

   _____

2. What are the seven critical issues to be addressed in staffing nonprofit organizations?

   _____

   _____

3. Describe what nonprofit board members do for the organization and be prepared to discuss how each role and responsibility helps accomplish the mission:

   _____

   _____

   _____

   _____

4. What can an ED do to integrate volunteers into the work of a nonprofit organization?

   _____

   _____

   _____

5. Which is the most important board committee and what is its role?

   _____

   _____

6. Describe the two factors affecting the interaction environment in successful communications?

    _____

    _____

7. In what ways can conflict produce positive rewards for a group?

    _____

    _____

    _____

    _____

8. How do people typically respond to conflict?

    _____

    _____

9. What are the most effective approaches to building teams in nonprofit organizations?

    _____

    _____

    _____

    _____

■ References

Bermann, H. (2010). *Making a Difference: The Management and Governance of Nonprofit Organizations*. (2nd Ed.) CCE Publications.

Black's Law Dictionary (6th Ed.). (1990). St. Paul, MN: West Publishing.

BoardSource (path: *http://www.boardsource.org*)

Bokeno, R. M. (2002). Communicating other/wise: A paradigm for empowered practice. *Reason in Practice: The Journal of Philosophy of Management*, 1(2), 11-23.

Bokeno, R. M. and Bokeno, J. K. (1998). The cultivation of participative change: Managerial development influences on employee communication practice. *Compendium of winning papers from the IABC Reseach Foundation* 1997-1998. 37-67.

Bokeno, R. M. & Gantt, V. W. (2000). Dialogic mentoring: Core relationships for organizational learning. *Management Communication Quarterly*, 14(2), 237-270.

Borisoff, D. and Victor, D. A. (1998). *Conflict Management: A Communication Skills Approach* (2nd Ed.). Boston: Allyn and Bacon

Caputo, J. S., Hazel, H. C., and McMahon, C. (1997). *Interpersonal Communication: Using Reason to Make Relationships Work* (2nd Ed.). Dubuque, IA: Kendall/Hunt Publishing.

Certification competency requirements handbook. Kansas City, MO: American Humanics.

Chait, R. P., Ryan, W. P., and Taylor, B. E. (2005) *Governance as Leadership*. Hoboken, New Jersey: John Wiley & Sons, Inc.

Deetz, S. A. and Stevenson, S. L. (1986). *Managing Interpersonal Communication*. New York: Harper & Row.

DeVito, J. A. (1998). *The Interpersonal Communication Book* (8th Ed.). New York: Longman.

Gantt, V. W. (1997). Beneficial mentoring is for everyone: A reaction paper. Paper presented at the National Communication Association Convention, Chicago.

Hardy, J. M. (1990). *Developing Dynamic Boards: A Proactive Approach to Building Nonprofit Boards of Directors*. Erwin, TN: Essex Press.

Herman, R. D. and Associates. (2005). *The Jossey-Bass Handbook of Nonprofit Leadership and Management*. (2nd Ed.) San Francisco: Jossey-Bass.

Hocker, J. L., and Wilmot, W. W. (1985). *Interpersonal Conflict*. (2nd Ed.) Dubuque, IA: William C. Brown.

Levering, R. and Moskowitz, M. (January 7, 2003). How companies satisfy workers. *Fortune*.

Maravelas, A. (2005). *How to Reduce Workplace Conflict and Stress*. Franklin Lakes, NJ: Career Press.

Maxwell, J. C. (1999). *The 21 Indispensable Qualities of a Leader: Becoming the Person Others will Want to Follow*. Nashville, TN: Thomas Nelson Publishers.

Maxwell, J. C. (2001). *The 17 Indisputable Laws of Teamwork*. Nashville, TN: Thomas Nelson Publishers.

Naisbitt, J. and Aburdene, P. (1985). *Re-Inventing the Corporation*. New York: Warner Books.

National School and Community Corps. (1998). *Dr. Martin Luther King, Jr. Day of Service Packet*. Free Library of Philadelphia.

Pegasus Communications. (1998). *The Ladder of Inference Pocket Guide*. Waltham, MA.

Resources Unlimited. (2010). DiSC Personal Profile System. Inscape Publishing.

Satir, V. M. (1988). *The New Peoplemaking*. Palo Alto, CA: Science and Behavior Books.

Schutz, W. (1966). *The Interpersonal Underworld*. Palo Alto, CA: Science and Behavior Books.

Senge, P. M. (1990). *The Fifth Discipline: The Art and Practice of the Learning Organization*. New York: Doubleday.

Senge, P. M. (1994). *The Fifth Discipline Fieldbook*. New York: Doubleday.

Tuckman, B. W. (1965). Developmental sequence in small groups. *Psychological Bulletin*, 63, 384-399.

Weis, R. M. and Gantt, V. W. (2004). *Knowledge & Skill Development in Nonprofit Organizations*. Peosta, IA: Eddie Bowers Publishing.

Weis, R. M. and Gantt, V. W. (2002). *Leadership & Program Development in Nonprofit Organizations*. Peosta, IA: Eddie Bowers Publishing.

Wood, J. T. (1995). *Relational Communication: Continuity and Change in Personal Relationships*. Belmont, CA: Wadsworth Publishing.

Wood, J. T. (Ed.). (1996). *Gendered Relationships*. Mountain View, CA: Mayfield Publishing.

Worth, M. J. (2009). *Nonprofit Management: Principles and Practices*. Thousand Oaks, CA: Sage Publications, Inc.

Zoglio, S. W. (1993). 7 keys to building great workteams. (path: *www.teambuildinginc.com*, select: "Articles"; scroll down and select: "7 Keys to Building Great Workteams.")

4 Human Development, Competencies, Issues and Trends

Individuals go through an incredible range of developmental changes and situations throughout their lifetime, and it is critical that nonprofit leaders/managers understand the nature of human development and various other issues in planning programs that enhance people's lives.

Understanding human development provides leaders with a foundation of knowledge about what most individuals are facing in terms of developmental stages and how best to address these stages with supportive programs. Knowing for instance, that adolescents between the ages of twelve and seventeen are searching for a positive identity is important in structuring programs that would help them find a sense of self-worth, self- knowledge and some direction. Similarly, being aware of important issues and trends allows nonprofit leaders to structure programs that address specific individual, family, and community situations.

The first section of Chapter 4, Human Development, provides the reader with insight into the ways in which people develop including specific areas of competency development. The next section, Issues and Trends, presents information on important issues and trends that are developing. All three sections are intended to provide guidance for setting priorities in program planning.

■ Human Development

The highest goal of any youth, human service, or nonprofit leader is to develop programs that enhance people's lives and to provide supportive relationships for members/clients. With that in mind, it is essential to understand the nature of human development as individuals progress through various life stages.

The changes that occur between birth and death contribute to an amazing odyssey, and the saying "change is the only constant" is particularly true as individuals pass from one of life's many stages to another. Young children, for instance, often view their parents' commands as pronouncements to be accepted as what is right, but within a few years they begin to believe their parents are not always right. Then, in adolescence, a child may begin to think his or her parents are rarely correct; this often changes yet again into an appreciation of the parents' viewpoints in late adolescence or early adulthood. Mark Twain once wrote, "When I was a boy of 14, my father was so ignorant I could hardly stand to have the old man around. But when I got to be 21, I was astonished at how much *he* had learned in 7 years" (Rees 1994, 337). Physical changes, health, attitudes, beliefs, values, and behavior are continually evolving from one experience to another and from one time of our life to another (Weis and Gantt 2004).

Most experts believe developmental changes occur as a result of the interaction of genetic and environmental influences. The term **maturation** is most often used to describe the unfolding of the genetic plan, such as the appearance of baby teeth, facial hair in boys, and the oncoming of menstruation in adolescent girls. The maturation process is determined by internal signals. The concept of **learning**, however, involves changes that occur as a result of interaction with the environment. **Development,** then, is the interaction of genetic and environmental influences. With this in mind, it is easy to understand the responsibility and opportunities nonprofit leaders have in shaping human development.

Development does not happen in isolation, but occurs in the **context** of various circumstances and situations. The most important context is the **family**, which has tremendous influence on individual development. Other important contexts for healthy development include **school** and **community experiences**. To a degree, individuals are products of their school systems and neighborhoods. The **media** is another significant influence on human development. People are greatly influenced by what they watch on TV or experience at the movie theaters. Since most people's days are centered on their jobs, **career paths** are another important context for individual growth. **Culture** also has a great deal to do with who we are and who we become. A child growing up in China will have different experiences and values than a child who grows up in the United States of America. Children in rural settings often have different challenges and activities than those growing up in places like New York City. In complex societies, groups exist that differ from the majority in areas such as beliefs, attitudes, behaviors, values and traditions. These **subcultures** also have a legitimate and profound effect on individual development.

Considering the contextual nature of human development, nonprofit leaders have a tremendous opportunity to enhance areas of family structure and support, individual growth, and community development.

■ Developmental Theories

Theories explaining human development are important because they help us to explain various processes and stages of human nature, and they assist us in predicting what might come next. They also help us develop the kinds of programs necessary to address individual needs in various life stages and situations. Good theories can enhance understanding, they can help us make accurate predictions, and they are testable. There are a number of developmental theories worthy of consideration (Kaplan 1998).

Freud's Psychoanalytic Theory

Sigmund Freud postulated that there were three levels of awareness: the **conscious**, which consists of immediate awareness; the **preconscious**, which consists of memories that can readily become conscious; and the **unconscious,** which is beyond normal awareness and which sometimes manifests itself in dreams and inadvertent actions or words. Freud argued that behavior and actions could sometimes be caused by memories that had been stored and forgotten in the unconscious.

Freud used three constructs to explain the workings of the mind: the **id**, the **ego**, and the **superego**. The id is the construct that controls wishes and desires. It wants what it wants when it wants it and expects instant gratification. The ego interacts with reality and satisfies the needs of the id in a socially acceptable manner. The ego grows in importance as a child develops. The superego is similar to the conscious. It contains principles and compares behavior with the **ego ideal**, which is what individuals think they should be. The ego ideal tries to maintain a balance between the desires of the id, the constrictions of the ego, and the restraints of the superego (Kaplan 1998).

Anxiety can develop between the desires of the id and the restrictions of the ego that may lead to the ego creating **defense mechanisms** to protect itself. These mechanisms take the form of behavior designed to relieve stress and create emotional peace.

Early experiences, particularly those between parents and children, were considered to be very important by Freud, who thought bad experiences in childhood left irreversible impressions on children. More contemporary experts believe that subsequent positive experiences can ease the trauma of earlier negative experiences.

Although some of Freud's other theories, such as the **Psychosexual Theory,** are not as respected by modern theorists, his overall impact is unmistakable, and his theories are still used by developmental psychologists in understanding human nature.

Erikson's Psychosocial Theory

A proponent of many of Freud's theories, Erik Erikson has had a strong influence on the study of human development. Erikson developed a theory that holds that individuals pass through eight different stages of life. At each stage, each individual encounters the possibility of a crisis. If the crisis at each stage is handled relatively well, a positive outcome occurs, and the person develops into a healthy individual. Few people advance through Erikson's eight stages with an entirely positive outcome, but a mostly positive outcome is critical for healthy development. Passing through one stage successfully makes the next stage easier, and so on (Weis and Gantt 2004).

- **Trust versus Mistrust.** When caregivers and others support infants by expressing love and protection, a child emerges from infancy with a sense of trust for people and for their surroundings. Children may become distrustful if caregivers are perceived as angry and stressed. Infants who develop a sense of trust will feel more comfortable in their environment and will be more likely to develop positive attitudes toward all of life.

- **Autonomy versus Doubt.** Young children between the ages of two and three begin exploring their world by practicing new physical skills. When this exploration process is encouraged and supported by caregivers, the toddlers develop a sense of autonomy. If, on the other hand, this exploration process is discouraged, a child may begin to question his or her abilities. It is important that caregivers reward and encourage youngsters to explore and practice new skills.

- **Initiative versus Guilt.** When children around the age of four are encouraged to develop plans and to carry out these plans, they begin to develop a sense of initiative and often become self-starters. When plans are not encouraged and actions are often discouraged, a child may feel a sense of guilt and develop a lack of assertiveness.

- **Industry versus Inferiority.** Children between the ages of six and eleven who are rewarded for developing skills in such areas as reading, math, and socialization begin to develop a sense of industry and feel that their efforts are worthwhile. Children who feel that their efforts are not appreciated or who are compared unfavorably with other children could very well develop a sense of inferiority.

- **Identity versus Role Confusion.** Adolescents involved in healthy experiences who receive encouraging feedback for their actions usually begin to understand who they are and develop a positive self-image. Self-knowledge and a positive self-image provide adolescents with a sense of security and confidence. Adolescents who have less self-knowledge may begin to feel confused regarding their identity and could engage in negative behavior just to be noticed.
- **Intimacy versus Isolation.** Young adults who have entered into positive activities and who have developed a strong identity are often ready to share themselves in relationships that require commitment and sacrifice, such as a healthy marriage and close friendships. Individuals who are unable to form close relationships may become isolated and lonely, even despairing.
- **Generativity versus Self-Absorption.** Middle-aged adults who invest in the future through children, grand-children and/or community involvement generally experience a sense of fulfillment and gratification. Adults who concentrate on the acquisition of material possessions and physical well-being may fail to develop a similar sense of gratification.
- **Ego Integrity versus Despair.** Older adults who look back on their lives with a sense of accomplishment and gratification develop a sense that their lives have had meaning. Individuals who realize they have missed too many opportunities and made a number of significant mistakes may experience depression and despair.

According to Erikson, the resolution of each stage depends on the interaction between individuals and their culture, their relationships, and the historical context in which they lived. The development of identity, for instance, could be very different for someone growing up in Hollywood compared to a child's development in Afghanistan. In a similar sense, the development of industry for someone growing up in the industrial age would vary significantly from someone growing up in the twenty-first century. Erikson's theories have been difficult to test, but they are easy to understand, and they provide an excellent foundation of concerns at each stage of life.

Piaget's Theory of Cognitive Development

Jean Piaget spent his entire adult life studying the cognitive growth processes of children and determined that development occurs as people assimilate and organize their lives in relation to their environment. Development, according to Piaget, is defined by four principal factors: **maturation, experience, social transmission,** and the **process of equilibration.** Maturation involves the gradual unfolding of each person's genetic plan for life. Experience includes the interaction of the child with his or her environment. The traditions, customs, and information that parents and others pass on to the child make up social transmission or education. And the process of equilibrium occurs when children try to balance what they have learned with what they have experienced. When a disequilibrium occurs between what one has learned and what one has experienced, one develops abilities to deal with situations differently and in a mature and sophisticated manner.

Piaget created the term **functional invariants** to refer to the processes that individuals use to adjust to situations throughout their lives (Bjorklund 1995). He defined the two most important processes as **organization** and **adaption.** Organization refers to structuring knowledge in a way that makes knowledge helpful, and adaption means being able to use knowledge to adapt to the environment and to survive. Essentially, as the environment changes, individuals must change to meet environmental demands.

For Piaget, maturation was the result of experience, and he believed experiential educational processes were more important than formal education. Piaget's theories have been criticized because they were not proven in a controlled environment, but his theories include the most complete description of cognitive development from infancy to adulthood and have been very influential on developmental psychology.

The Behavior Theory

Behaviorists believe that behavior is determined in part by environmental influences and that when the environment changes, behavioral change will follow. For instance, when a neutral experience, such as seeing someone in a white lab coat, is paired with pain, such as getting a shot with a needle, then the neutral experience may become associated with the negative feeling. Repeatedly pairing the neutral experience with the negative experience until a similar response is elicited from both is referred to as **classical conditioning**. The sight of the needle prior to the conditioning process may have caused concern and is therefore referred to as an **unconditional stimulus**, and a response to the needle, such as grimacing, prior to the conditioning is referred to as an **unconditional response**. A **conditional stimulus**, then, is the pairing of the neutral stimulus with the negative stimulus, and the **conditional response** would be the individual's concern about the person in the white lab coat.

This kind of conditional process may help us to understand some emotional responses. For instance, if a newly married stepfather begins to berate and criticize his new stepson, the stepson may begin to associate stress and anger with the sight of the stepfather, whom he may have previously trusted and been happy to be around. **Operant conditioning**, in which a behavior is either reinforced or punished following its occurrence, is also important in understanding human development. With operant conditioning, if a behavior is reinforced with a positive response, it will continue and possibly increase in occurrence; if the behavior is followed by a negative response, it will decrease in occurrence.

The behavioral view has been criticized by some theorists who believe it is too mechanical and fails to include conscious thought and subjective experiences in the overall scheme of things, but it can be helpful in understanding some behavior and successful in modifying behavior in a number of situations.

Social Learning Theory

Social theorist A. Bandura postulated that individuals learn by watching and imitating others and learn from examining the consequences of what they are observing. For example, a person who watches someone else pick up a hot pan and then flinch in pain does not need to replicate the event to understand that the pan is dangerous. Bandura organized his theory into a four-step process. First, an individual must concentrate on the model. Then the model must be retained in memory. Next, the stored information must be used in an attempt to replicate the action in the model. For instance, a person watching a baseball player at bat may try to duplicate a certain swing. Finally, motivation in the form of reinforcement must occur in order for the person to learn the behavior and use the behavior again and again in the future.

According to social theorists, behavior is divided into two processes: learning and performing. Learning can occur through observation and other activities, but performance depends partly on what Bandura calls **self-efficacy**, or the belief one has about his or her ability to do something in a particular situation (Schunk 1996). When individuals believe a task is within their capabilities, they will attempt to do it; when they doubt their abilities with various tasks, they are more likely to avoid those activities. The Social Theory is helpful in understanding behaviors that are learned and imitated from others.

Ecological Theory

Urie Bronfenbrenner formulated the Ecological Theory in order to expand the viewpoint that human development is contextual in nature, involving families, communities, culture and even historical periods. According to Bronfenbrenner, individuals are influenced by four different environmental systems: the **microsystem**, the **mesosystem**, the **exosystem**, and the **macrosystem**. The microsystem includes an individual's immediate experiences, such as a child's experiences at home with the family. As the child develops, additional settings emerge and the mesosystem involves the child in two or more settings such as a day-care center or school. This entry of a child into a new setting invariably has an effect on other major settings. For instance, a child's attendance at day care will have some effect on family activities at home.

The exosystem describes settings the child is not actively involved in, but that have an effect on the child and/or the family, such as the actions of the local school superintendent or a sibling's involvement with the local theater group. Although the child is not directly involved with these activities, the activities may have a direct effect the child. For example, the sibling's involvement in theater may affect the opportunities the child has to play and interact with his or her sibling. It may also affect the amount of time the parents have to spend with the child, since they may have to spend time transporting the sibling to and from theater practice and participating in related activities.

Finally, the macrosystem includes the ideology or belief system inherent in the social institutions as well as the ethnic, cultural, religious, political, and economic processes of the country in which the child resides. These differing ideologies can have a profound influence on the development of a child. For instance, the increased percentage of single parent families, the changes in the welfare system, and the increased numbers of disappearing dads, separately and/or together, could have a significant effect on a child's life.

An advantage of this theory is that it provides us with the idea that individuals are always moving between one system and another, and then back again. This information allows us the opportunity to assist in the transactions from system to system. The interaction an individual has with each of these systems has a profound effect on each person's life.

∎ Developmental Competencies

Edginton and Edginton (1994) subscribe to five basic areas of importance for the development of youth (as adapted from Pittman 1991), and they include:

- **Health/physical competence.** Youth need to have good health and to maintain knowledge, attitudes and behaviors to ensure good health for the future. This includes exercising, maintaining a healthy diet, and being aware of nutritional requirements.
- **Personal/social competence.** It is important that youth develop several good *intrapersonal skills*. They need the ability to understand and deal with personal emotions and to maintain-self discipline; they need to develop effective *interpersonal skills*, including the ability to work with others, to develop friendships and to understand and empathize with others; they need *coping skills* and the ability to adapt and assume responsibility; and they need *judgement skills*, for making good decisions and solving problems.
- **Cognitive/creative competence.** Youth need to have a broad base of knowledge and the ability to appreciate and participate in creative expression, good oral and written *language skills*, problem solving and *analytical skills* and an interest in learning and achieving.
- **Vocational competence.** It is important that youth develop an understanding and awareness of vocational and avocational opportunities. It is also important for youth to grasp the function and value of work and leisure time and for them to learn how to prepare for both.
- **Citizenship competencies (ethics and preparation).** Youth need to understand their nation's history and values and develop a sense of personal responsibility for community and national enhancement.

As young people move toward these competencies they develop a sense of self- confidence and self-efficacy and feel good about being themselves. Although Pittman focused on youth and competencies, it is easy to see that individuals develop competencies throughout their lives. Leaders of nonprofit organizations need to understand and incorporate these developmental competencies and other developmental theories into goal setting, program planning, and other relevant aspects of organizational operations when appropriate (Weis and Gantt 2004).

Understanding situations that people might face throughout their lives is equally important and will be discussed in the next section.

∎ Issues and Trends

Over the centuries, life has become more complicated with each passing year. Individuals, families, and communities are facing unparalleled challenges and opportunities in areas of health and fitness, education, family structure and patterns, cultural diversity, communication, social interaction, and technology, to mention several. The leaders of nonprofit organizations must be well-versed in the issues and trends their members and clients are facing and be capable of shifting strategies and resources to address issues and trends as they become relevant to the organization's mission.

Households, Families, Children, and Youth

Households can be distinguished from **families** in that a household is considered to be a residential and economic unit, whereas families imply a construct of meanings and relationships (Osmond and Thorne 1993; Rapp 1982). The U.S. Census Bureau defines households as taking one of three basic forms: **family**, **non-family**, and **single-person** household. Family households are considered to be two or more persons living together who are related through marriage, birth, or adoption. The most common type of family household is a married couple with or without children. Non-family households consist of two or more unrelated individuals who are residing in the same living area. Single-person households are made up of those individuals who live alone in a residential unit (Weis and Gantt 2004).

U.S. households continue to change in important areas. For instance, the number of households is still growing, but at a much slower rate, and there were approximately 115 million households in the year 2005. Another important change is the average size of a household which has gotten smaller and smaller over the last fifty years and now represents an approximate average of 2.6 individuals per household. Two trends that may work to counteract this are the growing number of adult children who are living with their parents, and the growing number of elderly mothers and fathers who reside with their children. There are more single-parent families, childless married couples, and people living alone than ever before, and no household arrangement can be classified as typical. A noteworthy trend is the percentage of households headed by married couples, which has declined significantly over the decades.

As with households, families have also changed in some important ways. For instance, there is a greater variety of family circumstances than ever before. **Traditional families**, in which there is a working father, children under the age of eighteen, and a mother who is not in the work force, have diminished in number. Social forces, such as high divorce rates, an increased number of women in the work force, and declining fertility rates, have added to the growing variety of family situations.

Some of these social forces have also added to the numbers of **single-parent families**, at least ninety percent of which exist with a woman as the head of the household. In spite of the fact that teenage pregnancies have declined in recent years, teen parents lead a significant percentage of single-parent families. Although a number of children from single-parent families become successful adults, children from single-parent families have comparatively poorer academic achievement and are more likely to drop out of school. They are more likely to be poor, to marry early and more likely to divorce. They are also more likely to become involved in criminal activity, including the use of illegal drugs. Since there is a strong correlation between single parenting and living in poverty, it is difficult to separate the effects of these two factors. In many single-parent families, the father is absent, and there is minimal interaction or financial support, if any. In families with **absentee dads**, the children are at much greater risk of dropping out of school, getting in trouble in school and having poor grades.

When a parent cannot or will not take responsibility for a child, a **skip-generation** family often develops in which a grandparent becomes the primary caregiver. This can become emotionally and financially difficult for grandparents, who may have to raise two generations of children but be unable to receive public assistance because they often do not have legal custody of their grandchildren. A large number of skip-generation families have the mother living there as well, but not as the head of the household. Family court judges and social workers often link drug and alcohol abuse to the skip-generation phenomenon.

Children staying at home longer and aging parents living longer due to advanced health technologies indicate there will be more **multi-generational** families in which the parent or parents are wedged between at least one child at home and their own frail and elderly parents. This is also sometimes referred to as the **sandwich generation** and has become more intense since families are smaller and the burden of care giving falls on fewer siblings. Fortunately, more and more corporations are providing elder care assistance to their employees (Hewitt Associates 2004).

Approximately half of all marriages end in **divorce** and that percentage has plateaued and even declined in recent years. The median duration of marriage before a divorce is about seven years, and over half of all divorces involve children who will experience a permanent disruption. Many divorces involve tremendous emotional, psychological, and financial upheaval for everyone involved. A large number of divorced fathers will let this upheaval become a reason for them to become completely absent from the lives of their children. Fortunately, divorce is expected to continue to decline since it is viewed with less favor as its disruptive and damaging impacts, especially on children, are increasingly recognized. There is also an increased disenchantment with the single lifestyle and a continuing fear of sexually transmitted diseases. One-fifth of all married couples with children make up **stepfamilies**, in which at least one child under the age of eighteen is involved. Stepfamilies often have their own special dynamics and provide unique challenges for parenting and developing relationships. Most stepchildren live with their biological mothers and stepfathers.

Another demographic with significant implications is the growing number of senior citizens over the age of eighty-five, which has increased at a rate three times that of the general population. These citizens seek to live independently, but the frailty that comes with old age catches up with them, and **elder care**, in which seniors require assistance to remain somewhat independent, is a growing consideration. Many of these citizens are cared for at home, but the main caregiver often works a full-time job and care giving can be difficult for the caregiver as well as for the recipient. Although nursing home care is a consideration, only a small percentage of seniors ever live in a nursing home. Adult home-care programs, foster-care, day-care programs, Meals on Wheels, and telephone reassurance are just some of the programs that provide seniors with the support necessary to remain in their homes.

Most experts agree that the care-giving and educational preparation for children from birth to age eighteen in this country is too often inadequate. Youth face other challenges as well, such as alienation, loneliness, social depravity, and a lack of connectedness. Low-income families, in particular, face hardships that include inadequate health care, crime and drugs, lack of successful role models, financial hardships, and a sense of hopelessness. An incredible twenty percent of all children in the United States live in **poverty**, which is often due to parental job loss and to the increase of children living in ingle-parent families. These families, usually with a female at the head, have a poverty rate of approximately five times the poverty rate of married-couple families.

In order to escape poverty and low income, most mothers work out of economic necessity, and the lack of affordable and effective **day care** for children under the age of six has become a serious problem. Many studies, including a study involving Head Start enrollees and a control group, concluded that the children involved with Head Start were more likely to become high school graduates, enroll in college or be employed. And they were less likely to become involved in crime or be on welfare by the age of nineteen (Eitzen, Zinn and Eitzen 2009).

Each year, tens of thousands of infants die before they reach the age of one. The infant morality rate for the United States is one of the highest among the industrialized nations, and the main reason for this is **low birth rate**, often a result of inadequate prenatal care. A significant portion of these children will end up with permanent disabilities. Many other children will have chronic and disabling conditions as a result of being born **HIV positive** or as a result of **cocaine exposure**. Spiraling health care costs make it difficult for many families to receive proper care, let alone incorporate preventive measures. Another health concern is the immunization process for preventable diseases. Although the vast majority of children are immunized against measles, mumps, and rubella, there are still a significant number of children who are not, particularly in inner cities. For instance, there are still tens of thousands of measles cases reported each year, which in severe cases can result in death. In spite of numerous diseases and other conditions, the number one cause of death among children is **accidents**, which can also result in permanent disabilities.

Another serious health concern for children is the lack of **proper nutrition**, which often leads to iron-deficiency anemia and is closely associated with poverty. Proper nutrition for low-income pregnant women, new mothers and infants is critical. This is often provided by **WIC**, which was created to do just that, but WIC is seriously under-funded and cannot meet the needs of all of those who meet the criteria. Incredible as it may seem, **hunger** is another serious problem for children: between five and six million children will go hungry nearly every day, and that number increased throughout the 2000s. The rate of hunger is closely related to childhood poverty.

Another area of risk for children is the area of **education**, in which American students often lag behind students in developed and developing countries, particularly in math and science. A significant percentage of students fail to graduate from high school, or they graduate without the knowledge and skills necessary for acquiring and keeping a job. There is a strong correlation between dropping out of school and crime and poverty. Factors sometimes associated with **dropouts** include being poor, belonging to an ethnic or racial minority, having limited English proficiency, and being a child from a single- parent family. Though often interrelated, any one of these factors can cause problems in school. Each year, about one million teen girls become **pregnant**, and a significant number of these will conceive again in one to two years. These young mothers are overwhelmed with responsibilities and are unlikely to finish high school and more likely to face a life of economic hardship and dependency. Statistically, the children of teen mothers are less likely to finish high school and more likely to achieve lower levels of education, become involved with crime and drugs, and to become teen parents as well.

Nearly one million children are considered **discarded**, which means they live in foster homes, detention centers, hospitals, and mental health centers. These living arrangements are necessary for a number of reasons, including family breakup, homelessness, child abuse, and alcohol and drug abuse. Teenagers are going through a rapidly changing period of life and require strong support. **Suicide** is the second leading cause of death among adolescents. Additionally, there are over a million **runaways** living on the streets or in less than desirable shelters, and tens of thousands of youth are classified as **lost, injured**, or **missing**. And in a country that prides itself on its diversity, about half of all teenagers have witnessed racist acts, and a significant portion of teens have been the victims of bias.

Although most families are healthy, functional units, researchers sometimes consider families to be the most violent social group, next to the police and the military, and **child abuse** is too often the result of this violence. Child abuse is an act carried out with the intent of injury or acts of omission that place children in danger. The incidents of child reported abuse increased in the 1980s, 1990s and 2000s. **Neglect** is another type of abuse directed toward children. Neglect includes inadequate feeding of children, poor sanitary conditions, and leaving children in a potentially dangerous setting.

Health and Education

Americans are living longer than anytime in history with **life expectancies** ranging from early sixties to high seventies, depending on race and gender. On the average, men die younger than women do, and African Americans die younger than whites, primarily due to cancer, heart attack, and strokes. **Heart disease** still causes more deaths than any other disease, with **cancer** second. One of the reasons that life expectancy rates are so high is that **infant mortality** rates have been reduced so significantly from the beginning of the century. Poor and rural communities maintain higher infant mortality than urban settings, and life expectancy is lower for racial and ethnic minorities, many of whom live in poor communities with inadequate medical care.

Acquired Immune Deficiency Syndrome (AIDS) is caused by the **HIV** virus which damages the body's immune system and leaves the body more susceptible to infections and cancer. AIDS is spread through sexual contact, needles or syringes shared by drug abusers, infected blood or blood products; it is also passed from pregnant women to their offspring. People who are at high risk for contracting AIDS include those who practice unprotected sex with infected partners and drug abusers who share needles. AIDS has also spread among groups not previously thought of as high risk, such as crack smokers, women, and teenagers. AIDS has also increased in rural communities, where residents are often ill-equipped to handle the disease medically or socially. African Americans and Hispanics are disproportionately affected by AIDS, and the estimates of those infected ranges from the hundreds of thousands to several million. **Sexually Transmitted Diseases (STDs)** such as syphilis, gonorrhea, and pelvic inflammatory disease (PID) remain serious health threats and can cause a great deal of suffering and even death.

Another disease, **tuberculosis**, was once the leading cause of death in the United States, but it has been in decline for decades. Unfortunately, it is making a comeback in major cities, and drug addicts, the homeless, and people with AIDs are especially susceptible to it. Airborne bacteria spread tuberculosis, which has led some cities to forcibly hospitalize patients and test schoolchildren. In the future, viral conditions that are not curable with conventional therapies are predicted to be on the rise as are bacterial infections that become resistant to commonly used antibiotics.

It has been suggested that as many as one in four American workers suffer from **stress-related** illnesses or **anxiety disorders**, and **depression** is thought to affect a similar number of individuals. Increasing competition, advanced technology, work-family issues, and job uncertainties are just a few of the variables contributing to these conditions. Electronic monitors that count the number of keystrokes made by some computer operators and electronic surveillance of telephone conversations are also causing increasing stress in the workplace. Medical experts generally agree that workers who are under electronic surveillance suffer higher levels of stress-related medical problems such as fatigue, ulcers, depression, and even heart disease.

Millions of Americans are addicted to **drugs** and millions more suffer from **alcoholism** or **alcohol dependence**. An estimated five to ten percent of the population have experimented with marijuana, the most popular illegal drug (Caplow, et al. 2001; Drug Enforcement Administration, 2007), and millions of Americans use or experiment with cocaine, heroine, hallucinogens and inhalants. Illegal drug use seems to have peaked in the 70s and 80s and has leveled off since. Factors contributing to drug abuse and addiction include boredom, social and work pressures, and medical needs. In moderation, alcohol is considered to be relatively safe, but when abused it is the leading cause of accidents and accounts for about half of all traffic related deaths. Criminals, prior to committing a criminal act, often use alcohol and drugs. There is a strong correlation between abusing alcohol and the overall suicide rate, and it is a big factor in drowning. Consumed in large quantities over long periods of time, alcohol almost always results in serious health consequences.

Although **tobacco** smoking has been on the decline for years, millions of Americans still use tobacco and there has been a disturbing, steady usage by women, young people, teens, pre-teens and minorities. Additionally, there has been a movement on the part of tobacco companies to market tobacco overseas, which increases health and financial problems in other countries that result in global consequences for all of us. **Second-hand smoke** also causes significant health problems and deaths from cancer and heart disease for thousands of individuals each year. Premature deaths as a result of smoking are possibly the most preventable kind in the United States, and the cessation of tobacco use results in almost immediate health benefits for individuals of all ages.

Alternative health care methods, such as holistic medicine and self-help groups, have grown in popularity in the United States. Some of these techniques include biofeedback, acupuncture, chiropractic medicine, meditation, yoga, massage, hypnosis, and homeopathic medicine. Many experts define health in terms of mind and body balance or harmony.

Health care is one of the most complicated, highly political and emotionally charged issues our nation is facing. Health care costs represent a significant percentage of the gross national product (GNP) and are rising steadily. While most people look to job-related insurance to cover the majority of their health costs, insurance costs reflect the increased rise in health care costs, and a significant portion of the population simply do not have insurance coverage. And while health care costs are spiraling upward, the availability of services (**health care delivery**) has declined, particularly in rural and poor sections of the country. Although the Health Care Reform bill of 2010 was intended to change both of these aspects of health care along with a number of others. The need for long-term care is increasing as American become older on the average. **Medicare** is the governmental health care program that assists senior citizens with these costs and others and **Medicaid** was implemented to address the health care needs of the poor. The level of support from Medicare and Medicaid varies depending on circumstances and current policy. Free clinics for the working poor, volunteer nursing visitations, and programs to help individuals save on medical costs are just a few of the ways nonprofit organizations are addressing needs that are not now or in the foreseeable future addressed through health insurance, Medicare, or Medicaid.

Education will remain one of the highest priorities on the national agenda, and the correlation between excellence in education and quality of life has been proven again and again. For decades, **educational reforms** have been taking place in school systems around the nation. The most recent wave of reforms includes the concept of **school-based management**, in which there is a transfer of decision-making power from a centralized authority to instructors, parents, and administrators of the schools. These decisions range from developing the curriculum to deciding how a school will spend its money. With reform in mind, many school systems are also incorporating **service learning** into the curriculum. Service learning combines community service with specific learning objectives and has proven to be an invaluable pedagogy for teaching values and character and for bridging the gap between theory and practice. Other school districts have adopted an option of a **choice** for parents as to which school their children will attend. This concept is designed to develop competition among schools and to stimulate curricula and facilities improvement. Still other educational systems have adopted **year-round school** programs in an effort to expand educational opportunities and provide additional support systems for students and parents the entire year. Having met with some opposition initially, this program continues to gain favor because of its flexibility and continuity of academics and extra-curricular activities.

A number of studies indicate that high quality early-childhood education programs make a significant difference for at-risk youth, and more and more experts are stressing the importance of early-childhood education. **Preschool** has been integrated into many educational systems, and the majority of all three- and four-year-olds take part in some form of early childhood education. The federal preschool program **Head Start** has helped millions of children since its creation in 1965 and is regarded as one of the government's most successful programs. Enrollment in both elementary and secondary schools has steadily increased, and more opportunities will develop for after school activities. **Home schooling** continues to be on the rise as some parents contend that public schools have poor academic standards, poor discipline and crowded conditions. Post secondary enrollment has been up and down so far in this decade, particularly among eighteen-to twenty-four-year-olds, and the average age of college students continues to rise.

The American way of life is still highly valued by many worldwide. Consequently, immigration has led to a **mosaic classroom** in which a significant number of students have limited English proficiency. This generally makes instruction much more challenging, and the combination of language and cultural differences sometimes leads to clashes in the school system. Even when **bilingual-education** programs are introduced, it takes about seven years for a non-native to reach national norms on standardized tests. **English-as-a-Second-Language (ESL)** has also been expanded, and many non-English speaking students have been mainstreamed into regular classrooms with ESL-trained instructors. A major concern remains regarding the educational underachievement among minority racial and ethnic groups. The situation is critical, since approximately one in three elementary and secondary school children are minorities. Clearly, there are numerous opportunities for nonprofit organizations to step in and assist in developing foundations for academic achievement.

About one in four students **drop out** each year, and that number is often higher in urban centers and a number of studies identify a correlation with difficulties in school and family problems (Walsh 2006). Dropout rates are costly for individuals and for society. Jobs require higher skill levels than ever before, unemployment rates are twice as high for high school dropouts as for graduates, and dropouts are more likely to become involved in crime and drugs. Dropouts are also more likely to come from a single-parent family, live in a household that is considered at the poverty level, and be at home alone more than three hours a day. Having limited skills in English and/or coming from a home where the parents are dropouts adds to the potential of dropping out. The nation's number of **illiterates** is in the millions and illiteracy is increasing at an alarming rate. Millions of Americans are classified as **functionally illiterate**, which means they are able to read at a fourth grade level; there are even more people referred to as **marginally illiterate**, who read at the eighth grade level. This is frustrating and demeaning for individuals; it costs them billions of dollars in unrealized earnings and costs the country billions of dollars in welfare and unemployment compensation each year. There are a disproportionate number of African American and Hispanic children living in poverty who also have trouble reading.

The ratio of computers to students in the classroom has moved ahead at a rapid pace and **technology** has made **distance learning**--video courses with a two-way hook-up between teachers and students--an established pedagogical method. **Global classrooms** in which students search the Internet for information and interact with individuals online could help develop technical expertise, cultural understanding, and knowledge.

Population and Aging

The American population has nearly quadrupled in the past century, and the number of people in the country has exceeded 270 million (Weis and Gantt 2004). The combination of falling death rates due to **medical advances,** massive **immigration**, and **increased birth rates** has led to significant population growth, although population has declined somewhat in percentage of growth over the last several decades. The 1990 Immigration Act led to significant increases in immigration, and medical advances have made it easier for women to become pregnant and for individuals to have longer, healthier life spans on the average. Approximately 600,000 individuals immigrate to the United States each year and an estimated 200,000 to 1,000,000 people enter the country illegally on an annual basis (Caplow, et al. 2001). As a matter of fact, it has been reported 485,000 undocumented Mexican immigrants crossed into the U.S. in 2004 (Bailey 2006). This influx of immigrants creates a number of cultural, educational, vocational, and financial challenges as new citizens prepare for a life sometimes far different from that in their native land.

Fertility rates have increased due to a number of factors, including the increased number of women bearing children in their middle to late thirties, the increased number of female immigrants who have higher fertility rates than native-born Americans, and an increased number of unplanned and too often unwanted births. Minority birth rates exceed that of the population in general.

About a third of the overall population was born between the years 1946 and 1964. These individuals are usually referred to as **baby boomers**, since many were conceived following the end of World War II, when people were putting their lives and families back together. Over the past century, the proportion of children and adolescents in the population has decreased as the proportion of older Americans has increased. As people live longer on the average and the proportion of births decreases, the average age of Americans will increase. The percentage of people seventy-five years old and older has increased and the proportion of **centenarians** increased more than any other age group in the last two decades of the past century. This trend will create tremendous challenges and opportunities for the social security system, health care, families, and certainly for nonprofit organizations.

Social Security is a major source of income for most seniors, and in many cases it is the only source of senior citizens' income. But Social Security is coming under increased pressure by the growing number of applicants, and people in certain occupations, such as agriculture, are often exempt from the Social Security program. Additionally, women who have worked as homemakers receive no credit for their work, and a woman who is widowed will not receive benefits until she is sixty, unless she has a child under sixteen or a disabled child, or unless she herself is disabled.

Although the majority of older people are in good health, the elderly are more affected by poor health than any other group. Both physical and mental conditions affect older people, and **Alzheimer's disease** is the leading cause of dementia in old age afflicting millions of senior citizens. Older people usually have more contact with physicians than other age group. Their prescription drug cost represents the largest out-of-pocket health-care expense for the majority of the elderly and their medical expenses are three times greater than those of middle-aged adults, yet their incomes are significantly lower (Eitzen, Zinn and Eitzen 2009). When senior citizens need to be institutionalized, an affluent minority receives **therapeutic care**, an approach that focuses on meeting the needs of patients and providing for their treatment. On the other hand, homes with welfare recipients tend to provide **custodial care**, which too often focuses on meeting the needs of the institution, rather than those of the patients.

The majority of the elderly are not institutionalized, and since senior citizens are living longer, family members will spend longer periods of **elder-caregiving.** Because there are fewer siblings in families than in decades past, caretaker responsibilities will fall to a very few individuals, usually daughters or daughters-in-law. Although most of the elderly benefit from family caretakers, there can also be an increased likelihood of **elder abuse.** Abuse can take a number of different forms. Physical abuse involves individuals being slapped, hit, or restrained. Psychological abuse includes verbal assaults or threats. Drug abuse may occur when seniors are encouraged to over-medicate. Material abuse includes theft or misuse of money. And a violation of rights occurs when an elderly person is forced into a nursing home against his or her will. Abuse may occur more often when the caretaker is overwhelmed physically, emotionally, and financially.

Poverty, Housing, and Homelessness

A family of four is considered living in **poverty** if their pre-tax income is approximately $20,650 per year (U.S. Department of Health and Human Services 2007), which includes about fifteen percent of all families. A study by the U.S. Bureau of the Census found that families living in poverty were twice as likely to divorce as families not in poverty; thus poverty can be a significant factor in the break-up of some families (Eitzen, et al, 2009). The picture is even bleaker for single-parent families, who often have to get by on the income from one parent when child support is not available for whatever reason.

The number of children living in poverty has more than doubled in the past several decades with approximately fourteen million children living at the poverty level. Child poverty has been reduced by other industrialized nations, but the United States has failed significantly in this regard. Poverty can effect health, physical and intellectual development, and a number of social conditions, and there is a growing number of children living in **extreme poverty**, in which the family lives at half or less of the official poverty level. Extreme poverty can put a child at serious risk of malnutrition or some other threat. It is estimated that as many as one in five children live in poverty.

Individuals between the age of nineteen and twenty-four are more likely to live in poverty than older individuals, and families with the head of the household under the age of thirty are more likely to live in poverty than families with older heads of households. Two out of three adults living in poverty are likely to be women. Poverty rates for minorities are disproportionately high compared to whites, but the overall number of whites living in poverty is still higher. Immigrants have a higher rate of poverty than do native-born individuals, and a larger percentage of rural families live in poverty than do people living in cities. With fewer business and commerce centers, it is difficult to move out of poverty.

The poverty rates for senior citizens over the age of sixty-five has improved significantly over the past several decades, as America has done a better job of re-training and supporting the older generation. However, there is a higher percentage of the elderly living just above the poverty level than those that are non-elderly. Senior citizens are therefore over-represented among the **near poor**. In spite of all of the improvements, the United States is still in the lower tier of success stories with poverty among senior citizens.

With more than forty million people in the United States living in poverty and another thirty million or so living just above the poverty level, more effort needs to go into eliminating poverty. Welfare reform, school breakfast programs, school reforms that include family resource centers, Head Start, the United Way's Success by Six program, job- and business-related investment initiatives, and other public and private assistance programs have made a marked impact on poverty. Still, America lags behind most of the other industrialized nations, and until national policies are changed to address poverty genuinely and effectively, the nonprofit sector must make a strong initiative to address the needs of the poor.

Most Americans cannot afford to purchase a home because of the often-required down payment (approximately twenty percent) and/or high mortgage payments that go along with **home ownership**. Individuals and families who own their home often develop a greater sense of personal and community pride and benefit financially from home equity and tax incentives. Some individuals are able to purchase a home only with the aid of governmental, private, or nonprofit programs that assist with the down payment, interest rates, or construction costs. A significant number, about one-third of all Americans, are **shelter poor**, which means they spend so much of their income on home ownership that paying for necessities like food, clothing, and utilities is difficult.

Poor families must often live in **public housing**, which is often substandard and inadequate, and housing for poor minorities, the elderly, and households with females at the head is twice the average of substandard housing in general. Nearly a fourth of all **rural poor** live in substandard housing, and even though the cost of rural housing is less than for urban housing, the income of rural families is typically lower.

Incidents in which senior citizens share their homes with unrelated people, referred to as **shared housing**, for the purpose of rent, companionship, assistance with daily living and/or security, has increased and will continue to do so in the future. The government's definition of "disability' now includes the de-institutionalized mentally disabled, as well as some classifications of drug addicts and alcoholics, and public housing for the **disabled** has increased significantly. Advocacy groups often make a point of working for fair housing for the disabled, the homeless, and the very poor. These efforts often run counter to the unwritten policies of housing managers who prefer residents with more options for paying rent.

Homeless families have increased in number and will probably continue to do so in the future. About one-third of all homeless families include children. Homelessness may come about through a variety of causes, including low-paying jobs, terminations and layoffs, domestic problems, alcohol and drug addictions, old age, and disabilities to mention several. There can be a number of solutions that involve shelters, job training and re-training, support, and sobriety programs.

The World of Work and Technology

Changes continue to take place at a dizzying pace as a mostly **information-based** economy replaces an industrialized one, and technology becomes more and more integrated into the way we conduct business and our personal lives as well. Businesses and organizations that are designed to incorporate information resources and electronic networks into their operating procedures can be responsive to changing customer demands and will have a decided edge over less enlightened organizations.

Individuals with specialized skills are in greater demand to work in information-based organizations. People who are innovative in developmental and problem solving areas will continue to be sought after by organizations. Individuals with critical skills and innovative character will find the highest paying jobs in all areas of work.

One of the benefits of enhanced technology has been that organizations have developed **flexible working environments** for employees who are unable to work a nine-to-five schedule, or are unable to work at a corporate headquarters. This flexible workplace also includes **job sharing**, in which several people share the same position. Working a **compressed work week**, working forty hours in less than five days, has become more popular and seems to enhance morale and efficiency, while reducing absenteeism. **Telecommuting** via computers from home provides individuals flexibility and provides opportunities for productivity and collaboration they may not have otherwise.

Changing demographics have made **managing diversity** a critical concern for organizational leaders. The rising number of women, minorities, and senior citizens in the workplace has made it a mosaic of different cultures and has led to a need for programs designed to empower and enhance a culturally diverse work force. These types of programs are important and demand for them will continue to grow.

As an increasing number of mothers come into the workplace, there is a growing need for more high quality, yet affordable, preschool, before school, and after school **child- care** programs. A significant number of parents believe that present day affordable child-care is often inadequate in staffing and content and a demand for better child-care will continue to grow. Organizations that recognize and address this need should be in great demand.

Employees can experience a sense of **alienation** when working conditions become such that individuals feel separated from others, from themselves, and even from the work they do, if there is a lack of satisfaction and personal accomplishment. Additional factors, such as the transition to an information-based economy, inadequate child-care, increased responsibilities, ambiguous job descriptions, and lack of security, have taken their toll on many employees who report significant **stress** and **fatigue** at the business site.

Unemployed workers whose skills are obsolete can be **trained** and **retrained** by companies who find themselves in partnerships with educational institutions more and more. Transitional approaches such as **school-to-work** initiatives can be critical for the millions of individuals for whom high school is the end of their formal educational experience. A number of programs including **cooperative education, monitored work experiences,** and **vocational education** are sometimes necessary for establishing important connections for this transition.

A wired world, in which machine-to-machine communication has become faster and less expensive, began to develop when telephone transmission was converted from analog to **digital** and **fiber-optic** phone lines were installed. The investment, transfer, and distribution of finances will occur more and more often through **electronic mediums** as will the design, production, installation, and sale of goods and services.

Computers will continue to become smaller and less expensive while providing more and more functions. **Artificial intelligence processes** provide support for human problem-solving processes, rather than mimic them and will continue to assist in analyzing complex data such as with space travel and medical diagnostic procedures. **Wireless phone service** has become the preferred communication process worldwide, and **multimedia technology** connects different technologies for use in business, entertainment and home.

Interactive design procedures have become a multibillion dollar business by making it possible to create **manufactured materials** for health care, agricultural, and other technologies that have completely revolutionized various problem solving processes.

Knowledge of and skills in technology are critical for success in nearly all aspects of work and many aspects of home as well. A schism already exists between the information-rich--those with access to electronic technology--and the information-poor, whose access is difficult at best. One way to manage the issue is to make it a national, even international, priority to encourage the establishment of **information utilities** to ensure equal access by everyone.

Crime

Crime, particularly violent crime among teenagers, grew in the past decade as family structure and support diminished. Children need role models and guidelines for values and behavior. This may be particularly true for teenagers who are attempting to understand the world around them and their role and purpose in the world. When these guidelines are not available through the family structure, individuals sometimes look elsewhere and **gangs** too often take the place of the family. Gangs provide security and a sense of belonging and are most often driven by drug sales as a means of financial stability. Gangs, who represent all ethnic and racial groups, recruit both male and female members.

Hate crimes related to race, religion, sexual orientation, and ethnicity, and organizations that support one group's beliefs and values over another have continued to flourish in spite of the great strides that have been made in equal opportunities and cultural diversity. **Family violence** remains a constant reminder for the need for family enrichment, support, and intervention programs. This can be one of the cruelest kinds of violence, since the individuals causing pain are those who are supposed to protect and support, and it can take the form of **child abuse, spousal abuse**, and violence against **elderly** relatives.

Only one country, Northern Ireland, has a murder rate comparable to the United States, making this country one of the most violent countries of all. **Homicide** is a part of both large cities and mid-sized cities, and gang-related crime continues to be a factor in almost all cities regardless of size. **Gun control** remains a volatile issue with individuals and groups taking a strong stance on both sides. State and local gun control bills are constantly being challenged and changed, and the issue will continue to remain volatile in the future. A disproportionate number of young African-American men between the ages of sixteen and twenty-four become the victims of crimes involving hand guns. Homicide is often the number one cause of death in this age group.

The production, transfer, and sale of **illegal drugs** is a crime, and there is a significant correlation between dealing in drugs and other criminal activities. Drug trafficking and sales has emerged as a huge business involving tens of billions of dollars in revenue annually and often including high-powered weaponry in the battle for control. There has been some shift away from imported drugs, such as **cocaine, heroin,** and **marijuana,** and toward more domestic drugs that can be made cheaply in home labs with easily available products.

A get-tough policy on crime as a way of **punishment** and **deterrence** by the United States has led to seriously overcrowded jails. America has the highest incarceration rate of any country, with a disproportionate number of those prisoners being African- American men. Nearly one fourth of all black men between the ages of twenty and twenty-nine are incarcerated or under some form of supervision from the criminal justice system, as compared to one out of every sixteen white men and one out of every ten Hispanic men (Weis and Gantt 2004).

Over four million people are being supervised in some way by the criminal justice system, and the cost for corrections is often the largest financial item in a state's budget. Alternatives to prison can be effective and less costly and include **half-way houses, community service programs, revised sentencing policies**, increased **electronic monitoring**, and a fairer system of **matching the punishment to the crime.**

Environmental Issues

Some environmental concerns, such as earthquakes and tornadoes are natural occurrences and beyond human control, but others, like water and air quality are very much a byproduct of mankind and human interaction, with national and often global consequences.

The **biosphere** is made up of the surface of our planet and surrounding atmosphere.

Together they provide the air, land, water and energy necessary for life. The **ecosystem** is the mechanism that supplies human beings with the essentials to sustain life and involves plants, animals, and microorganisms interacting with each other and the physical environment. These ecosystems are being disturbed by a number of forces. The tremendous growth in human population (approximately seven billion people) takes a tremendous toll on the supply of food, energy, and minerals. The concentration of so many people in urban areas makes it difficult for the air, water, and land to handle waste and other toxic elements. And finally, some environmental problems are the result of modern technology and its uses.

Pollutants are a major cause of various health hazards and are an example of how humanity is fouling up its world. Specific examples of mankind's polluting the environment include **chemical pollution**, in which toxic chemicals are released into the air, water, and land during the development of chemical products; **solid waste pollution**, which includes the disposal of billions of tons of glass, plastics, textiles, and other materials each year; **water pollution**, involving contaminants, sewage, and oil spills that pour into rivers, lakes and oceans; **radiation pollution,** which occurs through x-rays, nuclear fallout from weapons testing, and nuclear accidents; and, **air pollution**, which is caused primarily by automobile emissions and industrial plants.

The burning of fossil fuels and the destruction of tropical forests contribute to the **greenhouse effect**, in which harmful gases, such as carbon dioxide, nitrous oxide, chlorofluorocarbons, and methane accumulate and act much like the glass roof in a greenhouse. When sunlight reaches the earth's surface, this "roof" traps heat radiating from the ground and causes a warming of the earth, the melting of the polar ice cap, and other significant changes in climate. Although still theoretical, the greenhouse effect is supported by the fact that sea-level has risen gradually of late, indicating that the earth is warmer now than it has been in the past 6000 years.

Trends in Philanthropy

Americans are among the most giving people in the world. Approximately fifty percent of all American adults formally **volunteer** in a nonprofit organization each year. Nearly half of teenagers volunteer to provide service, usually through their school, church, synagogue, or mosque. Nearly forty percent of senior citizens volunteer their time and an almost larger percentage are willing but have not been asked. Of those who volunteer, the majority take part on a regular basis, monthly or more often. This translates into more than ninety million individuals volunteering approximately twenty billion hours of service each year (Independent Sector 2002).

There is a correlation between being asked to volunteer and volunteering and a correlation between those who attend some kind of religious service and volunteering. Women are more likely to volunteer than men, and there is a correlation between volunteering and contributing financially to an organization.

People with certain values and attitudes, such as those who want to help the less fortunate, those who gain personal satisfaction from giving and volunteering, and those who want to increase opportunities for others, are more likely to contribute financially to a nonprofit organization. Approximately ninety percent of all American households **contribute to charities** each year with an average household gift of over $1000. Individuals who volunteer and contribute generally give more than those who just contribute financially (Weis and Gantt 2004). A higher percentage of adults who become involved with volunteering and giving in their youth are more likely to continue that pattern later on than those who do not. Individuals who attend religious services on a regular basis give twice as much as those who do not. And family members who worry about the economy give about half as much as those who are not worried about the economy in general (Independent Sector 2002).

Religious organizations generally receive the greatest dollar amount in gifts. Education receives the second largest amount, followed by human services. These are followed by health, arts, culture, humanities, and public/society benefit groups. Americans have demonstrated a willingness to work together in addressing problems in their communities and nonprofit organizations need to tap into this spirit by implementing innovative volunteer programs and creative financial development plans.

∎ Summary

The goal of most nonprofit organizations is to enhance the quality of life in communities, and understanding human development is important for effective program planning. Organizational leaders must understand that human development is contextual in nature, meaning that development occurs in the context of various circumstances and situations, and leaders must understand developmental theories as well. Developmental theories provide information on how individuals pass through various processes and stages and provide a foundation to develop approaches tht will assist individuals in addressing life situations.

Nonprofit leaders must incorporate their knowledge of human development with their awareness of issues and trends that individuals and communities are facing and will face in the future. Educational concerns, such as illiteracy and technology in the classroom, and health problems, such as AIDS, STDs, drugs and alcohol, and the complexity of the health care system are staggering issues. A growing population and aging continue to present challenges and opportunities for nonprofit leaders. Children, individuals, and families are often devastated by poverty, housing costs, and homelessness that can and must be addressed effectively. Technology and other changes taking place in the workplace are occurring at a dizzying pace, leaving some employees stressed and feeling disenfranchised. Although aspects of crime have ebbed and waned over the last several decades, the family structure and support are too often diminished, creating opportunities for criminal behavior and leaving a huge gap for nonprofit organizations to fill. Environmental systems have suffered the consequences of human greed and thoughtlessness and will continue to require a special area of attention.

Throughout time, societies have been faced with challenging situations. There are no "quick fixes" to the numerous problems and situations that confront families, children, and individuals daily. Nonprofit organizations have a unique opportunity and responsibility to work with educational institutions and governmental agencies to address the needs of all citizens through programs.

This chapter addressed, in part, the Nonprofit Leadership Alliance Certification Competency Requirements of Youth and Adult Development.

■ **Reflection and Application**

1. What is the relationship between human development and context?

    _____

    _____

    _____

2. Which developmental theories can you identify with, and why?

    _____

    _____

    _____

3. What is the connection between the id, ego, and superego?

    _____

    _____

    _____

4. Which of Erikson's stages can you identify with, and why?

    _____

    _____

    _____

5. Describe a situation in which you have incorporated the Social Learning Theory?

    _____

    _____

    _____

6.   Which issue or trend is most important to you, and why? How should it be managed?

   _____

   _____

   _____

7.   Using Erikson's Psychosocial Theory as the foundation, develop an idea for a program directed toward individuals in a specific stage.

   _____

   _____

   _____

■ References

Bailey. *A border war*. Washington Post Weekly Edition (October 23-29, 2006).

Bronfenbrenner, U. (1979). *The Ecology of Human Development*. Cambridge, MA: Harvard University Press.

Caplow. T., Hicks, L., and Wattenberg, B. (2001). *The First Measured Century: An Illustrated Guide to Trends in America, 1900-2000*. Washington, D.C.: The AEI Press.

Drug Enforcement Administration, (2007). Online: Available: http://www.drugsense.org/html/modules.php?name=wodclock.

Edginton, Christopher R., and Ford, Phyllis M. (1985). *Leadership in Recreation and Leisure Service Organizations*. New York: John Wiley and Sons.

Edginton, Susan R. and Edginton, Christopher. R. (1994). *Youth Programs: Promoting Quality Services*. Champaign, IL: Sagamore Publishing.

Edginton, Christopher R.; Hudson, Susan D.; and Ford, Phyllis M. (1999). *Leadership in Recreation and Leisure Service Organizations*. 2nd ed. Champaign, IL: Sagamore Publishing.

Ehrlich, P., and Ehrlich, A. (1991). *The Population Explosion*. New York: Simon and Schuster.

Eitzen, D. Stanley, Zinn, M.B. and Eitzen K.S. (2009). *Social Problems*. Upper Saddle River, NJ; Pearson Publishing.

Erikson, E. (1958). *Young Man Luther: A Study in Psychoanalysis and History*. New York: Norton.

_____(1963). *Youth and Society*. New York: Norton.

_____(1969). *Ghandi's Truth*. New York: Norton.

_____(1975). *Life and the Historical Moment*. New York: Norton.

Erikson, E. H. (1963). *Childhood and Society*. Rev. ed. New York: Norton.

Feagin, J. R., and Feagin, C. B., (1994). *Social Problems*. 4th ed. Englewood Cliffs, N.J.: Prentice-Hall.

Freud, S. (1923). *The Ego and the Id*. New York: Norton.

Hewitt Associates (2004). *Worklife Benefits Provided by Major U.S. Employers, 2003-2004*, Lincolnshilre, Ill.; Hewitt Associates.

Independent Sector (2001). *The New Nonprofit Almanac*. Washington, D.C.

Kaplan, Paul S. (1998). *The Human Odyssey: Life Span Development*. Pacific Grove, CA: Brooks/Cole Publishing Company.

Mills, C. W. (1959). *The Sociological Imagination*. New York: Oxford University Press.

Piaget, J. (1970). *The Child's Conception of the World*. Totowa, N.J.: Littlefield and Adams.

_____ (1972). Intellectual evolution from adolescence to adulthood. *Human Development* 15:1-12.

Pittman, K. J. (1991). *Promoting Youth Development: Strengthening the Role of Youth Serving and Community Organizations*. New York: Center for Development and Policy Research.

Rubington, E., and Weinberg, eds. (1995). *The Study of Social Problems: Seven Perspectives*. 5th ed. New York: Oxford University Press.

Spector, M. and Kitsuse, J. I. (1987). *Constructing Social Problems.* Hawthorne, N.Y.: Aldine de Gruyter.

U.S. Department of Health and Human Services, (2007). *HHS poverty guidelines.* Washington, DC: Author. Available: http//aspe.hhs.gov/poverty/07 poverty.htm

United Way Strategic Institute (1992). *What Lies Ahead.* Alexandria, VA: United Way of America.

Weis, R. and Gantt V. (2004). *Knowledge and Skill Development in Nonprofit Organizations,* Peosta, IA; E. Bowers Publishing

Weis, R., and Gantt, V. (2002). *Leadership and Program Development in Nonprofit Organizations.* Peosta, IA: E. Bowers Publishing.

Walsh, F. (2006). *Strengthening family resilience* (2nd ed.). New York: Guilford Press.

Worth, M.J. (2009). *Nonprofit Management: Principles and Practice.* Thousand Oaks, CA: Sage Publications Inc.

5 Program Development, Marketing and Promotion

Programs developed by organizational leaders and managers are the means by which organizations achieve many of their objectives and goals as they work to fulfill their mission. In addition to exploring program development in Chapter 5, we will also take a look at some classic approaches to marketing and promoting programs in organizations and discuss ways to improve customer service.

■ A Customer-Centered/Benefits Approach to Program Development

Programs communicate to customers what the organization is trying to accomplish. A **customer-centered/benefits** approach to developing programs implies that leaders strive to develop programs that not only meet the needs of their customers, but often exceed them and provide customers with some form of positive outcome or benefit. This approach to program development communicates a quality organization with quality staff members. Quality programs must be carefully planned, implemented, and evaluated. Programs of all kinds can be developed for organizational members as long as they fall under the umbrella of the overall purpose of the organization (Weis and Gantt 2004).

Staff and volunteer members who are responsible for developing programs should meet certain **criteria** that include (1) believing in and being committed to the purpose of the organization; (2) being knowledgeable and skilled in program development; and, (3) being aware of the situations, needs, and desires of the constituents of the organization (Weis and Gantt 2004). Programs should meet the needs of the organization's constituents in the context of the organizational mission or purpose.

In addition to meeting certain criteria, it is important that leaders in nonprofit organizations commit to developing programs of the highest quality. More and more citizens are relying on nonprofit organizations to provide services to assist them in reaching their goals or in times of need, and these individuals deserve program services of the highest possible quality (Weis and Gantt 2004).

Quality. Once the need for a program is established, it is time to turn attention to establishing programs of the highest quality. **Quality programs** are those programs that meet or exceed the standards and expectations set for program activities (Russell and Jamieson 2008). They are programs of excellence that focus on the needs of the customers and make them feel as if they are valued members of the organization; such programs also provide members with a positive outcome or benefit (Edginton and Edginton 1994). Meeting and exceeding the expectations of the members of an organization is the hallmark of a competent, caring, and dedicated staff with the knowledge and skills to develop exceptional programs.

Programs that meet or exceed expectations are rare, and customers take note when their expectations are exceeded (Weis and Gantt 2004).

Developing programs that meet and exceed customer expectations is the responsibility of the organization's leaders. These guidelines should include, but not be limited to the following (Walton 1988):

- **Innovation.** Programs should be developed that meet the changing needs of organizational members and remain fresh by offering new and interesting activities to keep them exciting.
- **Continual improvement.** Constantly looking for ways that programs can be improved keeps them fresh, energized, and meaningful. Program development is a dynamic process that should always be evolving toward relevant methods and processes.
- **Continuous Education.** Good organizations commit to continuous educational opportunities for staff members. College classes, seminars, and workshops should be supported and encouraged for staff members to ensure competency and effectiveness in program and administrative areas.
- **Attention to Detail.** Programs in which details are important are generally superior to programs in which details are not an issue. Paying attention to details helps to ensure quality and success. There is an old saying that goes: "The devil is in the details," which reminds us those problems can occur when details are not attended to.
- **Pride.** Staff and volunteer members must have a strong feeling about the programs they are planning and must work diligently to provide customers with the best services possible. Pride is contagious, and it begins when everyone in the organization prides himself or herself on what the programs are accomplishing for their members. Pride includes planning and implementing new programs with as few mistakes as possible and eliminating mistakes or unnecessary aspects from existing programs.
- **Anticipatory Planning.** Program developers must be proactive in the sense that they look ahead to program needs for the future as well those of the present. In order to do this, leaders must be on the cutting edge of program development and must maintain knowledge of issues and customer needs.
- **Teamwork and Responsibility.** Programs are by necessity developed and implemented in a cooperative process. Program leaders must have skills in developing effective teams of professional staff members, volunteers, invested staff members of other organizations, consultants and even program participants in the overall development of programs. Shared input and responsibility requires leadership that is competent in developing collaborative, successful ventures.
- **Performance Measurements.** Program successes and outcomes can and should be validated through an evaluation process. Interviews, focus groups, surveys, pre/post tests, and observation are all legitimate ways to determine whether programs are meeting their objectives and whether they are successful from the participants' standpoint. Evaluations can be time-consuming but the results can assist the organization in developing better, more effective programs. They help staff

Figure 5.1
Stages of Program Development:
Planning, Implementation and Evaluation (PIE)

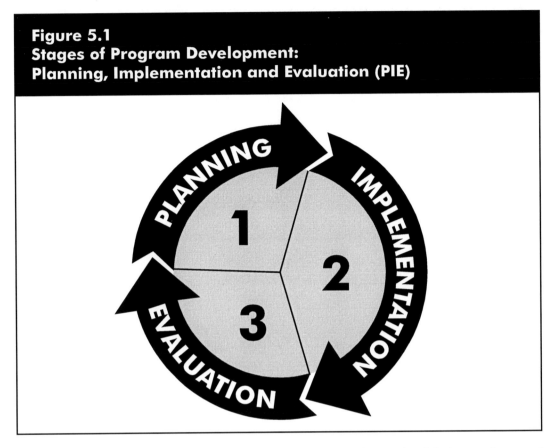

members determine whether they are meeting the needs of their members, and they provide useful information when seeking support from outside funders.

Providing programs of the highest possible quality that meet or exceed the expectations of customers is the only way to ensure that an organization maintains integrity in its mission while providing opportunities of enhancement for its members.

A commitment to programs of the highest quality is the responsibility of everyone in an organization, and once this commitment is established, the focus of attention turns to the developmental process itself. There are three major areas or **stages** of program development (Weis and Gantt 2004): (1) **Initial (Planning) Stage**, (2) **Middle (Planning/Implementation) Stage**, and (3) **Final (Evaluation) Stage** (See PIE, Figure 5.1 above):

■ Initial (Planning) Stage

Careful planning in this stage is important since it sets the groundwork for other activities throughout the program development process. Good planning should be a step- by-step process (Russell and Jamieson 2008), although the sequence of steps and modification or simplification of steps depends on particular situations, and some steps may not even be necessary.

Action steps are specific work segments or activities that are necessary to accomplish program objectives (Hardy 1984). The development of action steps is the responsibility of the program or planning committee, and members of this committee are determined by the

Figure 5.2
Program Planning Worksheet

Date____/____/____

Name of Organization _____

Name of Program/Project _____

Program Coordinator _____

Program Members:

	Name	Address	Phone Number	e-mail address
1				
2				
3				
4				
5				
6				

Program Objectives _____

_____

_____

Estimated Direct Expenses	Estimated Direct Income	Gain (Deficit)
Actual Direct Costs	Actual Direct Income	Gain (Deficit)

Action Steps or Work Tasks	Person(s) Responsible	Completion Dates

Evaluation Results _____

_____

Recommendations for Future Programs _____

_____

organization's leaders, usually a program director or another senior staff member. Action steps typically specify (1) which tasks are to be completed to accomplish program objectives, and in what order; (2) who is responsible for completing various tasks; and (3) when these tasks are to be completed. Although tasks for specific programs may vary considerably, some standard tasks for consideration are listed below (Weis and Gantt 2002):

Step 1 – Selection of a Planning Committee. Groups often have greater potential for creativity and thoroughness than individuals because of enhanced expertise, synergy, and opportunity to attend to details. Selecting an effective planning committee to develop specific programs is essential for successfully meeting organizational goals and planning programs that meet and exceed the expectations of its members. Planning members should include:

- staff and volunteer members who have knowledge and skills in program planning as well as in the particular content area of the program.
- individuals with particular knowledge and skills in areas of specific expertise relevant to program planning, such as marketing, finances, and volunteer coordination and risk management when these are needed.
- Individuals, such as the members of the organization, who will benefit from the program, since these individuals can often add insight into the needs and desires of the membership in general.

Planning committee members are *responsible* for the following:

- developing a schedule of program planning meetings
- identifying and prioritizing other tasks or action steps according to what needs to be done first, second, and so on
- assigning a responsible person or persons to accomplish each task
- recording each aspect of the program plan on a **Program Planning Worksheet (PPW)** (see Figure 5.2 below)
- implementing, monitoring, and reporting the progress of the program to the appropriate organizational leaders(s)

Step 2 – Needs Assessment. The needs and desires of constituents should be identified and assessed so programs can be developed to focus on appropriate areas. **Needs** are usually considered as an individual *physiological, psychological, or social imbalance.* Edginton and Ford (1985) note that when an individual recognizes a deficiency in any of these areas, he or she has a need. Physiological needs might include deficiencies associated with the need for food, water, sleep, and sex. Psychological and social deficiencies might be harder to assess, but would include the need for companionship, social interaction, recognition, safety, love, achievements, and self- esteem.

A need, then, is the assessed difference between the ideal state of an individual and the actual condition of an individual as he or she is functioning in their environment. Communities, too, have needs as do states, nations, and all of society, and program planners should be aware of collective needs in developing programs. **Desires**, on the other hand, are considered wishes *that are perceived as something necessary* (Edginton, et al. 1998). In this context, desires are differentiated from needs in that they are not necessary to sustain life, but they can also be considered in determining future programs.

In the 1940s, Abraham Maslow advanced a general theory of human needs and motivation that still serves as a foundation and guide to understanding basic human needs. He identified physiological needs, safety needs, affiliation needs, esteem needs, and the need to become self-actualized. These needs are discussed in detail below:

1. **Physiological needs.** These include basic human needs for food, water, shelter, sleep, sensory gratification and could be satisfied by a supportive environment.
2. **Safety needs.** This category includes being relatively free from danger and might involve a safe home, neighborhood, or work environment.
3. **Affiliation needs.** These needs can be expressed in the desire to join with others in completing a project, making a family, or achieving a sense of belonging (fraternities or sororities). This need implores individuals to explore and develop relationships with friends, family, and co-workers.
4. **Esteem needs.** These needs are expressed in individual and collective desires for a sense of accomplishment or achievement. This satisfaction can be received externally, internally, or both. External esteem satisfaction comes from visible rewards such as a salary increase. Internal esteem satisfaction results when individuals realize a sense of accomplishment, success, and being counted on.
5. **Need for self-actualization.** Maslow described this need as a desire to become everything that one is capable of becoming. As self-actualization occurs, individuals reach out to assist others in becoming all that they are capable of becoming through empowering or mentoring activities.

(Maslow 1943)

Maslow posits that individuals will work to satisfy needs in that order and it is only when basic needs such as safety and food are met that higher needs for esteem and self-actualization can be considered. Although research has failed to conclude a clear separation

L E V E L S	5	**Self-Actualization** Work which allows for independent decision making
	4	**Esteem** Internal: feeling good about how you help others External: bonus pay, family allowed at fun events
	3	**Affiliation** An organizational bowling or softball team
	2	**Safety** Working conditions which protect staff and customers
	1	**Physiological** Enough money to pay the bills – rent, food, health-care

between the categories and the validity of Maslow's theory in general, it remains a foundational treatise on human needs and motivation.

Programs should only be developed that address important issues and needs of organizational members and should take into account the various life stages that individuals may be passing through. For instance, teenagers are passing through a very difficult stage of their lives as they struggle to develop and understand their identity, as noted in Erikson's Stage Theory in Chapter 4 of this text. At the same time, they are also often confronted with a number of issues such as smoking, alcohol and drug use, and premarital sex. A program that is designed to strengthen their system of values by offering them the opportunity to make a difference in someone else's life, for instance, could become a critical aspect to their personal development. These kinds of programs help teens develop a positive sense of **self worth** and the knowledge that they can and do make a difference (**self-efficacy**). Programs that also confront important issues head-on with facts, methods of handling situations, and the opportunity to teach these to others, such as younger children, can be an invaluable experience with lifelong implications. These experience can allow them to develop communication and teamwork skills and even provide insight into future vocational possibilities.

An **assessment of needs** should be made prior to further program planning, and that can be done in a number of ways: (1) Researching and assessing existing data, such as published reports in newspapers, magazines, journals, and institutional bulletins can be essential in understanding the needs of individuals in general (Russell and Jamieson 2008).

Figure 5.3
Needs Assessment Survey

Kingston Community Center
Survey for New Programs

Please help the Kingston Community Center determine new program interests for the upcoming activity year. Complete the following anonymous survey and place it in the survey box located at the North entrance to the facility. Once you have done this, the front desk clerk will give you a coupon for 20% off any special class, workshop, or seminar. Thanks for helping your center be the best it can be!

PLEASE CHECK YOUR AREAS OF INTEREST:

☐ Aerobics	☐ Bowling	☐ Golf class	☐ Trips
☐ Aquatics	☐ Computer class	☐ Karate	☐ Softball
☐ Arts & Crafts	☐ Culinary class	☐ Racquetball	☐ Volleyball
☐ Athletics/fitness	☐ Cycling	☐ Scuba	☐ Youth activities
☐ Basketball	☐ Education	☐ Senior activities	

Comments and other suggestions: _____
_____
_____
_____

(2) Assessing the needs and desires of organizational members firsthand can and should be done through interviews, focus groups, and and/or surveys that can be implemented periodically or at set times throughout the year. Interviews can be face to face, or a sampling of telephone interviews can be initiated. Individual interviews provide a focus of insight that cannot be duplicated by other methods. On the other hand, focus groups sometimes provide collective information that cannot be found through an individual process. And surveys can provide confidentiality that is virtually non-existent with the interview and focus group format and may provide for more open and honest responses (an example survey can be found in Figure 5.3 below). (3) A third method of understanding the needs and desires of constituents is through information already gathered for organizations that are a part of a state-wide, regional, or national association. These organizations often receive pre-planned programs addressing the needs of the general membership, which can be valuable and time saving.

Step 3 – Review Developmental Theories, Competencies, Stages and Issues. After assessing the needs of the constituents of an organization, it is also important to have an understanding of developmental stages they may be experiencing, along with an understanding of significant issues and trends that members may be challenged with (see Chapter 4). It is important to review developmental theories, competencies, stages (Erikson) and issues relevant to the needs of the membership and the mission of the organization. Although needs and desires are important, understanding developmental processes is equally important to crafting effective programs.

Maintaining an awareness of current and significant issues and trends provides program planners with the opportunity to address some of these issues through programs. Programs that address recognized needs, confront important issues, and focus on the overall development of individuals strikes a chord with members who realize the organization is focusing on their situation and providing programs directed toward their well-being (Weis and Gantt 2004).

Step 4 – Incorporating Values and Character Education. Nonprofit organizations have a significant responsibility to assist members in becoming responsible individuals and citizens. This mandate dates back to the early part of the twentieth century when organizations such as the Boy Scouts of America, Girl Scouts of the USA, Boys and Girls Clubs of America, Camp Fire Boys and Girls, Girls, Inc., and the YMCAs and YWCAs focused a great deal of attention on character development, as they still do today (Edginton, Hudson, and Ford 1999).

Values can be thought of as principles that guide our lives and the constructs that are important in our lives (Edginton, et al.). **Values education** occurs when nonprofit leaders assist members in defining and developing their values through select, organized methods. Values education should reflect: (1) the basic values of the community and society; and (2) parallel the values of the organization, but they (3) should not impose values upon members. Values such as honesty, justice, equality, and freedom, to list several, are values that can and should be encouraged by organizations, but must be accepted freely by participants, not forced upon them.

There are several effective ways to introduce values in a program. In the **direct-programmatic approach** values clarification and development is the main focus of the program. In other words, the program is designed and promoted as a values clarification/ development program. This can be a very honest and effective approach, although some participants may be hesitant to be open regarding their value system.

Another effective way to introduce values education is through an **integrated-programmatic approach.** In this approach, values are introduced as part of the structure of the program and occur more *naturally* within the program's framework. This makes this approach very functional and prevents compartmentalization. For instance, the an indoor-soccer league might support the concept that all children make the team and there are no try-outs. It could also include the concept that all children will play an approximately equal amount of time and that all participants will shake hands with the opposing team members at the end of the game. Fairness, sportsmanship, and teamwork are just some of the values that can be presented within this framework. And finally, values are taught by **role modeling**. Organizational leaders inevitably provide examples of values for participants to consider through their decisions and actions, so it is important for these leaders to assess and monitor their actions in all facets of operational activities (Weis and Gantt 2004).

Another important concept to consider in program development is the concept of **character education**, or helping individuals internalize values such as honesty, integrity, equality, and fairness. It is one thing to clarify and develop a healthy system of values but it is another thing to live one's life in accordance with that system of values. Nonprofit leaders have the opportunity to develop programs that allow individuals to internalize values by clarifying, using, and reflecting upon them over and over again in various situations. Clubs and organizations, service learning opportunities (see Chapter 2), and other programs that promote continual use and reflection of values are essential to healthy individual development.

Quality programs combine (1) constituent needs with (2) an understanding of developmental stages along with (3) a focus on important issues or trends, and include (4) values and character education which can have a powerful impact on the lives of the members of any organization.

Step 5 – Determine Program Objectives. Most nonprofit organizations have a **purpose** or a **mission statement** that spells out their reason for being in a general way (Weis and Gantt 2004). This statement usually refers to enhancing the quality of life of specific individuals in the community in some way, but it is so broad that organizations usually designate a number of definitive **goals** they plan to accomplish as a part of their purpose. For instance, an organization that plans to enhance the quality of life for socially/economically disadvantaged children might have goals of helping children develop competencies in health, education, recreation, and vocations. More specifically, the organization could set a number of **program objectives** or outcomes for each of these areas (goals) (Hardy 1984). For instance, in the area of health, a program objective could include having children become competent in personal hygiene, or in nutritional guidelines of some kind. An objective for education could be to improve the literacy rate or the percentage of high school graduates in a particular community. Program objectives are both measurable and capable of being accomplished in a set amount of time.

Setting program objectives provides motivation and direction for the program staff, who can begin concentrating on developing action steps necessary for achieving set objectives. Having program objectives also provides a basis from which to measure whether or not goals have been achieved. The measurement process will be discussed in the evaluation phase of program development.

There are generally two types of program objectives: (1) **Qualitative.** This type of objective includes the various areas the program is designed to address or change, including needs, issues, situations, values, competencies, and/or life stages; and (2) **Quantitative.** This type of objective includes areas of the program that can be counted and observed, such as the number of program participants, the length and meeting times of the program, and financial considerations. Both types of objectives need to be considered and documented on the Program Planning Worksheet prior to implementing a program.

Program objectives should be written in a certain way and include certain criteria (Edginton, Hanson, and Edginton 1992):

- **Specific.** Program objectives should be clear and succinct.
- **Measurable.** There needs to be a way in which to measure whether or not program objectives are met.
- **Reality-based.** Objectives should be challenging yet reachable.
- **Useful.** Objectives provide program staff with direction and therefore must be helpful in guiding staff members toward achieving the purpose(s) of the program.
- **Linked to Needs.** Obviously, objectives must be linked to the needs, issues, competencies, values and so on that the program is addressing and is designed to affect.
- **Inclusion of Program Concept and Format.** Including the program concept or idea and the program format in the objective helps to connect the purpose of the program to the overall program process. The program concept and format will be discussed in Steps 6 and 7.

Setting purposeful objectives provides a foundation for the rest of the developmental process, and it is vital that objectives are well-written and defined. An example of a clear and effective **objective** follows:

The Teens for Seniors program provides teenagers in the Morganfield Boys and Girls Club opportunities to assist senior citizens attending the community center's day care program. Teens are trained to participate with seniors in social and recreational activities. Some of the intended objectives include:

- **Involvement of a minimum of 10 teenagers in a program with a minimum of 25 senior citizens meeting at least once a week for social and recreational activities for a 3 month period**
- **Improved inter-generational understanding**
- **Increased flexibility on the part of senior citizens**
- **Decreased depression on the part of senior citizens**
- **Enhanced self-esteem of teenagers and senior citizens**
- **Increased sense of responsibility and caring on the part of the teenagers**
- **Improved teamwork, communication, recreation, socialization and leadership skills on the part of the teenagers.**

This kind of program provides opportunities for improving the overall health and well-being of both teenagers and senior citizens and allows the teenagers to develop a number of important skills and character traits that will be useful throughout their lives. This objective includes the program concept and format and addresses needs, issues, competencies, values, and life stages. The objectives for this program include both qualitative and quantitative areas that can be measured in various ways and the program is designed to be realistic, yet challenging in nature.

    Step 6 – Selection of Program Concept. Once the program objectives have been established, a program idea or concept must be determined that results in an effective process for reaching objectives. There are a number of ways or program *approaches* that can be considered in determining the program concept (Edginton and Edginton 1994):

- **Traditional Approach.** Relying on past successes within the organization to determine a program concept is referred to as the traditional approach. Reviewing past programs to determine how they can meet current objectives can be valuable for two reasons: (1) Less time and energy needs to be expended on the planning process, since the program has been implemented previously; and (2) organizational members who have appreciated programs from the past often look forward to a repeat of those programs with anticipation.

   One disadvantage to planning programs from a traditional approach standpoint is that if current programs rely too heavily on past planning they may become uninspired by not taking into account changes in interests, issues, trends, and lifestyles. Taking traditional program ideas and adding new twists can help keep the program fresh and exciting.

- **Current Practice Approach.** Programs that are effective in one part of the country can often be effective in another part as well. Nonprofit leaders are usually open to sharing successful program ideas with each other in the field. This type of approach can save a good deal of planning time, and lends legitimacy to the future success of the program. One disadvantage, however, is that sometimes a program that works in a large metropolitan area of the country may not work in a rural area, or vice versa. In a similar manner, a program that succeeds in the northeastern part of the country may not be as acceptable in the southwestern part, and so on. Both sides of the situation need to be taken into consideration before employing the current practice approach.

- **Expressed Desires Approach.** Offering members opportunities to express their desires for program selection through surveys, interviews, and focus groups provides them with a feeling of involvement and may provide the program staff valuable insights for program development. This information can also be valuable in reducing risk of developing programs for which there is little or no interest. Information provided by members is important and
   should be weighed with other factors in determining the program concept.

- **Prescriptive Approach.** This approach is directed toward developing program concepts focused on members of the organization with special needs or special situations. This concentrated focus on specific individuals can have very important and far-reaching consequences and should always be considered in the overall scheme of program development. However, consideration should also be given to the fact that these programs are usually time-consuming and resource intensive and address the needs of only a select number of members and the approach may need to be used accordingly.

- **Innovative Approach.** Creating new programs from scratch can be challenging, exciting, and rewarding. Members of the planning committee should convene to discuss alternative program ideas in *brainstorming* sessions. These sessions include expressing any and all ideas without qualification, recording the alternatives, and returning later to discuss the feasibility of each idea. Each member of the planning committee should feel that his or her ideas are welcome while they are being expressed. The newness of the resulting program concept often creates a level of excitement and anticipation that other, more traditional program ideas may not incur. A possible disadvantage of this kind of program approach is that because of the newness of the program idea, more time and confusion in the planning and the implementation process may occur and some uncertainty may exist as to the potential outcome.

- **Combined Approach.** *Good organizational leaders incorporate some or all of the approaches above for creating options for program concepts* (Weis and Gantt 2004). Using successful program ideas from the past provides some continuity, certainty, and tradition. Incorporating program ideas that have been successful in other places may decrease the amount of time necessary for planning and provide a sense of certainty regarding the outcome. Inviting members of the organization to express their desires and needs gives them a sense of involvement while providing program staff members with valuable information. Developing specific programs for certain individuals in an organization indicates to those members that they are important and that their needs are being addressed. Finally, creating new program ideas can cause a sense of excitement throughout an organization. The combined approach to program development can be highly successful because it brings together information from numerous sources in making program decisions. Finding just the right approach to program development can be time-consuming, but being able to develop programs that create interest and excitement and that meet the intended objectives has a great deal of merit and is certainly worth the effort.

Step 7 – Program Format. The selection of a program format is important because different program structures or formats provide different kinds of experiences for individuals. The way in which a program is structured is linked to the likelihood that customers will achieve desired benefits. For instance, a program for self-improvement may be structured as a workshop or seminar. A program designed to include physical competition may take the format of a sports league. Farell and Lundegren (1991) posit that the program format chosen should be directly linked to the experience desired for the customers and suggest five program formats:

1. self-improvement
2. competition
3. social
4. participant spectator
5. self-directed

A great deal has been written about program formats in the leisure services field and Russell (1982) suggests more common approaches to program formats:

1. clubs
2. competition
3. trips and outings
4. special events
5. classes
6. open facility,
7. voluntary service
8. workshops, seminars and conferences.

Each of these formats vary in terms of general characteristics and provide for a wide selection on program structure. Yet another approach to categorizing program formats is offered by Kraus (1985), who identifies eight program structures to choose from in meeting customer needs:

1. instruction
2. free play or unstructured participation
3. organized competition
4. performances, demonstrations or exhibits
5. leadership training
6. special interest groups
7. other special events
8. trips and outings

Most experts agree that the program format is the structure or form the activity takes and that the format is one of the key ingredients in meeting customer expectations.

Step 8 – Evaluate Resources. Another important consideration in the overall development of a program is the assessment of resources necessary for program delivery. Necessary resources may include any or all of the following (Weis and Gantt 2004):

- **Space availability.** One of the first things to consider regarding resources is determining what type of space is necessary and then exploring the use of existing space within the organization, or other areas and facilities.
- **Personnel.** Planners should develop a list of staff and/or volunteer members who are competent and available to develop a specific program. If an expert specific to a particular program is not already a part of the organizational team, one might be recruited as a volunteer or a part-time consultant or expert might be hired.
- **Finances.** Sometimes a program fee may need to be assessed to cover some expenses. It is also important to research the availability of sponsors to cover program costs.
- **Collaboration.** Some programs can be more successful if they are planned in collaboration with other organizations. Collaboration may take a little more time in the beginning, but often brings with it enhanced resources, increased services for more people, and more excitement and enthusiasm.
- **Supplies.** Planners must envision the supplies necessary for a successful program and develop a list. They must also determine which materials are already available and which materials can be borrowed, donated, or paid for through sponsorship.

Businesses and service organizations often sponsor nonprofit organizations for several reasons: (1) it helps develop the community, (2) it enhances public relations, and (3) it builds morale among its members.

- **Equipment.** The equipment necessary for the program must meet the needs of the program and the participants, and must be in good, safe condition.

■ Middle (Planning/Implementation) Stage

This is also a vital stage of program development, since the steps necessary for planning and implementing the program are designated and developed further. This is also the stage in which a supervisory plan is selected and the program is actually implemented (Weis and Gantt 2004).

Step 9 – Risk Management is Priority #1. Risk management is the prevention, control, and handling of risk associated with programs. Because individual and group safety and health are at stake, it is the most important step in the implementation of programs and should be the number one concern of all staff and volunteer members. Anything that could involve a loss of resources is considered a risk. A **risk management plan** involves looking at potential problems before they develop, eliminating them if possible, or managing them through training, warning, controlling, and/or insurance; all of this is to prevent injury, illness, damage, or another kind of loss.

Risk management is the most important step in program development, and the risk management plan for the program must be carefully thought out and implemented with clear instruction and communication. The main focus of the plan is to protect the program participants and the organization and involves three essential components:

1. **Identification of Risks.** Each program should be examined carefully for conditions or situations that could present risks. Program staff and volunteer members should become aware of obvious risks as well as not-so-obvious risks. Risks can include potential losses, accidents, injuries, illnesses, health threats, or damages. For example, a service learning project that includes cleaning up a section of the shoreline at a lake could involve the risk of being around water as well as potentially dangerous materials along the shore.

2. **Evaluation of Risks.** All risks are relative in terms of importance, and two questions can be asked in determining this:
   - What is the probability that the risk will develop into an accident, injury, loss or damage of some kind?
   - If a loss of some kind occurred, how severe could it be?

3. **Handling Risk.** There are essentially three ways to handle risk:
   - *Prevention (Avoidance).* One of the first and most important areas of managing risks is to match participants with appropriate experiences. Following that, participant orientation, training, and appropriate communication and supervision are keys to preventing and avoiding risk (Russell and Jamieson 2008).
   - *Risk Reduction.* Examples of risk reduction include clearly defined and communicated safety rules and well-thought-out procedures, including emergency procedures. In the case of the shore line clean-up, having water safety equip-

ment readily available, including life jackets, and advising participants to stay away from potentially dangerous cliffs or deep areas of the water would be examples of effective risk reduction approaches.

- ***Risk Retention or Transfer.*** This refers to how a loss will be handled should it occur. In other words, which entity is responsible for the loss and responsible for payment of any damages (Van der Smissen 1990).

  There are a number of forms to be considered in various stages of program activities and throughout the risk management process. The organization's legal counsel must review all written forms. Some examples of forms are included below:

- **Agreements** should be written between the organization and other community organizations that are involved with the program activity or where the activity may be conducted. This is done so that there is a clear understanding of expectations and roles between the sponsoring organization, the participant, and the community organization to which the service is provided, or for which an activity is conducted.

- **Participant Agreements.** These forms can be used to document that the participant understands that risks might be involved in the activity, agrees to abide by set safety rules, and agrees to perform as trained or instructed. These forms are also referred to as *Assumption of Risk Agreements.*

- **Waivers/Releases.** These two terms are often used interchangeably. Ordinarily, these forms state that the participant agrees not to hold the organization responsible if a loss of resource should occur. This kind of form is only valid if it is signed by an adult, and parents/guardians **can never legally sign the rights of children away (under the legal age of majority).**

- **Insurance.** Maintaining effective insurance coverage is the standard way of handling risk to prevent excessive or even devastating financial loss to an organization or entity. Insurance policies should be checked carefully to determine coverage prior to each program or activity.

Managing and keeping risk to a minimum and being certain that liabilities are adequately covered through insurance should be the highest priority of each and every staff and volunteer member of the organization. Once risk management policies have been established by the organization, each individual **should make every effort to follow the risk management policies relating to program development and other activities.**

Managing risk is a fluid and ever-changing process, and risk management procedures should be reviewed periodically to keep them up to date. Experts in the field of risk management, legal counsel, as well as key board and staff members should be involved in the development and periodic review of risk management procedures. Further information on liability, risk management, and insurance relevant to nonprofit organizations can be found in Chapter 7 of this text. Additionally, the following references are suggested: *Leadership in Recreation and Leisure Service Organizations* (1999) by Christopher R. Edginton, Susan D. Hudson and Phyllis M. Ford, Champaign, IL: Sagamore Publishing; and *Legal Liability and Risk Management for Public and Private Entities* (1990) (Vol. 2) by B. Van der Smissen, Cincinnati, Ohio: Anderson.

Step 10 – Marketing and Promoting Programs. Bagozzi (1975) defines marketing as the facilitation of some form of exchange. Defined as such, marketing is an important process that can link nonprofit organizations with entities within their environment. These entities can include program participants, donors, governments, media, service collaborators, and others. Marketing is a vital process in a nonprofit organization because (1) the success of marketing campaigns often determines whether or not the organization will thrive; (2) it is not an optional process; whether it is done amateurishly or professionally, it inevitably will occur in some form; and (3) the exchange concept signifies that there is more to marketing than communication and that advantageous exchanges of something of value also occur (Moyer 1994).

In the context of nonprofit organizations, the something of value is usually a type of community service offered to the public. In conjunction, individual members of the community have something of value to offer nonprofit organizations: their membership and participation in programs. These individuals may also serve as volunteers from time to time, so there is an exchange of value when the organization needs assistance and offers the opportunity for individuals to assist through their specific expertise and involvement. Anytime two parties like this have something that might be of value to each other it is referred to as a **market exchange.** The process that brings these two parties together is usually referred to as **marketing** or **promotion** (Hardy 1984). The marketing and/or promotion committee of the board of directors should be involved in this process and should be able to be very helpful in developing strategies

Marketing and promotion are very important steps in the program development process, since programs are of little importance unless they are joined with individuals who need or desire to participate. In order to understand how individuals become attracted to particular programs, it is important to look at something commonly referred to as the four *Ps*, or the **marketing mix** (Wolf 1999):

- **Product.** One of the most important elements in the marketing mix is the product and the quality of the product. In nonprofit organizations this typically means a program or service. In order for a program or service to be desirable, it must meet or exceed the expectations of the participants for them to be willing to pay for and participate in it. Staff members focusing on developing programs that individuals need, want, and desire and then ensuring that those programs are of the highest quality possible helps to effect strong and continued program participation. The reputation of the organization and of the staff is another important consideration in order for the product to be successful. Since people often select programs from organizations with a history of success and quality, this may be the most important consideration in product selection.
- **Promotion.** Some of the best programs are often *best-kept secrets* as well when they are not promoted aggressively and effectively. Promotional material for programs should obviously be directed toward potential program participants, but it should also be directed toward other members of the public who may become interested in the organization as volunteers, potential sponsors, on in some other capacity. It is important to remember that some of the best potential program participants include current members. One of the most successful forms

of promotion is to current members, and this is referred to as **market penetration**, since the promotional activities are designed to further penetrate an already established group. *This group is also an excellent group to ask to convey program information to others.* Promoting programs to individuals who are not already members of the organization is called **market development** and can also be a very successful process. Making promotional material available to target groups that have a high probability of participation and providing similar promotional material to groups that are less likely to become involved is referred to as the **80/20 principal.** In other words, significant time, energy, and money may be spent on getting results that can be counted on in a big way while also spending time, energy, and money on lesser results, because those results are also important. For example, meager results may occur by spending a good deal of time and money to place flyers promoting programs for children on the windshields of cars in a local mall parking lot. The same and possibly less money could be spent on flyers that are delivered directly to children at the local schools, churches, or youth organizations. Both methods can be successful, but one will be more successful and cost less and should be given a higher priority. There are a number of ways to promote program opportunities:

- **Flyers.** Flyers need to be created that are attractive and appealing. They should contain appropriate information, graphics, and have some *open space* to make them easier to read and more appealing. Flyers should answer standard questions, such as (1) *What* is going to happen during this activity and *why?* (2) W*here* will the activity occur? (3) *Who* is organizing the activity? (4) *How* will it benefit the program participants? (5) *How much* will it cost? (6) *What* is the date and time(s) of the activity? (7) *Is there anything* the program participant should do in preparation for the activity? (8) Is *transportation* available for the activity? Any other questions that are applicable to upcoming events should also be answered. Graphics appropriate to the activity should be added, and sometimes a **registration form** may need to be added with spaces for appropriate information about when participants must register for an activity. Colored paper can be eye-catching and add to the appeal of a flyer. Most local printing companies can enlarge flyers to poster size when necessary. Flyers should be posted in highly accessible places well in advance of an activity, typically three weeks to a month. More advanced notice may be required for some programs. Members can be helpful in posting and passing out flyers in their neighborhoods, schools, or places of work. Contests and prizes for volunteers who bring participants in for program activities can also be effective. An example of a program flyer can be found in Figure 5.4 on the next page:

- **Public Service Announcements (PSAs).** Promotional announcements should be provided to local newspapers, television and radio stations with information regarding upcoming services and program opportunities. Including local media in the overall marketing and promotion strategies is an excellent way to promote opportunities and most media organizations are more than will-

Figure 5.4
Promotional Flyer

Make a Difference
in the life of a
Senior Citizen

You can make a difference in the lives of senior citizens in our community by joining the program at the Morganfield Boys and Girls Club. The Boys and Girls Club is located at 1618 Seawall Dr., behind the Southwest Cinema.

The teen program participants meet Thursday evenings from 7-8 p.m. to plan the project beginning April 19.

The project includes recreational activities, crafts, health and fitness, and joint service outings. The project will last 6 months culminating with a big splashdown pool and pizza party.

There is no program fee, but you must be between the ages of 13 –17 and be a member of the Boys and Girls Club.

Call today for more information: Stefani Dowell, **762-3808**.

TEENS
for Seniors

Morganfield Boys and Girls Club

ing to assist in promoting community activities. It can also be advisable to include a member of the local media as a **media sponsor** for a program. As a media sponsor, a radio station for example, might agree do some extra on-air promotional spots and a live segment on the day of the activity. In return, the organization could mention the radio station as one of the sponsors on flyers, t-shirts (if there are any) and in public service announcements. The chances of an organization's programs being included in newspaper and radio spots depend on the excitement generated around a particular activity, the reputation the organization has for providing community services, and the relationships that have been developed with members of the media. The same type of appropriate information should be included in the public service announcement that would be included in a flyer (above). An example of a public service announcement is included in Figure 5.5, on the next page):

- **Displays, Exhibits, and Demonstrations.** Displays are generally two- dimensional, while exhibits are typically three-dimensional, and both can serve as a great way to let the public know about upcoming events as well as about the organization in general. They can be used to attract program participants, volunteers, donors, or other interested parties to the organization. A simple display could be a flyer in the form of a *tent* left on the table of a business, school, doctor's office, or other appropriate location. A more sophisticated display might include a Velcro board with attractive materials attached. An exhibit could include some of the equipment used in various programs, such as life saving apparatuses, and can be displayed appropriately on tables or floors. Demonstrations are a more dynamic approach and can include past program participants demonstrating something they have learned or experienced or it could be the program leader(s) demonstrating an aspect of the upcoming activities. Demonstrations should be rehearsed in order for them to be successful.

- **Newsletters.** Businesses, service associations, and other organizations will sometimes let nonprofit organizations include program activity information in their monthly, quarterly, or biannual newsletters for free. This not only assists the nonprofit organization, but it also provides an additional service to their members. By using publishing software or obtaining sponsors, nonprofit organizations can also develop their own newsletters, which can become excellent outlets for program and service information.

- **Advertising.** It may sometimes be necessary for nonprofit organizations to pay for advertisements in local newspapers and on radio and television stations. Media organizations typically assist the nonprofit organization with content and layout and often provide advertising for a reduced rate. Many media organizations will also provide advertising if they sponsor a particular event or they may provide a **gift-in-kind**, which means that the advertising is the media's way of contributing to the nonprofit organization.

- **Personal Contact.** One of the most effective ways of letting the public know what is coming up programmatically is by word of mouth. People who have

Figure 5.5
Public Service Announcement

Morganfield Boys and Girls Club

1618 Seawall Dr.
Farmington, DE 22904
Phone: 277-762-3808
E-mail: **MBCGA@ORG.COM**

N E W S   R E L E A S E

(For Immediate Release)

The Morganfield Boys and Girls Club is proud to announce the Teens for Seniors program beginning Thursday, April 19, 7 – 8 p.m., in the club facility located at 1618 Seawall Dr. just behind the Southwest Cinema. This program will involve teens between the ages of 13 – 17 spending quality time with senior citizens in local nursing homes and the community seniors center. The program will consist of recreational activities, arts and crafts, health and fitness activities, and a joint service project. The 6-month long project will conclude with a huge splashdown pool & pizza party at the Morganfield Boys and Girls Club swimming pool. There is no cost for the program, but you must be a member of the Morganfield Boys and Girls Club. For more information on the program and membership into the Boys and Girls Club, contact Stefani Dowell at 762-3808.

had good experiences within an organization often willingly and voluntarily tell others about program opportunities. A more formal way of communicating program information is through a **speaker's bureau** made up of staff members and/or volunteers who present program information at club and organizational meetings. This process is an excellent way to provide program information as well as to recruit volunteers and financial support.

- **Informational Packets.** Information in the form of packets, brochures, or newsletters can often be left with the local Chamber of Commerce, United Way, Better Business Bureau, and other key places throughout a community where families and businesses that are new to the community can find out about the organization.

- **Web Site.** Creating and maintaining a web site with current program and organizational information gives both members and prospective members quick access to opportunities within an organization. Promoting the web site through informational packets, flyers, signs, and any other means available will provide the organization with a great deal of exposure.

- **Social Networking.** By incorporating Facebook and Twitter, for example, organizations can promote events by posting information and inviting individuals to join groups in an effort to keep informed on activities, special offers, volunteer opportunities, internships and even career possibilities. Social Networking can be a quick and easy way to promote just about anything an organization wishes to promote.

Designing and implementing promotional material and promotional campaigns is often done by staff members in association with volunteers who possess expertise in marketing and promotion. Most nonprofit organizations have a board committee or group of volunteers created with the primary purpose of promoting the organization, program activities, and any other services. When effectively designed and implemented, promotional activities can be both fun and rewarding.

- **Price.** Price is a significant aspect in the selection process of choosing a particular program, and if all things are equal, price can be the determining factor. Generally speaking, individuals select the product, service, or program that is the least expensive if quality and other factors are fairly equal. However, cost is sometimes associated with value, and a program must be perceived to have *real value* in order to be desirable. So it is important for an organization to keep cost at a minimum in order to be competitive and be cost-effective for its members, while establishing a sense that the program is of *real value*. The cost of the program must also fit into the budgetary requirements established for programs. Staff members of nonprofit organizations usually set pricing for programs, sometimes with input from board members, and with the approval of the board of directors. Organizations with national and/or regional affiliations often receive assistance in setting fair and effective prices. Most nonprofit organizations set up scholarships, a sliding scale system, and/or payment plans for individuals who qualify for financial assistance.

- **Place.** The location of the facility or space where programs or services are offered is a significant consideration. The location must first be accessible to the targeted group of potential participants. Sometimes this means making programs and services *outreach* activities that are delivered to the targeted group through mobile or satellite units. The facility or space must be a desirable location for programs and services and, above all else, it must be clean and safe and be perceived as clean and safe by the community. Program space must also adhere to local health, safety, environmental, and fire codes.

Promoting programs and services for a nonprofit organization is a vital and exciting aspect of program development and must be well thought out, comprehensive, and focused both on the present and the future. Organizations with an eye toward quality, which are effective at program and service promotion, are generally successful in attracting participants, volunteers and financial support.

Step 11 – Program or Project Budget. Successful nonprofit organizations require a **program** or **project budget** prepared in advance of each activity. This should be a separate budget from the **operating budget**, the budget the organization uses to operate on for a **fiscal** or financial year, but it folds into the operating budget. The program budget includes a total of the **estimated expenses** and a total of the **estimated income** or **revenue.** Estimated expenses include any projected costs for a specific program. These expenses might include such items as supplies and materials, equipment, postage, food, travel, and personnel hired just for a specific program. Estimated income would include any fees or contributions that are received for the use of a specific program. Estimated expenses and income can be summarized on a PPW such as the one in Figure 5.2.

Programs may be projected to have a **gain**, which means there is more income projected than expenses, or to have a **deficit**, which means the expenses are projected to exceed the income. Deficits are almost always listed in parentheses. Programs are usually planned to realize a gain or at least to break even, but some programs are considered so important they will continue to be implemented by an organization with the idea that the money will be made up in some other way. Once a program is completed there is a place on the PPW (see Figure 5.2) to include the **actual income** as well as the **actual expenses** and a space for the **actual gain** or **deficit.** This provides staff and board members with financial information regarding each program. For instance, the Teens for Seniors program mentioned previously might have an income based on projected sponsorships and expenses projected on the basis of planned activities. This would provide some budgetary guidelines for the program staff to work with. The actual income and expenses would be listed once the program was completed and would provide much-needed financial information for the program (See Figure 5.6 on the next page):

Income and expenses can be broken down further on a separate ledger for a detailed analysis of costs versus revenue. Recording expenses and revenues for each program on the PPW as well as in a ledger also provides financial information if and when similar programs are considered in the future.

Some organizations also keep an accounting of how much time professional and volunteer staff members spend with specific programs, along with how much overhead expense, such as utilities and rent, is incorporated in each program. This is sometimes referred to as **indirect** or **functional** cost.

Figure 5.6
Program or Project Budget

Program Budget for Teens for Seniors

	Income	Expenses	Gain/Deficit
Estimated	$500	$300	+ $200
Actual	$580	$380	+ $200

Step 12 – Walk-Through/Rehearsal. Before the actual implementation of any program or activity, it can be a good idea to do a visual and/or physical walk-through or rehearsal. This provides the program committee a chance to visualize and prepare for most aspects of the program, such as where equipment is to be set and where staff and volunteer members are to be stationed. It provides the committee with the opportunity to estimate spatial needs and examine equipment, materials, and supplies. A walk-through allows committee members an opportunity to review checklists and to become familiar with the layout of the program areas. Most importantly, it provides them with time to review the risk management plan and to be certain all aspects of the plan are in place.

Step 13 – Implementation and Supervision. The implementation step is the time in which the program or activity actually begins. The plans and steps that have been developed up to this date provide a structure and some guidelines on how to proceed with the program or activity. This is the time to follow carefully developed plans, monitor the progress of each aspect of the program, and make changes if necessary. Almost no program goes exactly according to plan, and ingenuity and flexibility are necessary character traits if and when things go awry.

Determining which leadership or supervisory style to adopt with specific programs is a lifelong endeavor (see Chapter 2). Studies indicate there is really no ideal leadership style for a given program (Edginton and Ford 1985), which means the leadership or supervisory style depends on the circumstances, the maturity of the staff and volunteers, and other dynamics that are involved with each activity. It means that individuals in leadership positions must develop leadership skills and knowledge and be flexible enough to incorporate appropriate concepts and actions when necessary. For instance, incorporating the Tri-Dimensional Leader Effectiveness Model (Situational Leadership), described in Chapter 2, Figure 2.4, as a supervisory strategy allows a supervisor to be flexible and lead differently under different circumstances. The same thing can be said of Collaborative Leadership, discussed in Chapter 2 along with Comprehensive Leadership, which is also outlined in Figure 2.6.

Good nonprofit organizations encourage leadership training for administrative program staff. These organizations typically provide training in the form of workshops, seminars, and conferences, sometimes offered as in-service opportunities. Some nonprofit organizations also support advanced, formal educational opportunities by offering financial assistance for tuition and/or rewards for advanced educational work (Weis and Gantt 2004).

Step 14 – Special Considerations. Staff and volunteer members should have training and should always be well prepared for special situations and individuals with special needs. Programs must be designed to meet the special needs of individuals, and often the diversity of individuals with special needs adds depth to program intent. Special needs may take the form of **medical problems,** such as diabetes, AIDS, or epilepsy. They could take the form of various **physical disabilities,** such as cerebral palsy and multiple sclerosis, or **psychological disorders** that include autism and psychosis, as examples. Severe **behavioral maladjustment** would include a condition such as attention deficit disorder (with hyperactivity). There are a number of **communication problems** that need to be considered, such as speech difficulties, hearing impairments, and language barriers (Weis and Gantt 2002). Some of these conditions may require staff and volunteers with specific training and qualifications. Others may require a certain staff-to-member ratio, and even special materials and equipment. Policies and procedures for handling individuals with special needs must be in place prior to program development. These policies and procedures must be inclusive, fair, effective, and within legal guidelines. They must be reviewed and approved by the board of directors of the organization.

Another special consideration when developing programs is the issue of **abuse** and **neglect.** In the course of offering programs and services, nonprofit leaders sometimes encounter children, senior citizens, spouses, and others who may have been or are being abused or neglected. Some **characteristics** of individuals who have been abused may include (Weis and Gantt):

- Feelings of inadequacy
- Listlessness and depression
- Lack of joy and excitement
- Unexplained bruises and abrasions
- Difficulties with relationships
- Aggressiveness
- Reluctance to receive praise and/or physical affection
- Thin or emaciated appearance

It is important to note that there might be other characteristics to suggest abuse or neglect and that the presence of any of the characteristics above doesn't necessarily mean that abuse or neglect is occurring. However, if a program leader suspects abuse or neglect he or she should follow the guidelines listed below:

- Report the suspected abuse or neglect to a supervisor.
- The supervisor should contact the organization's director.
- The director may decide to gather further information if further information seems necessary. Oftentimes, however, immediate action is called for.
- If abuse or neglect is still suspected, it must be reported to the

appropriate, local authorities as quickly as possible. In most instances, reporting possible abuse and neglect situations is a legal responsibility as well as being the right thing to do.

- An incident report should be completed documenting what occurred and what procedures were taken.
- Some organizations may require incidents of abuse and neglect be reported to a specific board member or committee.

If there is ever any question of abuse or neglect, it is imperative to follow the guidelines above and report suspected incident(s) without delay.

■ Final (Evaluation) Stage

The final stage of program development includes an effective and thorough evaluation process, which is important for a number of reasons: (1) it helps determine whether the program was successful and the program objectives were met; (2) the information is important in helping staff and volunteer members make constructive changes for the future; (3) it provides board members with the type of information important in determining if the organization is on the right track; (4) it gives program participants an opportunity to express their concerns, suggestions, and praise regarding activities that affect their lives; (5) the results may be reported to the media so that community members are kept abreast of the benefits of the organization; and (6) evaluation results are essential for accrediting bodies and financial sponsors, such as corporations or the United Way. This stage also includes the process of analyzing and reporting program results and making recommendations and changes for the future.

Step 15 – Evaluation Process. There are essentially four activities that need to occur in an evaluation process (Edginton and Edginton 1994):

- Determining which individual(s) should be involved in the process
- Determining what exactly needs to be evaluated
- Selecting the type(s) of evaluation
- Implementing the method(s) of evaluation

Which individuals should be involved in the evaluation process? There are a number of individuals who can and should be involved in the evaluation process. To begin with, the participants of the program are the primary individuals who need to be involved in the evaluation process because they are the individuals most affected by the program. If the participants are too young, or for some reason they are unable to respond to the evaluation, parents, guardians, or caretakers may be asked to assist. In addition to the participants, program staff, volunteers, collaborating agency members, sponsors, and anyone associated with the program can participate in the evaluation process.

What needs to be evaluated? Two major areas need to be measured regarding the success of the program to determine if the program met the program objectives and to what degree: **quantitative** measurements and **qualitative** measurements. In other words, did the program meet the numerical objectives, and did it make a difference and have a positive impact?

Numerical (quantitative) measurements could include the number of participants, the number of activities, and any financial objectives. Qualitative measurements help determine whether the program made a difference in specific areas such as knowledge, skills, health, and attitude.

In addition to providing information that helps to determine if objectives were met, evaluation processes can provide information regarding the overall quality of the staff, facilities, supplies, and materials. Other areas that can be examined include program accessibility and affordability, and any other aspect of a program that needs to be assessed.

Selecting the Type(s) of evaluation. In general, there are two major types of evaluation. The first type can be incorporated at various stages of the program; the second type is used at the end of a program:

- **Formative Evaluation.** A formative evaluation can be implemented at various stages while a program is being implemented to help determine whether changes need to be made while activities are in process. The advantage of this type of evaluation is obvious: constructive changes can be made before the program ends. The disadvantage is that it is one more task that can be time-consuming and therefore difficult to include.

- **Summative Evaluation.** This type of evaluation is done at the end of the program and provides feedback to determine whether the program met its objectives, and it provides information for making changes to a program in the future. Incorporating a summative or final evaluation at the end of a program is simpler and less time-consuming, but the disadvantage is that it will not help address changes that may need to be made during the implementation of an activity.

Implementing Methods of Evaluation. Programs can and should be evaluated incorporating a number of different methods. Select methodology is discussed below:

- **Observations.** Observation can be a legitimate form of evaluation that provides the evaluator with personal and immediate information. Although not as objective and often not as formal as other methodologies, observation provides a sensory assessment that cannot be duplicated.

- **Interview.** Conducting interviews provides the evaluator with a broad range of information. Questions should be designed from general to specific, and flexibility should be built in to ask other questions based on the responses. Interviews can be done in person, via telephone and e-mail or any other viable way, and the issue of confidentiality should be addressed up front. As an evaluation tool, interviews can be highly focused and valuable, but can be time-consuming. Example interview questions are listed in Figure 5.7. The evaluator should remember to remain flexible and to insert other questions based on the responses of the interviewees.

- **Focus Group.** Recruiting several people together at the same time for interviews provides the evaluator with a broad range of information and a synergy that is difficult to duplicate with interviews. Again, questions should be designed from general to specific, and flexibility should be built in to ask other questions based on the responses of the participants. Questions can be patterned after the interview questions in Figure 5.7.

- **Evaluation Survey.** Providing program participants with a way to report their experiences and assuring anonymity with a survey increases the likelihood the responses will be objective and more honest (Russell and Jamieson 2008). As

Figure 5.7
Example Interview Questions

1. What did you think of the Teens for Seniors program?
2. Was the program beneficial? For whom?
3. What did you like best about the program? Least?
4. Was it offered at a convenient time?
5. Was the program accessible for you?
6. Were the trainers/counselors helpful?
7. What would you change about the program?
8. Would you recommend this program to others?
9. Is there anything else you would like to say about the program?

with interviews and focus groups, questions should go from broad to specific and seek to assess any important aspect of a program. Questions can be turned into statements for use with the Likert Scale, and each statement should address only one aspect of the program. An example evaluation survey to be administered to the teenage participants is included in Figure 5.8 on the next page.

- **Pre/Post Test or Survey.** Providing a pre-test to participants prior to a program and then providing the same test following a program is an excellent way of determining whether real changes and impact have been made (Russell and Jamieson 2008). Knowledge, attitude, character, and skills are just a few areas that can be tested with a pre/post test to determine change. The pre-test and post-test must have correlative identification such as numbers and be completed by the same individual and scored accordingly. An example pre/post is included in Figure 5.9 on page 169.

The pre/post test above measures the participants' perception of knowledge, attitude, skills, and self-esteem regarding their experience and would be given to teenagers prior to the beginning of the program and again once the program was completed. The resulting scores will help the evaluators determine the degree of effectiveness of the program in a number of different areas.

Effective evaluation processes can be very helpful in determining whether or not programs are meeting their objectives and whether they are quality programs. The process also encourages communication between program staff members, volunteer members, and participants and provides helpful program information for the future. This information can also be used to develop funding, as a part of the promotion process, and for marketing processes as well.

Step 16 – Record and Report Results. Evaluation results need to be assimilated and recorded on the Program Planning Worksheet and maintained in a permanent file for future reference. This can provide invaluable information for future programs. The results

Figure 5.8
Example Evaluation Survey

Teens for Seniors Program Evaluation

In order to help us evaluate the Teens for Seniors program and plan for future programs, we would like you to complete the following survey. The survey is anonymous and no one will know the result of your responses. When you have completed the survey, please drop it in the box marked "Surveys" on the table near the exit. Thank you for participating in the Teens for Seniors program and for completing the survey.

Indicate the number that reflects your response to each statement based on the following scale:

	1 Strongly Disagree	2 Disagree	3 Undecided	4 Agree	5 Strongly Agree
1. The Teens for Seniors program was effective.	☐	☐	☐	☐	☐
2. I am now more comfortable with senior citizens.	☐	☐	☐	☐	☐
3. The recreational aspects of the program were successful.	☐	☐	☐	☐	☐
4. The crafts aspect of the program was important.	☐	☐	☐	☐	☐
5. The health and fitness aspects of the program were effective.	☐	☐	☐	☐	☐
6. The joint service outings were successful.	☐	☐	☐	☐	☐
7. The trainers did a good job in preparing us.	☐	☐	☐	☐	☐
8. The meeting location was convenient.	☐	☐	☐	☐	☐
9. I would recommend the program to a friend.	☐	☐	☐	☐	☐

Comments/suggestions: _____

_____

_____

Figure 5.9
Example Pre/Post Test

Teens for Seniors Program
Pre/Post Test or Survey

In order to help us determine various changes that might have occurred during the Teens for Seniors program, we would like you to complete the following Pre/Post Test. Be certain that your Pre-Test number correlates with your Post-Test number and thank you for participating in the survey and the program.

Indicate the number that reflects your response to each statement based on the following scale:

	1 Strongly Disagree	2 Disagree	3 Undecided	4 Agree	5 Strongly Agree
1. I am comfortable being around senior citizens.	☐	☐	☐	☐	☐
2. Senior citizens can make a positive contribution to their community.	☐	☐	☐	☐	☐
3. I am making a positive difference in my community.	☐	☐	☐	☐	☐
4. I am able to lead recreational activities with senior citizens.	☐	☐	☐	☐	☐
5. I am able to lead crafts activities with senior citizens.	☐	☐	☐	☐	☐
6. I can work effectively with senior citizens in making a difference in our community through service projects.	☐	☐	☐	☐	☐
7. I feel good about myself.	☐	☐	☐	☐	☐

Comments/suggestions _____

_____

_____

_____

_____

of each program should be discussed by the program and volunteer staff members and with the participants when applicable. Program evaluation results are sometimes reviewed by the program committee of the board of directors and even by the entire board of directors. They may also be used as a part of personnel evaluations. The results of successful programs should also be reported to the media and included in the organization's promotional material.

Step 17 – Formulate Recommendations for Future Program. Program staff and volunteer members, along with a select group of program participants should discuss recommendations for future programs based, in part, on the resulting program evaluations. Recommendations for future programs will provide insight for the focus of programs and can be recorded on the Program Planning Worksheet and filed for future reference.

Providing programs that meet and exceed the expectations of customers and provide them with positive outcomes is both exciting and rewarding, and it requires a good deal of expertise in planning, implementation, and evaluation. This customer-centered/benefits approach to program development provides a step by step planning process intended to offer guidance and support for program development. Action steps or work tasks can be derived from the program planning steps. As mentioned earlier in this chapter, programs can and often do change directions in all stages for one reason or another, and flexibility and innovation are required characteristics for leaders in the nonprofit area. A simplified, simulated program plan is included in Figure 5.10 on the next page.

■ A Plan to Improve Customer Service

In addition to providing the best programs possible, organizations must also strive to deliver the best **customer service** as well (Russell and Jamieson 2008). Customer service is anything that helps a customer or member realize the full value of a product or service (David and Uttal 1989). This could include providing effective information and assistance whenever and however it is needed. Davidow and Uttal (1989) developed a six-point plan to address customer service:

1. **Devise a service strategy.**
   This involves understanding what customers or members expect then developing services to match those expectations. This helps an organization prepare plans for many different scenarios.
2. **Encourage top management to set examples.**
   It is important that top level management walk the talk and have a genuine passion for great customer service and demonstrate that passion every day. It needs to be understood that customer service is everyone's job not just those working on the line.
3. **Concentrate on motivating and training employees.**
   The first step in this part of the process is to hire the best personnel possible then train them in the most effective ways of solid customer service for the organization. Always acknowledge personnel when they succeed with good customer service strategies and activities.
4. **Design services that make good customer service possible.**
   The kind of services that will most often be needed can be anticipated and a

Figure 5.10
Simulated Program Plan (page 1)

Date **09** / **25** / **11**

Name of Organization   **Morganfield Boys and Girls Club**

Name of Program/Project   **Teens for Seniors**

Program Coordinator   **Julie Weston**

Program Members:

	Name	Address	Phone Number	e-mail address
1	**Julie Weston**	**1407 Wall St.**	**762-4791**	**j.weston@b&gca.org**
2	**L.W. Perdue**	**131 Camile Dr.**	**762-0101**	**lw.perdue@bas.org**
3	**Vivian Perdue**	**7229 Opal St.**	**753-1098**	**v.perdue@bas.org**
4	**Virginia Kenova**	**1413 Carol Dr.**	**759-2038**	**v.kenova@lol.org**

Program Objectives **The Teens for Seniors program provides teenagers in the Morganfield area opportunities to assist senior citizens attending the Westview Day Care program. Teens will be trained to participate with seniors in social, cultural, service, and recreational activities. Intended objectives include**

- A minimum of 10 teenagers involved in a program with a minimum of 25 senior citizens meeting once a week for activities

- Improved inter-generational understanding

- Increased flexibility on the part of senior citizens

- Decreased depression on the part of senior citizens

- Enhanced self-esteem of teenagers and senior citizens

- Increased sense of responsibility and caring on the part of teenagers

- Improved teamwork, communication, recreation, socialization and leadership skills on the part of the teenagers

Estimated Direct Expenses $340	Estimated Direct Income $500 (sponsorship)	Gain (Deficit) $160
Actual Direct Costs $270	Actual Direct Income $480	Gain (Deficit) $210

Action Steps or Work Tasks	Person(s) Responsible	Completion Dates
1. **Formulate Committee**	**Weston**	**October 1**
2. **Conduct Needs Assessment**	**V.Perdue**	**October 9**
3. **Review Developmental Theories, Issues, and Values**	**Weston**	**October 11**
4. **Determine Program Objectives**	**Committee**	**October 13**
5. **Develop Program Concept & Format**	**Weston**	**October 14**
6. **Evaluate Resources**	**Committee**	**October 15**
7. **Identify Potential Program Risks**	**Committee**	**October 20**
8. **Prioritize Program Risks**	**Committee**	**October 20**
9. **Develop Plan for Handling Risks**	**Committee**	**October 21**
10. **Evaluate Insurance Coverage**	**Weston**	**October 22**

Figure 5.11
Simulated Program Plan (page 2)

Action Steps or Work Tasks	Person(s) Responsible	Completion Dates
11. Prepare Participant Waiver Forms	Committee	October 23
12. Meeting to Develop Plan for Promoting Program	Committee	October 25
13. Develop Flyers & PSAs	L.W. Perdue	October 26
14. Develop Promotional Event	V.Perdue	October 27
15. Establish Program Budget	LPerdue	November 1
16. Plan for Special Considerations	Weston	November 5
17. Post Flyers	L.W.Perdue	November 9
18. Release PSAs	L.W. Perdue	November 9
19. Conduct Promotional Event	V. Perdue	November 9
20. Walk-Through/Rehearsal	Whole Committee	November 10
21. Participants Sign Waiver Forms	V. Perdue	November 15
22. Implement and Monitor Program	Whole Committee	December 1
23. Conduct Formative Evaluations	V.Perdue	January 15
24. Conduct Final Evaluations	V. Perdue	March 1
25. Record Results on PPW	Kenova	March 5
26. Report Results to Board & Media	Weston	March 6
27. Formulate & Record Future Recommendations (PPW)	Whole Committee	March 15

Evaluation Results   **The Teens for Seniors program was evaluated primarily through observation and a final evaluation. A summary of the evaluation administered to the teenage participants follows:**

Summary of Evaluation

Number of Respondents: 10

Statement	Average Score
1. The Teens for Seniors program was effective.	4.9
2. I am more now more comfortable with senior citizens.	4.5
3. The recreational activities were successful.	4.3
4. The crafts aspect of the program was important	4.4
5. The health & fitness aspects of the program were effective	4.6
6. The joint service outings were successful.	4.8
7. The trainers did a good job in preparing us.	4.1
8. The meeting location was convenient.	4.7
9. I would recommend the program to a friend.	5.0

Comments/Suggestions: **I loved the program and would do it again!**

Need more time for preparation.

Training could have been more comprehensive

Recommendations for Future Programs **Based on observation, informal interviews, and the final evaluation, it seems that the program basically met the objectives and in some cases exceeded expectations. It is recommended that the program be repeated annually or more often if appropriate. Suggestions for changes include a longer preparation time and a more thorough training period.**

system designed to meet needs efficiently and effectively (Weis and Gantt 2004). Constantly reviewing customer service strategies helps an organization stay in touch with customer and membership needs.

5. **Invest in service infrastructure**.

   To be successful, organizations must invest in the kinds of resources that will help employees deliver the best customer services possible. Computer hardware and software need to be updated constantly with a good support system and training readily available. Leaders must consistently assess that the infrastructure matches the needs of customers.

6. **Monitor achievement of customer service goals.**

   Continuous monitoring of the success of customer service is essential in being certain that customer service goals are being met. The monitoring process can take the form of focus groups, individual interviews and evaluation surveys for example and should be a priority of any organization that wants to succeed. This kind of information can be essential for improving processes and activities and maintaining a strong base of customer respect and support.

◼ Summary

Programs should be designed to meet the objectives and goals of the organization and to meet and exceed the expectations of the customers while providing them with positive outcomes. This customer-centered/benefits approach to program development requires that staff and volunteer members be committed to the organization, to quality programs, and to the customers or members. Programs must be designed to meet and exceed the general standards and expectations of the constituents.

Program development can be divided into three interrelated stages: (1) Initial (Planning) Stage, (2) Middle (Planning/Implementation) Stage, and (3) Final (Evaluation) Stage (PIE). Each of these stages can be divided into specific steps that can be modified or simplified depending on the circumstances. The sequence of steps can also be changed if necessary.

The Initial Stage of program development is important because it builds the foundation for later stages. This stage includes selecting a program committee to organize the project, surveying membership needs, reviewing developmental theories and relevant issues, including values and character education, and then determining objectives for the program. Once program objectives have been decided, a program concept and format must be developed to ensure the objectives are achieved. This stage is concluded once resources necessary for the program, such as personnel, time, space, and money, are evaluated.

The Middle Stage of program development begins with the most important step in the whole planning process, developing a system to keep all risks involved in any program to an absolute minimum. The next step in this stage is to create a comprehensive marketing plan for generating promotional material. Another step in this stage is to design a Program Budget in order to record the estimated and actual expenses and the income for each individual program.

Conducting a walk-through or rehearsal for each program allows the program staff to visualize and prepare for most aspects of a program. Understanding leadership and supervisory styles is also important, so nonprofit leaders can incorporate appropriate concepts and actions when necessary in supervising others in program delivery. And finally, being trained and prepared for special situations and individuals with special needs is vital to the overall success of program development.

In the Final Evaluation Stage, the program must be evaluated to help determine whether it was successful and met its objectives. This information can also be helpful for staff and volunteer members in making changes for future programs as well as for sponsoring organizations to determine if their sponsorship is worthwhile. Some ways programs can be evaluated are through observation, interviews, focus groups, and surveys.

Program results should be recorded on the Program Planning Worksheet and reported as is appropriate. Reports might be made to a board of directors or to a committee within the board. Other reports may be presented to sponsoring entities, to the news media, and they may be included in the organization's communications materials. It is particularly important that recommendations for the future be recorded and kept readily available for future programming staff.

This chapter addressed, in part, the Nonprofit Leadership Alliance Certification Competency Requirements of Nonprofit Program Planning, Nonprofit Marketing, and Nonprofit Risk Management.

■ **Reflections and Application**

1. How can the concept *customer-centered/benefits approach* help you in planning effective programs?

_____

_____

_____

2. What are the advantages to this kind of approach?

_____

_____

_____

3. Describe the key parts of a program objective?

_____

_____

_____

4. What is the difference between a program concept and a program format?

_____

_____

_____

5. How does a program budget fit into the fiscal, operational budget?

_____

_____

_____

6. Design a needs-assessment plan to develop a program scenario.

_____

_____

_____

7. After developing a program scenario, design a risk management plan.

_____

_____

_____

8. Using the same scenario, develop a comprehensive marketing plan.

_____

_____

_____

9. Finally, develop a plan to evaluate the program.

_____

_____

_____

10. Develop a list of nonprofit leaders to see about shadowing the staff during a day a program is implemented. Describe what you experienced:

_____

_____

_____

■ References

Albrecht, K. M., and Zemke, R. (1985). *Service America!*. Homewood, IL: Dow Jones-Irwin.

Bagozzi, R. P., (1975). Marketing as exchange. *Journal of Marketing* 39:32-39.

Bush, P. (1972). *A Program Course for Writing of Performance Objectives*. Chico, CA: North California Program Development Center.

Covey, S. R. (1989). *The Seven Habits of Highly Effective People*. New York: Simon and Schuster.

Davidow, W.H. and Uttal, B. (1989) *Total Customer Service: The Ultimate Weapon*. New York: HarperCollins.

Edginton, C.R., Ford, P.F., and Hudson, S.D. (1999). *Leadership in Recreation and Leisure Service Organizations*. Champaign, IL: Sagamore Publishing.

Edginton, C. R., Hanson, C. J., Edginton, S. R., and Hudson, S. D. (1998). *Leisure Programming: A Service-Centered and Benefits Approach*. Boston, MA: McGraw-Hill.

Edginton, S. R., and Edginton, C. R. (1994). *Youth Programs: Promoting Quality Services*. Champaign, IL: Sagamore Publishing.

Hardy, J. M. (1984). *Managing for Impact in Nonprofit Organizations*. Erwin, TN: Essex Press.

Jordan, D. J. (1992). Risk management guidelines. *Journal of Physical Education, Recreation, and Dance*. Cedar Falls, IA: University of Northern Iowa.

Kaplan, P. S. (1998). *The Human Odyssey: Life Span Development*. Pacific Grove, CA: Brooks/Cole Publishing Company.

Kotler, P. (1982). *Marketing for Nonprofit Organizations*. 2d ed. Englewood Cliffs: N.J.: Prentice Hall.

Maslow, A. H. (1943). A theory of human motivation. *Psychological Review* July, 370-96.

Mohr, L. B. (1988). *Impact Analysis for Program Evaluation*. Chicago: Dorsey Press.

Purpel, D. and Ryan, K. (1976). *Moral Education: It Comes with the Territory*. Berkeley, CA: McCutcheon Publishing Corporation.

Rathmell, J. M. (1974). *Marketing in the Service Sector*. Cambridge, MA: Winthrop Publications.

Russell, R., and Jamieson, L. (2008). *Leisure Program Planning and Delivery*. Champaign, IL: Human Kinetics.

Rea, L. M., and Parker, R. A. (1992). *Designing and Conducting Survey Research: A Comprehensive Guide*. San Francisco: Jossey-Bass.

Stern, G. J. (1990). *Marketing Workbook for Nonprofit Organizations*. St. Paul, MN: Amherst H. Wilder Foundation.

Thomas, J. C. (1994). "Program evaluation and program development." In *The Jossey-Bass Handbook of Nonprofit Leadership and Management*. San Francisco: Jossey-Bass Publishers

Van der Smissen, B. (1990). *Legal Liability and Risk Management for Public and Private Entities* (Vol.2). Cincinnati, OH: Anderson.

Walton, M. (1998). *The Demming Management Model*. New York: Perigee.

Weis, R.M., and Gantt, V.W. (2004). *Knowledge and Skill Development in Nonprofit Organizations.* Peosta, IA: E. Bowers Publishing.

Weis, R. M. and Gantt, V.W. (2002). *Leadership and Program Development in Nonprofit Organizations.* Peosta, IA: E. Bowers Publishing.

Weiss, C. H. (1972). *Evaluation Research: Methods of Assessing Program Effectiveness.* Englewood Cliffs, N.J.: Prentice-Hall.

Wolf, T. (1999). *Managing a Nonprofit Organization.* New York: Prentice Hall.

6 Financial Resource Development and Management

The role of financial resource development and management in successful nonprofit organizations continues to gain importance and appreciation as a result of a number of significant changes in the nonprofit sector. What started as one of the natural strategies through which people expressed their early voluntary spirit and organized to build the country, has become a measurable part of the gross domestic product, employment, and human services delivery system. The sector has grown into what many call the "third sector," taking its place of importance along side of the for profit business and government sectors of society.

What was once considered to be an afterthought or necessary evil, finding the money to pay the costs of voluntary actions, is now considered one of the most important elements of effective nonprofit sector leadership. Nonprofit programs once operated from a perspective that good work would naturally translate into sustainable funding. A lot has changed and continues to change nonprofit funding. Difficult economic times bring a pressure that can promote a **zero-sum** perspective that makes nonprofit leaders feel like they are competing with each other for a limited and shrinking pool of funds. Shifting political focus often accompanies economic challenges and can promote devolution of government relationships with human services. Government devolution is a complex process involving changes in regulation, funding, and service delivery. It is a shift in the responsibility for providing and funding services from government to the community. In some cases, if a profit can be generated, the business sector responds to the opportunity. However, for the vast majority of human service programs and services, the nonprofit sector is the only system available to respond. The financial resources of the nonprofit sector are significantly less than those in government. So, the nonprofit sector needs the highest possible quality financial development and management to respond to the shift in funding support.

Nonprofit sector leaders recognize the critical intersection of the organization's successful response to community needs and the **public will** necessary to support and sustain the work. The case for sustainability is based on the value the community places on the services provided, regardless of the funding sources. The assumption is that if the services are valued, the financial resources will follow. While it may not always be the case, it is one basis upon which leadership is increasingly committed to demonstrating program value and effective **financial stewardship**. This framing of the role of financial resources in the nonprofit sector requires everyone working in the sector to have an appropriate level of related appreciation, understanding, and skills. For example, people working in the delivery of programs and services for large nonprofit organizations, at a minimum, need to be able to participate in program budget development and appreciate the role their programs play in building and maintaining public support for the organizations. A large proportion of the nonprofit sector is composed of small to mid-sized organizations in which most staff members are required to play a range of financial roles that may include fund raising, budgeting development, and financial reporting, among other responsibilities. A lot of the detailed financial resource development and management work may be done by specialists, including book keepers, accountants, tax preparers, financial managers, etc. However, a successful career in the nonprofit sector, regardless of role, is supported by quality financial resource development and management skills and the ability to work effectively with specialists. Nonprofit leaders want staff who understand the importance of financial resource development and management and who have related skills to bring to the organization.

This chapter is dedicated to promoting a fuller appreciation and understanding of the role of financial resource development and management in the ongoing leadership and operation of nonprofit organizations. There are three major areas to consider in this chapter regarding fiscal matters: (1) financial management or budgeting, (2) financial processes or accounting, and (3) financial development or fundraising. The chapter will explore these three areas, how they relate, and how they are integrated with other aspects of organizational leadership and development.

■ Financial Management

Good nonprofit financial management involves an annual planning process that is typically a part of a five-year rolling plan for financing the organization. At the end of each year, the plan rolls forward one year so that at any given time the organization has a financial plan for the next five years. The financial plan describes how the organization will cover the cost of its operations. The term "budgeting" is often used to describe this planning process. The resulting **operating budget** is an organization's plan for the financial or **fiscal** year, that specifies how much **income** or **revenue** it expects to generate and how much it anticipates it will cost in **expenses** to operate for the same period. A typical "income and expense" operating budget is present in Figure 6.1 below.

A fiscal year often aligns with the calendar year, from January 1 to December 31. Other fiscal years are chosen because the work of the organization aligns with other budget processes, like the traditional school year of September 1 to August 31, the typical government budgeting year of July 1 to June 31, or a different fiscal period dictated by another funding source like United Way or a grant making foundation. A nonprofit organization can select any dates for its fiscal year as long as it specifies these dates in its articles of incorporation and has a financial management system that allows it to track and report budget activity at any given time during the period.

As shown in Figure 6.1, the operating budget is generally divided into two major sections, **income** or **revenue** and **expenses**. These sections are often further divided into additional levels of detail by identifying **income categories** and **expense categories**. Each specific expense and income category is listed on a "separate line" with a certain dollar amount shown to the side, and for this reason these categories are referred to as **line items.** It is up to the organization to decide which line items (or categories) to include. For instance in the expense section, all salaries may go in one line item and employee benefits may make up another. In the income section, all membership fees may be listed as one line item while program fees may make up another. (Weis and Gantt 2004)

Figure 6.1
Simulated Operating Budget for a Fiscal Year

Income		Expenses	
Membership fees	$95,000	Salaries	$93,000
Program fees	27,000	Benefits	17,000
Special Events	20,000	Activity Supplies	14,000
United Way	15,000	Utilities	24,000
Foundation Grants	12,000	Facility cost	10,000
Annual Campaign	25,000	Telephone cost	9,000
Total	194,000	Postage	3,000
		Contingency/reserve	23,000
			194,000

Developing a Budget

Budget development is the core of the financial planning process, and it is important to have specific guidelines to follow when developing the budget that will help support the organization for the coming fiscal year. Each nonprofit organization needs to develop its own budgeting guidelines, to alignment with the size and scope the organization's finances, to most effectively engage the human resources available, and to complement the management and leadership approaches in practice. The following steps are recommended in preparing a budget and are derived in part from Wolf (1999), Weis and Gantt (2004), and Zieltow, Hankin and Seidner (2007):

Step 1: Develop a List of Expenses. Budgets need to be prepared months in advance of a fiscal year by the administrative staff, with input from the program staff and guidance from financial committee members of the board of directors. These individuals must consider and make a projection of all of the expenses necessary to operate the organization for a fiscal year.

Administrative staff members should (1) look at expenses from previous budgets to develop a sense of what costs have been in the past, (2) estimate any changes in those costs, and (3) envision future needs and what those needs will cost the organization to operate effectively. To be as accurate as possible, leaders should seek input from all staff members of the organization, as well as from board members, before making projections about expenses. Expenses should be estimated on the high side, with room for unexpected expenses to be considered.

Step 2: Determine Sources of Revenue. Once a list of projected expenses is developed, a process follows to determine sources of income. Administrative leaders, with input from the program staff and guidance and approval from the financial committee of the board of directors, develop a list of sources of revenue to pay for the projected expenses. This can be accomplished by (1) looking at revenue sources from previous budgets to get an idea of potential areas of income generation and by (2) looking at new areas of financial development. Many organizations have a financial development committee comprised of staff and board members whose job it is to generate potential revenue sources. Income projections should be kept on the low side, and allowances must be made for possible discrepancies in income projections and lower-than-projected actual income outcomes.

Step 3: Comparing Expenses with Revenue. Once the projected revenue and expense lists have been developed, it is time for the administrative staff and financial committee members of the board to determine whether the projected revenue will cover projected expenses. If the projected revenue covers or exceeds the projected list of expenses, then the budget could move forward toward the approval phase of the budgeting process. If, on the other hand, the projected revenue does not cover the projected list of expenses, then a number of considerations can be undertaken.

First of all, each administrative and program need should be evaluated carefully. After close scrutiny, some of the expenses may be eliminated, or at least the cost reduced. One way to do this would be through a process referred to as **zero-based budgeting** in which no historical base is recognized for expenses and each expense line begins with a clean slate. This process provides an opportunity to examine exactly what is needed to cover the cost of each organizational need. For instance, in looking at telephone costs, it could be advantageous to consider other, less expensive telephone service providers, as long as the service is still effective. A change in providers can save an organization hundreds or even thousands of dollars each year.

The same process could be used in hiring a consulting firm for accounting and bookkeeping processes or any number of other organizational operations, rather than maintaining full-time staff for these functions. Even though it is generally more time consuming, zero-based budgeting can be very effective in eliminating unnecessary expenses and should be considered when balancing expenses with income. Another way to meet organizational costs would be to look at the revenue side of the budget to determine other ways to enhance or develop new income streams to cover expenses.

Step 4: Setting Administrative and Program Priorities. Once expense and revenue potential have been reviewed and assessed, organizational leaders should schedule a priority-setting session. This session should help in determining the need for specific programs and administrative operations. Several key questions need to be asked in this session:

- Which programs are central to the purpose of the organization?
- Which programs are cost effective and how important is this consideration?
- Which administrative operations are essential to the overall success of the organization, and which ones can be altered or eliminated, if any?

When these questions have been addressed thoroughly, organizational leaders will be better prepared to select the best path for the organization to pursue for the coming fiscal year.

Step 5: Adjust and Balance. Once projected expenses and revenue potential have been carefully examined and a list of priorities selected, the next step involves listing expenses and income figures on a budget sheet and balancing those figures. Generally speaking, the projected expense side of a budget should balance with the total figure for revenue. Each program may not be cost-effective, or even cover all of the expenses for the program, but the overall budget must balance.

The budget process so far has skewed the figures so that expenses are projected on the high side and revenue estimates are projected on the low side. If the budget actually ended up as projected, the "extra" money for a fiscal year could not be used as a form of profit to be distributed to individuals. This money must be used within the organization in some manner, so that the expense side of the budget balances with the revenue side. This is often done by incorporating this money in a contingency or reserve fund that will be discussed later in this chapter.

Step 6: Budget Approval. Following the development of a budget, only the board of directors can approve the budget. This is often done by first having the finance committee of the board review a proposed budget and then forward their recommendation to the full board for final approval. Board members must be fully knowledgeable regarding any expenses that are to be incurred and confident about the revenue that is to be generated. Members should have an opportunity to ask questions about the legitimacy of any and all expenses and the accuracy and certainty of income projections. Board members are ultimately accountable for fiscal matters of an organization, and therefore they should challenge each line of the budget to be as certain as possible the organization is on a responsible fiscal path.

When they sign off on a budget, members of the board are exercising their fiduciary responsibility to set parameters for the budget and therefore for the operation of the organization and its programs and services. When the board votes to approve a budget, they are implicitly agreeing to a level of financial development necessary to sustain expenses for programs and administrative operations.

Step 7: Monitor and Amend. Once the budget has been approved and put into place, it must be continually monitored. A budget is only a carefully thought out fiscal projection for the coming year, and a number of things can and often do happen to warrant monitoring and sometimes alteration. It is important that key members of the staff and board monitor the budget at least on a monthly basis. It is also important that provisions are made to amend the budget when necessary and possible.

Most organizations have included in their constitution, charter, and/or policies as to when budget amendments can be made. Amending the budget once or twice a year provides an organization with some flexibility without necessarily going to extremes. Revisions should be carefully thought out and should reflect the changes that necessitated the revisions in the first place. "Revised budgets" must also be presented to, studied and approved by the board of directors, as designated by the policies regarding budget revisions.

Project or Program Budget

Nonprofit organizations typically pursue their missions by delivering programs and services to the community. Developing a budget for each program or service is an important part of the overall financial management process and is referred to as **project or program budgeting**. A separate budget for each program allows the organization to estimate income and expense lines for each and then to analyze these income and expense lines once the program is completed. Allocating the right amount of financial and human resources to each program the organization provides, links the budgeting process directly to the strategic planning. An organization with a high quality strategic plan has already done some of the work to create a program budget. (Zietlow, Hankin and Seidner 2007) This budgeting

Figure 6.2
Project or Program Budget

Direct Income		Direct Expenses	
Registration fees	$13,000	Part-time salaries	$4,000
Concession fees	9,000	Materials and supplies	3,000
T-shirt sales	8,000	T-shirt costs	5,000
Total	$30,000	Promotion	3,000
		Total	$15,000
			$30,000
			-15,000
		Gain/(Deficit)	$15,000

process is also known as **functional accounting**, or **cost center accounting** when referring to record-keeping procedures, and it allows an organization to assess income and costs on a project-by-project basis.

A program budget includes the **direct income** and **direct expenses** associated with conducting a specific program. For instance, CPR classes presented by the local American Red Cross require specialized instructor skills, equipment, and space rentals and are often paid for through a fee paid for by the participants. It is fairly simple to estimate the direct expense and income for these types of programs and to determine actual expenses, income, and gain or deficit once the classes are completed. It is a good practice to analyze program budgets once completed in order to continue to learn about the costs of related expenses and the level of interest and capacity or willingness to pay fees among the target populations. This practice helps program staff conduct effective budgeting over time.

The projected income and expenses, as well as the actual income and expenses of each program, can be placed on a Project or Program Budget (see Figure 6.2) and added or attached to a Program Planning Worksheet (Figure 5.2) with the total figures recorded on the worksheet. Quality budgeting involves formal commitments and guidelines to planning, implementing, reporting, and analyzing program budgets. In most nonprofit organizations, project or program budgets are combined in the development of the operating budget, which also includes the other expenses and income beyond the projects or programs. (Weis and Gantt 2004)

Some nonprofit organizations require program budgets to include the management and support costs (administrative/overhead) that are associated with the conduct of each program, and the organization often devises a formula to determine these **indirect costs** for each program budget. Costs can be calculated for the percentage of staff time, space and utility allocation, marketing material development, phone service, and others designated as indirect costs to each program. This information provides leaders with an idea of the overall costs, direct and indirect, associated with each program and may help in determining the program's overall financial desirability.

Project or program budgeting has a number of benefits:
- It provides a detailed analysis of each program for the purpose of cost effectiveness and priority setting.
- It helps determine the revenue-generating possibilities of each program.
- It can be used as a tool to seek financial support from community service groups, foundations, and/or corporations if program are determined to be important, but not necessarily cost effective.
- It provides leaders of organizations with a program-by-program analysis of specific budgets and tells them how the estimates and results fit into the overall budgeting process.

Contingency/Reserve Funds

The financial health of a nonprofit organization can be significantly impacted if there is a plan to generate excess income that can be used for unexpected needs or expenses--the contingency part--as well as for new equipment, renovations, or growth of any kind--the reserve part (Wolf 1999). When heating units break down, roofs leak, and community outreach vans wear out, a contingency fund is vital to ensuring the continuation of needed programs, regardless of unexpected circumstances. Most organizations allocate a certain percentage, such as between five and ten percent of their annual income, to this fund, although it may be higher depending on the probability of need. This extra income is listed on the expense side of the budget and may be divided up as a contingency and a reserve fund or combined as in Figure 6.3.

Several factors need to be examined prior to creating a contingency/reserve fund (Weis and Gantt 2004):
- **Probability of need.** The larger, more complex, and more facility/equipment-based an organization, the more possible flexibility in programs and the more repairs or replacements for facilities and equipment could be required.
- **Probability of growth.** The more probable some kind of growth is in the foreseeable future, the greater need for significant contingency/reserve funding sources.

Figure 6.3
Contingency/Reserve Fund

Income		Expenses	
Membership fees	$430,000	Salaries	$520,000
Program fees	270,000	Benefits	213,000
United Way	128,000	Materials/supplies	119,000
Special events	96,000	Contingency/reserve	72,000
Total	$924,000	Total	$924,000

- **Consistency of income or revenue.** The less consistent income predictability and reliability, the greater the need for contingency/reserve funds to maintain operations.
- **Cash-flow concerns.** Organizations also may experience cash-flow problems when bills need to be paid before there is adequate income. With a reasonable reserve fund, an organization can borrow from itself.
- **Relative stability of the organization.** If the organization is constantly changing leadership and/or is a relatively new organization, the fund should be larger to support unanticipated changes that may occur.

When an organization has adequate financial resources in the contingency fund, it should allocate the rest to a reserve fund that is kept in a carefully selected interest-bearing account, approved by the board of directors. A number of organizations maintain as much as twenty-five to fifty percent of a year's budget in the contingency fund, and others maintain a good deal more. Evidence of financial health is found in the thoroughness of planned contingency/reserve funds and the commitment the organization has to their long-term development.

Sometimes an organization's contingency/reserve funds become significantly large and may become a disincentive to funders and supporters, because it could look like the organization has more money than it needs. One way to manage this dynamic is to place a portion of these funds in an **endowment** which has special rules and restrictions. Generally speaking, only the interest generated from this kind of an account can be used for the designated purposes for which the endowment was established. This means that the principal will remain in perpetuity (forever). With good management, it can also grow over time. Nonprofit organizations often establish endowments to support a portion of their ongoing operating budget to insure financial health when other sources of funding decline and/or to allow them to put a larger portion of their other funds into the delivery of programs and services. It is also common practice for endowments to be established to support particular programs that are important to the organization's mission but difficult to fund. The funds contained in endowments can be switched to other uses by an action of the board of directors, if and when it becomes necessary. However, effective financial management involves the establishment and long-term maintenance of endowments as a way of helping insure financial sustainability of the organization and its programs. (Zietlow, Hankin and Seidner 2007)

Cash Flow

In the budgeting process, income and expense projections are made for an entire fiscal year, as a part of the broader or rolling multi-year financial planning process. An annual budget can only indicate how things are supposed to come out at the end of a year, but it does not indicate how much money is needed or available at any given point in the year. Since organizations may incur more expenses in one part of the year than in another, and since the level of funds coming into the organization may vary significantly from one month to another, it is important to know how much money is available for expenses throughout the year. **Cash-flow** projections, or projecting and maintaining an organization's expenses and income on a month-to-month basis, help to keep the organization solvent and able to cover its expenses.

To conduct a cash-flow analysis, both expenses and income are laid out on a computer-generated spreadsheet (if possible), with separate columns for each month. The first column lists the total yearly budget, and each horizontal row lists each budget line item. Listed next to each item is the amount of expense or income expected for that item in each particular month. For example, if salaries for the organization total $360,000, and if that is consistent from month to month, then the line item for salaries would read $360,000 as the annual total, followed by the monthly totals of $36,000 for each month. The first three months would appear accordingly:

	Total	January	February	March
Salaries	$360,000	$30,000	$30,000	$30,000

On the other hand, if all the money for a special event came in March, the line item "Special Event" would look like this:

	Total	January	February	March
Special Event	$37,000	0	0	$37,000

A careful projection of cash flow requires that each expense item and each income item be calculated to determine the availability of money in relation to expenses for each month. There can be uncertainty regarding the exact amount of an expense item, and it is best to be conservative and estimate on the high side. It is also advisable to be conservative with the income items, to underestimate the amount, and to estimate the time of the deposit later than expected.

Once all of the projected monthly income and expense items have been listed, a monthly net income (or deficit) is calculated by subtracting total expenses from total income for that particular month. For example, if the organization anticipates $45,000 of income for the month of January and anticipates spending $44,500, then there is a net income for January of $500. If in February the anticipated income is $43,000 and expenses are anticipated to be $43,500, then the anticipated net deficit is $500 for the month of February (see Figure 6.4 on next page).

Monthly financial projections are important because each one affects a cumulative flow of cash. The cash-flow summary is indicated at the bottom of Figure 6.4 and begins with an opening cash balance or the amount of money on hand at the beginning of the month. The net monthly income (or loss) is added (or subtracted) from this amount for the ending or cumulative cash balance for the month. This bottom line indicates the amount of money the organization should have to begin the next month.

Developing cash-flow projections approximately six months in advance of the coming fiscal year helps to prepare for and prevent any potential shortfalls. If the organization still falls short at some point, money can be borrowed or moved from a contingency/reserve fund. If this is not possible, money can be borrowed through a commercial lending institution. The board should take the lead in this process and seek a low or no-interest loan.

This chapter began with the idea that financial resource development and management practices and skills are becoming increasingly important to the success of nonprofit

Figure 6.4
Cash-flow Analysis

Expected Income	January	February
Membership fees	$25,000	$25,000
Program fees	16,000	14,000
United Way	4000	4,000
Total	$45,000	$43,000
Expected Expenses		
Salaries	$31,000	$31,000
Benefits	6,000	5,000
Utilities	4,500	4,500
Facility rent	3,000	3,000
Total	$44,500	$43,500
Monthly net income (or loss)	$500	($500)
Cash-flow summary		
Opening cash balance	$200	$700
Monthly net income (or loss)	500	(500)
Ending (cumulative) cash balance	$700	$200

organizations and for careers in the sector. Everyone who works in the nonprofit sector has some level of fiscal responsibility, and it is important that all staff members have at least some knowledge of and input into financial matters. It is equally important that senior staff and board members are highly knowledgeable in the fiscal matters of the organization, particularly since senior administrators are responsible for preparing budgets and other financial processes and since board members are ultimately responsible for overall finances and the approval of finances. Delivering quality, effective programs from a financially sound foundation is a major factor in assuring organizational success, demonstrating quality stewardship of the public trust, and sustaining the programs and services needed in the community.

■ Financial Processes

Since so many people rely on nonprofit organizations for the delivery of important programs and services, it is essential that these organizations maintain accurate financial records and that these records be open for review and examined annually by an independent auditor. **Accounting** is the term used for financial record keeping, and there are two main types of accounting methods. One is called **cash-basis accounting** and the other one is called **accrual-based accounting.** (Weis and Gantt 2004)

Cash-basis accounting may be the most familiar type of accounting being practiced in nonprofit organizations, since most people use this type of approach with their personal finances. With cash-basis accounting, financial transactions are recorded only when cash changes hands. Records are made only when money is deposited in an account or when money is withdrawn from an account or a check is written from an account. This system is beneficial in its simplicity, straightforwardness, and quickness. It does not, however, take into account any unpaid bills that are outstanding or any money that might be owed to the organization.

With an accrual-based accounting system, on the other hand, money that actually changes hands, whether through a deposit or a withdrawal, is recorded, and money that is owed to an organization and owed by an organization is recorded as well. The advantage of this system is that it represents an organization's actual financial status at any given time much more accurately (see Figure 6.5). The disadvantage is that it is a more complex and time-consuming process.

Still another option for an organization is to incorporate a **modified cash-basis accounting** system. With this system most accounts are kept on a cash basis with the exception of a few accounts that need to be monitored closely because of the amount of funds that may move in and out of the account throughout the fiscal year. For example, an organization might incorporate a cash-basis system for all of its income lines with the exception of membership fees, if membership fees can be paid over a period of time. This system would provide information on memberships that have been paid in full, yet keep track of those that are being paid over a period of time. This same system can be used for paying bills. Bills that are paid in full using a cash-basis accounting system would be recorded, while select bills that may take some time to pay could be recorded through an accrual-based system. For instance, major equipment purchases that are being paid over an extended time period could be recorded with the accrual-based system. This modified cash-basis accounting system is often used for paying federal and state taxes as well, which involves withholding money from employees' salaries on a regular basis and using that money for paying the appropriate taxes. (Weis and Gantt 2004)

Fund Accounting

Income and expenses that are designated for the sole purpose of operating the organization are sometimes referred to as **operating funds** or **unrestricted funds**, which means they can be used for almost any aspect of the organization's operations. Some smaller organiza-

Figure 6.5
Cash Versus Accrual

	Cash	Accrual
Beginning cash in bank	$10,000	$10,000
Purchased materials (payable)	0	-500
Membership commitment (receivable)	0	5,000
Ending cash in bank	$10,000	
Net worth		$14,500

tions that operate exclusively on unrestricted funds are often able to develop a budget for income and expenses on a simple format referred to as a **single fund budget.** Larger, more complex organizations have unrestricted operating funds and often have fund accounts that are used for a number of other areas as well. One such example might be a special project in which funds would be **restricted** just for that project. Another reason to have an additional fund account is to separate the accounting for grant funds from the accounting for operating and other funds.

Operating funds and additional funds can be recorded on the same budget sheet, which is referred to as a **multiple fund budget.** Each fund is separate from the other, each with its own categories of revenue and expenses (see Figure 6.6).

The operating budget is listed first on the left-hand side of the budget. A special project (restricted) is summarized in the second column, and the third column represents a project sponsored by a grant. The sum of the three columns is represented in the fourth column. A multiple fund budget is more beneficial than a single fund budget when more than one fund is necessary because it provides quick access to the records of separate funds at one time and allows a review and comparison of all funds at the same time.

Figure 6.6
Multiple Fund Budget

	Operating fund	Project fund	Grant fund	Total
Income				
Membership fees	$800,000			$800,000
Program fees	320,000			320,000
United Way	32,000			32,000
Annual campaign	64,000			64,000
Contributions		$87,000		87,000
Grant			$212,000	212,000
Total	$1,216,000	$87,000	$212,000	$1,515,000
Expenses				
Salaries	$720,000	$47,000	$132,000	$899,000
Benefits	253,000	24,000	43,000	320,000
Supplies	57,000	15,000	32,000	40,000
Utilities	66,000			66,000
Facility rent	47,000			47,000
Contingency/reserve	72,000			72,000
Total	$1,216,000	$86,000	$207,000	$1,509,000

Financial Statements

Two types of financial statements provide information relevant to the financial well-being or financial condition of organizations, the **balance sheet** and the **income statement** (Zietlow, Hankin and Seidner 2007). The balance sheet (see Figure 6.7) is like a snapshot of the organization's financial condition, providing information as of a particular date, and that date is usually the last day of the month of the last month of the fiscal year. Half of the balance sheet lists all of the organization's assets or those things it owns. The other half lists the organization's liabilities (all that it owes) as well as its net assets or fund balance. Each half adds up to the same total number, hence the term *balance sheet*.

The **balance** exists between the assets on the one hand and the liabilities and net assets on the other. Mathematically speaking, it would look like this:

Assets equals Liabilities plus Net Assets, or $A = L + NA$

This formula makes calculating the **fund balance** easy, since it is determined by subtracting the amount the organization owes from how much it owns:

Net Assets equals Assets minus Liabilities: $NA = A - L$

Balance sheets may first appear to be complicated, but understanding each section helps to reveal the overall financial picture of an organization. Reviewing the **asset** section of the statement in Figure 6.7 indicates what the organization owns in terms of cash in the bank, land, buildings, and equipment, as examples. Since most balance sheets are prepared on an accrual basis, they also include all the money owed to the organization as an asset. These are often referred to as **accounts receivable** and might include money owed to the organization by way of membership payments that are on a schedule or grant money that has been committed but not received. The asset section may also indicate a line for **prepaid expenses** that might include expenses for an activity or event that is occurring in the next fiscal year or some other expense that had to be prepaid.

The asset section of the balance sheet is divided into **current assets** and **noncurrent assets**. Current assets include cash or any item that is expected to become cash within the next year; noncurrent assets are those items that are not as liquid (currently available to be used) and may not be paid for two years or more in the future, like those from grants or pledged contributions from individuals.

The other half of the balance sheet includes the organization's **liabilities**, or what it owes to others. This section is divided up as well, into **current liabilities** and **noncurrent liabilities**. Current liabilities include money that the organization owes in terms of unpaid bills (**accounts payable**) and any revenue or income that has been collected for activities that will not occur until the next fiscal year (**deferred revenue** or **income**). Longer-term obligations, such as **mortgages**, are classified as **noncurrent liabilities**, since they are not due in the next fiscal year.

Once all of the liability categories are totaled and subtracted from the total assets, the difference results in the **net assets**. Net assets are classified into one of three categories as established by the Financial Accounting Standards Board, which establishes financial accounting and reporting standards that are followed across the sector:

- **Unrestricted net assets** include income from contributions and grants and any other earned income or income from investments that is not restricted for use and can be used for any purposes as determined appropriate by the organization.

Figure 6.7
Balance Sheet

Assets

Current Assets

Cash	$13,300
Accounts Receivable	15,200
Prepaid Expenses	16,300
Total Current Assets	$44,800

Noncurrent Assets

Fixed Assets (land, buildings)	$110,000
Grants Receivable	16,300
Total Noncurrent Assets	$126,300
TOTAL ASSETS	$171,100

Liabilities and Net Assets

Liabilities

Current Liabilities

Accounts Payable	$17,200
Deferred Income	10,500
Total Current Liabilities	$27,700

Noncurrent Liabilities

Mortgage	$91,000
Total Noncurrent Liabilities	$91,000

Net Assets

Unrestricted	$23,000
Restricted	$7,700
Net income/(loss) YTD	
	$22,000
Total Net Assets	$52,300
TOTAL LIABILITIES AND NET ASSETS	$171,000

- **Temporarily restricted net assets** are those assets that are temporarily restricted by donors until that restriction has been met in the future.
- **Permanently restricted net assets** include donor-imposed requirements that will never be removed.

Looking at the total net assets in Figure 6.7, it would appear the organization is in good financial shape with a net worth of $52,300. Closer examination of the balance sheet shows that only $13,300 is actual cash in the bank and $15,200 is listed as accounts receivable. A large portion of the asset section includes fixed assets such as land and buildings ($110,000), which is not liquid (not available) and would have to be sold in order for funds to be available to cover any debts the organization might have.

Since the balance sheet must include all the assets and all liabilities of an organization, it is an excellent tool for board and staff members to use when making major financial decisions. It is also an important barometer for prospective board members, funders, and regulators to determine the financial health of an organization prior to any commitments or designations. It is a much better indicator of financial health than a financial statement, which will be examined next, but because individuals are often mystified by all of the numbers and jargon, most people are content to review only the financial statement. But an organization can have a significant net worth and look healthy on a financial statement, yet have a large amount of money invested in a non-liquid asset, such as a building, and therefore appear less healthy on a more detailed balance sheet. This is why the balance sheet should be examined prior to any important financial decisions.

While the balance sheet provides us with information about an organization's financial health at a particular moment in time, the **income statement** summarizes financial activity over a period of time, usually a month or a year. It contains historical financial information and information about the sources of an organization's revenue and expenditures. Since revenue and expenditures are divided into sub-categories, it provides detailed information on each source of revenue and where expenses are going. The income statement indicates whether an organization has a surplus or a deficit over a period of time, and it is calculated by subtracting expenditures from total revenue and is carried forward to the balance sheet. An income statement can include the fund balance at the bottom portion of the report, particularly in the case of year-end audited statements.

A monthly financial or income statement designed like the one in Figure 6.8 (on the next page) provides a view of the progress being made on revenues and expenses, as well as activity for the month that was recently completed and all of the activity thus far this year, and it compares both to a monthly and annual budget. The sample in Figure 6.8 presents an organization that is half way through the fiscal year, since the statement covers the period from July 1 through December 30. Focusing on the revenue half of the budget, it might be expected that approximately 50 percent of the budget would have been met half way through the fiscal year. The income or revenue that is indicated in for the first six months totals $144,000 of an annual budget of $264,000, which equals 54 percent. This is a good sign that the organization is progressing well toward its overall goal of $264,000 in revenue for the fiscal year.

Looking at the expense half of the budget, the organization has spent $121,000 of an annual budget of $264,000 this equals 46 percent of the budgeted amount for the first half of the fiscal year. Based on the information provided by this financial statement alone, revenue seems to be accruing in a reasonable fashion, and expenses seem to be under control for the first half of the fiscal year. But a more accurate fiscal picture can be determined by looking "behind the numbers" at each category to understand the organization's fiscal status in depth. For instance, $74,000 has been generated in membership fees, which is 59 percent of what is budgeted in the membership line for the year ($125,000). This appears to be a positive figure, but what if the organization has completed a major membership campaign and expects far fewer members in the next half of the year? It still needs $51,000 in this category to meet the budget, and it needs to be certain that plans are in place to generate this income. Similarly, the organization has only spent 46 percent of its allocation for expenses

Figure 6.8
Income Statement from July 1 to December 31

Revenue	Current Month		Year to Date	
	Actual	Budget	Actual	Annual Budget
Membership	$12,000	$12,500	$74,000	$125,000
Program	5,000	4,000	27,000	53,000
United Way	2,000	2,000	12,000	24,000
Annual Campaign	5,400	4,000	31,000	62,000
Total Income	$24,000	$22,500	$144,000	$264,000
Expenses				
Salaries & Benefits	$14,000	$13,700	$84,000	$171,000
Supplies/Telephone	700	800	4,200	9,000
Postage	1,600	1,200	8,800	15,000
Travel Expenses	1,100	1,000	7,000	16,000
Mortgage Interest	3,000	3,000	18,000	36,000
Contingency/ Reserve	0	0	0	17,000
Total Expenses	$20,400	$19,700	$121,000	$264,000
Net income (loss) YTD	$4,000	$2,800	$23,000	0

in the first half of the year, which is also a good indication of positive fiscal health. Key board and staff members need to monitor the expense side of the budget continually to be certain that expenses are kept at the same conservative level for the remainder of the year to insure fiscal health.

Continually examining balance sheets and income statements provides board and staff members with the information they need to make effective financial decisions that often have a direct bearing on the overall success of the organization. Providing a narrative with statements offers additional, in depth information on financial categories and helps prevent any unwanted surprises down the road.

Controls

In handling money within an organization, a number of irregularities can occur, either intentionally or unintentionally. One of the most important responsibilities of the board of directors is to establish **fiscal controls** that protect individuals and the organization from irregularities and mistakes. For example, it is generally accepted that fewer fiscal irregularities will occur if there are at least two people involved with financial transactions, each double-checking the decisions and actions of the other. Similarly, the board should design all financial processes and policies with a significant number of **checks and balances** to insure fiscal integrity. (Weis and Gantt 2004)

One of the most important steps in establishing reliable financial procedures is for the board to require that two people be involved in processing all payments. For example, a key administrator who is familiar with the budget and with specific financial expenditures should approve payment. A board member involved with the financial committee should receive the approval for payment and be responsible for writing checks and monitoring this procedure for other board members.

Each payment transaction requires documentation, and one simple way of providing this is to create a stamp that is placed on each invoice that arrives with the following designations and then filled in with the required information as the transaction moves through the established process (Wolf 1999):

```
Date Received:
Date Paid:
Account:
Check Number:
Approved:
```

On the day the invoice is received, it is stamped and the date is recorded on the first line. The assigned staff member determines which budget line item account is to be used to make the payment, records the appropriate account title or number on the third line, and signs or initials to indicated approval for the payment to be made. The assigned board member receives the invoice with all the information in place and writes the check, recording the check number and the date it was written in the appropriate stamped space on the invoice. All payment records should be systematically filed for future referral and review by an auditor.

Another important control on writing checks is to set a policy that checks cannot be made out to the same individual who is signing checks, or that at the least there must be a counter signature on those particular checks. This process--of having two people sign certain checks--could also apply to expenditures exceeding a certain amount, such as $1,000, or whatever amount the board deems appropriate. A formal policy to this effect, with the names of those approved to sign checks when needed must be on file and available for consultation.

With a similar commitment to formal procedures, a system of careful controls must also be incorporated for the handling of incoming money so that both a staff and board member are included. Incoming funds must be received, recorded, and deposited promptly. Deposit slips should be checked with records periodically, and any significant irregularities must be reported to the board.

The organization must be protected from loss of income through either intentional or unintentional irregularities. One way to do this is through the process of **bonding**, which is a form of insurance for fiscal matters. Because premiums for the bonding process vary with the amount of money under protection, careful consideration should be given to determine this amount to be covered and the cost of bonding. One way to designate this amount would be to determine the largest amount of money that could be in the bank at one point and increase that figure by twenty percent (Wolf 1999). This amount should comfortably protect the organization, its staff, and its volunteers without excessive bonding premium costs.

Physical controls and security measures are equally important in protecting organizations from financial loss, or worse. Financial transactions that are conducted with electrical or mechanical equipment, such as cash registers, have a small likelihood of error. Equipment must be checked regularly for proper functioning and accuracy. Financial transactions that are conducted online must follow security protocols and include appropriate protections. Financial records should be kept in fireproof cabinets. Offices should have adequate fire and burglary protection and should install properly functioning security systems. If large amounts of money are expected to come into the organization at one time, as with a special event, hiring security police should be considered.

Reporting Requirements

Nonprofit organizations must file a number of reports each year to maintain their nonprofit status and demonstrate fiscal responsibility. Financial reporting procedures for organizations vary from state to state, and it is important that each organization check individual state regulations regarding reporting requirements.

Most nonprofit organizations are required to complete an **annual tax return** with the IRS that is called a **Form 990.** This form includes information on all income and expenses of the organization in support of its tax-exempt status. Failure to comply with this requirement could lead to significant civil and criminal penalties. If an organization receives income exceeding $1000 that is not related to the tax-exempt purpose of the organization (excluding income from investments) it must be recorded and filed on a **Form 990-T** with its Form 990. Determining which income this might include can be difficult and is best determined by the individual who does the annual audit and who knows the related tax regulations.

Some general understanding of tax regulations will help illustrate the importance of having knowledgeable people involved in this aspect of the organizations financial management. For example, all organizations that have employees must withhold income taxes, social security, and Medicare from their pay and report this amount to the IRS. If a nonprofit organization is not a 501 (c) 3, it must also pay federal unemployment taxes (**FUTA**) on salaries that are reported on **Form 940.** Employers must prepare a **W-2 Form**, which is the annual wage and tax statement, for each employee. This must be mailed to each employee by January 31, and a copy must be filed with the IRS no later than February 28 of each year. Non-employee compensation paid in amounts exceeding $600 must be reported on **Form 1099-MISC**, filed with **Form 1096** and filed with the IRS annually. If an organization receives a gift of property, other than money or securities, it must file a **Donee Information Report Form 8282** with the IRS if the amount of the gift exceeds $500. These examples illustrate the importance of having an in depth understanding of the tax regulations in order to insure that the nonprofit organization is in full compliance.

Recording and Reporting Systems

It is essential that nonprofit organizations have quality policies and procedures for recording and reporting all aspects of their financial processes. This often starts with how the recording and reporting process is designed. Prepackaged accounting computer software is readily available to handle accounting needs and even the smallest of organizations can benefit from the use of these often-inexpensive programs. Customized accounting software packages that include links to membership and fundraising packages can also be purchased through accounting or software firms that specialize in the work of nonprofit organizations. Computerized spreadsheets are an important tool in recording and analyzing income and expenses, determining cash flow, and maintaining membership and fund-raising records. They are also readily available as prepackaged software, or they can be obtained in a more customized fashion. Affiliates of national nonprofit organizations may also be able to acquire software packages designed specifically for their organization from their national headquarters. Another good source of such resources can be found in the state association of nonprofit organizations and their National Council of Nonprofit Associations.

Some organizations find it less expensive and/or more expedient to contract accounting procedures, payroll systems, and other record-keeping and meeting form requirements to firms that specialize in these processes. These firms are generally more accurate and can relieve the organization of unwanted and often time-consuming tasks.

Organizations with the best of intentions and purposes can help develop their effectiveness, in part, by maintaining appropriate financial records and reporting those accounts in a timely and appropriate manner. An effective accounting and reporting process adds to the overall success of the organization and helps to assure staff and volunteers, participants, contributors and other community members of the organization's financial integrity.

■ Financial Development

The development of the financial resources needed to successfully operate a nonprofit organization includes an increasingly sophisticated field of practice. Financial development and fundraising are not synonymous. Fundraising is just one aspect of financial development. The nonprofit sector has its roots in a number of traditional methods of acquiring financial support. The notion of individual financial contributions was a key to the early years of the founding of this country by the way in which successful voluntary action generated charitable contributions of support. The tradition continues as individual donors contribute enormous sums of money to nonprofit organizations. The idea that people would pay a fee for a valued program or service from a nonprofit organization has been a common practice throughout most of the modern history of the sector. And, government departments and other organizations have provided funding to nonprofit organizations in support of the delivery of important programs and services to the community for decades. Nonprofit sector financial development includes these and many other methods of acquiring the resources needed. Increased value is being placed on nonprofit organizations that have a strategic and diversified set of sources of funding support. A nonprofit organization with diversified sources of support is considered to be healthier and better able to withstand shifts in funding from any one stream of revenue. Therefore, this section will focus on the range of funding strategies nonprofit organizations incorporate into their financial development.

Modern nonprofit organizations must construct a thorough and comprehensive financial development plan in order to successfully meet their financial needs. Some pre-requisites for that the financial development plan include the following **criteria** (Weis and Gantt 2004):

- *A clear and focused mission or purpose.* It is much easier to generate income and gain support for a nonprofit organization when the purpose of the organization is clear and highly desirable. The mission must be clear, understood, and important to community members.

- *An overall reputation for integrity.* Before any fundraising efforts are initiated, the organization must have developed a reputation for dependability and quality. For new organizations, the reputation can be associated with that of the volunteer board members and staff members.
- *A history of program success.* Individuals like to support organizations that are successful and that enhance their communities. Some history of program success implies the probability of future success.
- *Professional staff members and committed volunteers.* Individuals like to support organizations that have competent and committed leaders. Proven leadership provides confidence in community support.
- *Clear and proven needs for financial support.* Community members are more likely to provide financial support to an organization that is generating money for specific needs that have been clearly established.
- *Administrators with experience and skills in financial development.* In addition to having clear needs for financial support, an organization must have individuals with specialized skills in developing support. Technical and people skills are essential in building a financial base.

There is some truth to the axiom "actions speak louder than words." Organizations with a proven record of success and with the potential to develop and maintain a financial base will have a much easier task developing financial support. In order to have organizational information readily available for financial development efforts, many organizations prepare a **case** or **case statement** in advance of such activities. Aspects of a case statement are discussed next.

Case Statement

The case statement tells a compelling story of the importance and relevance of the organization to the community. It has many uses, from providing a framework for continuity among all public relations and program promotion efforts to attracting partnerships, collaborations, and donors. Sometimes referred to as the organization's "elevator speech" (a powerful story that can be told at any moment by any member of the organization during a short elevator ride), the case statement attracts interest and advances the potential of a value connection with the listener. Basically, the case statement includes (1) the history of the organization, 2) mission of the organization, (3) constituents and their needs, (4) current goals, (5) money needed to meet those goals, and (6) ability to use funds effectively (Bray 2008).

The case statement should describe the importance of the organization and list some of its projects or activities that work toward its purpose or reason for being. It needs to include a specific list of projects that, with appropriate funding, could make further differences in the lives of individuals in the community. And it should include a list of program or project successes as proof of consideration for support. A good case statement provides a bases for preparing a tailored request to a potential donor, with a particular interest and giving level, illustrating how a gift of a particular amount will meet specific needs. (Bray 2008)

Tim Seiler (2003), the long-time director of The Fund Raising School at the Indiana University of Philanthropy, proposes that when writing a case statement organizations should focus on the following types of questions:

- What is the problem or social need?
- What special services or programs do we offer?
- Do we have a written plan with a statement of philosophy, objectives, and a program?
- What are the specific financial needs?
- Who are the people associated with the organization?
- Who should support the organization?

Whether the case statement is a written document or a data-base of information on the organization and the community, it should be a fluid instrument capable of being changed quickly as new data is revealed. It can save individuals within the organization a great deal of time searching files for effective information, and it provides potential participants, partners, and contributors with invaluable assistance in making decisions for engagement or support.

The Board's Role in Financial Development

The involvement of board members is critically important to the overall success of developing finances in a nonprofit organization. There are typically **five (5) ways board members get involved in financial development**. First of all, (1) as the primary stewards of the organization, board members have an overall fiduciary responsibility. This is not a day-to-day assignment, but is generally realized by working through the chief executive officer or assigned administrator or Executive Director (ED). Additionally, (2) board members can play a strategic role in helping to determine both the kinds of financial development activities that will occur and the goals of those activities. They can bring expertise, experience, connections, commitments, and their time and energy to the diverse set of financial development activities that the organization engages to fund its ongoing operation and sustainability. Organizations that do not include board members in financial development meetings are missing out on valuable resources and may be acting contrary to organizational by-laws.

Board members can (3) also provide key leadership in fundraising activities by their participation, guidance, and inspiration. Some board members are selected because of their experience and expertise in generating funds and should be called upon accordingly. Other board members may not have significant financial expertise but (4) their connections with community leaders provides access to other potential donors, linkages to prospective partners and collaborators, and support for other types of investments (such as contracts for services). Board members can help identify donors and can serve as door openers for prospective gifts. With few exceptions, (5) board members should be asked to contribute financially to the organization and should be a part of the process in organizing and soliciting other contributions.

Although staff members have developed more and more expertise in financial development, not involving board members can leave a tremendous void in the overall development process. An explanation of the board member's role in financial development should be one of the first things the nominating committee provides when recruiting potential board members. Once a member has been selected, this same role must be reiterated in the board's orientation and training sessions. Committed and informed board, staff, and volunteer members along with organizational integrity combine to make the best formula for financial stability.

The Development Committee's Role

One of the most important factors in successful financial development is the creation of a cohesive development committee that has effective leadership, vision, and commitment (Conway 2003). The *core* **development team** is made up of board members that include representatives from the development and finance committees, the development committee chairperson, and the board chairperson. Other volunteers from the community may also be included on the development team. Key individuals from the staff side of the organization should be involved, including the ED, the development director, other professional and support staff members and paid consultants, when appropriate. It is always good to have professional staff members involved who are leading key programs that are central to the organization's mission. Since all board and staff members are expected to contribute to financial development in one way or another, everyone needs to be involved in the development process at appropriate times.

In many nonprofit organizations, the **development committee** works with the development director (or a staff member assigned the responsibility) to (1) determine financial needs, (2) develop a plan that strategically integrates all the methods of financial development, (3) implement that plan, and (4) monitor and amend the plan when necessary as the plan unfolds. This would often include financial plans for the short term such as a fiscal year as well as strategic, long-range development plans. The case statement, mentioned previously, is an invaluable tool in assisting with all of the steps above.

Some organizations seem blessed with great leadership when it comes to matters of finance, while others struggle in their **recruitment** of quality staff and board members. Good leaders are generally attracted to an organization because of the mission or purpose and the organization's reputation for success and integrity. Recruitment of development committee members should be done just as it is with other board members, incorporating job descriptions and a matrix of specific skills and tasks. Once development committee members have been recruited, they can be *empowered* by a number of strategies (Grace 2003):

- broad participation in the overall process, from planning, to setting goals, to implementation, to evaluation
- training
- coaching and practice
- clear and effective communication process
- providing experienced mentors with each team
- continually reminding team members of the importance of the development activity to the overall mission of the organization

Because of the nature of their work, it is essential to organize the development committee into an effective team. Successful teams often demonstrate a number of the same qualities (Rosso 1996):

- highly productive teams have developed a similar vision and are able to share that vision with others
- hierarchy is almost nonexistent, and communication is open and respectful
- the organization is highly supportive of the committee's work
- team members rely on empowerment of each other and develop an effective level of synergy

• the team is open to new ideas and works hard to reduce misunderstandings

Recruiting and maintaining a highly effective development committee needs to be one of the top priorities of the ED, development director, and the board chair. They must understand what kinds of individuals are important in building an effective development team, and they must be able to maintain that committee at the highest level of success. The development committee can and should be involved in one way or another in all of the activities discussed below.

Developing a financial base for any organization should be a comprehensive process involving the following possibilities, where appropriate: membership fees, program fees, special events, product sales, residential campaigns, United Way support, annual campaigns, capital campaigns, deferred gifts, and grant support. A key to long-term financial health is the selection of a strategic set of these financial development methods, which are closely monitored and adjusted periodically to respond to changing circumstances and the revenue generated by each method. (Weis and Gantt 2004)

Membership and Program Fees

It is common for facility-based and a number of non-facility based organizations to use a membership fee and some additional program participation fees in order to help insure that their operating costs are paid on an ongoing basis. A membership fee (1) provides funds for operating the organization and (2) gives members the sense that they belong to the organization and are committed enough to pay a fee. It also (3) provides members with a sense that they are supporters of the organization's core values and mission. Program fees can be used to cover some of the direct expenses associated with certain programs, such as specialized instructor skills that are not typically found on the staff. There are a number of questions that need to be asked regarding membership and program fees (Weis and Gantt 2004):

• **Who should make up the membership of an organization?**

Membership in organizations is generally based on (1) the purpose of the organization and (2) the guidelines established by the board in the by-laws and/ or membership policy of the organization. For example, a nonprofit organization whose purpose it is to enhance the lives of children in the community should specify age, geographical parameters, and any other considerations.

• **How many members should an organization have?**

Organizations generally set a limit on the number of members and program participants that can be served effectively:

- **Space analysis.** The number of participants allowed for a given space is first of all determined by community policies, usually by the local fire department. Beyond this legal control, organizations may wish to limit the number of participants so there is adequate space for effective and safe program implementation.

- **Resources.** An analysis should be done to determine an effective staff, faculty, and/or volunteer ratio with program participants. In most cases, a predetermined ratio of staff to program participants is set by organizational policy and in some cases, such as therapeutic settings, the ratio may be set by law or professional standards. It is also important to assess the quantity of supplies, materials, and equipment available for adequate programming.

- **Budgetary considerations.** It is important to consider the number of members and program participants necessary to meet the specific line items of the budget dealing with membership and program participation. This is essential if the program budget is based solely on a program fee or as a part of the membership fee. If the program cost is being supported by other sources of funding, the number of members and participants can still be useful to have a sense of what to charge or what needs to be raised in additional funds.

- **Tradition.** Some organizations have a tradition that limits the number of members and program participants and others have a history of including a larger number of members. Traditions can be changed, but they should at least be considered in the overall discussion to determine individual numbers for an organization and for specific programs.

- **How are membership and program fees determined (pricing)?**
  Determining the cost for memberships or a fee for a specific program in any organization is tricky, but a number of aspects should be considered:

  - **Mission and policy.** If the mission of the organization is to serve economically disadvantaged individuals, then this must be considered in establishing any fee, membership or otherwise. Many nonprofit organizations set some of their fees on a **sliding scale** basis, meaning that the fees for individuals who need assistance can be based on their income-to-expense margin or cash availability. Additionally, some organizations set up a **scholarship program** for people in need. Even if the organization's mission has nothing specifically to do with serving the economically disadvantaged, nonprofit organizations are created to provide a service and should be priced accordingly.

  - **Budgetary requirements.** Just as budgetary requirements must be considered when determining the number of members or program participants an organization should engage, it must also be considered when setting a price for membership or specific programs. Membership and program fees often make up a substantial portion of an operating budget and are therefore necessary for the overall financial health of the organization. The amount of the budget being generated by other financial development methods informs the pricing process.

  - **Tradition.** The organization's history should also be considered in the mix of determining membership and program prices. If an organization has a tradition of setting memberships or program fees at a certain level, the community comes to expect that range of pricing. Pricing can and often does change, but gradual, conservative changes are much easier to accept and deal with than radical, major changes in pricing. This can impact the overall blend of financial development methods and goals set for each.

- **What does a membership campaign consist of?**
  Many organizations develop a special campaign, referred to as a membership campaign, to recruit new members. Whether motivated by a need to increase

membership or to respond to an opportunity to provide new or additional programs to different parts of the community, a membership campaign should be
designed to stimulate a great deal of enthusiasm and interest in the organization
and can last from a few weeks to several months, and even longer. A well-
designed membership campaign can be a way of increasing the flow of funding
through this financial development method. The goals set for this method must
be closely coordinated with the other methods that make up the overall financial
development plan. Quality membership campaigns consider the following:

- **Special Offers.** Membership campaigns often include special offers during
  the campaign. These may include a reduced cost for membership, extended
  membership for a standard cost, additional memberships at a reduced rate (see
  Figure 6.9), current members receive a discount for their annual fee when they
  bring in new members, and free or reduced program fees for sign-ups during
  the campaign. Any innovative special offers that will attract new members to
  the organization should be considered.

Figure 6.9
Reduced Membership Promotional Flyer

Buy One Membership in the Morganfield YMCA and get the Second Membership at 1/2 Price!!

That's right. When you sign up for membership in the Morganfield
YMCA, you can bring along a friend for just half price if you
both register during the month of June! This 12-month offer is
good for current and new members.

Membership includes full use of the facility:

■ Olympic size pool ■ Giant whirlpool
■ Fitness center ■ Racquetball courts
■ Youth center ■ Adult and youth sport leagues
■ Career development center

For more information on this great offer,
contact Darcy Young at 750-9622.

Hurry, offer ends soon!

- **Kick-off.** Effective membership campaigns often have a *kick-off* event, an activity that begins the campaign with a whirl of excitement and activity. The kick-off can be an event that includes information on the organization and special offers involved with the campaign. Door prizes, entertainment, surprises, and free food are all likely to enhance the excitement surrounding the campaign. Local celebrities and the media should be invited along with the members of the organization. The kick-off event can also be an opportunity to bring broad public attention to the mission of the organization and a source of attention and support for other methods being used in the financial development plan. For example, materials and media activity being prepared for the membership campaign can be designed to also support ongoing individual donor development and cultivation. Potential donors can also be invited to the kick-off as an opportunity to get quickly acquainted with the mission.

- **Flyers, Public Service Announcements (PSAs), and Signs.** Attractive, informative flyers should be created and posted strategically throughout the community several weeks prior to the kick-off and the beginning of the campaign. Public service announcements should also be sent to the media prior to the beginning of the campaign. Businesses will often donate space for display and marquee signs to promote the campaign. Any materials developed for a membership campaign can also have uses in other financial development methods if designed with multiple uses in mind.

- **Contests.** Introducing contests for the campaign adds excitement and interest, helps create a sense of ownership for staff members, volunteers, and members, and has a strong potential for increasing membership enrollment. Prizes can include days off for staff members and t-shirts for volunteers and members. Grand prizes or drawings for contest participants can include free trips donated by local travel agencies.

Special Events

A special event fundraiser is an activity designed with the primary purpose of generating income for an organization and with secondary objectives that could include increasing public awareness, entertainment, health and fitness, enhanced knowledge and awareness, and fun. Special events have the potential to generate enormous interest in the organization while also developing funds. Special event fund raisers come in many, many forms and are limited only by imagination. There are a lot of resources available to help development committees make decisions about the methods they will undertake and about the process of planning for these activities. (Mintzer 2003) When planning special events, the following criteria should be considered (Weis and Gantt 2004):

- **Safety.** The most important aspect of a special event or any activity in an organization is keeping risks and health hazards to an absolute minimum. For all special events, a conscious effort must be made to follow the guidelines for managing risks listed in Chapter 7.

- **Community Need.** The most successful special events are those that most effectively fulfill needs of the community or a targeted group. Events that focus on sports, health and fitness, or the arts, as well as any activity that fulfills specific need in a meaningful way--such as an educational event--are popular.

- **Creative and distinctive.** Special events should be distinctive in order to appeal to a wide range of interests. For instance, *-thons* have a long and proven history of being successful and a twist on a *–thon* might be to have a *volunteer-a-thon* instead of a *walk-a-thon.* It is a little different than a typical *–thon* and it provides services to the community. The notion is that participants get pledges of a set amount of money for each increment of the event that they accomplish to be paid upon completion of the event, such as a set amount for each mile walked, each hurdle jumped, hours volunteered, and so on. Special events vary as widely as people's imaginations, from carnivals to bingo and from "pies in the face" to silent auctions. Choosing the right kind of event to best match the interests and energies of those who are sought as participants/donors is the real trick to successful special events.

- **Natural Connection.** Special events that have some kind of a natural connection to the organization can sometimes be easier to implement than others. An example might be a YMCA that develops a bicycle or running race. Health and fitness are two areas that YMCAs typically incorporate in their programs, so they would have access to expertise in those areas as well as access to members with those interests.

- **Organization and Promotion.** To be successful, special events have to be planned and promoted well, just like any other program. The program development section in Chapter 5 contains detailed steps to follow in developing a program. To goal here is to make sure that the people who are targeted as participants/donors for the special event are aware that it is happening and motivated to engage and donate.

- **Fundraising Potential.** Regardless of how creative or well-planned an event is, it has to have the potential to raise money. Finding a high quality fit between the interests of those who are targeted as participants/donors and the special event being planned is the primary key to success. Corporate and association sponsorships can be solicited to cover many or all of the costs. It is also important to keep expenses as low as possible, while maintaining a quality event.

Product Sales

The Girl Scouts of America have taken product sales to great heights with their acclaimed Girl Scout cookie campaign that results in tens of millions of dollars for local councils around the country each year. It has a double benefit in that it is also an educational program for participants who are learning about small business management while selling cookies and generating funds for the organization. Other organizations are successful selling candy, calendars, popcorn, teddy bears, and fruit, to mention only a few of the items sold each year for nonprofit causes. Selling products can be very successful if a few key factors are incorporated (Weis and Gantt 2004):

- Make safety the number one priority.
- Be certain to have a large and responsible sales force.

- Develop an effective communication system.
- Select products that are popular and easy to sell.
- Provide appropriate and adequate incentives.
- Establish a clear beginning and end date.
- Try to buy products on consignment.
- Develop an effective control system for money.

Product sales also help promote the organization and provide members of the organization an opportunity to develop ownership by assisting the fundraising process.

Residential Campaigns

A number of nonprofit organizations, particularly national health organizations with high visibility, have great success with **residential campaigns**, in which individuals in specific communities are asked to approach their neighbors requesting support for an organization. This type of campaign is highly organized, yet personalized at the same time, as neighbors are approaching neighbors for support and participation.

Residential campaigns usually begin with paid or volunteer staff members within the organization calling individuals in various neighborhoods using a specialized phone book that is divided by neighborhoods within communities. Any advance work that can be done to identify potential supporters by neighborhood will increase the success with the first level of recruiting participants for the campaign. Since the first level of participation requires a sizeable commitment, any advanced connection to the organization or the person doing the calling can increase the potential for agreement to join. The individuals who are called are asked to represent the organization within their neighborhood and are then sent a packet of material that may include the following:

- A letter of explanation describing in detail the campaign and the volunteer's role
- Information on the successes of the organization in addressing specific problems
- A list of names and addresses of other individuals in the neighborhood
- A solicitation letter to be given to each individual on the neighborhood list along with a return envelope
- A large, return envelope where all checks can be sent to the organization upon completion of the campaign

Once an individual has been recruited to coordinate the neighborhood campaign, he or she may be reminded occasionally by the organization about the campaign goal and any deadlines. There is usually a packet or kit goal for each neighborhood that is set at a reasonable level. Residential campaigns designed as such can be very successful, particularly when (1) the organization is recognizable and the purpose desirable; (2) the campaign is well organized; and (3) the solicitation approach is personalized, such as neighbor to neighbor. Once people have had a good experience participating in a residential campaign and are celebrated and recognized for their success, they make good candidates to serve in this capacity again or to be interested in moving into other financial development roles with the organizations. Successful residential campaigns result in tens of millions of dollars for nonprofit causes across the country each year.

United Way

Local United Way organizations are designed in part to be umbrella organizations that collect contributions for distribution to other organizations. The money United Way raises is **allocated** to organizations based on (1) need, (2) numbers of individuals served, and (3) types of programs. An organization such as a community-based health and wellness center that has a strong capacity for fundraising through membership or program fees may not receive as much United Way support as a Big Brothers Big Sisters organization that provides important services with no membership or program costs to its members. United Way is increasingly focusing its allocation decisions on community issues that are determined by input from the community. This process is typically narrowing the focus of its funding and reducing the number of organizations and/or the amount of funds received by each organization.

An organization that is interested in becoming a United Way affiliated agency should review the organizational funding requirements prior to making application to see if it meets the standards and to understand any restrictions. Organizations that apply and become affiliates of the United Way must reapply for support each year. An **allocation committee** made up of local, community volunteers determines the amount of money allocated to each organization. Most United Way funds are generated through a **payroll deduction** process in which individuals designate that a certain amount of money be withheld from their paycheck and contributed to the United Way or a specific organization affiliated with the United Way. In many communities, United Way also allows individuals to select among its affiliates the organization that will receive its donation. This has the impact of reducing the amount of money available for United Way to distribute. This financial development method has proven to be one of the most successful in history.

Annual and Capital Campaigns

An **annual campaign** is designed to generate funds for operating expenses and these funds can be passed on to members in the form of reduced membership and program fees, or in some cases fees may be eliminated (Weis and Gantt 2004).

Annual campaigns are highly organized with a chairperson, division leaders, team captains, meeting dates, fundraising material, and financial goals (see Figure 6.10, next page). One hundred percent of the board of directors should be involved in the annual campaign, from participating as chairperson or division leaders, to recruiting division leaders on or off the board, recruiting team members, and making donations. **Campaign leaders** must be respected members of the community with a commitment to the organization and can be made up of board members and other members of the community in general.

The overall **campaign chair** should be someone who has a great deal of respect from the community, is committed to the purpose of the organization, and is able to organize and motivate others. The chair is sometimes a board member of the organization, but not always.

The community should be divided up into segments that make sense in the given community. Segments could include such divisions as small, middle-sized, and large business divisions, an educational division, a professional division, an organizational division, a division that includes city, state, and federal employees, and so on. Each division should

Figure 6.10
Annual Campaign Organizational Chart

Boxwood, Illinois – Big Brothers Big Sisters
"Buddy Campaign"
Annual Campaign Organizational Chart
2004 (Goal $500,000)

have a leader who can organize his or her segment into teams with team captains. Each team is responsible for generating a certain amount of money from an assigned section of the division, and that amount, combined with other teams, is the goal for the division.

A **prospect list** must be established for each division. Special consideration should go to individuals, corporations, and associations with natural ties to the organization, such as board members, staff and volunteer members, members, parents of members, firms represented by members, previous members, previous contributors, community-minded corporations, and service associations. Prospects may also be selected from the Chamber of Commerce list and even from the yellow and white pages of the phone book, although this should be a lesser priority as a method of developing prospect lists. Lists should be reviewed after each annual campaign and cultivated by the members of each team to reflect the results of the experience. This provides a list of donors or prospective donors based on the experience of the team, increasing the odds of meeting future fund raising goals with the annual campaign.

The **solicitation process** for an annual campaign should be highly organized, but personable. Telephone calls, face-to-face meetings, and direct-mail contacts between team members and prospects are very important and produce the best results. Often, a campaign will have an appealing **theme** and purpose, such as the "Buddy Campaign" in Figure 6.11, and this theme and purpose will be reflected and explained in the campaign material. This provides some focus for potential prospects and helps assure them that their money is going to make a difference in a specific area within the organization. Meetings should include an informational and inspirational **kick-off** event followed by a number of **update** or **report**

meetings. All of these meetings should be both informative and inspirational. Although annual campaigns should be planned a year in advance, the actual campaign is relatively brief, lasting from two to four weeks.

Organizational staff members usually play support roles in an annual campaign, developing materials (see Figure 6.11), organizing meetings, keeping records, supporting the volunteers in their fundraising efforts, and organizing the kick-off event and closing celebration.

Figure 6.11
Flyer for Annual Campaign

Boxwood, Illinois – Big Brothers Big Sisters (BBBS)
"Buddy Campaign 2004"
CAMPAIGN GOAL: $500,000

The Boxwood, Illinois, Big Brothers Big Sisters program matches children from single-parent families with caring, adult mentors for the purpose of friendship and guidance. The organization averages approximately 350 matches each year. The Big Brothers Big Sisters program of Boxwood is affiliated with the National BBBS organization. The Boxwood program has proven to be a deterrent to unacceptable behavior, drugs and alcohol abuse, and school absenteeism. It has fostered positive character development and provided opportunities for young children between the ages of 6 - 17 that might not have them otherwise. Won't you help? BBBS charges no fees to the families who participate, and the organization operates primarily through corporate and private contributions. You and/or your organization can choose to be a "Buddy" at several different levels:

Universal Buddy	$5,000
Galactic Buddy	$2,500
Solar Buddy	$1,000
Super Nova Buddy	$500
Super Buddy	$200
Buddy	$100

Just fill in information below, attach it to your check, and return it to the BBBS Buddy Campaign team member who contacted you. Any amount is greatly appreciated. Thank you so much for being a buddy to children who really need one!

_____   _____
Your Name   Corporation (if applicable)

_____   _____
Address   Phone Number

_____
Amount Contributed

A **capital campaign** is designed to generate funds for capital expenditures, such as new buildings, renovations, major equipment purchases, and endowed educational positions (Weis and Gantt 2004). A capital campaign is highly organized, like an annual campaign, and involves the selection of a chair, division chairs, teams, and team captains. It also has a financial goal, campaign materials, and scheduled meeting dates. Unlike an annual campaign, a capital campaign is typically designed to raise larger amounts of money and the campaign period is usually longer. This period can last from several months up to one or two years, and even longer in some circumstances. This is in part the result of the challenge typically encountered in raising funds for capital development.

Fundraising **consultants** are often hired to coordinate capital campaigns because of their expertise and so that staff members can concentrate on other duties, although the staff should be involved in a support role. The consultant may first conduct a **feasibility study** to determine (1) whether the community believes in the goal the campaign is addressing and (2) whether the community would be willing and able to support the campaign. If the feasibility study results are positive, the consultant often serves as the overall advisor and/ or professional coordinator of the campaign. Capital campaigns can result in some great opportunities to serve communities, but they can also extract a great many resources from the community and should only be considered if real needs exist and if the community is willing to support the campaign. One potential negative side effect of a successful capital campaign is that donors may choose not to contribute to the organization when other requests for support come their way, and should be considered when identifying prospect lists for a capital campaign.

Corporate and Service Club Support

Whether the support is for a special event, an annual campaign, capital campaign, or some other financial development method, corporate and club support can be essential. If cultivated effectively, corporations and service clubs, such as the Rotary or Lions Clubs, can become key allies for nonprofit organizations. First of all, service clubs have a primary interest in the well-being of a community. Local corporations are also typically invested in the quality of life in the community. Increasingly, corporations are considering a dual bottom line of profit and social good. Their employees and colleagues, along with their families live and work in the communities in which they are located, and it is in their best interest to provide support to nonprofit organizations. Another reason corporations and clubs often support nonprofit causes is that this support usually boosts the morale of the employees and members. Supporting nonprofit causes can enhance loyalty and positive feelings among employees and club members. Finally, supporting nonprofit organizations establishes a strong public image and influences public opinion favorably.

When seeking funding support from a corporation or club, it is important to research the organization regarding their work and community involvement. Prior to seeking an interview to present a case for support, a proposal should be carefully prepared listing reasons the corporation or club should support the organization. The corporation or club will also want to know what the benefits to its organization will be if it supports the organization.

It's a good idea to offer the corporation or club sponsorship at several different levels and to seek an introduction through a board member or other community leader. Regardless of the results, the organization should be gracious in its relationship with the corporation or club, because a decision not to provide support today could be different the next time a request is presented. Individuals should always be thanked for their support in the most appropriate manner.

Planned Gifts

Planned gifts come in three forms, (1) **current outright gifts,** (2) **expectancies, and** (3) **deferred gifts** (Regenovich 2003). **Current outright gifts** of assets such as stock, real estate, and personal property are consider planned gifts because of their value and that they are combined with other assets. The organization can keep the asset or sell it, as they choose. Another current outright gift is a **charitable lead trust** that pays income to the organization for a set period, and when completed the principal returns to the donor. An **expectancy** is a promise from a donor to make a gift at a future date, which can be revoked at any time. Bequests, retirement plans, IRAs, and life insurance are all expectancies that allow a donor to promise a contribution. The funds pass to the organization named as a beneficiary at the donors death. Expectancies may be revoked by the donor at any time.

Deferred gifts involve the irrevocable transfer of money or property that will not be available to the organization until a set time in the future. Once established, the deferred gift is complete, providing an income tax deduction for the donor. The organization receives its benefit at a future event (the donor's death) or the expiration of a specified term. There are two common forms of deferred gifts, (1) a **charitable gift annuity** and (2) a **charitable remainder trust.** The charitable gift annuity is a contract where the donor transfers cash or property to the organization. The organization agrees to pay a set amount each year until the donor's death. The charitable remainder trust created with a legal trust document that transfers cash or property to the organization. In return the donor receives income from the trust for life or a specific term not to exceed twenty years. (Regenovich 2003)

Since donors benefit from tax incentives and from the feeling that they have helped the community, and since organizations benefit from the financial aspects, deferred giving is a mutually beneficial process, but it has to be organized and promoted. The first step in organizing a deferred gifts program is to (1) form a committee consisting of an attorney, a banker and/or an accountant, and a marketing specialist. These committee members can be board members or other members of the community, with staff members in supporting roles.

The committee members must then (2) decide the type of deferred gift plans the organization would like to initiate and (3) design marketing material that describes the plan and the ways donors can be involved. (4) A prospect list needs to be developed along the same lines of developing a prospect list for an annual or capital campaign. Once the list is ready, (5) contact should be made in person, over the telephone, and/or through a mail campaign. (6) Seminars describing the plans should also be considered, with the public invited.

Although a deferred gift program usually does not benefit an organization immediately, the long term-benefits can be astounding, and the benefits to donors are significant. Because of the minimal cost invested, the volunteer nature of the process, and the financial potential, seeking deferred giving should be an organizational priority.

Grant Support

Grant funds are typically viewed by the funding source as support for innovation in their specific fields of interest. The underlying assumption is that individual donors and program participants are unlikely to be able or willing to pay for the start-up costs of developing new programs and services, but once proven effective, they will be more likely to support the ongoing operation. Given that framing, most grant making organizations view their funds as a rare source of support for testing new programs, reaching out to new populations, or experimenting with creative approaches to program delivery.

A wide range of organizations use competitive grant making processes to distribute their resources in pursuit of their missions and interests. Different levels of **government** frequently use a grant making to distribute funds to promote innovation in addressing a critical social issue or challenge. **Corporations** often engage in grant making to distribute resources from their profits to help improve the community in which they do business and to participate in cause-related marketing to help enhance their public image. Individuals, families, corporations, and communities create philanthropic organizations (foundations) to focus funding attention on selected issues, needs, or communities. Many of these efforts are organized as **operating foundations**, which generally means that they do not have endowments and must acquire the funds that are distributed through grant making and/or by operating programs and services in support of their interests. **Endowed foundations** place funds in endowments, using the interest generated by the investment of the principal for grant making. IRS regulations promote philanthropy by allowing a tax deduction for donations made to foundations with their public benefit missions. The IRS promotes endowed philanthropy by requiring that a minimum of five (5) percent of the net asset value to be given for public purposes each year. Over time this means that the endowment is able to generate more than that amount, with the difference being added to the principal and supporting its growth. (Orosz 2000)

Foundations accomplish their missions through the successful efforts of the organizations that they fund, so they are typically very eager to connect with those working in their fields of interest. Lists of foundations and descriptions of what they support can be found online and in hard copies located in libraries around the country. The Internet facilitates connections and most grant making organizations have quality sites that offer detailed information about their interests and processes. The same commitment to transparency encourages organizations to be members of the Foundation Center and participate in their online directory, www.fdnenter.org. The directory is an electronic clearinghouse search engine that facilitates locating grant opportunities. (Sargeant and Shang 2010)

The government is not designed to address actively all of the needs of each individual citizen. Billions of dollars, therefore, are set aside each year for government agencies to provide funding in the form of grants to individuals and organizations that propose to address some of the needs in communities. With the same commitment to facilitating quality communications and promoting ease of connection to grant making opportunities, most government funding sources turn to the Internet. For example, the U.S. Department of Health and Human Services manages *www.grants.gov* which offers a quality search engine for a very large portion of Federal funded grant making open to nonprofit organizations. In addition, the Catalogue of Federal Domestic Assistance (www.cfda.org) maintains information on almost all federally funded grant programs. With the success of such Internet sites as a model, more and more government departments at all levels of government are using their official Web Sites to help promote grant making opportunities. Connecting to government funding opportunities can be supported by developing relationships with local, regional, and national political representatives whose job it may be to provide funding for worthwhile projects. Developing and maintaining communications can help insure connections whenever resources become available.

The sheer volume of grant making opportunities can make the search process challenging, particularly for small nonprofit organizations with limited staff resources. One frequently used approach to identifying potential grant making opportunities is to **participate in professional networks**, asking other nonprofit organizations in the local area and that work on similar issues to learn what foundations they have applied to with success. Cultivating these types of relationships with other organizations can pay dividends over time. Look for opportunities to network through professional associations and community gatherings, like the United Way Agency Directors Association and its regular meetings. Grant making organizations often use these associations and gatherings to promote their goals and opportunities to apply for funding support.

There are resources available to support the grant seeking process. Many nonprofit organizations have grant development departments that maintain this information and also provide instructional methods on completing applications and writing proposals for funding. Network organizations, associations, and educational institutions frequently offer support to the grant making process for their members, including grant writing training. Consulting firms and individuals are available to support grant seeking efforts for a fee. In addition, most grant making organizations are eager to support the application process in order to facilitate effective connections to those doing the most creative work in their areas of interest. Once a potential grant source has been identified, it is important to invest time in building a quality relationship with the organization's representative to help insure that the resulting application for funds meets all expectations and is successful.

Traditionally, an application for grant funds is presented in the form of a **proposal** that makes a compelling case for the alignment between what the project needs funded and the interests of the funding source. In addition to a written proposal, many grant makers (foundations and government) have a number of forms that must be filled out exactly as they are requested. With the increasing use of the Internet online applications, the forms include the typical prompts, space limits, and information requirements, not allowing submission until they are completed correctly. This type of online application may replace or be synonymous with the proposal for some funding sources. In completing an application or developing a proposal for a grant, it is always essential to *follow the directions* just as they are listed.

Although the requirements for grant proposals may vary greatly across funding sources, there are some typical sections proposals often include. The following are recommended to help guide the develop of grant proposals and are derived in part from Weis and Gantt (2004), Orosz (2000) and Sargeant and Shang (2010):

- **Introduction, Abstract, or Summary.** This section is usually brief and to the point. It should include the name of the applicant, the name of the funder from which the money is requested, the amount of money requested, and for what time period. Beginning the content area with detailed information regarding the problem or situation can be a strong start. It is a good idea to describe the program or method that is being proposed to address the problem, along with the program objectives. The program should be innovative and should clearly address the problem or problems. Information should be provided regarding the credibility of the organization and the credibility of the staff that would be developing the program. This section should be written in clear and concise language.

- **Problem Statement or Statement of Need.** The problem statement or statement of need often follows the introduction. This section asks for expanded information regarding the problem or opportunity on a local basis and a description of the constituencies being served. The applicant may include quotes and paraphrases from local experts and officials if they emphasize the importance of the problem or opportunity. Information can point to community members affected by the situation, and quotes from some of these people can be provided. Incorporating vital statistics is also important. If the situation exists in other areas, regions or localities, this information may also be included. If possible, a connection should be made here with the organization's background and the problem or opportunity.

- **Program Objectives.** Program objectives describe *what* is to be accomplished through the program and is therefore an *outcome-based* concept. Objectives should be clear, specific, and measurable and should include established time lines for completion. They should be challenging, yet realistic. The evaluation of the project will assess the achievement of these objectives. Results anticipated beyond the funding period and information regarding the evaluation process may also be mentioned.

- **Program Description or Methodology.** This section should describe the program activities in detail and answer the question of *how* the objectives will be reached. The program section describes the project staff and often includes resumes from key individuals, particularly the coordinator, attached as appendices. Timelines for activities need to be included and schedules for activities can be a part of the methodology section or attached as appendices.

- **Evaluation.** The purpose of an evaluation is to determine whether adjustments need to be made to a project (**formative evaluation**) and whether the project was effective in achieving the objectives (**summative** or **final evaluation**). Also, it is often important to provide accountability to funders. A good practice is to provide a set of **key evaluation questions** that align with the program objectives. Providing the answers to these questions will all the organization to demonstrate progress and success experienced during the grant. Evaluations may be done through a number of methods, including surveys, interviews, focus groups, and journals. Pre/post tests can also be administered to participants to determine changes from the beginning of a project to the end.

Specific data, which might come from an educational institute or a health organization, for example, can also be recorded at the beginning of a project and then be recorded again at the end to calculate any significant changes. For more detailed information on conducting evaluations, see Chapter 5, "Program Development." This section should express a willingness to work with an external evaluator and describe how the results of the evaluation are to be recorded and reported.

- **Organizational Expertise.** This section is used to demonstrate why the organization is the right one to take on the proposed project. There are several things that can be included to support this case, such as the mission, the qualifications of the staff, established expertise, and particular skills, technologies, or capacities.
- **Future Plans.** If there is a need for a project to continue, many foundations and governmental sources like to know what will happen when the grant ends. Sometimes this can be accomplished by pulling the project into the organization's operating budget. Rearranging staff responsibilities and re-prioritizing existing supplies, materials, and other costs might do this. Another possibility is to institute some program fees, develop special events to support the project, and/or develop corporate sponsorships. Yet another proven method for future funding is to seek additional grant support. There is almost always a way to continue funding a project that should continue.
- **Budget.** The budget for a project is guided by what is needed for a successful project and by what is available from the funder and other sources. The budget should indicate that all expenses for the project will be met in some way. The income side of the budget should include income that has been confirmed, as well as income that is anticipated. Expenses should be realistic and as minimal as possible without sacrificing quality or important aspects of the project. The budget for a grant includes specific expenses and does not usually include a miscellaneous line. The budget should also include a narrative description where additional information will help explain any unusual or critical items.
- **Additional Support.** Funders typically prefer that they are not being asked to fund the total cost of a project and want to see a description of any other sources of support, including funds from the organization itself. Support from other sources can demonstrate a sense of credibility and value others have placed in a project, and, where appropriate, show how the project may be funded after the grant funds being requested.
- **Appendixes.** This section should be used sparingly but provide copies of pertinent documents that support the case made in the proposal, such as related policies, reports, financial statements, key staff resumes, etc.

In addition to the counsel offered in the above outline, a grant proposal needs to demonstrate to the funding source (Long and Orosz 1995):

- the creativity and innovation of the project
- how the project fits the funders interests
- the commitment to doing the project whether grant is funded or not
- that the organization has the expertise need to succeed
- that the goal is on improving the lives of people and not just making the organization better
- that the organization is working with people and not doing things to them

- that the organization is taking a comprehensive approach to the problem or opportunity and show how the project fits
- that the organization is working collaboratively with other organization that is working with the same problem or opportunity

In addition, it is good advice to keep the proposal concise and to the point, do not oversell the project, and personalize the proposal to the funding source's interests. It is never a good idea to write one grant proposal and sent it to a bunch of grant making organizations. It is definitely worth the effort to write the proposal so that the reviewers can see that the applicant believes that there is a strong fit between their need for funding and the grant making organizations interests.

■ A Final Thought

In all aspects of financial resource development and management, it is critical that staff, board, and volunteer members follow the guidelines and policies of the organization regarding financial matters, and that the integrity of the individuals involved and that of the organization are always maintained. The **ethical culture** that is described in Chapter 2 is exactly the culture that must exist in all areas of finance. Maintaining openness will result in the community developing a confidence and trust in the organization and the individuals who are a part of it. Being able to explain and be accountable for financial activities also leads to community trust and is an integral ally in all financial matters.

A high quality ethical culture on all financial matters is integrated with the other aspects of organizational leadership and development. The integrity, honesty, and character that it reflects is a direct product of ethical organizational leadership. As presented in the Chapter 2 description of the importance for nonprofit leadership to incorporate generative or creative elements into their work, this chapter also seeks to promote a balance among fiduciary, strategic, and generative roles for leadership. (Chait, Ryan and Taylor 2005) For nonprofit leaders to focus too much attention on any one of the three areas of organization development will lessen the impact of their work. High quality practice in financial resource development and management is most effective when it is accomplished in close alignment with quality strategic planning and generative organizational development.

■ Summary

This chapter is divided into three major areas regarding fiscal matters: (1) financial management or budgeting, (2) financial processes or accounting, and (3) financial development or fundraising.

Managing finances includes the process of developing a budget, which is a financial plan for an organization. Creating a budget should follow certain steps, such as developing a list of expenses necessary for the organization to operate for a fiscal year. A next logical step in developing a budget should be to determine available resources for the coming year. Once this is done, a comparison of expenses to revenue should be made to determine whether the revenue projections are adequate for the anticipated expenses. Following this, organizational leaders must meet and set program and administrative priorities for the fiscal year.

Once these priorities are set, expense and income figures should be placed on a budget sheet and balanced. Following this, the board of directors approves the budget and, along with staff members, monitors, and in some cases adjusts, the budget at specific times in the fiscal year.

Other important budgetary considerations include a project or program budget that allows program leaders to project and calculate expenses and income lines for specific programs. A contingency/reserve fund is necessary so that nonprofit organizations can address unexpected expenses, potential growth, or other concerns and opportunities. Keeping a positive cash flow for expenses is important, and preparing a month-by-month cash-flow analysis is critical in managing a budget.

The term used for financial record keeping is *accounting*. Organizations either use a cash-basis accounting system, in which financial records are made only when cash changes hands, or they use an accrual-based system, in which records are made when money changes hands, and in addition, money owed by an organization and owed to an organization is accounted for as well. Many organizations also employ a modified cash-basis accounting system, in which some records are kept on a cash basis and others on an accrual-based system.

Unrestricted funds are funds that are designated for the sole purpose of operating an organization and are often kept on a single fund budget. Special projects and funds restricted for specific purposes must be noted separately and are often recorded on a multiple fund budget in a separate area from the operating funds.

A balance sheet provides a thorough look at the assets and liabilities of an organization at one particular point in time, usually the end of a fiscal year. An income statement summarizes financial activity over a period of time, usually a month or a year. Both provide valuable analytical information on the current and overall financial status of an organization.

Expenses and income must be controlled carefully. This usually entails having a specific checks and balances system involving at least two individuals within the organization. Bonding, which is a form of insurance, is a necessary process to protect the organization from loss of income through either intentional or unintentional irregularities. Other controls include making sure there is physical protection for records and finances.

Most nonprofit organizations are required to complete a number of forms that verify their tax-exempt status. These organizations must also withhold income taxes and social security from pay and report this amount to the IRS. Prepackaged accounting software is readily available to assist organizations with accounting needs. Some organizations contract accounting procedures to firms that specialize in these procedures.

Modern nonprofit organizations must construct a thorough and comprehensive financial development plan involving a number of revenue producing areas. Many nonprofit organizations require a membership fee to provide funds for operating the organization and providing members with a sense of ownership. Program fees may also be charged for special programs and are designed to cover some of the direct expenses involved.

Special events can also be effective in developing revenue and should be planned as carefully as all other programs. Product sales, if planned correctly, can provide substantial revenue, and United Way affiliation can be a significant source of funds. Annual campaigns provide money for the operating budget and help keep membership and program costs low.

Capital campaigns provide much-needed funds for new buildings, renovations, major equipment purchases and other major expenses.

Deferred gifts are mutually beneficial to nonprofit organizations as well as providing tax breaks for the donors, and grant support can infuse funds for special projects and community needs. Corporate and service club support is also mutually beneficial by providing support for organizations and providing a morale boost and good public relations to the corporation or club.

This chapter addressed, in part, the Nonprofit Leadership Alliance Certification Competency Requirements of Fundraising Principles and Practices and Nonprofit Accounting and Financial Management

∎ **Reflection and Application**

1. Describe how are financial budgeting, accounting, and development interrelated:

    _____

    _____

    _____

2. What are the steps in developing a budget? List the steps and be prepared to discuss.

    _____

    _____

    _____

    _____

3. How does a program budget fit into the overall budgetary scheme?

    _____

    _____

    _____

4. Define the roles of contingency and reserve fund and be prepared to discuss:

    _____

    _____

    _____

5. What are the differences between an annual and capital campaign? Discuss.

    _____

    _____

    _____

6. Describe how are membership and program fees determined:

_____

_____

_____

7. Make a list of what needs to be included in the case statement used to guide the creation of a comprehensive financial development plan:

_____

_____

_____

8. Develop a list of the sections of a grant proposal:

_____

_____

_____

_____

_____

■ References

Bray, I. (2008). *Effective Fundraising for Nonprofits: Real-World Strategies that Work.* (2nd Ed.) Berkeley, CA: Nolo.

Brinckerhoff, P. (1994). *Mission-Based Management: Leading Your Not-For-Profit into the 21st Century.* Dillon, CO: Alpine Guild Books.

Chait, R. P., Ryan, W. P., and Taylor, B. E. (2005). *Governance as Leadership.* Hoboken, New Jersey: John Wiley & Sons, Inc.

Conway, D. (2003). *Practicing Stewardship.* Edited by Eugene R. Tempel. San Francisco, CA: John Wiley & Sons, Inc.

Grace, K. S. (2003). *Leadership and Team Building.* Edited by Eugene R. Tempel. San Francisco, CA: John Wiley & Sons, Inc.

Konrad, P., and Novak, A. (2000). *Financial Management for Nonprofits: Keys to Success.* Denver, CO: Regis University, School of Professional Studies.

Long, R. F. & Orosz, J. J. (1995). *Approaching the Foundation: A Useful U. S. Model. Philanthropy*, Austrailian Association of Philanthropy, Inc., Sydney, Australia.

Mintzer, R. ((2003). *The Everything Fundraising Book.* Avon: MA: F+W Publications Company.

Orosz, J. J. (2000). *The Insider's Guide to Grantmaking: How Foundations Find, Fund, and Manage Effective Programs.* San Francisco, CA: Jossey-Bass, Inc.

Regenovich, D. (2003). *Establishing a Planned Giving Program.* Edited by Eugene R. Tempel. San Francisco, CA: John Wiley & Sons, Inc.

Rosso, H. A. (1996). *Rosso on Fund Raising: Lessons from a Master's Lifetime.* San Francisco: Jossey-Bass.

Sargeant, A., Shang, J. and Associates. (2010). *Fundraising Principles and Practices.* San Francisco, CA: John Wiley & Sons, Inc.

Seiler, T. L. (2003). *Developing and Articulating a Case for Support.* Edited by Eugene R. Tempel. San Francisco, CA: John Wiley & Sons, Inc.

Weis, R. M. and Gantt, V. W. (2004). *Knowledge & Skill Development in Nonprofit Organizations.* Peosta, IA: Eddie Bowers Publishing.

Weis, R. M. and Gantt, V. W. (2002). *Leadership and Program Development in Nonprofit Organizations.* Peosta, IA: E. Bowers Publishing.

Wolf, T. (1999). *Managing a Nonprofit Organization.* New York: Prentice Hall.

Worth, M. J. (2009). *Nonprofit Management: Principles and Practices.* Thousand Oaks, CA: Sage Publications, Inc.

Zietlow, J., Hankin, J. A. and Seidner, A. G. (2007). *Financial Management for Nonprofit Organizations: Policies and Practices.* Hoboken, NJ: John Wiley & Sons, Inc.

7 Risk Management

Providing a safe and secure experience for all constituents, volunteers, and staff members must be among the highest priorities for nonprofit leadership and their organizations. **Risk** is inherent in every aspect of life, and nonprofit organizations are certainly not exempt from this reality, but they need to develop guidelines for understanding and dealing with risk in the most effective ways. Although insurance acquisition is primarily a task for administrators, developing and maintaining an effective risk management plan is the concern of board members, administrators, and program leaders.

Across the nonprofit sector, organizational leaders accept the principle that no program is totally safe and that risk is an inherent part of doing business. In many parts of the world, program participants often assume a large part of the responsibility for risk. But in the United States, participants are far less likely to accept as much personal responsibility for risk, and acceptance of responsibility varies from activity to activity and from one age group to another. This perspective on risk has produced a climate of **litigation** where people are quicker to turn to the law and engage the court system to determine responsibility and accountability. The resulting increased legal action has pushed liability insurance costs higher. As a result, organizations are having to bear varying and increasing degrees of responsibility and are forced to be as prepared as possible with adequate insurance coverage and a comprehensive plan for managing risks. The more thoroughly the plan is implemented, the more effectively risk is managed. If the legal system is engaged, a high quality risk management plan that is being consistently implemented will help support the organization during the process.

The chapter explores the types of risk that are typically found in nonprofit organizations, the management of risk, the case for risk management planning, and the development of a comprehensive risk management plan. Specific risk management guidelines for program activities that involve complex logistics and unusual potential for risk will also be examined. The chapter concludes with a review of relevant risk management processes and forms and the role insurance plays in providing financial relief for losses.

■ What is Risk and Risk Management?

A **risk** might be considered as any threat to a nonprofit organization's ability to accomplish its mission (Jackson, White, and Herman 1997). Threats take a number of different forms including potential risk to people, property, income, and reputation in the community. Risk can never be managed away, but organizations can develop a framework and a *culture* for both understanding and addressing risk in the most effective manner.

Maintaining insurance coverage does not eliminate risk; it just transfers some of the financial responsibility for risk to the insurance company in exchange for a premium.

Purchasing insurance does not reduce the possibility that an accident or some other mishap will occur; it simply provides a method of payment for any damages or compensation.

Risk management is an attitude and the commitment of everyone associated with the organization for dealing with potential threats to individuals, income, property, or reputation. The willingness to take risk depends on many factors, including the people who are involved and in charge, the organization's history with risk, and the financial conditions (Brinckerhoff 2009). A culture of risk management in an organization is illustrated by the thoroughness and application of a comprehensive plan for managing the risk. Good risk management plans are carefully undertaken and result in well thought out implementation procedures that are successfully integrated into the ongoing operation of the organization. They should be aimed at protecting people, property, income and the reputation of the organization (Weis and Gantt 2004).

Too often nonprofit organizations delegate risk management to a second or even third level of importance because of the complexities and potential cost involved, when a good risk management plan often reduces other problems and saves money in the long run. The Nonprofit Risk Management Center (*www.nonprofitrisk.org*) proposes **ten reasons** why nonprofit organizations need **risk management plans**:

1. Risk management plans help the organization protect clients, staff and volunteers and other individuals in the community from harm.
2. Nonprofit organizations are like any other institutions: they are vulnerable to claims and lawsuits alleging damages and injuries due to operational activities and are not exempt from punishment because of their altruistic mission.
3. Accidents and other adverse situations can often be prevented with a carefully thought out plan.
4. Nonprofit organizations often undertake projects collaboratively with other entities, and it is essential that organizations have a comprehensive plan that protects collaborative partners as well.
5. Part of a risk management plan prepares organizations to forecast, prevent, and cope with difficulties stemming from a crisis in public confidence or negative publicity.
6. Prospective board, staff, and volunteer members will be far more attracted to an organization with an integrated risk management plan in place. All three groups are interested in strategies used to protect members and preserve the organization's assets.
7. A good risk management plan can preserve various categories of assets and enable the organization to concentrate its focus on fulfilling its mission.
8. Although some finances are necessary in funding the risk management plan, it will enable the organization to conserve financial resources in the long run by preventing the loss of finances in unexpected situations.
9. A risk management plan allows the organization to concentrate the majority of its financial resources on realizing its mission, rather than on accidents and other unanticipated incidents.

10. Having an effective plan for managing risks focuses attention on safe and productive operations and allows the organization to offer more programs and activities within the framework of a positive environment.

The implementation of high quality risk management plans over time is the only way to create the culture in which the organization can be free to pursue its mission without being limited by fear of risk. To complement the above list of reasons a nonprofit organization needs a risk management plan, the Nonprofit Risk Management Center provides a Hallmark Tool that allows organizations to examine the quality of its plan and its implementation. The Tool is designed to inspire thoughtful risk-taking, to illuminate **risk management hallmarks** in risk-aware organizations, and to provide specific and practical guidance for strengthening risk management practices. The following are the hallmarks of a risk-aware nonprofit:

- Takes more risk than it avoids
- Heralds a risk management champion
- Guided by reality, in addition to scary headlines
- Is bold but smart
- Cultivates a "can do" attitude among paid staff and volunteers
- Sees the whole iceberg not just the tip
- Understands that hindsight is not 20/20, but it is better than a blindfold
- Tells it like it is
- Is transparent with insurance partners
- Values the journey, not just the destination
- Engages the board in their battle
- Looks at risk from everyone's perspective

As with hallmarks in any arena that serve as goals and guides, these are offered to help nonprofit leadership measure the context in which they work with the issue of risk. A well-managed nonprofit organization is not limited by the fear of risk and is free to actively pursue its mission.

Another reason to develop an effective risk management plan is that the types of legal actions that can be taken against nonprofit organizations are almost without limits. Risk management planning can help prevent many situations that might lead to a lawsuit. Some of the more **common types of lawsuits** against nonprofit organizations are listed below (Weis and Gantt 2004):

- Accidents are the basis of the largest number of lawsuits filed against organizations. When someone causes an automobile accident, for instance, or creates some other dangerous condition that results in an injury, it is referred to as a **tort.** Under tort law, liability is typically based on negligence that implies the person causing harm did not exercise a degree of care that a reasonable person in a similar situation would exhibit.
- A negligent act may be an indirect cause of an accident. For instance, an accident might occur while taking children through leadership training at a high ropes course. The organization may be held liable for a broken limb, based on the fact the ropes course instructors had not been properly trained. The organization may also be held liable if the instructors had not been properly screened and did not have adequate certification. Improper screening of staff and volunteer members

is the basis of many claims against nonprofit organizations each year.

- Board members may be sued if practices based on organizational policy they have set resulted in negligence and/or injury or some other form of harm. If a program participant is hurt on the diving board of the local YMCA and the policy allows the diving board to be present, then board members as the legal body that approved that policy are open to a potential legal action.
- Unfair employment practices are a large source of legal action. Some areas that are frequently a part of such legal action include discrimination, wrongful dismissal, sexual harassment, and other employment-related acts.
- In addition to organizations and directors being sued by people who allege injury, the appropriate government office for fines and penalties can also sue them. Another arm of the government, the Internal Revenue Service, can also file claim against board members for the organization's failure to file tax forms or for breaching other IRS rules. Although board members should certainly take great care in their duties of board service, the number of lawsuits is relatively small and most claims derive from the area of employment.

Different experts in the field of risk management propose a variety of **strategies for managing risk**. However, there seem to be **five steps in the process of managing risk** (Herman and Head 2002) (Herman 2005):

1. **Consider the Context.** The environment in which a nonprofit organization operates is changing constantly and needs to be considered and reviewed on a regular basis and be a starting point when any risk management issues surfaces. Changes in staff and volunteers, funding patterns, appetite for risk, experience with legal actions, and economic and political shifts can all impact an organization's view of risk and how it manages risk.

2. **Identify Risks.** Each operation, program, or activity presents conditions or situation that might present risks. Both obvious and not so obvious risks must be explored. For example, a service program that involves cleaning up debris along the bank of a lake presents some potential risk of drowning along with the possible harm from dangerous materials. Identifying risk should be done on a regular basis to respond to changes in the context. A good practice is for a group with diverse perspectives to periodically review the organization's work and brainstorm to consider risks, both current and potential.

3. **Evaluate Risks.** There is no single or preferred way in which to analyze, review, or rank the list of risks identified in step 2. Determining the relative importance of risks can be accomplished by asking the following questions:
   - What is the probability that a risk will result in an accident, injury, illness, or damage?
   - How severe would the loss be if it occurred?

4. **Decide What to Do and Take Action.** This step requires the most commitment of time and diligence in making decisions about the actions that will be taken to address identified risks. It is important to start by considering the three basic ways to handle risk:
   - **Prevention (Avoidance).** Matching participants to appropriate experiences is

one key to preventing and avoiding risk, as is effective orientation, training, and appropriate supervision.

- **Risk Reduction.** Providing safety rules and well thought out emergency procedures are examples of risk reduction. In the case of the lake clean-up above, following safety procedures regarding how close individuals should get to the water's edge and providing effective materials such as gloves, orange vests and/or life jackets are ways to reduce risk. Clear communication is also important in risk reduction.

- **Risk Retention or Transfer.** Risk retention or transfer refers to how a loss will be handled should it occur. That is, who is responsible for the loss and who will pay for the loss?

5. **Monitor and Adjust.** It is important to regularly review risk management policies and practices, particularly after a risk issue has been handled. This allows the organization to learn from experience, improving the policies and practices or eliminating those that no longer apply. This step keeps the risk management plan current and easier to apply.

Experts with the Nonprofit Risk Management Center propose four somewhat different strategies for managing risk that align with and support the pursuit of the goals set with the use of the Hallmark Tool presented earlier in this chapter:

1. **Avoidance.** Most nonprofit organizations will simply not offer a service or conduct an activity if it is considered too risky and will curtail programs or services if risks cannot be managed well. For instance, providing a zip line at a Boys and Girls Club swimming facility could be great fun, but the inherent risk might far outweigh any benefits.

   A number of nonprofit organizations that transport members or clients are scrutinizing this activity more closely and deciding it may not be cost or risk effective. If the risk outweighs the benefits, but completely stopping an activity impairs the mission of the organization, another technique, modification, can be considered.

2. **Modification.** This implies changing the activity so that it can still be implemented, but within bounds, so the potential for harm is within acceptable limits. Modification might be as simple as screening volunteers more carefully, taking hazardous materials away from a fence next to a YMCA, or removing the diving board from the Salvation Army pool area.

   With the example of transporting clients or members above, some modifications that could keep a program within acceptable limits might include:

   - Making sure driver licenses are up-to-date and that no driver transporting members has an unsafe or unacceptable driving record.
   - Providing drivers with training relevant to safe driving, accident procedures, emergencies, and other proper vehicle operation procedures.
   - Conducting regular vehicle inspections and maintenance, and removing or fixing any unsafe vehicles.
   - Maintaining records on all risk management procedures.

   Modifying activities increases safety throughout operations and activities while still allowing activities to continue within the revised framework. These modifications are a clear message to members and personnel that safety is the number one concern of the organization and helps advance a quality risk management culture.

3. **Retention.** If an organization decides that it will retain the risk inherent with a certain practice, then it must be prepared to handle that threat if it occurs. For instance, if an organization decides not to purchase insurance for the loss of money, then it should consider a contingency fund that could handle financial losses that might occur from theft or some other manner. To manage risk, the organization should anticipate what losses could occur in various areas and decide the extent to which those risks could be handled. This type of projection and planning should be ongoing, since potential losses may increase or decrease, from case to case, and the organization must stand ready to handle them.

4. **Sharing.** Working with another institution to share the risk or the financial consequences is another method of managing risk. Agreements for sharing with other institutions may include other nonprofit organizations, insurance companies (through premiums), or through some other contractual agreement. This option is also referred to as "transfer," since it is possible to transfer risk to another party. It is, however, almost impossible to fully transfer the risk for an activity to another party and maintain responsibility for the activity.

   For instance, a nonprofit organization has purchased "adequate" fire insurance, and a fire occurs. The insurance may cover the cost of property and injury, but not cover the loss of membership or program fees if programs are not operating or the serious damage to the organization's reputation for poor safety practices and not managing risk effectively. In this case, financial loss has not been completely "transferred" and the organization may still experience damage to its reputation.

■ The Process for Developing a Risk Management Plan

Administrative leaders and board members should undertake the development and implementation of risk management plans with input from staff members, volunteers, organizational members, and other constituents. Another consideration is to involve a specialist in risk management to provide guidance in the development of a plan. The organization may wish to confer with other specialists as well, such as a human resource professional who could examine the employee handbook, an accountant who could help in developing financial and accounting controls, and an insurance professional who could review related policies and insurance coverage. Many nonprofit organizations seek to include people with this expertise among their board and committee membership. Ideally, representatives with this range of needed expertise will be included in a **risk management committee** to guide the planning process and oversee the long-term development of the plan (Herman 2005). Although there are any number of approaches to developing a quality risk management plan, this section will concentrate the four-step process recommended by the Nonprofit Risk Management Center (Jackson, White, and Herman 1999):

Step 1. Develop Risk Management Goals and a Policy Statement

The first step in developing a risk management plan is to determine the goals of the plan. The goals are set in collaboration with the Executive Director (ED) and the board of directors along with input from a Risk Management Committee, although *only board members can actually approve the final plan.* In addition to setting goals, this group must also design a brief (one or two sentence) risk management policy statement expressing the organization's commitment to managing risk and outlining what individuals throughout the organization can do to support the risk management plan. The risk management policy statement can also be used to demonstrate to others the seriousness with which the organization is taking this important issue.

One of the first steps in establishing goals is to review reasons that it is important to have a risk management plan. An extensive list is presented earlier in this chapter, which includes the desire to reduce accidents, which also lowers insurance rates. Other reasons may include the discussion of prevention activities that can occur before any threat or loss and activities that can occur in response to a threat or loss. A thorough review of how the organization's programs and services will help determine what can be done to address these risks and others.

Based on the list of reasons for taking action that surface from this initial review effort, the Risk Management Committee can develop three or four specific goals for the risk management program, such as:

1. To protect the organization's financial assets.
2. To provide a safe and healthy environment for staff members, volunteers and constituents.
3. To develop plans for any crisis that should occur.
4. To confirm that insurance is adequate and cost effective.

After determining the goals of the risk management plan, the next step is to write a **risk management policy.** The risk management policy is extracted from the program goals. The policy should reflect the goals of the program and point to actions that others can take in the risk management efforts. A simulated Scottsdale Salvation Army policy statement is included below:

> *The Scottsdale Salvation Army's number one priority is to protect its people, property, income, and reputation through the practice of effective risk management. The organization's board, staff members, and volunteers are dedicated to maintaining the safety and dignity of all constituents.*

A risk management policy can and should appear on all important documents associated with the organization, and it should be emphasized more than anything else the organization promotes.

Step 2. Determine Responsibility of the Risk Management Program

With consultation from the board of directors, the ED should assign responsibility for developing and implementing the organization's risk management program to the Risk

Management Committee. In addition to key staff, board members and constituents, experts from appropriate fields may be included in the committee to make sure that the needed expertise is available. Areas of expertise needed may include:

- insurance
- legal area
- public relations
- safety
- program development
- content areas aligned with the programs and services of the organization

The composition of the Risk Management Committee will vary with the type of risk associated with the organization and may change over time as programs and services change and risk change. There is also benefit to having people involved in the committee who have personal knowledge of the types of risks associated with the programs and services of the organization, which may be found among its constituent groups and program participants. (Herman 2005)

The Risk Management Committee should consider dividing into subcommittees to address various operational categories. These categories could include; program, finance, building and grounds, governance (board operations), and public relations, to mention several. The subcommittees would then be charged with designing materials for in-service training as well as be responsible for insuring that the training is conducted, which should be ongoing. The greater the involvement of everyone in risk management training, the greater the possibility that risk management will be understood as the highest priority and practices across the organization.

Step 3. Develop a Working Plan for the Program

The first step of the Risk Management Committee is to develop an action plan and assign responsibility and completion dates for each part of the plan. Committee and subcommittee tasks are listed next:

- Discuss the four steps of risk management.
- Identify key subcommittees and determine responsibilities.
- Begin risk identification and analysis by subcommittee.
- Review, analyze, and consolidate subcommittee findings.
- Set priorities for risk management (top, moderate, low).
- Determine appropriate risk management technique.

A. Discuss the Four Techniques of Risk Management

Determining techniques of risk management provides a framework for the work of the Risk Management Committee. A brief summary of the four stages in the typical risk management process follows:

1. Recognize and Identify Risk

The first stage in managing risk is to pull the Risk Management Committee together for a brainstorming session to determine what can go wrong in the organization. Such a session begins with a discussion of potential threats to people, property, income, and reputation. Many risks are generic in that they are virtually present within any organization, such as wet floors around a swimming pool, the potential for theft, and allegations of improper hiring or firing are typical kinds of threats. Other threats can be unique to specific organizations, such as sexual abuse within a youth organization, or a malpractice suit against an organization for providing free legal services. The facilitator for such a brainstorming session should be someone with expertise in both facilitation and risk management, when possible.

2. **Assess and Prioritize Risk**

   Once potential risks have been identified, the committee can begin evaluating the risks mentioned and determine the probability of certain risks materializing, how often they might occur, and what would happen if they did occur. Following this evaluation, the committee (or subcommittees within the committee) can begin assigning a high, moderate, or low grading for risks based on their probability and severity. Once labels of High, Moderate, or Low are assigned to each risk, the committee can look at those risks with a "High" grading to determine if the organization should avoid the activity, provide appropriate insurance for the activity, and/or manage the risk with specific actions. An activity that is placed in a "Low" priority might be postponed until those activities in the top and moderate categories have been addressed.

3. **Select and Initiate Effective Risk Management Techniques**

   The four risk management techniques explained earlier are briefly reviewed below:
   - *Avoidance.* Eliminate all activities that are deemed too risky.
   - *Modification.* Restructure the activity so any threats are within acceptable limits.
   - *Retention.* Accept all risk and prepare for potential consequences.
   - *Sharing* (transfer). Share potential consequences with another entity, such as an insurance company.

     This implementation phase is a critical part of risk management. Expectations for the results of using each technique should be clear, measurable, and easily observed. This entire process needs to be explained carefully to board, staff, constituents and anyone else who could be affected by the process.

4. **Continually Monitor and Change the Risk Management Program when Necessary**

   This stage of the risk management process is also important because it involves members of the Risk Management Committee evaluating the plan that is being implemented and determining if it is having its desired effect. The committee needs to assess whether or not the plan is working and if not, it needs to modify the plan to become more effective. Monitoring the plan requires a structured communication process in which members can interact with each other at scheduled times as well as at impromptu times to assess and make adjustments.

B. Identify Key Subcommittees and Determine Responsibilities

Because of the complex nature of developing a risk management plan, sharing the responsibilities with subcommittees simplifies the process and can make it more effective by having the right expertise involved in each element of the planning. Subdividing tasks by the organization's different operations is one way to address this complexity. Following are some of the typical subcommittees:

- **Programs.** All identified programs can be assigned to a subcommittee specifically established for this operation. Another way to do this would be to have a subcommittee assigned to categories of programs, such as special events, facility-based programs, or field trips. Each of these areas can involve unique and significant risk that may need to be addressed.

- **Fundraising activities.** Fundraising activities present a unique set of risks. Controls and security processes for handling money need to be carefully spelled out for all to know and follow. Careful consideration should also be given in developing a system of controls that virtually prohibits any possible impropriety.

- **Administrative operations.** Administrative activities actually have a great potential for threat or loss when areas such as physical facilities, employment practices, office policies and procedures, computer equipment and data, and the accounting and financial operations of the nonprofit organization are considered.

- **Governance (board operations).** The legal and fiduciary responsibilities of a board of directors is significant, and examining the operation of the board, including legal documents, bylaws and articles of incorporation, is an important part of risk management planning. The procedures for board minutes, orientation programs, and operating policies and procedures should also be a focus of risk management.

A Risk Management Project Task Worksheet can be used to assign responsibilities and to track progress. A sample task sheet similar to the one suggested by the Nonprofit Risk Management Center is presented in Figure 7.1.

C. Begin Risk Identification and Analysis by Subcommittee

Each subcommittee needs to begin analyzing risk potential for the assigned area of the organization. Committee members should be thorough in their efforts to identify risks. There are a number of tools available to help members identify risks. Several tools are discussed below:

- **Surveys, Checklists and Questionnaires.** Forms that help organizations identify risks are sometimes referred to as **exposure analysis forms** (as in "exposure to risk"). These forms are developed by insurance companies and businesses specializing in risk management and can be helpful to nonprofit organizations in identifying risks. Risks can sometimes also be determined by focusing on the questions asked with insurance applications.

- **Internal Documents.** Documents and records, including bylaws, employee manuals, the annual audit, policies and procedures manuals, board and committee minutes, annual reports, fundraising materials, marketing flyers, accident reports and other informational documents, can be valuable clues to where risk may be found in the work of the organization.

- **Financial Statements and Records.** Financial records, such as annual reports, monthly statements, and audit reports, may be helpful in determining whether there are any threats in financial controls and other risks.

- **Workflow.** Analyzing all of the processes involved with delivering core services

---

Figure 7.1
Risk Management Project Task Worksheet

Organization: Lexington Kentucky Family YMCA
Date: November 15, 2011

Task	Leader	Start/Finish Dates
Risk Identification		11/15 – 12/15
Special Events	Jeffery Howe	
Field Trips	Ann Sakona	
Sports Leagues	Jeremy Fishe	
Fundraising	Roland Gunn	
Administration	Sandy Lynd	
Governance	David Monahan	
Review Subcommittee Findings	David Monahan	12/15 – 12/31
Establish Priorities	David Monahan	1/10 – 1/30
Evaluate and Select Techniques		
Special Events	Jeffery Howe	
Field Trips	Ann Sakona	
Sports Leagues	Jeremy Fishe	
Fundraising	Roland Gunn	
Administration	Sandy Lynd	
Governance	David Monahan	
Document the Program	Sandy Lynd	3/15 – 3/30

---

will help determine if there are any problem areas. Areas to check include registration procedures, service delivery, complaints, grievance resolutions and the monitoring and supervision of staff and members. Marketing, employment, and fundraising procedures are other areas to be considered.

- **Personal Inspections.** Going over paperwork can assist in determining risks, but walking around and personally examining facility areas, financial safeguard systems, and other types of potential areas of risk can provide additional knowledge regarding possible losses. Personal examinations should be done at different times of the schedule so that numerous types of activities can be observed and assessed.
- **Interviews.** In addition to surveys and questionnaires, conducting personal interviews can provide an in depth level of information regarding potential risks. Interviews should be conducted with those individuals who know more about

existing risks than anyone else: staff members, volunteers, constituents, and any other parties that interact with the organization.

- **Loss Histories.** Identifying what kinds of losses have occurred in the past will help to insure that history does not repeat itself and that the organization can provide safeguards against any trends with particular situations. It is also a good idea to examine what has happened in similar organizations, a process referred to as **bench-marking** (establishing a standard of practice by which the organization will measure its results).

D. Review, Analyze and Consolidate Subcommittee Findings

Once the subcommittees have collected their information and recorded it on the Risk Management Project Worksheet (Figure 7.1), the full committee should review the information. A number of mutual risks may be common to most areas, such as potential for child abuse, automobile accidents, or injuries, and these can be consolidated on one worksheet. A separate worksheet can be kept for risks unique to specific areas, such as employment procedures.

E. Set Priorities for Risk Management (high, moderate, low)

After risks have been identified, subcommittees begin an assessment of the potential for each risk. Projections must be made for the chances a loss will occur (*frequency*) and its probable effect (*severity*). **Frequency** indicates the probability a risk will actually occur and how often it might occur. **Severity** measures the probable effect and cost and negative impacts to the organization if the loss occurs. Each risk can then be graded as high, moderate or low for both frequency and severity (see Figure 7.2 below).

Assigning grades to potential risks can be challenging, to say the least, but looking at past history and assessing current operations can help subcommittee members assess and project the frequency and severity. Looking at each past operation to see if there have been injuries--thefts and fires, for instance--and considering the effects of these losses can help determine the grading of potential losses. Although it is still only a projection of losses, it is a calculated and knowledgeable projection.

Once all risks have been graded, they can then be divided into high, moderate, and low priorities. For example, incidents within the category of sports leagues, where there is a

Figure 7.2
Risk Identification Grades

Risk	SEVERITY			FREQUENCY		
	High	Moderate	Low	High	Moderate	Low
Special Events		x			x	
Field Trips	x					x
Sports Leagues	x			x		

high potential for severity along with a high possibility for frequency, would certainly go to a high risk priority level. Something with a more moderate level of frequency and severity, such as a special event, would be listed as a moderate priority, and so on.

Categories that receive the highest priority have the potential of being highly detrimental to a nonprofit organization. These categories should be looked at closely to see if the organization should avoid the risk altogether or transfer a part of the responsibility of the risk to another party, such as an insurance company. Categories of risk that receive a lower priority for severity and frequency may not require such strong actions, but must still be assessed and evaluated. All three categories require close attention.

F. Determine and Establish Appropriate Risk Management Techniques

Once risks have been identified and prioritized, attention should turn to handling risk through various techniques. Sometimes each area requires a combination of techniques. For instance, field trips would certainly require the purchase of insurance covering travel and potential incidents that may occur during the trip. A screening and driver training program could also be put in place. This would help to promote safety and lower the cost of insurance premiums. The organization may, instead, choose to contract a part of the responsibility of the field trips to another party, such as a charter bus organization. This would still require some insurance, but some of the responsibility of the trip would have been transferred.

Once strategies have been identified and put in place for the high level risks, attention can be focused on other priorities, and techniques can be put in place for these as well. For instance, special events were assessed at a moderate level for frequency and severity (see Figure 7.2 above). Checking existing insurance may determine that it is adequate and that no additional insurance is required to satisfy the "severity" grade. Providing adequate staff and volunteer risk management training, along with appropriate waivers (discussed later in this chapter) for participants may be all that is required for this category.

Step 4 – Document, Implement, and Monitor the Plan

After techniques for every risk are established for managing risk, documentation processes need to be refined or put in place, along with plans to monitor the ongoing implementation of the plan. Piecing together worksheets and documents produced during the overall process will result in a Risk Management Manual to facilitate implementation. This manual can be invaluable for helping everyone in the organization manage risk effectively.

A number of items should be included in the manual:

- Risk management policy statement and goals
- Responsibilities of the Risk Management Committee
- Job descriptions for committee members and subcommittee members
- A list of all members including addresses, phones numbers and e-mail addresses
- A synopsis of the work that went into developing the manual
- A list of techniques and monitoring methods for each risk
- Crisis and emergency management plans
- Copies of Risk Management Committee reports
- A summary of the organization's insurance coverage

Figure 7.3
Risk Management Guidelines for Specific Activities

I.   GENERAL DESCRIPTION
       A. Name of Program
       B. Type of Activity
       C. Level of Activity

II.   DATES AND TIMES
       A. Dates
       B. Times

III.   GOALS AND OBJECTIVES
       A. Organizational
       B. Activity

IV.   LOCATION
       A. Site/Area
       B. Weather
       C. Routes
       D. Facilities

V.   TRANSPORTATION
       A. Mode
       B. Routes/Destinations

VI.   PARTICIPANTS
       A. Number
       B. Skill Level
       C. Characteristics

VII.   LEADERS
       A. Number/Roles
       B. Qualifications

VIII.   EQUIPMENT
       A. Type and Amount
       B. Control

IX.   CONDUCTING THE ACTIVITY
       A. Pre-Activity Preparation
       B. Group Control
       C. Teaching/Instruction Strategy
       D. Time Management

X.   EMERGENCY PREPAREDNESS
       A. Policies
       B. Health Forms
       C. Telephone Numbers

Source: Edginton, Hudson and Ford 1999

Putting together a Risk Management Plan and Manual will take some time, but it is an important investment in the long-term wellbeing of the organization and all of its constituents.

Once strategies have been developed and a formal plan exists, the committee must then decide how to implement the plan. Responsibilities, deadlines, and objectives for the plan need to be developed in order for it to be effective. An introduction of the plan and an explanation of the overall organizational approach and commitment to risk management must be presented to all involved with required training for staff and volunteer members.

The Risk Management Committee must monitor the plan continually through established methods of collecting information, and it must evaluate the effectiveness of the plan on a reoccurring basis. As the organization and the communities they serve change, all aspects of the plan should be reviewed and revised as frequently as is appropriate. This review and revision process should be done as needed, but with a formal review process occurring annually. Good risk management plans become a part of an organization's culture and are an integral part of helping it focus on its mission and improve the chances of success.

∎ Risk Management Guidelines for Specific Program Activities

Because of the nature of some programs, certain activities may require more specific guidelines. Program activities such as water sports, team sports, some special events, and other programs with complicated logistics seem to take on lives of their own and can be managed more effectively with guidelines tailored to the distinctive nature of each activity. In a sense, risk management guidelines for specific program activities become a *plan within a plan*. In other words, guidelines for specific activities fit into the overall risk management plan. Although each of these programs or activities need to be considered separately, the guidelines included in Figure 7.3 can be beneficial in managing risk for a number of different kinds of program activities (Edginton, Hudson, and Ford 1999).

Each activity should be examined carefully to make sure that all identified risks would be graded low enough to be acceptable or lower modifications (e.g., helmets, gloves, lifeguards, trail guides, and safety equipment). It is also important that personnel have the appropriate credentials and training, that participants are of the right age and skill level, that the facilities and equipment are safe and effective, and that no unavoidable risk exists prior to detailed planning. Consider the following when applying the guidelines in Figure 7.3 in developing plans for each program and activity (Weis and Gantt 2004):

I.   **General Description.**

A. **Name of Program or Activity**

Appropriately naming a program or activity helps staff members, volunteers, and participants to begin forming a mental picture of the what might occur, including any potential risk. Organizers can begin to brainstorm for potential risks. For instance, a swimming activity may conjure up images of drowning, hypothermia, or choking. A baseball league will include equipment--such as bats, bases, and fences--that can cause bruises or broken bones. Even something as seemingly harmless as an arts and crafts program might include potentially hazardous materials, such as cutting instruments, electrical tools, and heat from the use of a kiln.

B. Type of Activity

Determining what will take place with each program or activity will help in designing the appropriate risk management techniques.

C. Level of Activity

Using appropriate terms when describing the skill levels associated with each activity is also important. Terms such as *beginners*, *advanced-beginners*, *intermediate*, and *expert* may suffice. Sometimes activities have their own set of terms in describing skill levels, but the most important rule is to use terms that everyone understands, staff and participants alike.

II. Date(s) and Time(s)

The designation of dates and times is important so that contingency plans can be made for events that will be held out-of-doors, in case of inclement weather. Another consideration is timing: an event held out-of-doors in the summer will have a longer opportunity for daylight than if the same event were held in the winter. It is also important to plan things so that activities do not last so long as to unduly fatigue leaders and participants and so that each group receives adequate break time and adequate refreshment. The possibilities for fatigue and overstimulation should be considered when planning a long event, and adequate downtime and refreshment breaks should be built into the schedule.

III. Goals and Objectives

Listing and understanding goals and objectives is imperative to the   overall success of the activity. Understanding purpose gives direction to the activity and some guidelines for what risks might be acceptable or not acceptable. Objectives need to be clearly written with specific, projected outcomes. Objectives should be as inclusive as possible, stating skill, knowledge, emotional, spiritual, and/ or physical attainment when appropriate. Both leaders and participants should have a good understanding of the objectives.

IV. Location

The selection of a location for a program has a lot to do with the potential risk and the type of risk that may be involved.

A. Activity Site or Area

The activity site or area should be described by name and/or details may be listed that allow participants to find the site using a map. Information regarding any special hazards associated with getting to the site or the site itself should be identified in advance. Current, in depth information should be available regarding the site prior to the event, and every attempt should be made to visit a site prior to conducting the activity.

B. Weather and Climate

Weather should be assessed carefully prior to an activity, particularly an outdoor activity or one in which travel is involved. Being prepared for a change in weather during an activity is also extremely important. It is far better to be prepared for the worst-case scenario and to operate on the conservative side.

C. Routes

Activities that involve travel or moving from one place to another should be precisely described in the program plan, particularly when a trip of several days or more is planned. Emergency escape routes should be considered and communicated along with possible lodging sites, locations for food and liquids, and locations of medical facilities or services.

D. Facilities

Facilities that are to be used for an activity should be fully described. Directions should be provided if the facility is located away from the home organization. All facilities should be carefully inspected, especially those with high potential for risk, such as ropes courses, swimming pools, gyms, and playing fields. When visiting lakes, streams, and oceans, it is imperative to understand the tide movement, strength of the currents, the depth of the water, and any unusual occurrences associated with that particular aquatic area. Proper plans for fire emergencies are important for activities in buildings. Fire alarms need to be continually tested, and a fire emergency exit plan needs to be established and practiced. Periodic inspections of building systems, like electrical and air conditioning must be a priority. Other equipment that should be formally inspected as the risk management committee dictates includes diving boards, gymnastic equipment, swimming pool chemical and filter systems, and any other equipment or structure that may include a risk.

V. Transportation

A. Mode of Transportation

Transportation plans for activities need to be clearly devised and communicated. If a charter bus is chosen for a ski trip, then the company providing the bus should be carefully checked out for its overall safety record, screening of drivers, training requirements for drivers, insurance coverage, and scheduling procedures. An understanding of equipment maintenance records is important. Buses, vans, and cars that are maintained by the organization must also be properly serviced and documented. Drivers should be carefully screened, trained, and monitored.

B. Routes, Distance, and Time

Participants should understand prior to an activity that involves transportation which routes are going to be used, the distance to be traveled, and the time involved, as it can best be projected. Alternative routes and times should be discussed, as should emergency action plans. Often, the transportation of participants and staff members is the most dangerous part of an activity, yet it is too often considered as an afterthought. The risk management plan for transportation needs to be reviewed and followed diligently.

VI. Participants

A. Number

Most events will have both a maximum and a minimum number of participants set in advance. Minimum numbers are often set so that resources are not spent on events with little interest, and maximum numbers are set to insure quality and often to meet guidelines for space accommodation and safety. Both are valid concerns, but flexibility is important when possible and appropriate.

B. Skill Level

Participants should be aware in advance of what skill levels, if any, correlate with a program activity. In many instances, the terms *beginner*, *novice*, *intermediate*, *advanced*, and *expert level* are assigned to different activities and each will have a different skill requirement and a different risk management strategy.

C. Characteristics

Participant characteristics have to do with specific, individual attributes, such as whether a participant is an adult or a child, male or female, and in some cases, disabled, highly fit or just starting a fitness program. Knowing as many characteristics as possible regarding the participants makes it easier for program staff to assign the right kind of supervision. It also allows the participant a chance to understand more about the challenges of a particular activity. For instance, a ten-mile hike or a climb through a hillside covered with rocks would not work for a novice, but may be fine for an intermediate-level participant. Developing a participant profile helps to prevent mismatching lower level skills or other attributes with an activity that is too challenging.

VII. Leaders

A. Number and Roles

Describing the criteria necessary for activity leaders in the program plan is a wise concept, as is listing the number of leaders required for each activity. Most organizations have a required ratio of staff-to-participants for quality assurance and risk management purposes. Program staff members are usually the most expensive part of a program budget, but generally, the more qualified staff an activity has, the better and the safer the event.

B. Qualifications

It is important to maintain a current list of qualifications and years of experience of individual staff members. Hiring standards and requirements for staff members should be at least as stringent as those of comparable organizations in the region.

VIII. Equipment

A. Type and Amount

Listing the various types of equipment involved in an activity and certifying that the equipment meets acceptable guidelines indicates that activity leaders are making every effort to keep risk to a minimum. Maintaining the right number of tumbling mats, for instance, is important, because having a lesser number could raise a concern for safety.

B. Control of equipment

A system for controlling and maintaining equipment is essential to be certain it is kept clean, dry, and in good condition for the next usage. Equipment should be checked, both when it is returned and when it is checked out again, to maintain the best condition possible and to avoid any surprises during an activity.

IX. Conduct of the Program Activity

A. Pre-Activity Preparations

Pre-activity meetings should be included in the risk management plan for all activities to promote a culture that expects the plan to be integrated with the program implementation process.

B. Group Control and Communication

How communication will occur within a group activity, including roll and attendance keeping, should be included in the risk management plan. This, of course, includes any and all safety instructions, as well as a detailed account of who is responsible to whom and for what.

C. Teaching Strategy

Teaching strategies for developing various skills should be documented and notes kept on any variation from non-standard methods, with reasons for the variation. Teaching strategies affect risk levels, so they need to be understood and documented appropriately.

D. Time Management Plan

Setting beginning and ending times and dates for activities, along with times and dates for specific parts of the activity schedule, provides guidance for what is to happen, when it happens, and how long each part takes. This provides the program team valuable information for overall program development and is essential for good risk management.

X. Emergency Preparedness

Developing strategies for program emergencies is a critical part of any risk management plan. Plans for fires, storms, floods, first aid, missing persons, transportation breakdowns and other emergency situations should be developed and documented.

Each program and activity plan should also have a place to include emergency help numbers and emergency numbers for participants in case of an incident. If health forms are necessary, they should be current and attached with the plan. The risk management guidelines for specific programs described in the last section addresses most components of program activities and can be used as standard operating procedures for similar types of activities. Standard operating procedures or guidelines, as such, can be easily inserted in the overall risk management plan. Release forms and waivers will be discussed in the next section.

■ Reports, Forms, Waivers and Releases

There are a number of reports and forms that can help in the planning and organizing of program and activities. These forms can be prepared by the administrative and program staff, but they should be reviewed by the organizational legal counsel to help make sure that the information needed for legal issues and effective risk management is being collected. Examples of forms include the following (Weis and Gantt 2004):

- **Agreements.** Specific agreements can be developed between collaborating organizations, so that expectations are clear regarding which organization is responsible for specific aspects of the undertaking. These kinds of agreements clarify roles and make managing risk much easier.

- **Participation Agreement.** Sometimes called **Assumptions of Risk Agreements**, the document is developed to accurately reflect that the participant understands the risks, agrees to abide by safety rules, and agrees to a established behavior code.
- **Accident Reports.** Accident reports should be completed on any accident that occurs during a program or activity supported by the organization and details of any injury that results. The report must include a detailed description of what happened, a list of the parties involved, and an account of what was done to alleviate any pain or suffering.
- **Incident Reports.** Incidents that are out of the ordinary which pose potential risk to individuals, property, finances or reputation should be recorded and any disposition noted.
- **Personal Health Forms.** Health forms may be required of all participants in the programs and activities of an organization, or they may be required to complete a form prior to specific activities. Health forms should include relevant information such as the participant's limitations, medications, allergies, disabilities, and health status.
- **Waivers/Releases.** These two terms are interchangeable here, and each implies that the participants agree not to hold the organization responsible. For minor children, this form is only valid when signed by an adult, and parents or guardians **can never sign away the rights of children under the legal age of majority**, as previously mentioned in Chapter 5. Signing such a form for children indicates intent, but does not have a strong legal basis.

Signing a waiver does not eliminate the potential of being sued for negligence. Most U.S. courts have ruled that organizations providing a public service cannot absolve themselves from liability to the public to whom they are providing a service, particularly in cases of negligence. Regardless of this fact, it is important that organizations protect themselves and their members as much as possible by providing waivers to participants. Waivers indicate that the participant has at least stated that he or she will not hold the organization responsible and understands the risk involved, which may dissuade the participant from legal resolve. Release forms also remind participants of potential risks and make them more alert to hazards associated with activities. They are, therefore, well worth the effort.

■ Insurance

As stated earlier in this chapter, insurance does not eliminate risk; it just transfers some of the financial responsibility for risk to the insurance company in exchange for the premium the organization pays. Insurance is the typical way of handling risk to prevent excessive or possibly devastating financial loss to an agency or entity (Weis and Gantt 2004). Insurance policies assure the availability of some of the needed funds to pay for damages and to compensate victims following a loss. Just as for profit businesses, nonprofit organizations are vulnerable to losses stemming from accidents or negligence. Given this vulnerability, it would seem that most nonprofit organizations would be adequately insured, when in fact many organizations carry no insurance or are only marginally insured. Insurance rates are constantly increasing and budgets are often tight, so smaller organizations will sometimes take their chances that a loss will not be catastrophic.

Although insurance is important, it is not the only mechanism available to a nonprofit organization. Other options include setting aside **reserve funds** to pay for potential losses, or establishing a line of credit with a financial institution to cover something that might go wrong down the road. Both of these options need to be calculated with the cost of insurance versus the loss of readily available money through the establishment of a reserve fund, or the loss of money to cover a credit owed.

Insurance is usually divided property and liability coverage (Herman 2005). **Property insurance** typically covers tangible assets such as furniture, buildings, computers, documents and equipment. This type of coverage will often replace the losses. It can also pay the cost of a temporary office, if one is needed until a more permanent space can be provided, and it can covers loss of income during periods when programs and activities may not be possible. **Liability insurance** provides protection from claims and lawsuits against the organization. It also provides financial relief if the organization is found to be negligent and that negligence has caused damages to another person or organization. These general liability insurance policies--usually referred to as **commercial general liability**--do not cover all losses, particularly those arising from board decisions and the delivery of professional services. These types of claims can generally be protected by purchasing **directors' and officers' policies**, which provide financial relief in the event the organization and/or its officers and staff are sued regarding a loss as a result of a board decision or of a service provided. (Weis and Gantt 2004)

Because of the many different kinds of insurance needs and the number of types of insurance policies available, a committee consisting of administrative and program staff members, board members, and experts in insurance should be formed to help determine needed coverage. Often, insurance is either mandated by law and/or by the organization's national affiliate. Many times, branches of the same organization or organizations with similar missions and programs will band together to purchase less expensive group insurance policies. In addition, state and regional associations of nonprofit organizations typically provide the opportunity for nonprofits to participate in group insurance programs. The National Council of Nonprofits (www.councilofnonprofits.org) is a good place to find links to these types of group support systems. In most cases, it is far better to have adequate insurance coverage for all potential losses than to rely on other sources of relief.

■ Summary

A risk could be anything that is deemed a threat to an organization's accomplishing its mission. Threats usually take the form of potential risk to people, property, income, and reputation in the community. Risk can never be fully managed away, but organizations can develop ways to deal with risk effectively. Maintaining insurance transfers some of the financial responsibility for risk to insurance companies in exchange for a premium, but does not eliminate risk.

Risk management is a plan for dealing with potential risks. There are a number of reasons for developing organizational risk management plans, all of which are aimed at protecting individuals, income, property, and reputation.

There are a number of different strategies for managing risk, and they generally include identifying, evaluating, and handling risk. Experts at the Risk Management Center propose other strategies, including avoidance, modification, retention, and sharing, all of which make it easier for an organization to manage risk.

The development of an organizational risk management plan should be undertaken by a risk management committee made up of board members, staff leaders, constituents, and experts in the field of risk management. Developing a good risk management plan involves four steps:

- Developing risk management goals and a policy statement.
- Determining responsibility of the risk management program.
- Developing a working plan for the program.
- Documenting implementing, and monitoring the program.

Certain program activities may require more specific guidelines. In a sense, these guidelines become a plan within the overall organizational risk management plan. They include a general description and details of the program, including dates, times, goals, objectives, location, transportation, participants, leaders, equipment, activities, and emergency processes. Planning and assessing these details in advance adds a great deal of strength to reducing risks in each program activity.

There are a number of reports and forms that can help to plan and organize program activities and help to minimize risk. These include agreements between collaborating organizations, agreements for program participants, accident and incident reports, personal health forms, and waivers and releases.

Insurance is a way to transfer some of the financial responsibility for risk to the insurance company in exchange for a premium. Insurance is the typical way of handling risk to prevent excessive or possibly devastating financial loss to an agency or entity. Because of the many different kinds of insurance needs and the number of insurance policies, a leadership committee should examine the best possible coverage for the organization.

This chapter addressed, in part, the Nonprofit Leadership Alliance Certification Competency Requirements of Nonprofit Risk Management.

■ **Reflection and Application**

1. Relying on the textbook's definition of risk, describe the three key risks involved in a program activity in which you have recently participated:

    _____

    _____

    _____

2. Describe the five steps in the typical risk management process:

    _____

    _____

    _____

    _____

3. In one paragraph, summarize the ten reasons the Nonprofit Risk Management Center describes as important reasons to have a risk management plan.

    _____

    _____

    _____

    _____

    _____

4. What is the importance of a policy statement and how could it be used?

    _____

    _____

    _____

5. List and give reasons for including specific members on the risk management team or committee:

    _____

    _____

    _____

6. Write a brief description of the process for determining risk management priorities and be prepared to discuss:

    _____

    _____

    _____

7. Why is it important to have risk management guidelines for specific program activities? Give several examples of how guidelines might help reduce risks.

    _____

    _____

    _____

    _____

    _____

    _____

8. What is the role of insurance in managing risk, and what is the process for determining the right kind of insurance for an organization?

    _____

    _____

    _____

■ References

Brinckerhoff, P. C. (2009). *Mission-Based Management: Leading Your Not-for-Profit.* (3rd Ed.) Hoboken, NJ: John Wiley & Sons, Inc.

Edginton, C., Hudson, S., and Ford, P. (1999). *Leadership in Recreation and Leisure Service Organizations.* Champaign, IL: Sagamore Publishing.

Fishman, J. and Schwarz, S. (2000). *Nonprofit Organizations: Cases and Materials.* New York: Foundation Press.

Herman, M. and Head, G. (2002). *Enlightened Risk Taking: A Guide to Strategic Risk Management for Nonprofits.* Washington, DC: Nonprofit Risk Management Center.

Herman, M. (2005). *Risk Management.* Robert D. Herman Ed. (2nd Ed.) The Jossey-Bass Handbook of Nonprofit Leadership and Management.

Jackson, M., White, L., and Herman, M. (1997). *Mission Accomplished: The Workbook.* Washington, DC: Nonprofit Risk Management Center.

_____ (1999). *Mission Accomplished: A Practical Guide to Risk Management for Nonprofits.* 2nd ed. Washington, DC: Nonprofit Risk Management Center.

Patterson, J., Tremper, C., and Rypkema, P. (1994). *Staff Screening Tool Kit.* Washington, DC: Nonprofit Risk Management Center.

Tremper, C., (1994). Risk management. In Robert Herman & Associates, eds. *The Jossey-Bass Handbook of Nonprofit Leadership and Management.* San Francisco: Jossey-Bass Publishing.

Tremper, C. and Kostin, G. (1993). *No Surprises: Controlling Risks in Volunteer Programs.* Washington, DC: Nonprofit Risk Management Center.

Tremper, C., Lally, F., and Studebaker, D. (1994). *Insurance Assurance for Volunteers.* Washington, D.C.: Nonprofit Risk Management Center.

Van der Smissen, B. (1990). *Legal Liability and Risk Management for Public and Private Entities.* Vol. 2. Cincinnati, OH: Anderson.

Weis, R. M. and Gantt, V. W. (2004). *Knowledge & Skill Development in Nonprofit Organizations.* Peosta, IA: Eddie Bowers Publishing.

Weis, R. M. and Gantt, V. W. (2002). *Leadership and Program Development in Nonprofit Organizations.* Peosta, IA: Eddie Bowers Publishing.

8 Organizational Development: Building Capacity, Impact and Sustainability

Organizational development is the application of all of the principles and practices presented in the preceding chapters. Leaders need to understand the nonprofit context, the characteristics of quality organizations, and what can be done to make them more effective and efficient. Organizational development means building and improving the various components of the system so that each works as desired and they work well together. Improving the representation of needed skills and perspectives on the board is organizational development. Putting effective financial management controls in place is organizational development. Conducting a comprehensive financial development plan is organizational development. By comparison, **capacity building** includes all that the organization does to improve the impact of its programs and services in the community. It can include work being done to improve human resources and skills, systems and structures, strategies, and program and service approaches. As each of these areas of the organization's work are extended, expanded, and improved, capacity is built to increase and sustain impact on the issues and goals that are the organization's mission.

A great deal has been written about how to develop healthy and effective nonprofit organizations that are engaged in serving the needs of their communities and constituents. Many approaches to organizational development start with creating and improving the component parts of the system with the expectation that they improve the capacity of the organization to pursue its mission (Worth 2009). Developing leadership, improving human resources, integrating human development, refining programming, growing finances, and attending to issues like risk management makes nonprofit organizations more effective (Weis and Gantt 2004).

Many approaches to organizational development start with the end in mind by considering the strategic design and integration of all the component parts with the focus first and foremost on the intended impact of the organization's mission. Just like travel, the destination informs the journey! This means focusing more on the "results" of the work of the organization than just on what the organization "aspires to do" in its mission statement. Such approaches move deliberately from internally focused organizational development to strategic capacity building that targets improved impact in the community. This is the capacity building framework taken in this chapter and the entire book. Each chapter builds on the next, and each can be tied together in the applications associated with building the capacity of the organization to have impact that can be sustained over time.

Nonprofit organizations experience a great deal of pressure to demonstrate the quality of the results of their work. In tight economic times, individuals and institutions providing financial support tend to ask more often for evidence of impact on the quality of life in the community. Being able to demonstrate the relevance of what the organization is doing is increasingly important to support organizations like United Way. It is not enough to just demonstrate that an organization is run efficiently. As time has passed and many of the problems addressed by nonprofit organizations seem to be getting worse, more and more questions are being asked by all supporters about results as they decide where to place money, time, and support. The changing roles and relationships among the government, business, and nonprofit sectors discussed in Chapter 6 further illustrate the importance of focusing on building the capacity of nonprofit organizations to become more effective in serving the needs of the community. Therein lies the case for learning more about capacity building for nonprofit organizations. This chapter explores capacity building, planning for its applications, and links to resources that support effective practice.

■ Building Capacity

A nonprofit organization can view nearly everything it owns and does in pursuit of its mission as "capacity." For example, the equipment owned by a youth sports program can be considered a capacity needed to deliver programs. Building the capacity would seem as simple as acquiring more equipment, which could mean that they can reach more youth. Of course, it is not that simple. The sports equipment is among the most simple capacity associated with the delivery of the youth sports program. There are many things to consider. The ability to deliver the program and the quality of its impact are influenced by everything from the established developmental objectives which are influenced by an appropriate number of participants to the quality of training programs for coaches, which is limited by the number of qualified volunteers available and the time and money for training, and so on and so on. This example illustrates how capacity can mean many things but is not a simple matter of increasing one aspect of a program, like buying more equipment, in order to increase the desired impact. By itself that will not work! For any investment in building capacity to increase impact in the community, it must be strategically targeted where it can make a sustainable difference.

There is a logical sequence of actions that will help increase the potential of having the desired long-term results. (1) Identify a very specific impact of the organization's mission upon which to focus the capacity building effort. It should be an impact that if improved, the ability of the organization to fulfill its mission will be built. (2) Select aspects of the programs and services that target the specific impact. (3) Choose element(s) of the organization (capacities) that if improved, increased, or enhanced, it is reasonable to expect that the selected aspect of programs and services will be more effective in advancing the targeted impact. (4) One valued measure of effective capacity building is when the resulting impacts are sustained over time and the quality of life in the community will be better as a result.

In addition to sustainable impacts of one capacity building effort, nonprofit capacity needs to be considered in collective terms. As DeVita, Fleming, and Twombly (2001) report "This new vision of nonprofit development is based on nurturing and growing the sector's capacity as a whole" (5). To this end, "collective impact" on the broader community and society at large can become another big step. The old 1960s social activist expression "act locally and think globally" has new application with the potential for social good that comes from the positive contributions of any one nonprofit mission, let alone a systematic connection of the work of many organizations.

∎ A Case for Broader Impact

Imagine the leaders of a local youth sports program that get excited about becoming a part of a new national childhood obesity initiative being promoted by the White House. For years, their developmental objectives had included improving sports skills, leadership development, group cooperation, and general fitness. Over time the primary focus had shifted to the sports skills objective, which influenced the program model, the coaches preparation and support, and youth practices Like many youth sports programs, the attention was on producing skilled athletes, with winning as the primary measure of success. Their assumption was that the other objectives were being addressed by giving youth a quality team sports experience.

In order for the program to have any impact on the central goal of the new initiative, the organization has to get very clear on the specific impact being pursued and then build a new set of program supports to make sure that it happens. Nearly every aspect of the program needs some change. New objectives might include health related indicators like body mass index, heart health, and nutrition. New training regimens and related coaches education programs would have to be instituted that include specific exercises. New rules for practices and games would have to be put in place that promote specific levels and types of activity. The overall attitude will likely have to shift from "winning" to "everyone plays" in order to help insure that all participants gain the desired health benefits. The new approach would have to be aggressively marketed across the community to help insure that participation and support continued and even grew. A new set of partners in the community who are concerned about childhood obesity need to be cultivated and incorporated into the work of the program. And so on and so on! And, it all needs to be done in a way that will still look like great fun for the youth. Once all of this work is completed and the newly framed program is operating effectively, the organization can have increased confidence that it is now having a direct impact on the targeted issue of childhood obesity. As the leaders gather evidence of positive impact, they will increase the likelihood that they can sustain the program and its impact on the health of local youth. This type of impact will also help encourage support to sustain the operation of the program.

Building the new program framework in conjunction with a national initiative would include alignment with the work of other youth sports programs around the country. Being a part of this larger network will allow the impact of one program to be added to that of other programs, improving the quality of youth health nationally. The collective impact has the added benefit of helping the local community see itself in a larger context, which can help encourage support to sustain the program and encourage great participation.

This simple example is offered to show the difference in the work of nonprofits when they choose specific new impact targets that have to do with critical issues in their communities, and they do so in conjunction with other organizations. The choice leads to greater potential for impact and sustainability.

■ Planning for Effective Application

Connolly and Lukas (2002) provide a comprehensive framework that can help with the analysis of a situation and planning a strategic capacity building response. It includes five (5) elements of capacity a nonprofit organization can consider when designing a capacity building effort:

1. mission, vision, and strategy
2. governance and leadership
3. ability to deliver programs and ensure the impact of programs
4. strategic external relationships
5. internal systems and management

McKinsey and Company (2001) provide a framework of the elements of nonprofit capacity to help guide the analysis when considering a capacity building effort. It breaks down the nonprofit organization into human resources, systems and infrastructure, organizational structure, organizational skills, strategies, aspirations, and culture. The case is made that each element is critical to understanding what needs to be done to increase capacity and then how to best accomplish the goal. The resulting analysis would provide a deep understanding of the current reality in each area and how that may impact capacity building. From the potential constraints of organizational culture to the limits of current skills and from the level of support from the system to the resistance to change in the staff, each element must be considered in design to help improve the chances of success.

Building capacity can be a way of thinking about improving the overall effectiveness of an organization. An *effective and efficient organization* can more fully accomplish its own mission and meet the targeted needs of its constituency. Letts, Ryan, and Grossman (1998) describe how the results of strategic capacity building can be seen at three levels: (1) improvement in the capacity of the organization to do what it already does (**program delivery capacity**), (2) improvement in the organization's capacity to grow (**program expansion capacity**), and (3) improvement in the organization's ability to sense needs for change and respond to them with program improvements or innovations (**adaptive capacity**). All three types of capacity building are needed if the organization is to perform effectively and efficiently for the long term. To this should be added the notion that the most good for society is done when the work of high performance nonprofit organizations combine for greater impact.

Once the specific focus of a capacity building effort has been determined, the next step is to decide how to go about improving or expanding the work of the organization within the targeted area. Light and Hubbard (2004) examined how foundations that support capacity building typically invest their money in strengthening organizations. They report that funders promote capacity building through three types of interventions: (1) **consultation** that is focused on assessment or process issues, such as building a new program plan focused on the newly targeted area of the mission, (2) **training** that involves small-group seminars or classes in which staff or board members learn specific skills to improve their abilities to work on the issues associated with the target area, and (3) **technical assistance** that is a more hands-on process in which the nonprofit is provided support for a project, program, or problem-solving process. Whether the impetus for the capacity building comes from an external source, like a funder or a national initiative, or from an internal source, like a board that is pushing for expanding programs, selecting the types of actions to take is the most critical part of the process. Limited money and time, pressure to continue existing programs and services, and the challenges of making change of any kind in the organization should be considered when designing a capacity building effort.

There are some important cautions to consider when developing a capacity building effort. These types of perspectives can serve as guiding principles that support the group process of planning and implementing effective capacity building activities (Long 2010):

- First and foremost, do no harm. Be sure that the risks of any particular action have been taken into account before implementation. It is important to take risks, as explained in Chapter 7, but they need to be calculated risks where any resulting problems are known and managed.

- Guard against being overly prescriptive or "top-down" in the process and implementation. Engaging each of the different groups potentially impacted by the effort will both gain their creative contributions to the design and help insure their support for any resulting changes. Without the support of constituents, board members, and key staff, the process may be limited or fail.

- Use caution in selecting external resources to support capacity building. To do effective capacity building, an external resource must take into account all of the forces that shape an organization: its mission, its values and its organizational culture; the environment in which it has to navigate; and the culture(s) and circumstances of its constituents. Look for an intermediary with a solid track record of collaboration with and support of the targeted constituencies.

- Recognize the multidimensional roles of nonprofit organizations. They often have important roles to play within their communities beyond delivering services, as a part of the local fabric of support for the area in which they work. Any capacity building work that is undertaken will likely influence other aspects of the organization.

- Have clear expectations about the potential outcomes of capacity building:
  - there must be agreement among all involved groups on the targeted results
  - do not push beyond the capacity to assimilate learning and undertake changes while still carrying on its daily business
  - develop clear and manageable communication and reporting procedures to help track the process
  - keep a flexible timeline so that adjustments can be made and time is available for reflections and learning

There are a lot of resources available to help plan quality capacity building efforts in nonprofit organizations. In addition to those reference above, the Human Interaction Research Institute hosts a searchable database of capacity building resources being carried out by U.S. foundations at www.humaninteract.org/reports/pcbrdatabase.asp.

◼ Challenges and Opportunities

When considering a capacity building effort in a nonprofit organization, there are a number of important factors that will influence the decision and the resulting plan of action. Taking some time to explore such factors before the decision is made or time is spent in planning, will allow leaders to avoid potential challenges and take advantage of opportunities. To promote this sort of advanced thinking, three will be explored here: **readiness, building on strengths, and adequate resources.**

Readiness. It is important to think about whether or not an organization is ready and willing to undertake capacity building work before the process begins. There is a lot to consider. It all starts with a clearly identified problem that, if addressed, will increase the organization's capacity to have impact on its mission. If that is clear, then there needs to be a high level of commitment to the related changes among the staff, board, volunteers, and constituents. Key organization members must believe that capacity building will help to further the mission, particularly senior level leadership (ED and board chair in particular). Among those, it helps to have champions who help promote the process. With each group having the appropriate opportunity to participate in the design process, both the quality and level of support will develop. With support and commitment in hand, attention needs to turn to the goals, intended outcomes, approach being taken, and plan of action. They should all line up to offer everyone involved a strong sense that the goals can be achieved in the time allotted. In addition, it is important to know that the board and staff leadership have committed the funding and time needed to do the job effectively. And finally, it is important to know that the organization has the expertise needed for the activity or has access and funding support to bring it into the effort.

Build on strengths. Most of the time capacity building efforts focus on problems that seem to be limiting the success of the organization's mission. A deficit-based or problem-solving approach may limit the design and implementation. Instead, imagine the difference in what might occur if the effort was framed by focusing on sustaining and renewing areas that are strong, and using those internal organization strengths to address areas that are weak or need to be developed further. Referring to the Creative Tension Framing in Chapter 2, rather than focusing on "what we do not want," focus instead on "what we want" for the future. Building on strengths can have a very positive impact on all aspects of capacity building, from the quality of the support and positive energy from each group involved in the process to the resources and commitment to sustaining the resulting changes in the organization.

Adequate resources. It is important to balance expectations with the budget, time, and human resources needed for capacity building. While organizational effectiveness can improve with small investments in such things as technical assistance, like board training, it takes more money, time, and commitment to have lasting and substantive impacts on issues of importance to the organization's mission. Organizations require ongoing support and continuing education to sustain any gains in capacity. Time is money, and commitment to sustaining the changes that occur through capacity building efforts involve both. At the core of an effective balance of resources to support capacity building are quality relationships that promote shared learning. Effective leaders and organizations understand this and work to develop three kinds of learning relationships that help sustain the change: (1) networks of colleagues and peers who share their commitments, (2) coaches or mentors who help develop their potential, and (3) experts who provide specialized and objective assistance (Newman 2001). All of these relationships are important resources to successful capacity building.

∎ Sustaining Results

There are strategic points in the life of nonprofit organizations where capacity building makes sense and might be more effectively implemented and the results sustained. Within each, there are some specific considerations that will help with capacity building design and continuation of the resulting changes in the organization. (Long 2010)

Executive transition. Whenever there is a change in executive leadership, it can be an opportunity to consider capacity building. A board can look at an upcoming transition as a chance to make changes in its mission and goals and incorporate those desired changes into the search process when looking for new leadership. A new Executive Director can use the transition as an opportunity to engage the organization in developing a new shared vision for the future and to entertain any associated capacity building. Transitions, when appropriately supported and managed, provide powerful opportunities for nonprofit organizations to grow new leadership, make important strategic decisions about the future, and build the capacity needed to realize that future. (Teegarden 2005) Well planned change can breathe new life into an organization, re-energize staff and volunteers, and renew and build commitments with supporters.

Periods of growth and change. Responding to a desired change in mission and its impacts with a capacity building effort can produce growth in the organization. Growth can be disruptive and have negative impact on organizations. It can be difficult to pay for the ongoing improvements necessary to maintain effective and efficient operations *without* growth, since a large proportion of funding often comes from fees and contracts for programs and services. The challenge is that the money usually comes after the grow occurs and there are inadequate funds to get to that point in operations. One response to this situation is to raise funds to support the costs of the fundraising, planning, and financial management skills that come with growth. Investing in this type of capacity building can make all the difference when growth and change occur. Capacity building efforts can also require changes to programs that require shifts in staffing, organizational structure, and administrative systems. Training and planning assistance can be crucial in these times, but there are associated costs to consider. It is important to understand that program expansion requires a greater budget for the entire organization, not just for programs.

Times of crisis. Any crisis can be an opportunity to change the organization. However, organizations in trouble typically have outdated programs, poor morale, and limited funding. Regardless of what is driving the crisis, these types of symptoms may need to be addressed before the organization can work on bigger issues of long-term impact and mission. This situation poses a dilemma because it may be difficult to improve any of these types of conditions without first finding a stronger link between the mission and the current reality of its constituents and the needs in the community.

Keeping organizations strong. A quality, mature organization needs to continually evaluate its work to insure that its mission is relevant to the changing context of the community and its constituents. A strategic planning process that supports the needed adjustments in programs and services is essential. Quality evaluations can provide important information to periods of transition, growth, organizational development, and change, etc. Having these core processes in place supports effective capacity building.

Stagnant organizations. Even successful organizations can become complacent if they are not using quality processes to stay current and relevant in their communities. They may not know that their work is no longer meeting needs. Awareness of the situation must be followed with thorough and meaningful assessment and planning to use capacity building to move from stagnation to an effective and relevant future.

Capacity building is just like everything else that a nonprofit organization undertakes. It needs to be developed through an effective planning process, as presented for program planning in Chapter 5. The simple cycle of planning, implementation, and evaluation will bring a deliberate and intentional tone to the work.

■ Final Thoughts

In order to have the broadest possible impacts with capacity building efforts, it is helpful to show progress by a different set of indicators than simple measurements of inputs and outputs, like trainings conducted and new processes implemented or new program designs and numbers of new participants. For any one nonprofit organization or a group of nonprofits working on the same issue, it is important to be able to show evidence of intended positive impacts on the issue and sustainability of impacts over a period of time. Evidence is also valued that demonstrates key roles that the organization is now playing in the group of nonprofits and across the large social system as a result of capacity building. A new set of quality and valued partnerships that shows how the collective effort is having positive impacts on the issue are also valued. Together, this type of evidence goes a long way toward building support among all types of funding sources involved in the community and society in general, including government departments with responsibilities for the issue. A nonprofit organization that operates in this collaborative way to have an intentional collective impact on important community issues is demonstrating the six practices of high-impact nonprofits presented in Chapter 2 when describing quality nonprofit leadership. Crutchfield and McLeod report that great nonprofit sector organizations do these six things (2008):

- advocate and serve
- make markets work
- inspire evangelists
- nurture nonprofit networks
- master the art of adaptation
- share leadership

There are a lot of resources available to help nonprofit organizations help themselves with capacity building work. It is important to make sure that evaluation is incorporated into the process in order to both inform its development and implementation and to help determine its long-term effectiveness. The Nonprofit Good Practice Guide offers links to many useful tools at www.npgoodpractice.org. Grantmakers for Effective Organizations also offers a range of useful resources at www.geofunders.org. And finally, the National Council of Nonprofit Organizations is a repository of enormous amounts of experience with organizational development and capacity building, through its own resource collection as well as through its network of state associations of nonprofits. More information can be found at *www.councilofnonprofits.org.*

∎ Summary

Nonprofit organizations must continue to develop in order to stay current and engaged in valuable relationships with the community they serve. As the context and needs of the community continue to evolve, it is the responsibility of nonprofit leaders to make sure that the organization develops to stay relevant and important to the quality of life in the community. This is accomplished by constantly development the component parts of the organization so that they are efficient and effective and align with each other to support a quality enterprise.

Beyond this work to continually develop the organization, leadership must pay attention to building the capacity to have positive impacts on aspects of the mission that have a lasting positive effect on life in the community. **Capacity building** includes all that the organization does to improve the impact of its programs and services in the community. Challenging times and circumstances can press nonprofit organizations to improve their capacity to serve the community. However, nonprofit leaders needs to consider this kind of work as an important part of their responsibility to make sure that their organization is having a positive impact that is sustained over time. The case is strong for connecting capacity building to the work of other related organizations so that the collective impact may be more significant in the community and sustainable.

A simple framework for developing a capacity building plan should include steps that insure thoughtful consideration of the specific targeted impact, selected aspects of the programs and services that need to change or develop, elements of the organization to improve, and the ability to track progress. The chapter offers another element to the framework by focusing on the broader impact of capacity building to promote greater impact and sustainability of strategic partnerships and collaborations among organizations that are committed to the same results. To do this work effectively, five elements need to be considered: (1) mission, vision, and strategy; (2) governance and leadership; (3) ability to deliver programs and services and ensure the impact of programs; (4) strategic external relationships; and (5) internal systems and management.

In order to be successful with capacity building efforts, there are a number of factors to consider. The level of readiness in the organization, a commitment to building on the strengths of the organization, and access to adequate resources must be taken into account during the initial planning activity. Planning is also effected by a variety of situations and conditions that can influence the effectiveness and sustainability of capacity building, including executive transitions, periods of growth and change, times of crisis, commitments to keeping the organization strong, and dealing with stagnation within the organization.

Capacity building is an essential part of long-term organizational development that helps insure the relevance and value the organization will have in the community. If done well in partnership with a group of committed related organizations, the impact in the community can be significant and long-lasting.

This chapter addresses, in part, the Nonprofit Leadership Alliance Certification Competency Requirements of Nonprofit Management and Program Planning, Implementation, and Evaluation.

■ Reflection and Application

1. Describe the differences between organizational development activities and capacity building efforts:

    _____

    _____

    _____

2. What are the recommended steps to take in developing a capacity building plan?

    _____

    _____

    _____

3. List the five elements of a nonprofit organization that should be considered when developing a capacity building effort:

    _____

    _____

    _____

    _____

    _____

4. Define the three types of capacity that can be built in nonprofit organizations:

    _____

    _____

    _____

5.   Describe how "readiness," "building on strengths," and "adequate resources" are involved in the decision to conduct capacity building in nonprofit organizations:

_____

_____

_____

_____

6.   Develop a list and be prepared to discuss strategic points in the life of a nonprofit organization where capacity building makes sense to undertake:

_____

_____

_____

_____

_____

∎ References

Block, P. (2008). *Community: The Structure of Belonging.* San Francisco, CA: Berritt-Koehler Publishing, Inc.

Christine W. L., William P. R., and Grossman, A. (1998). *High Performance Nonprofit Organizations: Managing Upstream for Greater Impact.* New York: John Wiley & Sons, 1998.

Connolly, P. and Lukas, C. (2002). *Strengthening Nonprofit Performance: A Funder's Guide to Capacity Building.* Saint Paul, MN: Amherst H. Wilder Foundation/Grantmakers for Effective Organizations.

Light, P. C. and Hubbard, E. T. (2004). *The Capacity Building Challenge: A Research Perspective.* Foundation Center, http://foundationcenter.org.

Long, R. F. (2010). *Advanced Grant Portfolio Management.* (2nd Ed.) Johnson Center on Philanthropy, Grand Valley State University.

Mattessich, P. W. (2003). *The Manager's Guide to Program Evaluation.* Saint Paul, MN: Fieldstone Alliance Publishing Center.

Murray, V. (2005). *Evaluating the Effectiveness of Nonprofit Organizations.* Robert D. Herman Ed. (2nd Ed.) The Jossey-Bass Handbook of Nonprofit Leadership and Management.

Newman, A. (2001). *Built to Change: Catalytic Capacity Building in Nonprofit Organizations.* The David and Lucile Packard Foundation, http://www.packard.org.

Rodriguez-Campos, L. (2005). *Collaborative Evaluation.* Tamarac, FL: Llumina Press.

Teegarden, P. H. (April, 2005) *Leadership Change in Nonprofit Milwaukee: Making Transitions Work.* Research and Opinion, Vol. 18, No. 1. University of Wisconsin.

Weis, R. M. and Gantt, V. W. (2004). *Knowledge & Skill Development in Nonprofit Organizations.* Peosta, IA: Eddie Bowers Publishing.

Worth, M. J. (2009). *Nonprofit Management: Principles and Practice.* Thousand Oaks, CA: Sage Publications, Inc.

9 Career Planning and Professional Development

Life isn't about finding yourself.
Life is about creating yourself.

- Author Unknown

The need for qualified professionals in the nonprofit sector is growing at a very fast rate and is expected to continue for years to come. Working in a nonprofit organization and developing programs that enhance people's lives is one of the most important and exhilarating careers imaginable. Deciding which organization to work with, then obtaining a position with that organization, however, can sometimes be confusing and frustrating.

This chapter helps anyone assess his/her interests and skills relevant to nonprofit organizations and learn about specific nonprofit organizations; and, then, learn a process for developing effective résumés, refined networking skills, compelling cover letters, dynamic interviewing skills and strategies for assessing job offers. There are two critical aspects of career development and exploration. One centers on individual needs for a clear career plan and a view toward the future. The other revolves around organizational needs for specific and general skills and knowledge. In addition, this chapter will explore both individual and organizational issues related to career preparation and planning, as well as how to look to the future and be prepared to alter career paths both for individuals and an organization. Finally, this chapter's content can also assist students and current agency employees in organizing professional development strategies to meet short-term and long-term career goals.

What a person values largely determines how he or she will approach career development and career options. Is salary more important than what is being done? Is making a difference in the life of just one person enough? Is helping people more important than the pay scale? Arthur Ashe, tennis professional and founder of the Arthur Ashe Institute for Urban Health, put the issue in these words, "From what we get, we can make a living; what we give, however, makes a life."

The one preeminent word in finding and excelling in a career is: ***connectedness*** (Weis and Gantt 2004). A person must know or discover the connection between and among the following four areas:

1. **Abilities** – These are the things a person does well, their natural skills. They could include the ability to talk with anyone, the ability to help people avoid conflict, the ability to show compassion for people who are hurting, the ability to run fast, or the ability to speak in public with little fear of failure.

2. **Interests** – These are the things a person enjoys doing. These items could include enjoying working outdoors, working with your hands, working alone, working with people, working in stressful situations, working in a highly predictable position, or working at night.
3. **Learned skills** – These are the things a person has learned to do well. They could include anything from the abilities list which does not come naturally. A person can learn public speaking skills, learn to show compassion, or learn to help people manage conflict. In addition, people can learn budgeting skills, programming skills, fundraising skills or other technical skills.
4. **Interaction styles** – This is the way people like to communicate, the way they like for others to communicate with them. The consequences of a person's style determine how effective a person is as judged by others.

All four of these areas, along with all written correspondence, the résumé, networking contacts and interview content must be connected in order to "***tell your story***." The competition is often fierce and you have to convince potential employers they should hire you instead of someone else (Dahlstrom 2009). All the steps and materials prepared to support all applications for employment must be connected to each other. It is in this **connectedness** that an applicant gains power over those who see each step as an individual activity.

Abilities provide the natural base for any career. They set the stage for any success. What a person can't do limits options just as what a person can do creates options. A person with no compassion for the plight of the poor is ill advised to look at careers in the nonprofit sector. It should also be noted that because a person is good at something does not mean they would be happy doing that for a career. A person who runs fast may not like training well enough to commit to the preparation necessary to become an Olympic class athlete. For that reason, abilities must be combined with other qualities to determine the best career match for each person.

Interests should drive a person's search for a challenging career path. The other three factors are very important, but if a person has little genuine interest in an area of work, there will be little real reward. A statement attributed to Confucius offers sage advice, "Choose a job you love, and you will never work a day in your life."

Learned skills emerge from the knowledge of what a person **needs** to be able to do in order to combine natural abilities and interests to insure greater chances of success in a desired career. These skills are learned through career-related experience and specific, focused training.

Interaction styles reflect how a person prefers to communicate and interact with others. It is clear to anyone who has lived more than a few years that not everyone likes to give and receive information in the same way. Some people find teasing as a sign they are liked by others and some people are offended by any teasing. Some people desire the blunt, straightforward presentation of messages – make it clear. Some people want messages presented diplomatically and indirectly. There are several tools for assessing interaction styles and the implications of each style. Some of those tools are discussed later in this chapter (Weis and Gantt).

■ The Career Decision Process

It's important to understand the decision-making process relevant to career planning and develop a strategy for making effective decisions. The *Flowchart for Career Planning* in Figure 9.1 can assist anyone in making informed career decisions. In order to minimize the *confusion and frustration*, substantial *career research* is required. There are two major areas in which to develop and assimilate information for an effective career decision. The *Self-assessment Profile* area should include information regarding abilities, values and lifestyle, interests, and interaction style. The *Organizational Exploration* area should include information on professional settings and qualifications for positions in various nonprofit organizations (Weis and Gantt 2004). See **APPENDIX A** for an extensive list of national nonprofit organizations.

It is also important to select someone who is knowledgeable in career planning to assist in the assessment process. This individual should be an academic advisor; a counselor

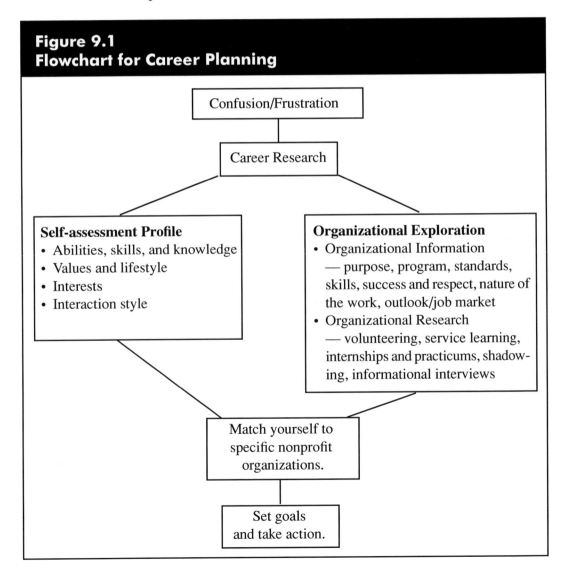

Figure 9.1
Flowchart for Career Planning

Confusion/Frustration

Career Research

Self-assessment Profile
- Abilities, skills, and knowledge
- Values and lifestyle
- Interests
- Interaction style

Organizational Exploration
- Organizational Information
  — purpose, program, standards, skills, success and respect, nature of the work, outlook/job market
- Organizational Research
  — volunteering, service learning, internships and practicums, shadowing, informational interviews

Match yourself to specific nonprofit organizations.

Set goals and take action.

with career services; a coordinator of youth, human service, or service learning programs; or any individual who is skilled in the area of career development. For students, the chair of an academic department or dean of an academic college should be contacted for suggestions on the appropriate advisor. For nonprofit professionals, contact a person who has been successful in nonprofit work. It is critical to choose a person who will take the necessary time to advise, review drafts of written work and assist in planning for interviews.

Using the *Flowchart for Career Planning* reduces confusion and frustration, provides a structure for career research and allows for informed decisions based on specific goals and clear action steps. The process works! As stated earlier, the two major stages in the career research process are the self-assessment profile and organizational exploration.

Self-assessment Profile

Like anything worthwhile, choosing a career path requires a good deal of time and commitment. Self-assessment processes can be useful in determining the right career path. Many of the following assessments can be taken at college and university career planning and placement centers, or student development offices. Some of the more popular and useful self-assessment processes include the following:

- **Personality Mosaic** – Based on the work of psychologist and vocational Counselor John Holland, the Personality Mosaic is an assessment tool that takes approximately an hour to complete. It takes about 30 minutes to complete its 90 questions and another 30 minutes to interpret the results.

  Holland theorizes there are six major personality types, or a combination of two or more types and the Personality Mosaic provides a profile of a person based on these results. The Personality Mosaic is a simple assessment, and students generally report the instrument is accurate based on personal observation.

  The assessment is included in the career handbook, *Coming Alive from Nine to Five*, by Betty Neville Michelozzi. (Check college or university libraries before purchasing a copy.)

- **Strong-Campbell Interest Inventory (SCCI)** – The SCCI is also based on the work of John Holland. It contains over 300 items requiring a "like," "indifferent" or "dislike" response. These items are then divided into groups of professional occupations, academic disciplines, activities, amusements, and types of people.

  The individual results are compared to successful individuals in over 70 occupations. Occupations are grouped into the same six categories used by the Personality Mosaic: Realistic, Investigative, Artistic, Social, Enterprising, and Conventional. Because individual responses are mailed to a testing firm for computerized results, an appointment is generally necessary with the campus career counselor for an interpretation of the results.

- **Discover** - This is a computer-based planning and information system that includes an interest inventory and activities to help identify individual abilities, experience, and values. These variables are then considered relevant to various occupations. The Discover system also contains modules on exploring various occupations, making educational choices, planning careers and making career transitions.

- **Personal Profile (DiSC)** – The DiSC is an interaction styles analysis tool. It is available through Inscape Publishing. This and other tools can be obtained from a number of independent consultants. One of these is Resources Unlimited (on-line at *www.resourcesunlimited.com*).

   By choosing the adjective which is most like you when you interact with people in a given situation and the adjective which is least like you in the same situation from several sets of adjectives, a profile is shaped. That profile then suggests the consequences of your style of interaction. The profiles allow a person to see not only the consequences of his or her interaction style but also allows for an understanding of the consequences of others style when the two are working together or in a relationship.

- **Myers-Briggs Type Indicator (MBTI)** – The MBTI is an excellent assessment which places individuals in one of sixteen different personality types based on responses to various questions. The MBTI then describes different variables involved, for each personality type, with respect to activities such as choosing a major, studying, playing and relaxing.

   The MBTI includes a list of careers most often chosen by individuals from each of the sixteen personality types along with a list of careers chosen the least by each personality type.

Each of the assessment tools above can provide valuable information for self-assessment. The results from each assessment should be discussed with someone who is experienced and competent in interpreting the results. Additional self-assessment activities designed specifically for individuals seeking a career in nonprofit organizations are located in **Appendix B.** The more self knowledge a person is able to assemble the better prepared that person is to **"tell his or her story."** Everyone works best in a situation where there is a match between the person and the organization.

Organizational Exploration

There are a number of effective ways to research and assimilate career information for youth, human service, and other nonprofit organizations. The exploration process that follows concentrates on direct, experience-based techniques for gathering information regarding various careers in nonprofit organizations.

As the examination of different kinds of organizations begins, it's important for students or nonprofit professionals to have some sense of who they are and the kinds of professional goals each hopes to accomplish. Exploring various organizations can help in understanding their purpose and the kinds of activities professional staff members engage in on a daily basis. First-hand exploration will provide opportunities to see how organizations really operate. This section of the flowchart concentrates on processes for researching organizational information and activities.

Organizational Information

- **Purpose** – One of the most important aspects of any organization is its purpose – what the organization stands for. The purpose of each organization varies, but generally speaking all are designed to enhance the quality of life for specific individuals in specific communities through some sort of program or process.

Identifying with the purpose of an organization is one of the essential elements of being comfortable and successful with a career within that organization.

- **Programs** – Nonprofit organizations will have a number of programs designed to achieve their purpose. It is equally important to have an idea of the kinds of programs organizations implement to determine if they are the kinds of programs that would be interesting and challenging to work with.

- **Standards, qualifications, and skills** – One should be aware of what an organization expects in the area of educational requirements, certifications, skills and experience in order to prepare to be a viable candidate for a position. One should also be aware of these expectations because the standards and qualifications an organization maintains provides an indication of the level of quality of the organization.

- **Success and respect** – Organizations that are consistently successful in achieving their goals in an effective and professional manner maintain a high level of respect in the community. This is an important consideration for employment.

- **Nature of work** – Being aware of an organization's mission and programs and having an awareness of the work individuals do daily to help the organization achieve its mission is essential.

- **Outlook/job market** – According to news reports, government and organizational reports, the need for professionals in the youth and human service field increases substantially each year. It is important, however, to research the need for specific positions in certain nonprofit organizations as well as in specific geographical areas.

After information about what the organization claims to do is collected, it is time to get information about how the organization actually works on a day-to-day basis. This is best done by hands-on contact with the organization. The following suggestions help conduct the most important organizational exploration.

Organizational Research

- **Volunteering** – Volunteering in a nonprofit organization has numerous benefits. Most importantly, a service is provided to a population in the community who needs assistance. At the same time it's also one of the most direct and effective methods of gaining information relevant to a particular organization. Volunteer opportunities can usually be found through the campus volunteer center or student development office. Included in Appendix A are the names, addresses, phone numbers, and mission statements of a number of national nonprofit organizations. Contact the national number to determine if there is a local affiliate.

- **Service learning** – More and more campuses are developing service learning course work in which students work in community service projects that incorporate learning objectives. Check with an academic counselor or the office of academic affairs to determine which courses these might be. Service learning is a structured and effective way to provide service, learn course content, and receive college credit.

- **Internships and practicums** – Internships and practicums are an excellent way to learn about an organization. Select an organization that could be of interest as a career choice to initiate an internship or practicum.

- **Shadowing** – Another way to gain information about an organization is to follow one or several of the employees around for a day or more. This can be an excellent way to determine what individuals do on a daily basis without a large commitment of time. Organizational leaders are usually willing to accommodate these kinds of requests.
- **Informational interviews** – It can be helpful to contact an organizational leader and request an interview to obtain information regarding the organization prior to getting involved. Informational interviews are generally more successful when they are done in person, but a phone interview can also be effective if a personal interview is not possible. Potential questions for an interview are listed below:
  - What is the mission of the organization?
  - Could you tell me a little about the programs?
  - How successful has the organization been in accomplishing goals?
  - How did you become interested in this field?
  - What do you like best about your job? Least?
  - What sort of qualities and qualifications do you look for when hiring employees?
  - What is the outlook for employment within this organization?

  NOTE: Always send a thank you note to the person who granted the interview.

Match and Act

Once an individual's interests and skills have been assessed and specific nonprofit organizations researched carefully, it's time to choose target organizations, set goals and design a plan of action. Which organizations are the best matches for your interests and skills? Which organization missions best match your values and style of interaction? What is the best way to approach each organization chosen? Can others help in the process? What is next?

The most important document for career planning is the résumé! What should go in a résumé? How should it look?

The résumé is a one or two-page summary of educational, service, and work history. In conjunction with the cover letter, it's the document employers typically use to determine if an individual's qualifications match those of a specific position in their organization. It will determine who they invite for interviews.

Generally, there are two types of résumés – a **chronological résumé** in which various activities are listed by date, with the most recently held position listed first, and a **functional résumé** in which skills and supporting activities are presented in segments (there is no emphasis on dates). Since it is the most commonly used, this text concentrates on the preparation of a chronological résumé.

■ The Résumé

Résumés should be divided into three main sections: header information, basic information, support information. There should be a good deal of white space in the margins to allow an interviewer to make notes. Paper needs to be white, gray or off-white and at least 50 percent rag content. This is not the time to use cheap paper. These sections should be included in the résumé in the order they are listed (Figure 9.2). A sample of an effective résumé is included as Figure 9.5 and should be referred to periodically as various sections of a résumé are discussed.

HEADER INFORMATION

Header information is contact information. It must be correct and current. Never list a phone number that will not be usually answered or does not have an answering machine or voice mail. If an e-mail address is listed, check for messages two to three times a day.

The perception of a person's professionalism starts at the top. Font size and style for contact information must be professional. Very large fonts and very graphic or ornate styles detract from the message of a professional image. Get some feedback from people who read résumés if you doubt this advice.

BASIC INFORMATION

This may be the most important section of the résumé because it's what employers see first. The quality and impact of this section may determine whether an employer continues

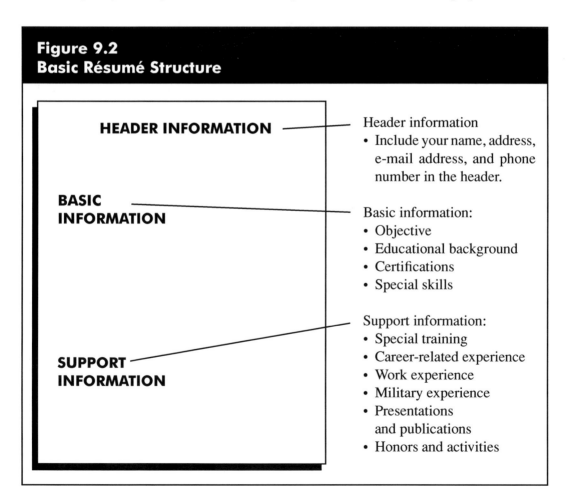

Figure 9.2
Basic Résumé Structure

HEADER INFORMATION

BASIC INFORMATION

SUPPORT INFORMATION

Header information
• Include your name, address, e-mail address, and phone number in the header.

Basic information:
• Objective
• Educational background
• Certifications
• Special skills

Support information:
• Special training
• Career-related experience
• Work experience
• Military experience
• Presentations and publications
• Honors and activities

reviewing a résumé further. Research indicates that a résumé will receive a 10-second glance to see if it deserves further attention (Dahlstrom 2009).

Career Objective

The career objective should be listed immediately after the heading of a résumé. If an internship is the objective rather than a job, the phrase "Internship Objective" can be substituted for this heading. The career objective is important because it enables employers to see the focus of professional intentions and a summary of an individual's strengths. This helps employers identify whether an applicant is truly interested in their field or if someone is applying randomly (Weis and Gantt 2004).

If a person has five or more years of professional experience, career summary can replace career objective. A career summary includes what the professional has been doing, for how long and lists some demonstrated personal qualities which would make them attractive to an employer.

Career objectives are frequently made up of two to three phases that form one cohesive statement regarding the career direction someone is interested in pursuing. For the purpose of this discussion, the objective statement is broken down into three sections.

- **First section of the career objective – field-focused phrase**

  The first section of the career objective is most effective when it's focused on a particular field. A **field-focused** objective is directed toward a specific segment of organizations which adds clarity to a résumé. For instance, if someone is interested in working for a youth and human service organization, then the initial portion could be written: *To obtain a position in a youth or human service organization.* By indicating the field of interest, employers are much more likely to be interested in a résumé with a field listed that is related to their work. Other sample starters for field-focused objectives are listed in Figure 9.3.

- **Second section of the career objective – skills-related phrase**

  The next section of the career objective statement is specific to the skills an individual brings to the organization. Skills listed here should be ones that have

Figure 9.3
Sample Starters for Field-Focused Objectives

To obtain a position in a health and wellness organization ...
To obtain a position in a performing arts organization ...
To obtain a position in a child care organization ...
To obtain a position in an educational organization ...
To obtain a position in a therapeutic recreational organization ...
To obtain a position in a career development organization ...
To obtain a position in a crime prevention organization ...
To obtain a position in an outdoor recreational organization ...
To obtain a position in an outdoor camping organization ...

been developed, or are being developed, and should be relevant for the organizations which will receive the résumé. These are skills that occur naturally or have been developed in the classroom, in class projects, during practicums, or internships, or in some other manner. Prospective employers expect college graduates to have acquired skills at a level of expertise required for an entry-level position.

The skills listed below are ones important to most nonprofit organizations, although the relative importance of each skill varies with each organization and position:

advising	financial management
analysis	leadership
communication	marketing
conflict resolution	program development
counseling	problem-solving
cultural diversification	public relations
evaluation	supervising/teaching
facilitation	team development
financial development	therapeutic assessment

Two or three skills should be listed in the career objective statement. These skills should be realistic and relevant to the job that is being sought. The most important skill should be listed first, and so on. Skills can be listed in several different ways. For instance, it is acceptable to list skills simply by stating: *... where skills in communication and leadership ... .*

If these skills have been developed significantly through class projects, class projects or some other means, it sounds stronger to include the word "proven" in the statement. For example: *... where proven skills in communication, program development, and leadership ... .*

- **Third section of the career objective – the "why" phrase**

   The third and last section of the statement should be written so there is an implied benefit to prospective employers. The last part of the objective should be stated positively, assertively and in a manner that indicates the organization will be benefited by hiring the applicant. For example: *... can be utilized to assist the organization.*

When these three parts of the career statement are written together, the objective will look something like this:

CAREER OBJECTIVE	To obtain a position in a youth or human service organization where proven skills in communication, program development and leadership can be utilized to assist the organization.

This objective focuses on a particular field, briefly summarizes the applicant's strengths relevant to a prospective employer's needs, and indicates the applicant wants to make a difference in the employer's organization. The career objective is the first area that prospective employers see, and it will provide them with some idea of the applicant's professional intentions, skills, and how well the applicant organizes concepts on paper.

Education

Educational experiences should be included in the basic information portion of the résumé. The following areas are suggested for the education section (Weis and Gantt 2004):
- The institution being attended (or graduated from)
- Location of the institution (city and state only)
- The degree that is being sought or has been acquired
- The date of graduation (or anticipated date of graduation)
- Major and minor fields of study
- Overall grade point average and/or the grade point average in a major – if the GPA is above 3.0 on a 4.0 scale (most career counselors recommend including these averages if they are above a 3.0).
- Any academic honors that are outstanding (for example, graduating Magna Cum Laude or being selected senior of the year in a department).

Although special honors are also included in the Honors/Activities section of the résumé, it is important to list them here as well because it will attract attention sooner and provide more reason to consider a candidacy. Samples of how educational experiences should be listed follow:

If someone has graduated from one institution, here is how it should be listed on a résumé:

EDUCATION	**Murray State University**, Murray, KY Bachelor of Science, May 2011 Health major, Human Services minor GPA 3.93/4.00 GPA in major: 4.00/4.00 Graduated Magna Cum Laude

If a student is graduating in the near future:

> **EDUCATION**   **Missouri Valley College**, Marshall, MO
> Bachelor of Arts, Expected in May 2011
> Health major, Human Services minor
>
> GPA 3.50/4.00
> GPA in major: 3.65/4.00

If the applicant has attended two different schools:

> **EDUCATION**   **University of Houston**, Houston, TX
> Bachelor of Science, May 2010
> Education major
> GPA 3.21/4.00
>
> **Perry Community College**, Perry, KY
> Associates degree, May 2007
> Social Services emphasis

If the applicant has two degrees from the same institution:

> **EDUCATION**   **Clemson University**, Clemson, SC
> Master of Arts in Recreation, May 2010
>
> Bachelor of Science, May 2006
> Recreation Major

Certifications

Being certified in areas of proficiency relevant to nonprofit organizations is important and should be included on the résumé. Often, certification in various areas is required for a particular job, and prospective employers always look upon this favorably when choosing employees. A list of example certifications is included below:

- Nonprofit Leadership Alliance Certification
- American Red Cross Basic Life Support (CPR)
- American Red Cross Advanced Lifesaving and Water Safety
- Certified North Carolina Emergency Medical Technician
    - State of California Provisional Certification, Grades K-12
- Certified Therapeutic Recreation Specialist
- American Canoe Association Certification

Certifications should be included on the résumé as follows:

CERTIFICATIONS: Nonprofit Leadership Alliance Certification
American Red Cross Basic Life Support (CPR)

Since certification is so important to some agencies, it is never too late to become certified in a certain area if it is important or required for a position.

Special Skills

Skills that have been acquired in areas such as computer technology, foreign language, or program development may be included in a special skills section immediately following the certification section. Some examples of special skills are listed below:

- Knowledge of IBM personal computer
- Familiar with WordPerfect and Microsoft Word
- Experience with Power Point and Excel
- Proficient in written and spoken Spanish
- Experience in administering the following tests:
    (List appropriate tests)
- Proficient in program promotion

Special skills should be included on the résumé as follows:

SPECIAL SKILLS: Familiar with Microsoft Word
Proficient in written and spoken Spanish

Figure 9.4
Common Action Verbs Used in Résumés

Accelerated	Created	Initiated	Reported
Accomplished	Designed	Inspected	Researched
Acquired	Developed	Maintained	Reviewed
Administered	Directed	Managed	Scheduled
Analyzed	Distributed	Minimized	Selected
Appointed	Edited	Modified	Serviced
Arranged	Engineered	Monitored	Started
Assisted	Equipped	Operated	Supervised
Attended	Established	Organized	Surveyed
Combined	Evaluated	Originated	Taught
Completed	Expanded	Planned	Tested
Composed	Facilitated	Prepared	Trained
Conducted	Generated	Presented	Used
Constructed	Guided	Produced	Worked
Controlled	Helped	Recorded	Wrote
Coordinated	Implemented		

SUPPORT INFORMATION

This section should include support information regarding any special training, career-related experience, work experience, military experience, presentations and publications, and honors and activities. All entries should reflect achievements and accomplishments to the degree possible. Show potential employers what to expect, based on past performance and accomplishments.

When listing various experiences, begin each descriptive statement with an action verb (see Figure 9.4). Each statement should describe an aspect of an experience and should express a level of responsibility, skill, initiative and/or success. Include two to four statements for each experience, beginning with the most important to the least important.

Special Training

This section should include specific knowledge and skill areas that have been acquired through workshops, seminars, special projects, conferences or lecture series. Special training in customer relations, leadership, public relations, finance, first aid, risk management, computer technology or any area relevant to a field of interest should be included. Each descriptive phrase should begin with an action verb. For example:

SPECIAL TRAINING: **American Red Cross, Tempe, AZ**
Disaster Relief Workshop, Spring 2009
Student participant:
- Attended lectures on community disaster preparedness and relief strategies
- Participated in simulated community-wide disaster preparedness and relief activities
- Awarded competency certificates in disaster preparedness and relief strategies

Career-related Experience

Career-related experiences are those experiences that relate to future professional directions and include experiences from class projects, internships, service learning and volunteer work, and part-time or summer jobs. An example is listed below:

CAREER-RELATED   **YMCA Camp Lakewood, Potosi, MO**
EXPERIENCE: **Youth Agency Intern/Leadership**
Development Coordinator, Summer 2009
- Planned and implemented leadership programs for over 500 campers
- Coordinated the activities of counselors in the delivery of leadership programs
- Developed evaluation processes to assess camper satisfaction and skill development

Work Experience

Jobs held during the collegiate experience may not be directly related to future professional experiences, but they do represent responsibility and should be included in the résumé. An example is listed below:

**WORK EXPERIENCE: Red Lobster Restaurant, Shreveport, LA,
Cashier, Summer 2008**
- Provided customer service and handled financial transactions
- Initiated and developed a customer assessment process that provided important service information

Military

Military experience may be directly related to a future career direction. It is important to include on a résumé, even if it is not directly related to current career plans:

**MILITARY
EXPERIENCE:**

**U.S. Army, Ft. Monmouth, NJ
Specialist, 4th Class, 2004-2008**

- Supervised a staff of six in the development of monthly newsletters
- Created a special section advising service men and women of educational opportunities in the community

Presentations and Publications

Presenting formally, conducting research and/or being published indicates a high level of achievement and should be included on the résumé following work experience. For example:

PRESENTATIONS:

Smart, Amy S. (2009). **The Implications of Service Projects for Student Development in Higher Education.** Presented at the American Humanics Management Institute, Orlando, FL.

PUBLICATIONS:

Smart, Amy S. (2010). A comparison of the grades of students involved in service learning projects with those not involved. *Journal of Leadership for Youth and Human Services,* 8: 4.

Honors and Activities

Employers want to know about student activities beyond the classroom and if those activities have been successful. Listed below are areas from which activities and honors should be considered:

- Social and service organizations
- Student government
- Student organizations
- Class projects
- Dean's list
- Service awards
- Leadership roles
- Academic activities and awards
- Athletic activities and awards
- Service and volunteer activities

Honors and activities should not be repeated if they appear elsewhere in the résumé. The ones included in this section should be listed in the order of importance, as indicated in the example below:

HONORS AND ACTIVITIES:	Girl Scouts of the U.S.A. – Gold Award Dean's List – six semesters American Humanics Senior of the Year All-Greek 4.0 Award Social Work Club Alpha Delta Pi Social Sorority

Personal information should not be included in the résumé. A person can unwittingly supply information that is not required or is illegal for the potential employer to ask about. While personal information can be used to establish connection with the interviewer, it can also give the person a reason for disqualification. Most often a résumé is used to knock people out of consideration. The reviewer is looking for a reason to reduce the pile of résumés.

There is also no need to take up space on the résumé to tell the reader that "references are available upon request." This is understood. Use the space for positive information that will increase the value of the résumé to the organization.

Developing a résumé is challenging, but it is an important step in starting a career. Once a résumé is developed, keeping it updated is much easier. The same basic format used for the **Sample Résumé** in Figure 9.5 can be used over and over again, although the "Career-related Experience" section should be renamed "Professional Experience." Various skills, experiences, and certifications will change and will need to be updated as well.

■ Networking

With the self-assessment profile and organizational exploration complete and the résumé in-hand, it is time to consider the most critical step of making productive use of your network to take the next step in the career process. A personal network is crucial. Often college students are selected for a position from campus interviews or internships, but most individuals must establish a networking and job search campaign to connect with individuals in organizations (Weis and Gantt 2004). Establishing a system of friends, family, and professional acquaintances for encouragement and guidance is of critical importance. Since over 75 percent of all positions are not advertised, it is very important that anyone

Figure 9.5
Sample Résumé — page 1

AMY S. SMART

Present Address
1405 Sycamore St.
Murray, KY 42071
(270) 759-1833
e-mail: amy.smart@murraystate.edu

Permanent Address
1721 Quarry Lane
Bath, ME 24112
(213) 475-4678

CAREER OBJECTIVE:
To obtain a position in a youth or human service organization where proven skills in communication, program development, and leadership will be utilized to assist the organization.

EDUCATION:
Murray State University, Murray, KY
Degree: Bachelor of Science, May 2011
Major: Recreation
Minor: Youth and Human Services

Grade Point Average: 3.93/4.00
Grade Point Average in Major: 4.00/4.00

Graduated Magna Cum Laude

CERTIFICATION:
Nonprofit Leadership Alliance Certification
American Red Cross Basic Life Support (CPR)

SPECIAL SKILLS:
Familiar with Power Point and EXCEL

SPECIAL TRAINING:
Murray Family YMCA, Murray, KY
Risk Management Workshop, Fall 2009
Student Participant

- Attended lectures on all aspects of reducing and managing health and safety risks
- Participated in simulated high-risk scenarios and developed risk management plan

CAREER-RELATED EXPERIENCE:
Camp Wyman, Eureka, MO
Human Services Internship, Summer 2007
Leadership-Challenge Coordinator

- Developed leadership-challenge programs for 500 inner-city children
- Directed the activities of support staff and counselors in delivery of services
- Designed Leadership-Challenge Program Manual as a guide for future staff

Figure 9.5
Sample Résumé — page 2

AMY S. SMART

CAREER RELATED EXPERIENCE:	**Camp Wyman, Eureka, MO** **Human Services Internship, Summer 2007** **Leadership-Challenge Coordinator**

- Developed leadership-challenge programs
  for 500 inner-city children
- Directed the activities of support staff and counselors
  in delivery of services
- Designed Leadership-Challenge Program Manual as a guide
  for future staff

Boy Scout National Museum, Murray, KY
Recreation Internship, Summer 2005
Challenge Course Coordinator

- Planned and implementing team-building
  activities related to high ropes challenge course
- Developed team-building activities to enhance high ropes
  experience
- Supervised all part-time and full-time challenge course leaders

WORK EXPERIENCE:	**Office of Alumni Affairs, Murray, KY** **Murray State University, 2006-2009** **Student Worker**

- Coordinated alumni-faculty scholarship meetings
- Organized functions and meetings involving the Board of
  Trustees and the Alumni

PRESENTATIONS:	Smart, Amy S. (2009). **The Implications of Service Projects** **for Student Development in Higher Education**. Presented at The American Humanics Management Institute, Orlando, Florida.

HONORS AND ACTIVITIES:	Nonprofit Leadership Alliance Senior of the Year Dean's List – six semesters All Greek 4.0 Award Sigma Delta Honorary Fraternity Nonprofit Leadership Alliance Student Recruitment – Chair Girl Scouts of the U.S.A., 4-H, and YMCA – Volunteer Recreation Club Alpha Delta Pi Social Sorority

seeking employment should focus the greatest effort in the area where the unadvertised positions can be found: the network. Networking, simply stated, means using every contact the candidate knows and everyone each contact knows to find the hidden jobs. The following step-by-step approach to networking and job seeking can be helpful:

Step 1 – Understand and Prepare for the Task Ahead

Networking is the process of developing individual connections within professional settings, and promoting your potential as an effective candidate for vacancies. Networking helps people to get to know someone as a professional candidate so they can support that candidate for a position within their organization or someone else's organization. Networking is not actually applying for a job, but campaigning for a position that may be open sometime in the future. Candidates must be prepared for a job search that can be long, frustrating, and expensive. Finding a job is a full-time job.

Step 2 – Develop a List of People and Services

Developing a list of people and services with potential for providing ideas, strategies or leads on career opportunities can be very helpful. The following list of people should be considered for contact:

Category I – People
- Faculty members
- American Humanics Campus/Executive Directors
- Organizational leaders
- Boards of directors members
- Friends and classmates
- Family members
- Former employers
- College and university administrators
- Networking contacts generated from other persons listed above

Category II – Services and Lists
- University/College career planning and placement office
- Organizational vacancy lists (YMCA, Boys and Girls Clubs, etc.)
- Chamber of Commerce
- United Way
- Professional placement services
- Association Directories
- The Internet (Hot Jobs, etc.)
- Newspaper – Classified Ads

Step 3 – Organize a Networking Notebook

One of the most important tools a job candidate can have is a networking notebook, designed to keep records of all the people and organizations contacted during a job search. The notebook can be of immense help in organizing the job search and for future job searches in the years to come. It is also useful when memory fails. Record important data, such as who has been called, who has a résumé, who has provided other contacts, etc.

A thick, lined, spiral notebook can be divided into categories of **People** and **Services** (listed in Step 2). Record keeping should include names, addresses, e-mail addresses, phone numbers, dates, and information on the results of the contact. A loose-leaf, three-ring binder could be used since it makes it easy to move information around to generate a section of "hot" prospects. However, it is easy to lose sheets. This is not good.

Step 4 – Making the Connection

Once the networking notebook is organized, contacts should be made with those individuals or services that are most likely to have information on available professional opportunities. Introductory phone calls should be made explaining that you are beginning a career search and would like to meet with them to get some ideas on a career direction. Sending résumés prior to meeting can be helpful, but it is essential that you take copies of your résumé with you and shared with any and all network contacts. Face-to-face meetings are generally best, but a phone or e-mail meeting can also be helpful. A candidate should try to get the names and addresses of at least three people who might be helpful in the job search, and these names and addresses should be recorded in the networking notebook. A thank-you note should always be sent to the contact person after the meeting.

Step 5 – Developing a Support System

Since job searches can be long, frustrating and expensive, it is important to develop a support system from the outset. A candidate must realize the process can be daunting and that determination is essential. Temporary jobs are sometimes necessary and should be selected with flexibility, so interviews can be scheduled when needed. Family members and friends should be informed of the situation and recruited for support and encouragement. Faculty members, college administrators, career advisors and organizational leaders should also be recruited into the support group. It is important to remain focused and to recognize the process is normal and that we all survive it.

■ References

Successful organizations carefully screen potential employees by reviewing letters of recommendation and calling references. Potential references should always be asked if they are willing to be a reference and if they are willing to write a letter of recommendation. Provide each person who agrees to be a reference with a copy of your résumé. It is very appropriate for you to draft a letter which describes how the person knows you, items from your résumé which are related to the job for which you are applying, and personal characteristics the potential employer can expect from you as an employee. This reduces the risk that a reference might produce a bad reference and increases **connectedness**.

References may come from a number of areas, including these:

Professors	Advisors
Employers	Administrators
Co-workers	Organizational leaders
Coaches	

Thank you notes or letters should *always* be sent to individuals who agree to serve as a

Figure 9.6
Sample Cover Letter

2207 Carol Drive
Murray, KY 42071
(270) 371-9897

August 30, 2011

Mr. Brad Simmons
Executive Director
Wilmington YMCA
Wilmington, NC 47501

Dear Mr. Simmons:

　　I would like to submit my résumé for your consideration for the position of Program Coordinator, which I recently saw advertised in the YMCA Vacancy List. I graduated in May of this year from Murray State University with a major in Therapeutic Recreation and a minor in Youth and Human Services. I am very interested in working for a youth and human service organization.

　　I believe my educational and career-related experience is ideally suited for this position. As an intern for the YMCA of Jeffersonville, Indiana, I was responsible for supervising the Counselors-In-Training (CIT) program. This program was so successful that I was asked to write the operating manual for the CIT program. I have also had successful program and supervisory experience with the Murray Family YMCA and the American Humanics program at Murray State University (MSU). As the Program Chair
For College Day, I successfully organized fellow students in the planning and implementation of a complete day of activities for 8th grade students on the MSU campus. I was recently honored for my accomplishments by being selected the American Humanics Student of the Year. The enclosed résumé lists my qualifications in more detail.

　　I am very interested in making a career with the YMCA. I am certainly interested in being considered for this position and working with the Wilmington YMCA. Thank you for your consideration, and I look forward to hearing from you in the near future.

Sincerely,

Jeffrey A. Student

Enclosure

reference. It is never a waste of time to send a thank you note. A handwritten note is best, but a typed one is better than nothing.

The names of references are never included on résumés, but a list of references should be a part of every job search toolkit. Take a list of references with name, address, phone number and the nature of their relationship. Four or five is enough. No more than one personal reference is necessary. Most employers are interested in professional associations.

■ Cover Letters

The cover letter has several purposes. It serves as a letter of introduction for a résumé, informs individuals in organizations which position a candidate is interested in and provides insight regarding a candidate's experiences and skills. Cover letters should be written specifically for the position that is being applied for. In other words, it should reflect the educational and career-related experiences a candidate has had that are relevant to a particular position.

The cover letter is the first document a prospective employer reads and it should be well written and error free. There are three main paragraphs that make up the content of the cover letter.

In the first paragraph a candidate should:
- Explain the résumé is being submitted for review.
- Describe the specific position being applied for.
- Identify oneself in terms of the position.
- Indicate interest in the organization.

The second paragraph is generally the most detailed of the three paragraphs and describes:
- Career-related and educational experiences relevant to the position (taken from the résumé).
- Levels of responsibility, leadership, initiative and successes a candidate may have had with these experiences.

The third paragraph is the concluding paragraph and should:
- Reiterate interest in this type of organization.
- Thank the individual reviewing the material.

The cover letter should include the return address, e-mail address (if applicable), telephone number, and the date as well as the name, title and address of the person to whom the letter is directed. A salutation (greeting) should be used before jumping to the body of the letter. See Figure 9.6 for a sample cover letter.

Tips for Cover Letters
- The same quality and color of paper should be used for the cover letter and the résumé.
- Take every opportunity to **connect** the content of the résumé with the cover letter content.
- The cover letter and résumé should be sent as soon as a position becomes vacant or a network lead is received.
- Contacting the individual to whom the cover letter and résumé were sent will

help insure receipt of the material. This should be done within seven to ten days after the material was sent.

- If possible, set a specific date and time to contact the person to arrange an interview.

■ Interviewing

The purpose of creating effective cover letters and résumés is to be offered an interview for a position that is of interest. With practice an interview can be as natural as having a conversation with a friend. Without practice an interview can be a professionally devastating experience. A person should prepare for an interview as she or he would for an important exam.

There are two main goals of an interview:

1. First, members of the selection committee or the interviewer want to see if a candidate is as promising in person as he or she seems to be on paper. Interviewers generally take note of dress and appearance, body language and voice, and even a candidate's handshake. As a matter of fact, the first few minutes of an interview are very important in establishing a positive impression. Interviewers are trying to determine whether a candidate seems like someone who can do the job and is someone they might like to work with.

2. An interview also provides the candidate with a chance to discover if the position and the people who work for the organization are right for him or her. A candidate should ask questions that will help determine if this position is the right position at the right time. The interview is a two-way street. It is just as important for the candidate to be comfortable with the situation and the personnel as it is for the others to be comfortable with the candidate.

Preparation

One of the biggest mistakes most people make is not preparing adequately for the interview. The more an individual knows about the position, the organization, the people who work there, his or her own personal goals and interests, and the interview process, the better chance the individual has of making a positive impression that will result in a job offer. Use a library or the Internet to research an organization before going for an interview.

Exploring the Position

Some information regarding the position is already available if the response was to a vacancy notice. Good organizations have clear and comprehensive job descriptions for each position and are usually willing to share these with candidates. A request can be made for a clarification of the job description from the interviewer(s). Asking for more information lets employers know that a candidate is interested in a position, and it provides the candidate with valuable information.

Exploring the Organization

It is important to find out as much as possible about the organization and the people who work there to assist a candidate in deciding if the organization is worthy of individual commitment. It is also important to gather information about an organization to be knowledgeable in the decision-making process and to indicate to employers a candidate is taking the position seriously enough to spend time researching the organization. There are several ways to gather information regarding a specific organization:

- Ask for and review a copy of the organization's annual report to get an idea of its goals, programs, and level of support and success.
- Contact the local United Way and ask for information about the organization.
- Contact someone who has received services from or has worked for the organization in the past, and ask his or her opinion of the organization.

Common Interview Considerations

Making the cut to the interview is a major accomplishment in and of itself. It is normal to be nervous at an interview. One of the best ways to calm down before and during an interview is to breathe deeply and slowly. If perspiration under stressful conditions is a concern, bring a handkerchief to the interview. Be aware of nervous habits (like running fingers through the hair or clicking a pen) and eliminate these practices from the interview. Throughout the interview, interviewers need to know the candidate is enthusiastic about the organization (without being overly zealous) and excited to be considered for the position.

The following categories of information can be helpful in making the interview process a success.

A. **Dress** – Dress should almost always be conservative. Men should wear suits or sport coats and be conservative with the length of their hair and facial hair. Women should wear business suits or a skirt and blouse, and be conservative with make-up, jewelry, lotions and perfumes. This is not the time to express a rebellious side or a creative flare.

B. **Interview Etiquette** – Copies of résumés should be brought to the interview for everyone, even though they may already have copies. Candidates should arrive at the interview 15 to 20 minutes early. The following etiquette is suggested (Dahlstrom 2009; Weis and Gantt 2004):

- Shake hands firmly (without excessive force) with each person involved in the interview. Be extra courteous and friendly.
- Always make eye contact when speaking with someone.
- Sit straight (yet comfortably) in a chair, and occasionally lean forward when emphasizing important points.
- Speak clearly and distinctly.
- Always express respect for the interviewers and the organization.

C. **Questions That May be Asked** - There is no rule on the number of questions that screening committee members can ask, so a candidate should be prepared to answer almost anything. Employers will sometimes present questions based on a specific problem scenario and ask how it can be solved. It is important to answer questions honestly, clearly, and as intelligently as possible. The following are standard questions asked in interviews.

- Tell me a little about yourself.
- Why do you want to work for this organization?

- What experience have you had that prepares you for this position?
- In what areas would you need to improve to be successful in this position?
- Describe a problem you've had in a career-related situation and tell us how you solved it?
- What would you hope to accomplish in this position?
- Why should we hire you for this position rather than someone else?
- What would you like to be doing professionally five years from now?

The first question in the list above is the most common and potentially the most deadly question asked in an interview. It is easily answered. It is an opportunity to focus the rest of the interview. It is an opportunity often squandered. An answer for this question should be practiced over and over. The question should be answered with a two- to four-minute response containing the following items:

- **The candidate's early history** (especially point to anything that relates to the position being applied for, such as interests and skills developed or nurtured)
- **Education** (with special focus on job related aspects – internships, etc.)
- **A brief description of career-related experience** (as much as possible, connect to the position being applied for)
- **How that experience qualifies the candidate for the position** (explain why you are a good match for the job)
- **Close the answer with a thank you for the opportunity to interview** (if it is the first or second question asked).

Too many people give their whole life history or say, "There isn't much to tell." Neither response gets jobs. A carefully thought-out answer **_connects_** the interviewee's training and experience with the job qualifications.

D. **Questions a Candidate May Wish to Ask.** – It is important for a candidate to ask good questions in order to have as much information as possible and to express a sense of knowledge and organization to the screening committee. The following questions should be considered during the interview:

- Why is this position open?
- What were the strong points of the person who last held the position?
- What exactly would be my responsibilities in this position?
- Who will be my supervisor?
- Could you describe his/her/your leadership style?
- Will I be supervising anyone, and if so, whom?
- Would you explain what a typical day would be like?
- What kind of person are you looking for?
- Would I have some flexibility to create new programs?
- Do you anticipate any changes for the organization in the future?
- What resources are available to me to do my job?
- Is further training and/or education available?
- How and when will I be evaluated?
- When can I expect to hear from you?

Questions regarding salary and benefits should never be mentioned in a first interview, unless the subject is introduced by someone else. There will be an appropriate time to do this.

E. **Practice, Practice, Practice** – No one ever did anything well without a lot of practice, and interviewing is no exception. Simulated interviews with a teacher or administrator can be very helpful. **Appendix C** contains an *interview simulation critique form*, which is useful in practice.

F. **Following the Interview** – A thank-you letter should be sent to the screening committee chair immediately following the interview. If the screening committee does not make contact within the designated time frame, a phone call may be appropriate.

■ Assessing Job Offers

An effective networking and job search campaign eventually culminates in job offers. The tendency for many people is to accept the first offer they receive. But accepting an offer without carefully evaluating it could be a major mistake. Create a list of all the important variables to consider in choosing a position. Assign weight to each variable in keeping with your values and of those affected by your choice. As offers come in, evaluate each offer objectively in light of the list. This will produce a better decision. There are several areas to resolve before a job offer is finalized:

- **Salary and Benefits** – Key benefits often included in a traditional benefits package include health insurance, life insurance, vacation and sick leave, a pension plan, tax shelters, and continued training and educational opportunities. Other benefits may include dental care, eye care, day care, and discounted or free facility use, if a facility is involved. When discussing benefits such as health or life insurance, candidates should ask what percentage of the costs they must pay versus what the employer pays.

- **Salary Negotiation** – If the demands of the job appear to outmatch the salary, or if the candidate thinks that the organization should offer more money for his or her skills and experience, the candidate may decide to negotiate for a higher salary. This can be done by explaining that he or she will accept the position at the salary offered, but that a higher salary (specific) would be more desirable for whatever the reason. Another option is to explain to the employer that the offer is appreciated, but it can only be accepted at a higher salary (again, be specific). This second option is obviously a risky strategy, and the candidate should be prepared for the possibility that the offer will be withdrawn.

Responding to Job Offers

Once a job has been offered and accepted, it is wise to send an acceptance letter. Acceptance letters are important because they provide written documentation regarding the acceptance of the job offer. They also provide an opportunity for clarification of the job offer. Besides, following up with a written letter of acceptance is the expected and courteous thing to do.

If a decision is made to turn down a job offer, it is also important to send a letter of rejection. This letter expresses consideration to the employer, and it helps keep the door open for future possibilities.

■ Professional Development
Training and Education

One of the most important aspects of developing professionally is to involve oneself in as many training and educational opportunities as possible. Good organizations offer numerous in-service training workshops or provide opportunities to attend training workshops elsewhere. Good organizations also encourage employees to continue their formal education, and some even pay for all or part of advanced educational pursuits. In the final analysis, training and education are not job benefits; they are personal necessities. They must be pursued, whether the organization provides them or they come at personal expense.

Professional Associations

Professional associations can be extremely helpful. They frequently offer support through a number of educational and informational workshops. They can also be helpful for career advancement opportunities. A person is not a professional if he or she is not connected with other professionals. Again, professional associates are not an option; they are a necessity.

Community Responsibility

Nonprofit leaders should always strive to have the best organization, with the best programs, and the best support systems possible. Of equal importance, leaders should strive to have the best relationships with colleagues, organizational members, volunteers, and other community members (Weis and Gantt 2004).

Leaders should also become involved in as many activities sponsored by the organization as possible. Most organizations are like big families. It is important for leaders to get to know and understand people in the organization.

Becoming involved with other organizations as a volunteer or as an interested community member is a good idea. "Practice what you preach" helps leaders remember to offer assistance to organizations other than their own. It is rewarding and fun, and it will ultimately benefit one's organization and career as well.

Just as it is important to continue learning and growing professionally, it's also important to balance professional pursuits with personal activities and responsibilities. Reserving quality time for oneself, family and friends is important. It helps to provide the support and strength needed to be a successful, professional leader.

An appropriate concluding statement for this chapter is found in another of those Successories motivational posters: "Great achievements are not born from a single vision but from the combination of many distinctive viewpoints. Diversity challenges assumptions, opens minds and unlocks potential to solve any problem we may face."

A wise person will spend five percent of every day preparing for the next step in his or her career—promotion, new employer, career change or retirement. Abraham Lincoln reportedly passed along this insight: "I do not think much of a man who is not wiser today than he was yesterday." To be totally content with today is to be foolish. The wise person positions himself or herself for the next bend in the road. A curve in a person's career path is not a disaster unless he or she fails to make the turn (Weis and Gantt 2004).

■ Summary

Success in career planning begins with a thorough knowledge of self. Without self-knowledge and understanding, planning a career and find a job is confusing and frustrating. The *Flowchart for Career Planning* reduces the confusion. The process begins with the construction of a *Self-assessment Profile,* ideally using more than one assessment tool. The next step involves organizational exploration by first collecting information about the purpose and scope of the organization. Then, one must do organizational research, which includes collecting data from volunteering, service learning experiences, internships, staff shadowing or informational interviews.

With a specific direction in mind and potential target organizations chosen, the next step is résumé construction. This is usually the most important step in the process. A résumé is a one- to two-page document providing a summary of education and experience. An effective résumé helps to get an interview. It must be error-free and completed before any other steps are taken.

The next step is personal and professional networking. This involves using contacts to locate potential positions and developing leads for open positions. Each person needs a copy of the résumé.

References need to be contacted based on their knowledge of the candidate's work experience and training. It is helpful for each reference to receive a résumé and a draft of a letter that they might be comfortable sending on behalf of the candidate. References often come from a person's professional network.

With a résumé constructed and contacts from networking activities in place, cover letters can be constructed to convey to potential employers how the candidate can meet the needs of the targeted organizations. These letters are specific but contain three basic paragraphs: a personal introduction of the candidate; an indication of which position is of interest and how the candidate qualifies for that position; and an expression of interest in moving forward with the employment process, along with a thank you for the agency's consideration. This too must be carefully written and error-free.

If all goes well, the next step is the interview. If effective preparation occurs, an interview can be an enjoyable experience. For all candidates, the same rules apply: Carefully collect background information on the target organization; prepare answers to commonly asked questions; select questions to be answered by organizational members; dress appropriately; control nervous habits; and give people a firm handshake.

A successful interview frequently results in a job offer. One should not accept the first offer unless it meets all the requirements of a dream job. Be knowledgeable regarding job market conditions, salary ranges and benefits packages for positions of interest. Be realistic and be prepared to negotiate for the things most important for a reasonable career progression.

The last section of this chapter discussed the role of professional development in the life of nonprofit staff members. Candidates should take every opportunity to gain additional educational credentials, acquire new skills and up-date old skills. In addition, he or she should seek every occasion to work with appropriate professional associations and community projects in order to expand network contacts for that next job search.

This chapter addressed, in part, the Nonprofit Leadership Alliance Certification Competency Requirements of Employability Skills and Career Development and Exploration.

■ **Reflection and Application**

1. Discuss ways in which you plan to use the *Flowchart for Career Planning* in your career search?

    _____

    _____

    _____

    _____

2. Discuss the value of self-assessment. How can others help in the process?

    _____

    _____

    _____

    _____

3. Discuss the skills you have developed that could be important for most careers in the nonprofit sector.

    _____

    _____

    _____

    _____

4. Select a campus or community leader to host a simulated interview for you. Be sure to prepare for the interview by studying the suggestions in that section of the chapter and incorporate the Interview Simulation Critique Form (Appendix D) in the process then discuss your results?

    _____

    _____

    _____

5. How can any and all work experience be valuable for your resume and for your career path?

_____

_____

_____

_____

6. Write a 2 – 3 page paper discussing your dream career path?

_____

_____

7. Choose a nonprofit organization in the community and plan and secure permission for a day of *shadowing*. What did you learn with this experience?

_____

_____

_____

8. Write a personal vision statement for 5 years from now, 10 years from now, and 15 years from now.

_____

_____

_____

9. Create a *networking* list of 20 - 25 individuals or organizational contacts.

_____

_____

_____

_____

∎ References

Dawson, K. M. and Dawson, S. N. (1996). *Job search: The total system.* (2nd ed.). New York: John Wiley & Sons.

Dahlstrom, H. (2009). *The Job Hunting Handbook.* Holliston, MA: Dahlstrom and Company, Inc.

Hirsch, A. S. (1999). *Interviewing.* (3rd ed.). New York: John Wiley & Sons.

Kennedy, J. (2000). *Job interviews for dummies.* New York: John Wiley & Sons.

Michelozzi, B.N., 1992. *Coming alive from nine to five.* Mountain View, CA: Mayfield Printing Company.

Lowe, D. (2002). *Networking for dummies.* New York: John Wiley & Sons.

Weis, R. and Gantt, V. (2004). *Knowledge and Skill Development in Nonprofit Organizations.* Peosta, IA: E. Bowers Publishing.

Weis, R. and Gantt, V. (2002). *Leadership and Program Development in Nonprofit Organizations.* Peosta, IA: E. Bowers Publishing.

Weis, R. (1996). *A lifetime of making a difference.* Kansas City, MO: Clevenger & Company Publishers.

A

**Appendix A
Directory of National
Nonprofit Organizations**

4-H

History

An informal organization established by Congress in 1914, the Cooperative Extension Service is a partnership of U.S. Department of Agriculture. 4-H is one of the extension's educational youth programs. Since 1914, 4-H has reached more than 40 million youth from all states, including more than 4.5 million boys and girls enrolled today.

Purpose

To help youth acquire knowledge, develop life skills, and form attitudes that will enable them to become self-directing, productive, and contributing members of society.

Programs

Cooperative Extension Service
Expanded Food and Nutrition Programs
Agriculture and Science Project
Home Environment Project

Leadership Programs
Honor Club
Public Speaking
Safety and Health Programs

Career Opportunities

Camp Managers
Camp Instructors
Medical Technicians
Home Economics
Recreation
Asst. Director for Youth Development

County Extension Agents
4-H Specialists
Extension Associates
Agriculture
Education
Management

Contact

Local offices are located in most counties with state offices based in state universities. Check the Internet for the latest news.

1400 Independence Ave., S.W.
Stop 2225
Washington, D.C. 20250-2225

Phone: 202-401-4114

http://4-H.org

Alcoholics Anonymous

History

AA was founded in 1935 by a New York stockbroker and an Ohio surgeon, both of whom had been "hopeless" drunks. It has grown from two members to more than 2,000,000. There are now 89,000 small groups.

Purpose

To stay sober and help other alcoholics to achieve sobriety.

Programs

TV or radio programs   Support Groups
AA Grapevine   Information dissemination

Career Opportunities

Therapy   Administrative
Counseling   Research
(Few paid positions)

Contact

Local groups are located in most communities. Check the Internet for the latest news.

P.O. Box 459   Phone: 212-870-3400
New York, NY 10163   Fax: 212-870-3003

http://www.aa.org

Alzheimer's Association

History

It was founded in 1980 by seven independent caregiver groups of dedicated family members. It is officially known as the Alzheimer's Disease and Related Disorders Association. The Association works through a network of more than 221 local chapters, more than 2,000 support groups and 35,000 volunteers nationwide.

Purpose

To lead in promoting awareness of Alzheimer's Disease and serving the diverse needs of the more than 400,000 affected persons and their families.

Programs

Adult Day Care Programs   Respite Care Programs
Support Systems   Research Programs
Memory Walk   National Education Conference
Safe Return   AA Newsletter

Career Opportunities

Fundraising   Medical and Scientific Affairs
Accounting   Management Information
Administration   Publicity

Contact

Local offices are located in many cities. Check the Internet for the latest news.

225 N. Michigan Ave., Fl. 17   Phone: 312-335-8700
Chicago, IL 60601   800-272-3900
                                 Fax: 866-699-1246

http://www.alz.org

American Association for Higher Education

History

It was founded in 1870. More than 7,800 educators are members today.

Purpose

To clarify and help resolve critical issues in post-secondary education through conferences, publications and special projects.

Programs

Educational Assistant Programs
Training Programs
Support of Academic Alliance

Career Opportunities

Clerical   Development Officer
Human Resources   Fundraising

Contact

Local chapters are located at many colleges and universities. Check the Internet for the latest news.

2020 Pennsylvania Ave. NW #975	Phone:	888-276-1299
Washington, DC 20006	Fax:	877-510-4240

http://www.aahea.org

American Cancer Society

History

In 1913, ten physicians and five laymen founded the American Society for the Control of Cancer. It was later named the American Cancer Society, Inc. The national ACS consists of 57 divisions and more than 3,400 units.

Purpose

To disseminate knowledge concerning the symptoms, treatment and prevention of cancer; to investigate conditions under which cancer is found, and to compile statistics in regard thereto.

Programs

Service Programs:
—Community Connection
—Transportation
—Home Care Items

Rehabilitation Programs:
—Reach to Recovery
—Laryngectomy Rehabilitation
—Look Good…Feel Better
—Children's camps

Patient and Family Education Programs:
—I Can Cope
—Anti-tobacco Programs

Group Support Programs

Career Opportunities

Management
Community Services
Public Education

Patient Services
Research
Fundraising

Contact

Local offices are located in most cities. Check the Internet for the latest news.

1599 Clifton Road NE
Atlanta, GA 30329

Phone: 404-320-3333
        800-227-2345
Fax: 404-325-1467

http://www.cancer.org

American Foundation for the Blind

History

Founded in 1921, the American Foundation for the Blind is recognized in the United States as Helen Keller's cause.

Purpose

To enable people who are blind or visually impaired to achieve equality of access and opportunity that will ensure freedom of choice in their lives.

Programs

Education Programs   Guide Dog Schools
Research   Client Assistance
Books on Tape

Career Opportunities

Medical   Fundraising
Research   Administrative
Dog Training   Readers

Contact

Local offices are located in many cities. Check the Internet for the latest news.

2 Penn Plaza, Suite 1102	Phone: 212-502-7600
New York, NY 10121	800-232-5463
	Fax: 212-502-7777

http://www.afb.org

American Lung Association

History

The National Association for the Study and Prevention of Tuberculosis was formed in 1904 by a group of doctors and concerned citizens dedicated to the elimination of tuberculosis. Its best-known funding program has been Christmas Seals. As tuberculosis was brought under control, the organization expanded its work to fight other lung diseases and pollution and adopted the name American Lung Association. More than 8,700 medical professionals take part in its medical programs today.

Purpose

To promote pulmonary health through research, education and patient assistance.

Programs

Medical Research Programs
School Health Education Programs:
—Lungs Are for Life
—Open Airways for Schools

Smoking Cessation/Intervention Programs:
—Freedom-from-Smoking Clinics
—In Control
—Healthy Beginnings
—Coping Without Smoking

Environmental Health Programs
Lung Disease Education Programs:
—Better Breathers Club
—Camp Superkids
—Alpha 1 Support Groups

Career Opportunities

Health Education Director
Communications Director
Development Director
Fundraising

Volunteer Coordinator
Clerical
Executive Director

Contact

Local offices are located in many cities. Check the Internet for the latest new.

Pennsylvania Ave. NW.
Washington, DC 20004

Phone: 800-LUNG-USA
Fax: 202-452-1805

http://www.lungusa.org

American Red Cross

History

In 1859, Henri Dunant, a Swiss banker, visited the battlefields of Solferino, in Italy. After seeing thousands of wounded and dying victims, he organized a group of peasant women to assist him in rescue operations. This was the first mission in what was to become the Red Cross Movement. In 1863, the International Committee of Red Cross formed. A few years later, Clara Barton founded the American Red Cross through her experience in the Civil War and the Franco-Prussian War. Today there are more than 3,000 chapters, 70 blood service regions, 300 field stations on military bases and in hospitals, three operation headquarters, and one national headquarters.

Purpose

The American Red Cross is a humanitarian organization whose volunteers provide relief to victims of disasters and help people prevent, prepare for and respond to emergencies.

Programs

Disaster	Blood Services
Tissue Services	Health and Safety Services
HIV/AIDS Education	Military and Social Services
International Services	Youth Services
…and many others	

Career Opportunities

Finance	Public Support
Biomedical Services	Human Resources
International Services	Health and Safety
Accounting	Corporate Planning and Evaluation

Contact

Local offices are located in most cities. Check the Internet for the latest news.

2025 E Street, NW	Phone:	703-206-6000
Washington, DC 20006		800-733-2767
	Fax:	202-639-3711

http://www.redcross.org

Big Brothers Big Sisters of America

History

The Big Brothers Big Sisters movement began at the turn of the century, when citizens in many American cities organized programs to stop the rising tide of juvenile delinquency. By 1917, the Big Brothers and Big Sisters Federation formed. It existed until 1937. In 1945, a national federation for Big Brothers agencies, Big Brothers of America, was formed. Big Sisters International, Inc. was formed in 1970. In 1977, the two national organizations merged to create today's Big Brothers Big Sisters of America. Today, over 600 agencies located throughout the United States help more than 100,000 children.

Purpose

To make a positive difference in lives of children and youth, primarily through a professionally supported one-to-one relationship with a caring adult, and to assist children in achieving their highest potential as they grow to become responsible men and women.

Programs

Mentoring
EMPOWER

Career Opportunities

Office Manager	Executive Director
Support Staff	Caseworkers
Field Managers	Finance
Marketing	Supervisor/Program Directors

Contact

Local offices are located in many cities. Check the Internet for the latest news.

230 North 13ᵗʰ St.	Phone:	215-567-7000
Philadelphia, PA 19107	Fax:	215-567-0394

http://www./bbbs.org/

Boy Scouts of America

History

The Boy Scouts of America was founded in 1910 by William D. Boyce, after he had been impressed by the young British Scout who had helped him find his way out of a dense London fog. The organization now serves more than four million members in programs ranging from Tiger Cubs for six-year-old boys to Eagle Scouts for older teens and with special programs for handicapped people of any age.

Purpose

To serve others by helping to instill values in young people and, in other ways, to prepare them to make ethical choices over their lifetime in achieving their full potential.

Programs

Trail Boss   Cub Scouting
Boy Scouting   Exploring
Learning for Life

Career Opportunities

Public Relations   Administration
Sales   Finance
Service   Psychology
Sociology   Human Relations
Management

Contact

Local offices are located in many cities. Check the Internet for the latest news.

   1325 W. Walnut Hill Lane   Phone: 972-580-2000
   Irving, TX 75038   Fax: 972-580-2502

http://www.scouting.org

Boys and Girls Club of America

History

In 1860, three ladies invited a group of street boys into their home. They saw a positive influence on the boys' behavior and extended their hospitality several more times. Along With others, the ladies resolved themselves to finding a facility where boys could go regularly. They called it Dashaway Club, which was the first Boys Club. Although this particular club was discontinued the following year, the idea grew. In 1897, the first building was planned specifically for a boys club in Fall River, Massachusetts. The movement then spread westward. There are now more than 4,000 Boys and Girls Club facilities that help more than 4.2 million young people.

Purpose

To help youth of all backgrounds, with special concern for those from disadvantaged circumstances, develop the qualities needed to become responsible citizens and leaders.

Programs

National Association of Keystone Clubs
Young Artists Program
National Photography Contest
Sectional Tournaments and Contests Programs

SMART Moves
Feed the Children
A Helping Hand

Career Opportunities

Educational Director
Social Recreation Director
Executive Director
Aquatics Director
Camp Director
Assistant Executive Director

Physical Education Director
Group Club Supervisor
Guidance Counselor
Industrial Arts Instructor
Program Director

Contact

Local offices are located in many cities. Check the Internet for the latest news.

1275 West Peachtree St. NE
Atlanta, GA 30309-3506

Phone: 404-815-5700
Email: info@bgca.org

http://www.bgca.org

Camp Adventure

History

The program began in 1985 for the Youth Activities Division of the U.S. Eighth Army's Recreation Service Operation, Korea. Later it was brought into partnership with the University of Oregon as a way to provide college-age students the opportunity to earn college credits while participating in a valuable service learning experience. Currently the program operates at 150 sites in 27 countries/territories and has expanded to 10 other college campuses with students from over 80 campuses nationwide participating.

Purpose

To provide opportunities to serve children and youth, integrate theory with practice, and develop new knowledge, skills and competencies.

Programs

Day Camps	Resident Camps
Sports Camps	Learning Adventures
Spirit Camps	Adventure Plus
Dance Pursuits	ArtFest
Performing Arts Camp	KinderCamp
Outdoor Rangers	Middle School Activities
Teen Program	Learn-to-Swim Programs

Career Opportunities

Human Resources	Programming
Staff Development	Marketing & Contracts
Administration	

Contact

Check the internet for the latest news.

2351 Hudson Road, HPC 106	Phone: 319-273-5960
Cedar Falls, IA 50614	Fax: 319-273-2058

http://www.campadventure.com

Camp Fire Boys and Girls

History

This organization was founded in 1910 as Camp Fire Girls by Luther Halsey Gulick, M.D., and his wife, Charlotte Vetter Gulick. It was the first national, nonsectarian organization for girls in the United States. In the 1970s, membership was expanded to include boys, and the name was changed to Camp Fire Boys and Girls. Each year, Camp Fire Boys and Girls serves more than 500,000 young children across the United States.

Purpose

To provide, through a program of informal education, opportunities for youth to realize their potential and to function effectively as caring, self-directed individuals, responsible to themselves and others; and, as an organization, to seek to improve those conditions in society which affect youth.

Programs

A Gift of Peace
Teens in Action
Teen Parent Program

Club Program
Teen Campaign on Suicide Awareness
Special Saturday Club

Career Opportunities

Executive Directors

Camp Administrators

Contact

Local offices are located in many cities. Check the Internet for the latest news.

1100 Walnut Street, Suite 1900
Kansas City, MO 64106-2197

Phone: 816-756-1950
Fax: 816-285-9444

http://www.campfireusa.org

Catholic Charities USA

History

The Catholic Charities USA was founded in 1910. The Catholic Charities Association has more than 1,400 local organizations with more then 300,00 staff members and volunteers, which serve nearly 10 million people in need.

Purpose

The purpose of the organization is for thousands of concerned volunteers and independent social service agencies to work together to reduce poverty, support families, and build communities in the United States.

Programs

Counseling   Education and Family Support
Health Services   Housing
Adoption Services   Neighborhood Support
Refugee Resettlement   Pregnancy Services
Residential Care

Career Opportunities

Administration   Communications
Development   Disaster Response
Facilities and Services   Social Services
Training and Convening

Contact

Local offices are located in many cities. Check the Internet for the latest news.

Sixty-six Canal Center Plaza, Suite 600 Phone: 703-549-1390
Alexandria, VA 22314   Fax: 703-549-1656

http://www.catholiccharitiesusa.org

Chamber of Commerce

History

The beginnings of the Chamber of Commerce movement can be traced back almost 6,000 years to the city of Mari, in Mesopotamia. The modern movement began in 1599, when merchants in Marseilles, France, formed an independent voluntary organization to represent commercial interests of the port. During the eighteenth century, chambers were established in many cities in France, England and Ireland. The first American Chamber of Commerce was organized in 1768 in New York, and five years later, businessmen from Charleston, South Carolina, united to form their Chamber of Commerce. Today there are more than 2,700 local, state and regional Chambers and American Chambers abroad, comprised of 1,100 trade and professional associations and more than 39,000 business members. It is estimated that approximately six million persons may be involved with Chambers of Commerce.

Purpose

To promote development of a community by pulling together its various elements: business, professional, industrial and artistic.

Programs

Communications   Small Business Assistance
Growth/Recruitment   Promotion of Tourism
Convention Center   Housing Bureau

Career Opportunities

Tourism Sales   Convention Planning
Sales Manager   Administrative Assistant
Executive Director   Director of Public Relations
Marketing Director   Business Services

Contact

Most communities have Chambers of Commerce. Check the Internet for latest news.

American Chamber of   Phone: 703-998-0072
Commerce Executives.   Fax: 703-212-9512
4875 Eisenhower Ave., Suite 250
Alexandria, VA 22304

http://www.acce.org

Council on International Educational Exchange

History

Founded in 1947, the Council on International Educational Exchange now has 276 members.

Purpose

To develop and administer a wide variety of study, work, travel and volunteer service programs for American and international students at secondary, undergraduate, graduate and professional programs.

Programs

Council Travel   Volunteer Service
Work Abroad Program   Summer Study Abroad Program

Career Opportunities

Program Coordinators   Administrative

(To qualify, applicants must have worked or studied abroad, have good language skills and have two to five years of experience.)

Contact

Check the Internet for the latest news.

300 Fore Street   Phone: 207-533-4000
Portland, ME 04101   Fax: 207-553-4299

http://www.ciee.org

Cystic Fibrosis Foundation

History

CFF was established in 1955 to raise money for research to find a cure for cystic fibrosis and to improve the quality of life for 30,000 children and young adults with the disease. Today it supports 12 CF research centers and finances 114 CF centers nationwide. There are currently 10 chapters across the country.

Purpose

To raise money for research to find a cure for cystic fibrosis and to improve the quality of life for those with the disease.

Programs

Research

Financial Assistance

Medical Care

GREAT STRIDES Walk-a-Thon

Career Opportunities

Medical

Financial

Pharmacy

Research

Fundraising

Communications

Contact

Local offices are located in many cities, especially at larger hospitals. Check the Internet for the latest news.

6931 Arlington Rd., 2nd Floor
Bethesda, MD 20814

Phone: 800-FIGHTCF
Fax: 301-951-6378

http://www.cff.org

Easter Seal Society

History

The Easter Seal Society, founded in 1922, serves a large number of children with special needs. More than 8,000 children and young adults benefit from their services annually.

Purpose

ESS is dedicated to helping children with physical disabilities achieve their full individual potential and future independence.

Programs

Camping
Financial Assistance
Integrated Preschools
Family Education Workshops

Parent-to-Patient Link
Respite Care
Parent Delegates

Career Opportunities

Nursing
Medical
Fundraising

Research
Administrative

Contact

Local offices are located in many cities. Check the Internet for the latest news.

233 S. Wacker Drive, Suite 2400
Chicago, IL 60606

Phone: 416-421-8377
Fax: 416-696-1035

http://www.easterseals.com

Family Career and Community Leaders of America

History

FCCLA was founded in 1945 for home economics students in junior and senior high schools of the United States, Puerto Rico and the Virgin Islands. Its current membership is 250,000 with 10,000 local chapters.

Purpose

To prepare young men and women in high school for careers related to home economics, family life and consumer education; to promote personal growth and leadership development through home economics education.

Programs

STAR events   Home projects
Chapter projects   School projects
Community projects   Youth for Understanding

Career Opportunities

Clerical   Administrative
Membership Services Assistant   Accountant
Computer Services   Meetings Manager
Program Manager   Adult/Chapter Relations Coordinator
Program Coordinator   Communications
Teacher/Chapter Adviser   Youth/Program Assistant

Contact

Local chapters are located in many high schools and colleges. Check the Internet for the latest news.

1910 Association Dr.   Phone: 703-476-4900
Reston, VA 22091   Fax: 703-860-2713

http://www.fcclainc.org

Fellowship of Christian Athletes

History

The Fellowship of Christian Athletes was founded in 1954. Currently there are more than 5,000 clubs with an estimated 250,000 – 400,000 athletes involved.

Purpose

To present to athletes and coaches, and all whom they influence, the challenge and adventure of receiving Jesus Christ as Savior and Lord, serving him in their relationships and in the fellowship of the church.

Programs

Rallies   Retreats
Camps   Sports Clinics
School Assemblies

Career Opportunities

Development/Public Relations   Camp Coordinators
Administrative/Executive Directors   Ministry Services
Finance   Publications
Data Processing

Contact

Local chapters are located in many cities and schools. Check the Internet for the latest news.

8701 Leeds Rd.   Phone: 816-921-0909
Kansas City, MO 64129   Fax: 816-921-8755

http://www.fca.org

FFA

History

Organized under the provisions of the Smith-Hughes Act of 1917, FFA's first national convention was held in 1982. Its current membership is 428,000 members with 52 state chapters and 7,300 local chapters.

Purpose

To motivate and vitalize the systematic instruction offered to students of vocational agriculture and to provide training and farm citizenship.

Programs

Vocational Agriculture Programs   Community Programs

Career Opportunities

Chief Operative Officer   National Adviser
National Executive Secretary   Team Leader
Administration Specialist   Co-team Leader
Clerical   Membership Services Specialist
Marketing Consultant   Management Information Systems Director
Distribution Resources Specialist   Partner Development Specialist
Teacher Services Specialist   Student Services Specialist
Alumni Services Specialist   Conference Program Director

Contact

Local chapters are located in many schools and colleges. Check the Internet for the latest news.

6060 FFA Drive   Phone: 317-802-6060
P.O. Box 68960   Fax: 317-802-6051
Indianapolis, IN 46268-0960

http://www.ffa.org

Fine Arts

History

Artists appear in the earliest recorded history and were the actual historians. Ancient cave drawings depict musicians and dancers. Jubal, the first maker and player of the pipes, is mentioned early in Genesis in the Bible; young David's harp skills were sought as therapy for the mentally disturbed King Saul, and his poetry is loved by millions. Today's arts include avenues unheard of only a few decades ago. Applications beyond pure visual and performance art are almost constantly developing.

Career Opportunities

Art Therapist*	Music Therapist*
Dance Therapist*	Performer
Graphic Designer	Program Planner
Symphony Conductor	Community Band Director
Community Theater Director	Puppet Therapist
Theater Director	Skit Writer
Creative Arts Project Planner	Teacher
Museum Curator	Civic Auditorium Manager
Concert Promoter	Fine Arts Center Director
Artist Manager	Agent
Fundraiser	Marketing Specialist

*Some career paths require special certification.

Contact

There are many local, state and national associations for the arts, which may be contacted through universities or specific disciplines. Most community arts groups are nonprofit organizations that may not be registered with any national agency. Job seekers are advised not to overlook such prospective employers as may be found through newspaper announcements, networking and Chamber of Commerce directories.

Future Business Leaders of America

History

FBLA was founded in 1942. Its current membership is 300,000 members with 12,000 local chapters.

Purpose

To promote competent, aggressive business leadership, establish career goals, encourage scholarships, promote efficient money management, and develop character and self-confidence.

Programs

Skills Competition   National Student Award
Educational Programs

Career Opportunities

Communications Specialist   Conference Assistant
Receptionist   Membership Coordinator
Executive Assistant   Membership Director
Conference Director   Publications Coordinator
Resource Center Coordinator   Mail Room Clerk

Contact

Local chapters are located in many schools and universities. Check the Internet for the latest news.

1912 Association Dr.   Phone: 800-325-2946
Reston, VA 22091   Fax: 866-500-5610

http://fbla-pbl.org

Girl Scouts of the U.S.A.

History

The organization was founded in 1812 by Juliette Gordon Lowe. The first club was formed with 18 girls. Today, it has more than three million members throughout the United States.

Purpose

To inspire girls with the highest ideals of character, conduct, patriotism and service so that they may become happy and resourceful citizens.

Programs

Daisy Girl Scouts   Brownie Girl Scouts
Junior Girl Scouts   Cadette Girl Scouts
Senior Girl Scouts

Career Opportunities

Marketing and Sales   Finance Services
Fund Development   Information Systems and Services
Communication Services   Legal Services
Human Resources   Field Director
Program Specialist

Contact

Local offices are located in many cities. Check the Internet for the latest news.

420 Fifth Ave.   Phone: 800-478-7248
New York, NY 10018   Fax: 212-852-6517

http://www.girlscouts.org

Girls Incorporated

History

The first Girls Club was founded in Waterbury, Connecticut, in 1854. The early clubs were safe havens and social and educational centers for the young women who worked in northeastern mill town during the Industrial Revolution. In 1990, the membership voted to change its name to Girls Incorporated. Girls Incorporated has grown to have over 200 centers in 121 cities. They serve a half million girls and young women, ages six to eighteen.

Purpose

The purpose of Girls Incorporated is to empower girls to be self-sufficient, personally fulfilled, and economically independent.

Programs

Friendly PEERsuasion   Preventing Adolescent Pregnancy
Going Places   Operation SMART
Teen Connections   Sporting Chance

Career Opportunities

Administrative Services   Program Services
Communication Services

Contact

Local offices are located in many cities. Check the Internet for the latest news.

120 Wall Street   Phone: 212-509-2000
New York, NY 10016   Fax: 212-509-8708

http://www.girlsinc.org

Goodwill Industries International

History

In the late 1890's, Methodist Minister Edgar J. Helms found ways to help his community's immigrant, jobless poor. His church's "industrial school" offered skills training. A job placement service developed in 1896. In 1902, a new facility was built and Goodwill Industries was truly born. The words "Goodwill Industries" were first used in Brooklyn, New York. During the 1930's, Goodwill Industries redirected its mission to helping people with disabilities. Today, there are 183 Goodwill organizations. Currently in the United States, Goodwill has 180 sites serving people with disabilities and special needs. They also served approximately 40,000 outside the United States and Canada.

Purpose

To achieve the full participation in society of people with disabilities and other individuals with special needs by expanding their opportunities and occupational capabilities through a network of autonomous, nonprofit, community-based organizations providing services throughout the world in response to local needs.

Programs

Employment & Training Services   Second-hand Retail Stores
Recycling Services

Career Opportunities

Rehabilitation   Vocational Training
Accounting   Retailing
Industrial Operations   Marketing and Sales

Contact

Local offices are located in many cities. Check the Internet for the latest news.

>   15810 Indianola Drive   Phone: 800-741-0186
>   Rockville, MD 20855   Fax: 301-530-1516

http://www.goodwill.org/

Habitat for Humanity International

History

Founded in 1976 by Millard and Linda Fuller, Habitat for Humanity International (HFHI) is a nonprofit, ecumenical Christian housing ministry.

Purpose

HFHI seeks to eliminate poverty housing and homelessness from the world, and to make decent shelter a matter of conscience and action. HFHI invites people from all walks of life to work together in partnership to help build houses with families in need. HFHI has built more than 300,000 houses around the world, providing thousands of people with safe, decent, affordable housing.

Career Opportunities

International Services
Accounting
Project Management

Contact

Local offices are located in many cities. Check the Internet for the latest news.

121 Habitat Street	Phone: 800-422-4828
Americus, GA 31709	Fax: 912-924-0641

http://www.habitat.org/

Hospice

History

The first modern hospice was founded in London in 1968. Cicely Saunders, the founder, believed that institutions were ignoring the special needs of the dying. The first American hospice was started in New Haven, Connecticut, in 1974. Now more than 2,000 hospices are serving people.

Purpose

To provide special care for dying people and their families.

Programs

Support Groups
Health Care Programs

Career Opportunities

Medical   Counseling
Nursing   Physical Therapy

Contact

Local offices are located in many hospitals. Check the Internet for the latest news.

1731 King Street, Suite 100   Phone: 800-658-8898
Alexandria, VA 22314   Fax: 703-837-1233

http://www.nhpco.org

The Humane Society of the United States

History

The Humane Society was founded in 1954. It maintains a regional office, an educational division, a team of investigators, legislative experts and an animal-control academy. There are more than a million members involved.

Purpose

To make the world safe for animals through legal, educational, legislative and investigative means.

Programs

Educational
Research
HSUS Adopt-a-Teacher

Wildlife Experts
HSUS News

Career Opportunities

Human Resources
Financial
Program Coordinators
Public Relations
Marketing

Accounting
Secretarial/Administrative
Executive Directors
Development Department

Contact

Local offices are located in many cities. Check the Internet for the latest news.

2100 L Street NW
Washington, DC 20037

Phone: 202-452-1100
Fax: 301-258-3079

http://www.humanesociety.org

Junior Achievement

History

Junior Achievement was founded in 1919. In 2009, four million children participated in the organization.

Purpose

To provide young people with practical, economic education programs and experiences in the competitive private enterprise system through a partnership with the business and education communities.

Programs

Project Business   Applied Economics
GLOBE   Business Basics

Career Opportunities

Field Services   Research and Development
Communications and Marketing   Human Resources
Management

Contact

Local contacts may be made through schools, businesses and local offices. Check the Internet for the latest news.

One Education Way   Phone: 719-540-8000
Colorado Springs, CO 80906   Fax: 719-540-6299

http://www.ja.org

Juvenile Diabetes Foundation

History

The Juvenile Diabetes Foundation was founded in 1970. Since then, it has given more than $200 million to diabetes research around the world.

Purpose

To support research in the cause, cure, treatment and prevention of diabetes and its complications.

Programs

Walk for the Cure   Promise Ball
Patient Camps

Career Opportunities

Fundraising   Research
Medical   Administrative

Contact

Local offices are located in many cities. Check the Internet for the latest news.

26 Broadway, 14th Floor   Phone: 800-533-2873
New York, NY 10004   Fax: 212-785-9595

http://www.jdrf.org

Leukemia and Lymphoma Society of America

History

It was established in 1949 as the de Villiers Foundation, in memory of Robert Roesler de Villiers, a young man who died of leukemia. In 1967, it was renamed the Leukemia Society of America. It now has 60 chapters, with branch offices in 40 states and the District of Columbia.

Purpose

It is dedicated to eradicating leukemia and its related cancers and improving the lives of patients and their families.

Programs

Research Programs   Patient Aid
Public and Professional Education   Community Service

Career Opportunities

Accounting   Public Relations
Communications   Administration
Research   Marketing
Finance   Medical

Contact

Local offices may be found through larger hospitals. Check the Internet for the latest news.

1311 Mamaroneck Avenue   Phone: 800-955-4572
Suite 310
White Plains, NY 10605

http://www.leukemia-lymphoma.org

March of Dimes

History

The March of Dimes has been dedicated to saving babies from birth defects and other infant health problems for more than sixty years. Since 1958, the March of Dimes has been funding cutting-edge research and innovative programs to save babies. It provides care for victims of polio, while aggressively working to develop vaccines against it. It represents the first large-scale, nationwide biomedical initiative led by a charitable organization.

Purpose

The March of Dimes researchers, volunteers, educators, outreach workers and advocates work together to give all babies a fighting chance against threats to their health, such as prematurity, birth defects and low birth weight.

Programs

Global Health Newsletter
Walk America
Mothers March

RIDE
Golf Tournaments
Jail and Bail

Career Opportunities

Assistant Director
Senior Designer
Manager

Program Coordinator
Special Events

Contact

1275 Mamaroneck Avenue
White Plains, NY 10605

Phone: 914-997-4488

http://www.marchofdimes.com

National Collegiate Athletic Association

History

It was founded in 1906 and reorganized in 1973 into three divisions, each with national championship competition. It has established 73 national championships in 21 sports. Today, nearly 1,000 education institutions are members of NCAA.

Purpose

To supervise regional and national collegiate athletics contests, adopt and enforce eligibility rules, and publish rule books for collegiate sports.

Programs

College Athletics	Statistics Services
National Youth Sports	Research
Life Skills Program	Youth Educational through Sports (YES)

Career Opportunities

Administrative	Research
Executive Director	Championship Staff
Sports Scientists	Professional Development
Education	Public Information
Marketing and Broadcasting	Finance
Compliance Services	Enforcement and Eligibility Appeals
Legislative Services	Publishing

Contact

Check the Internet for the latest news.

P.O. Box 6222	Phone:	317-917-6222
Indianapolis, IN 46206-6222	Fax:	317-917-6888

http://www.ncaa.org

National Geographic Society

History

Founded in January 1888 by thirty-three men from occupations ranging from explorer to meteorologist, the National Geographic Society now has a membership of nearly eleven million. Designed to increase geographic knowledge, National Geographic now issues four monthly publications in addition to books, atlases, maps, videos and documentary films.

Purpose

To disseminate information about the physical and social world by publicizing research of various natures in terms understood by lay people.

Programs

Map-making   Publication
Education   Seminars

Career Opportunities

Cartographer   Photographer
Administrator   Editor
Program Planner   Publisher

Contact

Check the Internet for the latest news.

1145 17th St. NW   Phone: 800-647-5463
Washington, DC 20036   Fax: 202-775-6141

http://www.nationalgeographic.com

National Wildlife Federation

History

Founded in 1936 as a nationwide network of grass-roots conservationists, the NWF now has a budget of $150 million and a staff of more than 500 professionals working throughout the United States and territories.

Purpose

To educate, inspire and assist individuals and organizations of diverse cultures to conserve wildlife and other natural resources and to protect the Earth's environment in order to achieve a peaceful, equitable and sustainable future.

Programs

Naturequest   Naturelink
Naturescope   Wildlife Camp & Teen Adventure
Conservation Summits   Washington Action Workshop
Animal Tracks

Career Opportunities

Conservationists   Public Relations
Administrative   Researchers
Writers
Artists

Contact

Local offices are located in most cities. Check the Internet for the latest news.

11100 Wildlife Center Dr.   Phone: 800-822-9919
Reston, VA 20192   Fax: 800-229-4532

http://www.nwf.org

Parks and Outdoor Recreation

History

America's parks include vast national acreage (such as Yellowstone National Park, established in 1872) and small town centers that provide little more than picnic table and softball parks. Wildlife and ecology programs have grown as the public has become more and more involved in conservation issues, and governmental and private agencies have proliferated.

Purpose

To provide recreational and conservation opportunities on local, state and national levels; to preserve natural resources.

Programs

Ecology
Community Recreation

Wildlife Preservation
State Parks

Career Opportunities

Recreation Director
Pool Manager
Program Director
Landscape Designer
Veterinarian
Marine Specialist
Firefighter
Volunteer Coordinator

Forest Ranger
Trail Guide
Finance
Ecologist
Biologist
Writer
Administrative Managers
Law Enforcement

Contact

Check the Internet for the latest news. Local, state and national parks may be contacted for career opportunities. The following agencies are suggested contacts: U.S. Fish & Wildlife Service, National Wildlife Refuges, National Park Service, U.S. Forest Service, Bureau of Land Management, Army Corps of Engineers, Bureau of Reclamation – all are based in Washington, D.C.; Tennessee Valley Authority (400 West Summit Hill Drive, Knoxville, TN 37902, phone 865-632-2101); individual state and municipal parks departments; and private organizations, many of which may be found in this book.

Peace Corps

History

The Peace Corps began as President John F. Kennedy sought to bring peace and prosperity to the world by sending American volunteers into third-world countries to teach their citizens how to use their own resources to support themselves. The first workers left for Ghana in August 1961. Today, nearly 6,000 volunteers work in 91 countries. While most volunteers are recent college graduates, many retired people are now opting to spend a few years in Peace Corps service.

Purpose

To aid less fortunate countries in their struggle to gain independence and prosperity by teaching their people basic skills and self-reliance.

Programs

Agriculture and Forestry   Adult Education
Fisheries   Language Skills
Master's Internationalist Program   Nutrition Programs
Medical/Nursing   Public Health
Special Education   Home Economics
"Life After Peace Corps"

Career Opportunities

Entering Peace Corps workers in almost any field are volunteers. Some administrative positions may be available through the national and regional offices, such as the following:

Recruiter   Office Administrator
Program Coordinator   Investigator
Clerical

Contact

There are currently sixteen regional offices. Check your local phone directory for the nearest office. The Peace Corps maintains several websites on the Internet.

1111 20th St.   Phone: 800-424-8580
Washington, DC 20526

http://www.peacecorps.gov

Special Olympics

History

In the early 1960's, Eunice Kennedy Shriver held day camps for people with mental retardation. Mrs. Shriver organized the first National Games in 1968 at Chicago's Soldier Field, and Special Olympics Inc., was established. Today ninety percent of U.S. communities and more than 140 countries around the world are involved with Special Olympics.

Purpose

To provide year-round sports training and athletic competition in a variety of Olympic-type sports for children and adults with mental retardation, giving them continuing opportunities to develop physical fitness, demonstrate courage, experience joy, and participate in a sharing of gifts, skills and friendship with their families, other Special Olympics athletes and the community.

Programs

Recycle for Gold   Standard Special Olympics
Unified Sports   Motor Activity Training
Senior Sports

Career Opportunities

Telemarketing   Management
Mail   Fundraising
Recreation   Public Relations
Administrative

Contact

Local offices are located in most cities. Check the Internet for the latest news.

1133 19th Street, NW   Phone: 800-700-8585
Washington, D.C. 20005   Fax: 202-824-0200

http://www.specialolympics.org

St. Jude Children's Research Hospital

History

Entertainer Danny Thomas once prayed to St. Jude Thaddeous, the patron saint of the hopeless, to "show me my way in life and I will build you a shrine." As his career prospered, he remembered his pledge and sought a way to fulfill it. The idea of creating a unique research hospital devoted to curing catastrophic diseases in children began to take shape, and he nearly single-handedly raised money to build the hospital. However, the larger problem of continued funding was bigger than one man could solve. That's why in 1957, he and other Arabic-speaking leaders founded the American Lebanese Syrian Associated charities specifically to raise operating funds for this research hospital, which opened in 1962. Today, it has grown to be America's seventh largest health-care charity. More than 5,000 patients are seen annually at no cost to their families.

Purpose

To save children's lives by finding the causes and cures for fatal diseases in children.

Programs

Math-a-thons   Bike-a-thons
Radiothons   Special Television Programming
Patient Care   Family Support Groups

Career Opportunities

Research   Medical
Physicians   Scientists
Executive Director   Board of Governors
Fundraising   Administration

Contact

Check the Internet for the latest news.

262 Danny Thomas Place	Phone:	888-419-5833
Memphis, TN 38105	Fax:	901-595-3103

http://www.stjude.org

Student Affairs Offices
on College and University Campuses

History

To promote retention, welfare, and growth and development in all dimensions of student life, including educational, vocational, social-cultural, civility and tolerance, psychological, values clarification, and physical. Student Affairs' offices also provide a variety of educational and administrative services, programs and activities in support of each university's strategic plan.

Programs

Judicial Affairs

Learning Center

Counseling and Testing

Women's Center

National Student Exchange

Educational Talent Search

Upward Bound

Health Services

Campus Recreation

Special Events

African-American Student Services

Ethnic Programs

Student Financial Aid

Career Services

School Relations

Veterans Affair

Admissions

Student Government Association

Student Organizations

Homecoming

Career Opportunities

Admission Counselor

Residence Hall Director

Academic Advisor

International Student Advisor

Greek Affair Coordinator

Coordinator of Intramural Sports Programs

Director of Health Education Programs

Coordinator for Sexual Assault Prevention

Career Development and Planning

Dean of Students

Director of Volunteer Programs

Director of Enrollment Services

Campus Life Coordinator

Director of Family Programs

Student Activities Director

Financial Aid Advisor

Multicultural Affairs

Contact

All colleges and universities have Student Affairs offices. The professional association to which many administrators belong is:

National Association of Student
Personnel Administrators
1875 Connecticut Ave. Suite 418
Washington, D.C. 20009
http://www.naspa.org

Phone: 202-265-7500
Fax: 202-797-1157

United Way of America

History

United Way originated in Denver in 1887, when four clergymen organized a single fund-raising effort to support community organizations. The idea of united fundraising spread to other areas of the community. As of 1993, there were approximately 2,500 United Way organizations in communities throughout the United States and Canada.

Purpose

To increase the organized capacity of people to care for one another.

Programs

United Way Management Training Program   Child Care Programs
Children's Program   Priority Program Fund
Homeless Family Prevention Project

Career Opportunities

Resource Development   Community Planning
Administrative Services   Communication
Social Work   Fund Distribution
Agency Relations   Management
Social Planning

Contact

Local offices are located in many cities. Check the Internet for the latest news.

701 N. Fairfax St.   Phone: 703-836-7112
Alexandria, VA 22314-2045   Fax: 703-519-0097

http://www.unitedway.org

Volunteers of America

History

The Volunteers of America organization was founded in 1896. Today, there are five regional groups and fifty-four local chapters.

Purpose

To provide social services for the homeless, disabled, senior citizens, etc.

Programs

Substance Abuse Programs
Elderly, Youth, Family Programs

Meals on Wheels
Programs for Disabled

Career Opportunities

Fundraising Officer
Executive Director
Accountant

Social Services
Program Director
Human Resources

Contact

Local offices are located in many cities. Check the Internet for the latest news.

1660 Duke Street
Alexandria, VA 22314

Phone: 800-899-0089
Fax: 703-341-5000

http://www.voa.org

World Vision

History

It was founded in 1950 and now has more than 5,100 projects in over 85 countries.

Purpose

To provide emergency relief for victims of national and man-made disasters and also to convey Christian love in action and Christian witness in deeds and words.

Programs

Emergency Relief   Disaster Aid Funds

Career Opportunities

Financial Assistant   Fundraising
Marketing Personnel   Communications
Data Processing Specialist   Clerical
Coordinator

Contact

Check the Internet for the latest news.

P.O. Box 9716   Phone: 888-511-6548
Federal Way, WA 98063-9716   Fax: 818-303-7651

http://www.worldvision.org

YMCA

History

In 1844, George Williams organized prayer and Bible studies for the shopmen at the store where he worked in London. The idea spread to nearby firms and the Young Men's Christian Association was formed June 6, 1844. By 1852, the first YMCA in the United States was formed in Boston. Today, YMCA is at work in more than 2,000 locations.

Purpose

To put Christian principles into practice through programs that build healthy body, mind, and spirit for all.

Programs

YMCA Youth Development Programs
Youth Fitness Programs
Aerobics
Family Programs

Teen Esteem
Aquatics
Youth Overnights
Day Camps

Career Opportunities

Marketing and Communications
Fundraising
Juvenile Justice
Physical Education Directors
Residence Managers

Finance
General Directors
Program Directors
Camp Directors
Executive Directors

Contact

Local offices are located in many cities. Check the Internet for the latest news.

101 N. Wacker Dr., 14th Floor
Chicago, IL 60606

Phone: 800-872-9622
Fax: 312-977-9063

http://www.ymca.net

Young Life

History

It was founded in 1941 by a young minister, Jim Rayburn, who saw the need to reach out to young people with the message of Jesus Christ. Today, it operates several resorts for teenagers in the western United States and Canada.

Purpose

To introduce Jesus Christ's love to students who otherwise would not be exposed to such a message.

Programs

Camps
Leadership Training
Campaigns

Career Opportunities

Clergyman
Fundraising
Accountant

Contact

Local offices are located in many cities. Check the Internet for the latest news.

PO Box 520	Phone:	877-438-9572
Colorado Springs, CO 80901-0520	Fax:	719-381-1750

http://www.younglife.org

Youth Villages

History

Founded in Memphis, Tenn., in 1986, Youth Villages has built a national reputation for offering the most effective programs and services to help emotionally troubled children and their families. The private nonprofit organization provides a fully integrated continuum of services, including residential treatment, in-home services, foster care and adoption, mentoring and a transitional living program for young adults aging out of foster care.

Purpose

Provides group homes and treatment centers to address the needs of children's emotional and behavioral health.

Programs

Residential	Foster Care
In-Home	Adoption
Group Homes	Transitional Living
Crisis Services	Project Safe Place

Career Opportunities

Counselor	Teacher
Administrator	Director
Program Consultant	Supervisor
Clinical Liaison	Human Resources

Contact

3320 Brother Blvd	Phone:	901-251-5000
Memphis, TN 38133	Fax:	901-251-5001

http://www.youthvillages.org

YWCA

History

The Young Women's Christian Association began its work in the United States in the mid-1850s. Today, there are community and student YWCAs in all fifty states, with some 400 associations operating at over 4,000 locations.

Purpose

To empower women and to eliminate racism.

Programs

Community and Leadership Programs

Youth Development Programs

Family Life Programs

Empowerment Programs

Health Promotion Programs

Career Opportunities

Executive Director

Business Manager

Branch Director

School-age Program Director

Association Network Specialist

Contact

Local offices are located in many cities. Check the Internet fort the latest news.

2025 M Street, NW, Suite 550	Phone:	202-467-0801
Washington, DC 20036	Fax:	202-467-0802

http://www.ywca.org

B

Appendix B
Self-assessment Activities for Career Planning in a Nonprofit Organization

Self-assessment Profile

Interests

It is important to have interests similar to the activities, programs and goals of a particular organization. On a separate sheet of paper, list 10 different activities or goals you are interested in doing in the context of a professional setting. These activities or goals may deal with issues such as substance abuse prevention, career planning, recreation, education, sports, the environment, fitness and health or something else. Once the list is made, prioritize these activities or goals below in the order of importance from 1 to 10; then set the list aside.

1.

2.

3.

4.

5.

6.

7.

8.

9.

10.

Values

What aspects of life are important to you and what principles guide your life? Just as it is important to express interests through a career, it is equally important to choose an organization with values similar to your own. Use the *Values Inventory* below to help rank values most important to you. Number each item in the order of priority to you, with 1 being the most important and 30 being the least important. Two spaces are available to fill in additional values. After this is finished, set the list aside for later.

—Integrity

—Enjoying the environment

—Making a lot of money

—Working with people

—Being close to your family

—Organizing activities/programs

—Helping special populations

—Working with money

—Living a long, healthy life

—Having a meaningful relationship with God

—Growing personally and professionally

—Having job security

—Living with meaning and purpose

—Being respected for achievements

—_____
    (fill in with your own value)

—Having the chance to be creative

—Autonomy at work

—Being the leader

—Having fun

—Planning and developing programs

—Working in crisis situations

—Helping others develop skills

—Determination

—Working in a relaxed environment

—Traveling

—Working with children

—Having a financially comfortable life

—Maintaining close friends

—Having equal opportunities for all

—_____
    (fill in with your own value)

Skills and Knowledge Exercise

Based on both classroom achievements and life experiences, write a brief reaction statement to each sentence under the three categories of skills; then put this exercise away for future analysis.

Human Relations Skills

1. I relate well to other people.

2. I communicate my ideas and feelings effectively to others.

3. I am a good listener, and I understand others well.

4. I can motivate and inspire others when I believe in something.

5. I can lead activities, yet I am also a good team player.

6. I can be effective in public speaking and presentations.

7. I communicate ideas well in writing.

Conceptual Skills

1.   I have been successful at visualizing how a program should be planned.

2.   I am able to assess problem areas and develop effective strategies to address these problems.

3.   I can assimilate information and make good, effective decisions.

4.   I am often creative in how I address problems and opportunities.

5.   I would rather plan and implement someone else's programs instead of my own.

6.   I am looking forward to developing my own programs when I begin working in an organization.

7.   I enjoy creating something from scratch.

Technical Skills

1. I like to organize programs and activities.

2. I have some experience with financial development, and I am familiar with budgeting and other financial processes.

3. I have had some success in supervising others as part of a program development team.

4. I am knowledgeable in the areas of promotion and marketing, and I enjoy this aspect of program development.

5. I have had experience in most areas of program development.

6. I am competent in program development.

7. I understand the way in which conceptual and human relations skills interrelate with technical aspects of program development.

Personal History

How do you want to be remembered? In the space below, describe the way in which you hope to be remembered at the end of your life. Describe your personal, family and community relationships as you hope they would have been. Then describe your professional activities and accomplishments. Be as specific and detailed as possible with your descriptions.

Once you have completed the entire Self-assessment Profile, review each section; then discuss the results with a faculty member, campus administrator or nonprofit leader.

C

Appendix C
Interview Simulation
Critique Form

Interview Simulation Critique Form

Your name _____

Interviewer's name _____

Date____/____/____

Score the interview on each item by rating him/her with a score from 1-5.	1 Least Satisfactory	2	3	4	5 Most Satisfactory
Appearance	☐	☐	☐	☐	☐
Communication Skills *Verbal*	☐	☐	☐	☐	☐
Nonverbal	☐	☐	☐	☐	☐
Listening/Understanding	☐	☐	☐	☐	☐
Preparation	☐	☐	☐	☐	☐
Answered questions effectively	☐	☐	☐	☐	☐

Enthusiasm _____

_____

Strengths _____

_____

Areas of Improvement _____

_____

Overall Impression _____

_____

Additional Comments _____

_____

_____

D Appendix D
Sample Organizational Chart

Sample Organizational Chart

Index